Abortion and American Politics

Abortion and American Politics

Barbara Hinkson Craig
Wesleyan University

and

David M. O'Brien
University of Virginia

Chatham House Publishers, Inc.
Chatham, New Jersey

ABORTION AND AMERICAN POLITICS
Chatham House Publishers, Inc.
Post Office Box One
Chatham, New Jersey 07928

Frontispiece: An individual's counterprotest against freedom of
choice on abortion. Washington, D.C., 5 April 1992. *Photo:*
Reuters/Bettmann Newsphotos.

Publisher: Edward Artinian
Production supervisor: Katharine Miller
Cover and jacket design: Lawrence Ratzkin
Composition: Bang, Motley, Olufsen
Printing and binding: R.R. Donnelley & Sons Company

LIBRARY OF CONGRESS CATALOGING-IN-PUBLICATION DATA

Craig, Barbara Hinkson, 1942–
    Abortion and American politics / Barbara Hinkson Craig
and David M. O'Brien.
        p.   cm.
    Includes index.
    ISBN 0-934540-88-8 (cloth). — ISBN 0-934540-89-6 (pbk).
    1. Abortion—Political aspects—United States. 2. Abortion—
Government policy—United States. 3. Abortion—Law and
legislation—United States.   I. O'Brien, David M.   II. Title.
HQ767.5.U5C73   1993
363.4'6'0973—dc20   92-41395
                                                         CIP

Manufactured in the United States of America
10   9   8   7   6   5   4   3   2

For our children,
Lathrop and Linsley Craig,
and Benjamin, Sara, and Talia O'Brien

Contents

Illustrations, viii
Tables, Figures, Boxes, ix
Acknowledgments, xi
Introduction, xiii

1. *Roe v. Wade,* the Burger Court, and   1
   American Politics
2. Interest Groups Battle over *Roe*   35
3. The States as Battlegrounds   73
4. A Reluctant Congress Faces the Abortion Issue   103
5. Abortion and Presidential Politics   157
6. The Tide Turns: The Rehnquist Court and   197
   Webster v. Reproductive Health Services
7. Public Opinion and Abortion   245
8. Abortion and State Politics after *Webster*   279
9. Abortion and National Politics   307
10. *Planned Parenthood of Southeastern Pennsylvania*   325
    v. Casey, the Rehnquist Court, and
    American Politics

Selected Bibliography   363
Index of Cases   371
Index of Names and Subjects   373

Illustrations

An Individual's Counterprotest against Abortion Rights   *Frontispiece*

The Burger Court, 1973   xviii

Justice Blackmun's Memorandum in *Roe* to the   21
Other Justices of the Supreme Court

March for Life Demonstration   34

New York Demonstration: "Human Rights for   72
Unborn Humans"

A Mock Cemetery Erected by the American   102
Coalition for Life

President Ronald Reagan Addressing a Press Conference   156

The Rehnquist Court, 1989   196

National Abortion Rights League: "I'm Pro-Choice   244
and I Vote"

Hollywood Stars and Feminist Leaders Head a Pro-Choice   278
March on the Capitol

NOW President Patricia Ireland Addressing a Rally   306

The Rehnquist Court, 1992   324

Tables, Figures, Boxes

Box 1.1	The Texas Abortion Law	11
Figure 2.1	Turnouts for Abortion Marches	51
Box 2.1	Rules for On-Site Participants	60
Table 3.1	State Abortion Laws before *Roe v. Wade*	75
Table 3.2	Women Obtaining Abortions Out of State	76
Table 3.3	States Restricting Abortions by Requiring Notification or Consent	86
Table 3.4	Public Financing for Abortions for Indigent Women	95
Box 3.1	Major Post-*Roe* Rulings on State and Local Abortion Laws	97
Table 4.1	Abortion Rates before and after *Roe*	111
Box 4.1	Major Legislation on Abortion Passed by the U.S. Congress	112
Table 4.2	Senate Votes on Bartlett Amendment	117
Box 4.2	Excerpts from Senate Debate on Abortion Funding Rider, 29 June 1977	122
Figure 4.1	U.S. Constitutional Amendment Process	138
Box 5.1	Supreme Court Upholds Ban on Federal Funding of Abortions in *Harris v. McRae*	162
Box 5.2	Abortion and Party Platforms	166
Box 5.3	President Reagan's Remarks at Annual Convention of National Religious Broadcasters	171
Table 5.1	Abortions and Abortion Facilities	191
Box 6.1	The Missouri 1986 Abortion Law, Excerpts	202
Table 6.1	Filers of *Amicus Curiae* Briefs in Support of Appellants, William L. Webster, Attorney General of the State of Missouri	205
Table 6.2	Senators Signing Antiabortion Briefs	207
Table 6.3	Filers of *Amicus Curiae* Briefs in Support of Appellees, Reproductive Health Services	214
Table 6.4	Senators Signing Pro-Choice Briefs	225
Table 6.5	Citation of Briefs by Justices in *Webster*	226

Table 7.1	National Opinion Research Center Abortion Opinion Poll Results	250
Figure 7.1	Abortion Opinion Poll Results, 1965, 1972, 1973: Trends in Affirmative Responses	251
Table 7.2	National Opinion Research Center Abortion Opinion Poll Results, Available Years, 1974–88	252
Figure 7.2	Abortion Opinion Poll Results, Available Years, 1974–88: Trends in Affirmative Responses	253
Table 7.3	National Opinion Research Center Abortion Opinion Poll Results, 1989–91	254
Figure 7.3	Abortion Opinion Poll Results, 1989–91: Trends in Affirmative Responses	255
Table 7.4	Demographic Characteristics of Women Obtaining Abortions	257
Table 7.5	Abortion Opinion Poll Results, by Demographic Category	258
Table 7.6	Abortion Support Opinion Poll Results, by Demographic Category	260
Figure 7.4	Public Opinion on Abortion, 1975–91: Trends in Affirmative Responses	263
Table 7.7	Two Abortion Opinion Polls' Results	265
Table 7.8	Feelings about Overturning *Roe*, Poll Results	271
Table 7.9	Abortion Activism, Poll Results	272
Table 7.10	Possible Abortion Restrictions, Poll Results	275
Table 8.1	Probable Abortion Action in the States after *Webster*	281
Table 8.2	Connecticut Abortion Statistics	287
Table 10.1	Abortion and the States	351

Acknowledgments

It is fair to say that we would not have undertaken to write this book were it not for the persistence and encouragement of our publisher, Edward Artinian, who after all these years remains a close friend. We are also grateful for the help of two of Ed's assistants, Katharine F. Miller and Christopher J. Kelaher, and to Betty Seaver and Irene Glynn for their fine work as copyeditors. Several of our students also deserve mention and their names in print for their cheerful assistance in researching this book: Stephen Bragaw, Richard Karat, and Alicia Bassuk. Finally, and most important, this book would not have been possible without the understanding and loving support of our spouses, Robert Gilmour and Claudine O'Brien.

Introduction

In the years since the Supreme Court handed down its ruling in *Roe v. Wade,* making a woman's decision to have an abortion a constitutionally protected right, the politics of the abortion controversy has affected every branch and every level of American government. Few issues more vividly illustrate how our political institutions actually operate in governing a nation of over 250 million diverse individuals.

Abortion is undeniably a controversial and divisive issue. Those who favor keeping abortion legal discuss the issue in terms of a woman's right to control her own body or as a matter of personal privacy that obtains to the doctor-patient relationship. Those opposed to abortion speak in terms of the rights of the unborn and of murder. There appears to be virtually no room for compromise between these highly emotional extremes. In a political system that depends on bargaining, negotiation, and compromise to create governing majorities, the abortion controversy was bound to be problematic and unyielding.

Many scholars and citizens bemoan the inefficiency and ineffectiveness of our governmental process. It is often hard to prod government into action on critical issues. And once public policies are adopted, it is next to impossible to get government to rescind programs that benefit powerful interests, even when changing circumstances no longer justify those programs. Also, government policies occasionally run in opposite directions at once, providing price supports for tobacco, for example, and at the same time aiming to regulate smoking out of existence. Decisions made in one branch or level of government may be subverted or reversed elsewhere. It is difficult to fix responsibility anywhere because so many actors seem to have a piece of the action. Foot-dragging is all too often the prime rule for politicians. Sometimes it appears that the only actors capable of making decisions are judges. Yet federal judges are unelected and not directly accountable to the people. And even their decisions typically take years and are then reviewable in higher courts or subject to evasion and even reversal by the legislative and executive branches.

The tyranny of the status quo is evident in our political system. Yet, fearing rule by mob passions and the all-too-human tendency toward aggrandizement of power, the Framers of the Constitution designed a complicated arrangement of governance with built-in checks and balances that provide opportunities for delay. The Framers first divided power between a national government and the state governments and then allocated the national government's power among three branches: Congress, the presidency, and the federal judiciary. These separate institutions share and compete for political power because the boundaries between them were blurred by giving each control over some of the other branches' turf. For instance, the power to make laws is vested in Congress, but passage of a law requires a majority vote in two bodies (the House of Representatives and the Senate) of different sizes, whose members serve terms of different lengths and represent different constituencies. Congress, moreover, does not have complete lawmaking authority: The president must sign a bill into law and has the authority to veto legislation. The presidential veto power is balanced by the power of Congress to override a president's veto by a two-thirds vote in both houses. The courts have a role both in checking the executive branch's interpretation and implementation of laws and in reviewing challenges to laws to ensure that they are constitutionally permissible. Judicial power is in turn balanced by restricting the courts' purview to cases and controversies brought by legitimate litigants. In addition, other branches may overturn court interpretations of legislation by passing new laws to clarify what is intended or, in the case of a ruling based on the Constitution, by passing a constitutional amendment subject to ratification by three-quarters of the states. Furthermore, the president has the power to appoint executive and judicial branch officials and thereby influence public policy. But the Senate, through its power to confirm the president's appointees, may reject his nominees and thereby also try to influence the direction of judicial policy making. These and other institutional checks and counterchecks amount to a prescription for political struggle that slows down the political process. Yet the Framers believed that slower, incremental change makes for a safer course, or at least gives time for passions to cool and all points of view to be heard. Delay was deemed a reasonable price to pay in order to protect the liberty of the people against hasty use or misuse of coercive governmental powers.

Despite all these seemingly inefficient and negative aspects of the American constitutional system, the structure and processes of government promote stability while allowing for change. The very fact that controversial decisions—whether by Congress, the president, or the federal judiciary—are subject to challenge, evasion, and overturning by other branches means that decisions on highly controversial matters are rarely final. "Losers" thus can realistically hope to become "winners" and are encouraged to work within the system rather than to try to overthrow it. The politics of abortion is a case in point. Although passions run high and the rhetoric is often fever-pitched, both sides have remained within the law. Both sides talk in terms of competing rights and use the legal and political processes for their own advantage.

Rhetoric has been a crucial element in the politics of abortion. As time has passed, the terminology each side uses to refer to itself has changed. The terms *pro-abortion* and *anti-abortion* were typically used by the media and others to describe the opposing positions in the years before and immediately after the *Roe* decision. In an effort to package their viewpoint more positively, the two sides coined the terms *pro-life* and *pro-choice*. These terms, at the urging of each side, were soon adopted by the press. Academic studies often referred to the activists as "supporters of abortion" and "opponents of abortion" in an effort to appear more neutral. Activists who favored permitting abortion found this terminology distasteful and pressed for the phrase *abortion rights supporters* to characterize their position more correctly. More recently, this phrase has been the designation most often used in scholarly works. In this book, we have attempted to use the terminology as it developed over time and to do so with balance. Though activists from both sides might at first find offensive our use of the earlier, now discarded labels, we hope that readers will understand our desire to reflect accurately the history of the terms used.

Many, if not most, elected officials probably wish the abortion issue would disappear, but it is not likely to do so. Indeed, as this book went to print the justices had recently decided under the Civil Rights Act of 1871 that federal courts may not enjoin Operation Rescue and other antiabortion groups from blockading abortion clinics. The Court still faces numerous other appeals of state laws aimed at limiting the availability of abortion. In the political controversy over abortion and other highly contested issues of public policy, the Supreme Court has its say, but not the last word. "Losers" may fight back, while "winners" are forced to fight on to protect their "gains."

This book does not aim to resolve the abortion debate. Nor does it present an argument in support of either side of the controversy. Rather, the purpose here is to use the abortion controversy as an illustrative portrait, even if in some ways a disappointing reflection, of the American governmental and political process. The first five chapters present an analysis of abortion politics as played out from the 1973 *Roe v. Wade* decision until the 1989 ruling in *Webster v. Reproductive Health Services,* in which the Supreme Court, whose composition had dramatically changed in the intervening years, gave its first clear sign of retreating from *Roe*. Each chapter focuses on different actors within the political system—the courts, interest groups, the states, Congress, and the president and executive branch. But because no actor or institution operates in a vacuum, the larger political environment and other competing forces are always present as well. Chapter 6 deals with *Webster* and covers the roles played by all the actors discussed in the preceding chapters. Chapter 7 then turns to public opinion on abortion as measured by polls, which are used and misused by the players in the abortion debate. Chapters 8 and 9 analyze abortion politics after *Webster* in the executive and legislative branches at both the state and national levels of government, showing how the strategies and apparent political advantages of interest groups were altered by that ruling. Finally, chapter 10 returns to the judicial arena with a discussion of court cases decided since *Webster*, including the 1992 ruling in *Planned Parenthood of Southeastern Pennsylvania v. Casey*. It then considers some consequences of Bill Clinton's election for the federal courts and for how the abortion controversy is likely to play out further in Congress and in the states due to policy changes and appointments made by the Clinton administration.

Abortion and American Politics

CHAPTER I

Roe v. Wade, the Burger Court, and American Politics

M edia coverage of the Supreme Court's announcement of its land-mark ruling in *Roe v. Wade*[1] was muted. On 22 January 1973, the day the Court struck down the century-old Texas law restricting the availability of abortions, former Democratic President Lyndon B. Johnson died. The next day, the *New York Times* ran this headline: "Lyndon Johnson, 36th President, Is Dead; Was Architect of 'Great Society' Program."[2] A smaller headline read, "High Court Rules Abortions Legal the First 3 Months." The headlines ironically symbolized the close of one political era and the coming of a new one in which the abortion controversy would become prominent on the national political agenda.

Johnson's death dramatized the end of the Democratic party's coalition of northeastern blue-collar workers, southern white conservatives, and religious and racial minorities. That coalition had largely dominated U.S. politics since the presidency of Franklin D. Roosevelt (1933–45). Johnson began his own political career as a freshman congressman from Texas and an ardent supporter of FDR in 1937, a year that was a turning point for the Court and the country. During FDR's first term in the Oval Office, an economically conservative Court struck down by bare majorities much of his early New Deal legislation, which aimed at speeding recovery from the Great Depression. Liberals attacked the Court's "judicial activism." After FDR's landslide reelection in 1936, he retaliated by proposing reforms that would have expanded the number of justices from nine to fifteen and thereby have enabled him to secure a majority on the bench favorable to the New Deal. But while the

Opposite: The Burger Court in 1973. *Standing, left to right:* Justices Lewis F. Powell, Jr., Thurgood Marshall, Harry Blackmun, William H. Rehnquist. *Seated, left to right:* Justices Potter Stewart, William O. Douglas, Chief Justice Warren E. Burger, Justices William J. Brennan, Jr., Byron White. *Photo:* Collection of the Supreme Court of the United States.

Senate Judiciary Committee debated his "Court-packing plan," the Court, by a 5–4 vote, upheld major pieces of New Deal legislation. That "switch in time that saved nine" in turn contributed to the Senate's eventual defeat of FDR's plan.

Despite losing his battle over the Court, FDR managed during the next six years to infuse his political philosophy into the Court by appointing eight justices and elevating Justice Harlan Stone to chief justice. The "Roosevelt Court"[3] had both immediate and long-lasting consequences for constitutional law and politics. Not only were more than a score of pre-1937 rulings on economic liberty and congressional power overturned, but the Court also gradually became more protective of civil rights and civil liberties; it thereby laid the basis for the Warren Court (1953–69) revolutions in constitutional law. Moreover, even with Republican President Dwight D. Eisenhower's four appointees—including Chief Justice Earl Warren (1953–69) and Justice William J. Brennan (1956–90)—for over thirty years the Court was dominated by those appointed by Democratic presidents[4] and incrementally assumed a new role in politics, that of "guardian of civil rights and liberties."

Johnson's political career tracked the rise and fall of the New Deal Democratic coalition. Priding himself on being FDR's protégé, he worked up through the ranks of Congress to become a powerful Senate majority leader and then John F. Kennedy's vice-president in 1961. Just short of two years later, after Kennedy's assassination, LBJ assumed the presidency. During most of his public life, the federal government had expanded, along with the post–World War II economy, amid rising social expectations for government services. FDR's New Deal had given way to Harry S. Truman's Fair Deal and later JFK's New Frontier, culminating in LBJ's Great Society programs—extensive social programs constituting a war on poverty, urban renewal, aid to education, conservation, and equal civil rights. As president, LBJ responded to the growing forces of the civil rights movement. He pushed through Congress the Civil Rights Act of 1964 and the Voting Rights Act of 1965, the first major civil rights legislation since Reconstruction.

In the 1960s, coincidentally, the Warren Court was carrying forth a "reapportionment revolution" by requiring state electoral districts to reapportion according to the principle of one person, one vote, forging a "due process revolution" in the area of criminal procedure by enforcing the Bill of Rights' guarantees for the rights of the accused,[5] and expanding the protection of a developing "constitutional right of privacy."[6] Indeed, between 1961 and 1969 over 76 percent of the Warren Court's rulings annually ran in a liberal direction toward protecting the rights of individuals and minorities.[7]

LBJ's championing of civil rights and the Warren Court's rulings embittered southern white conservative voters and ultimately eroded the Democratic party's coalition. Whereas thirty years earlier New Deal liberals had attacked "judicial activism"—that is, the Court's striking down congressional and state laws—and the Court's antidemocratic character, it now became the conservatives' turn to do so. Republicans and southern Democrats railed against the Warren Court. At the same time LBJ faced not only an increasingly divided Democratic party but growing discontent in the country. Riots erupted in ghettos, and antiwar protesters marshaled support against escalation of the undeclared war in Vietnam. By the spring of 1968, LBJ concluded he could not win reelection and announced he would not run again. The New Deal coalition was coming apart. And except for Georgia's former governor Jimmy Carter's victory in 1976, no Democratic candidate again won the presidency until Bill Clinton was elected in 1992.

LBJ was not alone in perceiving that "the times they are a-changin'." Chief Justice Warren feared that his old foe from his days as governor of California, Richard M. Nixon, would win the 1968 Republican presidential nomination and the national election. He therefore offered to step down upon confirmation by the Senate of LBJ's nominee to succeed him, Justice Abe Fortas. But Republicans and conservative southern Democrats in the Senate forced Fortas to withdraw. Republicans wanted to deny the "lame duck" president any appointments to the Court. And opposition from conservative southern Democrats focused on Fortas's support of the Warren Court's liberal jurisprudence. Virginia's Senator Harry F. Byrd, for example, charged that "the Warren Court has usurped authority to which it is not entitled and is not serving the best interests of our nation. Mr. Fortas appears to have embraced the Warren philosophy, which philosophy I strongly oppose."[8] As a result, Warren remained on the bench for another year, until after the presidential election and the Senate's confirmation of Nixon's proposed successor, Chief Justice Warren E. Burger. A moderately conservative Republican then sitting on the U.S. Court of Appeals for the District of Columbia, Burger had a reputation in the legal community for speaking out against the Warren Court's rulings on the rights of the accused and criminal justice.

Nixon's presidential election victory in 1968 owed much to his famous "southern strategy." Appealing to southern white voters disenchanted with the Warren Court and the Democratic party, his campaign denounced judicial activism and pledged to return law and order to the country. As did all subsequent Republican presidents, Nixon promised to appoint "strict constructionists"—that is, those who claim constitutional interpretation can be confined to literal readings of the text—and advocates of "judicial self-restraint"—who are deferential to the elected branches of government—to the Court.

With his four appointees, Nixon achieved moderate success in reorienting the Court. In 1969 Burger replaced Warren as chief justice, and Fortas resigned amid controversy over his accepting $20,000 for serving while on the Court as an adviser to a nonprofit foundation. A Democratic-controlled Senate rejected Nixon's first two nominees for Fortas's seat, Clement Haynsworth and G. Harrold Carswell, but the third nominee, Harry Blackmun, won confirmation. Blackmun was a conservative federal appellate court judge and a high school friend of Burger's; Burger had urged Nixon to appoint him to the Court. In 1971 FDR's first appointee, Justice Hugo Black (1937–71), and Justice John M. Harlan (1955–71) retired. Nixon's next (and last) nominees, Lewis F. Powell (1972–87), a prominent southern lawyer and former president of the American Bar Association, and William H. Rehnquist (1972–   ), a young and staunchly conservative attorney in Nixon's Department of Justice, were confirmed with relatively little opposition.

Nixon's four appointees had an immediate impact on the direction of the Court. In 1969, the first term of the Burger Court, the percentage of liberal decisions in civil liberties cases dropped over 25 percent from the preceding term, to just 54.5 percent. By the 1972 term the percentage was 46.3 percent. Only once again during the remaining years of the Burger Court (1969–86) did it rise above 50 percent.[9]

The Burger Court's ruling in *Roe* was thus surprising and ironic. Despite Nixon's four appointees, only Rehnquist and Justice Byron White, a Kennedy appointee, dissented. Contrary to predictions that the Burger Court would forge a "constitutional counterrevolution,"[10] it stemmed but did not reverse tides in constitutional law set in motion by the Warren Court. There were only modest "adjustments," as Chief Justice Burger put it when announcing his retirement in 1986, in the jurisprudential house built by the Warren Court.[11] Moreover, the generally conservative Burger Court, not the Warren Court, handed down *Roe* and thereby elevated the abortion controversy to the national political agenda.

—>*Roe v. Wade* remains politically symbolic and illustrative of the dynamics of the Supreme Court's decision-making process and its changing role in U.S. politics. How the Burger Court came to decide *Roe* illustrates the struggles that may take place within the high court. *Roe* was both an extension of the developing constitutional law of privacy and an invitation for more litigation and larger struggles within the country over abortion, as well as over the course of constitutional law and politics. *Roe* also transformed the abortion controversy. Like other landmark rulings on politically controversial issues of public policy, *Roe* marked only a stage—not the beginning or the end—of a continuing dialogue within the Court and struggle between the Court and competing political institutions and forces.

A Test Case for Changing Times

Landmark rulings often reflect larger social movements and the forces of history. *Roe v. Wade* was a test case for the times and registered an ongoing political struggle by women for equal rights and self-determination. Yet *Roe* was not an outcome of the kind of organized special-interest litigation that remains identified with the National Association for the Advancement of Colored People's systematic assault on racially segregated public schools that began in the 1930s and ran through the 1970s, or the kind of orchestrated antiabortion litigation that came after *Roe* (see chapters 2 and 6).

"Jane Roe," the plaintiff who challenged the constitutionality of the Texas abortion law, was Norma McCorvey. A twenty-one-year-old high school dropout, McCorvey was divorced and had a five-year-old daughter and little money. She was neither a member of any women's organization nor politically active, but her life changed in the summer of 1969 when she became pregnant and unsuccessfully sought an abortion. Texas, like most states at the time, prohibited abortion unless it was necessary to save the woman's life. "No legitimate doctor in Texas would touch me," McCorvey remembered years later. "I found one doctor who offered to abort me for $500. Only he didn't have a license, and I was scared to turn my body over to him. So there I was—pregnant, unmarried, unemployed, alone and stuck."[12]

McCorvey carried her pregnancy to term and then gave up the child she bore for adoption. A Dallas lawyer, Henry McCloskey, Jr., found someone to adopt the baby she never saw. McCloskey also introduced her to two recent graduates of the University of Texas Law School, Sarah Weddington and Linda Coffee. Both had graduated in the late 1960s, when the Warren Court was making sweeping changes in constitutional law and the federal courts appeared to be attractive forums for changing public law and policy. They were also deeply interested in women's issues and were connected with others in Texas who wanted to challenge the constitutionality of that state's abortion law in the courts.

To challenge the Texas law, Weddington and Coffee needed to establish "standing" to sue. That is, to bring suit, they needed a woman (e.g., McCorvey) who could show that she had suffered injuries as a result of the law. They also had to be certain of the woman's commitment to what might turn out to be a lengthy battle in the courts. Thus Weddington and Coffee met several times with McCorvey before they decided to go ahead.

Standing and the Developing Constitutional Law of Privacy

In the 1940s doctors and others who believed in family planning sought to change state laws that had originated in the nineteenth century banning the dissemination of information about, and the use of instruments of, contraception. In most states they were initially unsuccessful in persuading legislative majorities to revise state laws and therefore sought litigation to challenge the constitutionality of those laws in the courts.

Between 1943 and 1965, the Supreme Court consistently refused standing to individuals attacking the constitutionality of the Connecticut law prohibiting physicians from giving advice about contraceptives and virtually all individuals, single and married, from using them. In *Tileston v. Ullman,* 318 U.S. 44 (1943), a doctor sued, charging that the statute prevented him from giving information to patients. The Court ruled that he had no real interest or personal injury—and thus no legal standing to bring a lawsuit—because he had not been arrested.

Almost two decades later, in *Poe v. Ullman,* 367 U.S. 497 (1961), a doctor and a patient were denied standing on the ground that the law had not been enforced for over eighty years, even though the state had begun to close birth-control clinics. The justices split 5–4, and only Chief Justice Warren and Justices Clark and Whittaker joined Justice Frankfurter's opinion for the Court (Justice Brennan concurred in the decision but not in the opinion). But the Court changes with the times. The following year, Justices Frankfurter and Whittaker left the bench. In their places were John F. Kennedy's two appointees, Justices White and Goldberg.

Finally, after Dr. Buxton and Estelle Griswold, executive director of the Planned Parenthood League of Connecticut, were found guilty of prescribing contraceptives to a married couple, the Warren Court in *Griswold v. Connecticut* (1965) struck down what Justice Stewart called Connecticut's "uncommonly silly law." In his opinion announcing the Court's ruling, Justice Douglas explained why Griswold and Buxton were now granted standing:

> 🔊 We think that appellants have standing to raise the constitutional rights of the married people with whom they had a professional relationship. *Tileston v. Ullman,* 318 U.S. 44, is different, for there the plaintiff seeking to represent others asked for a declaratory judgment. In that sit-

uation, we thought that the requirements of standing should be strict, lest the standards of "case or controversy" in Article III of the Constitution become blurred. Here those doubts are removed by reason of a criminal conviction for serving married couples in violation of an aiding-and-abetting statute. Certainly the accessory should have standing to assert that the offense which he is charged with assisting is not, or cannot constitutionally be, a crime. 🔲

When Justice Douglas turned to the merits of Griswold's attack on the Connecticut law, he proclaimed that the law infringed on individuals' constitutional "right of privacy." Although such a right is not specifically enumerated in the Bill of Rights, Douglas drew on prior cases recognizing that the enumerated guarantees in the Bill of Rights have penumbras, or shadows, that protect individuals' privacy interests. Together, he argued, they created a basis for a constitutional right of privacy. In Douglas's words,

🔲 [prior] cases suggest that specific guarantees in the Bill of Rights have penumbras, formed by emanations from those guarantees that help give them life and substance. See *Poe v. Ullman,* 367 U.S. 497 [(1961)] (dissenting opinion). Various guarantees create zones of privacy. The right of association contained in the penumbra of the First Amendment is one, as we have seen. The Third Amendment in its prohibition against the quartering of soldiers "in any house" in time of peace without the consent of the owner is another facet of that privacy. The Fourth Amendment explicitly affirms the "right of the people to be secure in their persons, houses, papers, and effects, against unreasonable searches and seizures." The Fifth Amendment in its Self-Incrimination Clause enables the citizen to create a zone of privacy which government may not force him to surrender to his detriment. The Ninth Amendment provides: "The enumeration in the Constitution, of certain rights, shall not be construed to deny or disparage others retained by the people." ...

We deal with a right of privacy older than the Bill of Rights—older than our political parties, older than our school system. Marriage is a coming together for better or worse, hopefully enduring, and intimate to the degree of being sacred. It is an association that promotes a way of life, not causes; a harmony in living, not political faiths; a bilateral loyalty, not commercial or social projects. Yet it is an association for as noble a purpose as any involved in our prior decisions. 🔲

The Court's ruling in *Griswold* was limited to the privacy and contraceptive decisions of married couples. It did not apply to single
women, nor was it certain that the ruling would extend to strike down
restrictive abortion laws. Consequently, in *Eisenstadt v. Baird,* 405 U.S.
438 (1972), in order to gain standing to assert that single individuals
also have a right to acquire and use contraceptives, a doctor arranged to
be arrested after delivering a public lecture on contraceptives and handing out samples to single women in the audience. Relying on *Griswold,*
the Burger Court ruled that single women also have the right to acquire
and use contraceptives and that to deny them that right violated the
Fourteenth Amendment's equal protection clause.

Weddington and Coffee aimed to build on the developing constitutional "right of privacy" in two ways. First, they had to persuade a federal district court, and perhaps eventually the Supreme Court, that Roe
(McCorvey) had standing to challenge the Texas abortion law. To do
that, they had to build on recent developments in the law of standing in
order to gain access to the courts and then to assert their claim that the
Texas law denied Roe's interests as protected by a constitutional right of
privacy. Second, they hoped to persuade the judiciary to expand on the
Supreme Court's precedents that acknowledged some constitutional protection for privacy and reproductive freedom. They hoped ultimately to
establish a woman's constitutional right to "control of her own body."

Privacy and Reproductive Freedom

The Supreme Court in the 1920s first acknowledged protection under
the Fourteenth Amendment's due process clause for personal privacy and
freedom from governmental intrusions into the areas of marriage, reproduction, and child-rearing. *Pierce v. Society of Sisters,* 268 U.S. 510
(1925), overturned an Oregon law requiring primary and secondary
school children to attend public rather than private schools on the
ground that it interfered "with the liberty of parents and guardians to
direct the upbringing and education of children under their control."

The first major ruling building on those rulings' recognition of some
constitutional protection to reproductive freedom, however, did not
come until *Skinner v. Oklahoma,* 316 U.S. 535 (1942). Indeed, in *Buck
v. Bell,* 274 U.S. 200 (1927), the Court had upheld a Virginia law,
passed in response to the eugenics movement, that compelled the sterilization of persons confined to state mental institutions. By contrast, in
Skinner the Court unanimously overturned a state law providing for the
sterilization of "habitual criminals." Jack Skinner had been convicted of
stealing chickens in 1926 and of robbery in 1929 and 1934. In 1936 the
state attorney general instituted proceedings against Skinner under the
Oklahoma 1935 Habitual Criminal Sterilization Act, which authorized

the sterilization of individuals convicted two or more times of "felonies involving moral turpitude." Skinner challenged the constitutionality of Oklahoma's law as a violation of the Fourteenth Amendment's due process and equal protection clauses. When striking down the law for running afoul of the equal protection clause because it permitted the sterilization of those convicted of crimes such as embezzlement but not those convicted of larceny, Justice Douglas explained:

> We are dealing here with legislation which involves one of the basic civil rights of man. Marriage and procreation are fundamental to the very existence and survival of the race. The power to sterilize, if exercised, may have subtle, far-reaching and devastating effects. In evil or reckless hands it can cause races or types which are inimical to the dominant group to wither and disappear. There is no redemption for the individual whom the law touches. Any experiment which the State conducts is to his irreparable injury. He is forever deprived of a basic liberty.

Later, *Loving v. Virginia,* 388 U.S. 1 (1967), struck down a state miscegenation law forbidding people of different races from marrying.

These cases, along with *Griswold* and *Eisenstadt,* were the principal precedents, Weddington and Coffee would argue in *Roe,* for striking down the Texas abortion law.

The Suit Is Filed

In the process of challenging the Texas law, McCorvey, Weddington, and Coffee became part of a larger historical movement and political struggle. Throughout the turbulent 1960s, the movement to liberalize abortion laws was growing with the so-called sexual revolution and demands for women's rights. Yet the legal reforms pushed by abortion rights advocates were in some respects little more than a return to the legal status of abortions a century earlier. Until the mid-nineteenth century most states permitted abortions until after "quickening," or the first movement of the fetus; even then, abortions were usually considered minor offenses. In 1845 Massachusetts became the first state to make abortion a criminal offense. After the Civil War, the medical profession and antiabortionists persuaded states to toughen their laws. By 1910 every state except Kentucky had made abortion a felony. The overwhelming majority of the states permitted abortions only to save a woman's life. But in the late 1960s and early 1970s, fourteen states liberalized their laws to permit abortion when the woman's health was in danger, when there was a likelihood of fetal abnormality, or when the woman had been a victim of rape or incest. Four states—Alaska, Hawaii, New York, and Washington—had gone so far as to repeal all criminal penalties for abortions performed in early pregnancy. These changes reflected the changing status of American women after World War II: Women were increasingly prominent in the workforce, they were having fewer children, and they were emerging as a distinct economic and political force.

When filing their suit on 3 March 1970 against Henry Wade, the criminal district attorney for Dallas County, Texas, Weddington and Coffee had to show, first, that "Jane Roe" had suffered a legal injury and that her constitutional rights had been violated by the Texas law. To do so, they relied on the Warren Court's watershed ruling in *Griswold v. Connecticut,* which struck down the Connecticut law barring the dissemination of information about contraception. There, Justice William O. Douglas had proclaimed that a constitutional "right of privacy" was contained in the penumbras, or shadows, of the First, Third, Fourth, and Fifth amendments, and that it fell under the Ninth Amendment's provision for unenumerated rights "retained by the people" and the Fourteenth Amendment's prohibition against a state's depriving "any person of life, liberty, or property, without the due process of law."

What Weddington and Coffee had sought in their suit before a federal district court—the lowest trial court in the federal judicial system—was an expansion of the rationale for a constitutional right of privacy in *Griswold* and other rulings recognizing the importance of reproductive freedom and, thereupon, for the courts to strike down the Texas abortion law (see 1.1).

Weddington and Coffee subsequently amended their suit to sue on behalf of "all other [women] similarly situated." They thereby made the case a class-action suit that included all other women who might find themselves in the same predicament as McCorvey. If they won their case, that would mean that the Texas law would not apply to other women in the state.

As it happened, their lawsuit against Wade was joined by two other parties; each had different legal interests but the same goal, overturning the Texas law. Dr. James H. Hallford asserted that the law infringed on the rights of physicians because they were subject to criminal prosecution under the law. In addition, a married couple—"John and Mary Doe"—joined in another class-action complaint for all married couples. The Does were childless because Mary Doe suffered from a "neural-chemical" disorder that had led her doctor to advise her against becoming pregnant.

1.1 | The Texas Abortion Law

Article 1191 Abortion

If any person shall designedly administer to a pregnant woman or knowingly procure to be administered with her consent any drug or medicine, or shall use towards her any violence or means whatever externally or internally applied, and thereby procure an abortion, he shall be confined in the penitentiary not less than two nor more than five years; if it be done without her consent, the punishment shall be doubled. By "abortion" is meant that the life of the fetus or embryo shall be destroyed in the woman's womb or that a premature birth thereof be caused.

Article 1192 Furnishing the Means

Whoever furnishes the means for procuring an abortion knowing the purpose intended is guilty as an accomplice.

Article 1193 Attempt at Abortion

If the means used shall fail to produce an abortion, the offender is nevertheless guilty of an attempt to produce that result, provided it be shown that such means were calculated to produce that result, and shall be fined not less than one hundred nor more than one thousand dollars.

If the death of the mother is occasioned by an abortion so produced or by an attempt to effect the same it is murder.

Article 1196 By Medical Advice

Nothing in this chapter applies to an abortion procured or attempted by medical advice for the purpose of saving the life of the mother.

The Does declared that if Mary became pregnant, they would want her to have an abortion performed by a competent, licensed physician under safe medical conditions. But the Texas abortion law forbade women like Mary from obtaining safe abortions. *Roe* thus represented a challenge by an unmarried single woman, a married couple, a practicing doctor, and all similarly situated others who believed that the Texas law deprived "women of the right to choose whether to have children"—a right they asserted should be recognized as included in the developing constitutional right of privacy.

The Texas abortion law had been adopted in 1854. As incorporated in that state's penal code, it forbade any person from performing an abortion except for "the purpose of saving the life of the mother." It also made performing an abortion a criminal offense, punishable by up to ten years in prison. Notably, the law did not ban or criminalize a woman's self-abortion (see $\boxed{1.1}$).

McCorvey and the other parties in her lawsuit thus sought standing to challenge the Texas law. If granted standing, they planned to ask the court, first, for a declaratory judgment that the law was unconstitutional and, second, for an injunction—a court order—against enforcement of the law's provisions. Henry Wade countered that Roe and the other plaintiffs lacked standing to bring the case. None of the plaintiffs, he stated, had directly suffered injuries under the law. Roe and Doe were not pregnant, and Hallford's assertion was only hypothetical because he had not been charged with any crime. As to the merits of their challenge, Wade responded that the federal courts ought to abstain on the grounds that the issues should be left for state courts to decide. Neither side, however, entirely prevailed in the lower court.

A Federal District Court Declares the Texas Law Unconstitutional but Refuses to Enjoin Its Enforcement

In the federal judicial system, most cases originate in district courts, which are the trial courts of the federal judiciary. (There are ninety-four district courts and thirteen federal courts of appeals, which hear appeals from decisions of the district courts and administrative agencies.) Typically, cases initially come before a single district judge; but where Congress has specifically so provided, cases may be decided by a three-judge panel of district court judges. *Roe v. Wade* was one such case. (Congress has subsequently cut back on the number of cases heard by three-judge panels because of the growing caseloads of federal courts.)

Roe came before a three-judge panel of the U.S. District Court for the Northern Division of Texas, located in Dallas. Coincidentally, it was a panel that included one of the few female judges on the federal bench at the time: Sarah T. Hughes, an appointee of LBJ. After hearing brief oral arguments in the case, the panel entered a judgment on 17 June 1970.

In an unsigned (*per curiam*) opinion, the federal district court held that Roe and Hallford had standing to bring suit but that "John and Mary Doe failed to allege facts sufficient to create a present controversy and therefore [did] not have standing." On the merits of Roe's claims, the court ruled that the Texas abortion law infringed on the "fundamental right of single women and married persons to choose whether to have children." Although declaring the law void and unconstitutionally overbroad, the court declined to issue an injunction against the law's enforcement. The district court reasoned:

⚖ On the merits, plaintiffs argue as their principal contention that the Texas Abortion Laws must be declared unconstitutional because they deprive single women and married couples of their right, secured by the Ninth Amendment, to choose whether to have children. We agree. . . .

Since the Texas Abortion Laws infringe upon plaintiffs' fundamental right to choose whether to have children, the burden is on the defendant to demonstrate to the satisfaction of the Court that such infringement is necessary to support a compelling state interest. The defendant has failed to meet this burden. . . .

Not only are the Texas Abortion Laws unconstitutionally overbroad, they are also unconstitutionally vague. The Supreme Court has declared that "a statute which either forbids or requires the doing of an act in terms so vague that men of common intelligence must necessarily guess at its meaning and differ as to its application violates the first essential of due process of law." *Connally v. General Construction Co.*, 269 U.S. 385 (1926). . . . Under this standard the Texas statutes fail the vagueness test.

The Texas Abortion Laws [also] fail to provide Dr. Hallford and physicians of this class with proper notice of what acts in their daily practice and consultation will subject them to criminal liability. . . .

The grave uncertainties in the application of [provisions of the Texas statutes] and the consequent uncertainty concerning criminal liability under the related abortion statutes are more than sufficient to render the Texas Abortion Laws unconstitutionally vague in violation of the Due Process Clause of the Fourteenth Amendment. ⚖

The district court declined to issue an injunction against enforcement of the Texas law because it held that the "federal policy of non-interference [by federal courts] with state criminal prosecutions must be followed except in cases where 'statutes are justifiably attacked on their face as abridging free expression,' or where statutes are justifiably attacked 'as applied for the purposes of discouraging protected activities.' "[13] In *Roe,* however, no one had actually been arrested for performing an abortion nor, in spite of the law, had any doctor in the case been prosecuted for discussing abortion. The district court concluded that neither of those "prerequisites" was present in *Roe v. Wade* and added:

> ◫ While plaintiffs' first substantive argument rests on notions of privacy which are to a degree common to the First and Ninth Amendments, we do not believe that plaintiffs can seriously argue that the Texas Abortion Laws are vulnerable "on their face as abridging free expression." Further, deliberate application of the statutes "for the purpose of discouraging protected activities" has not been alleged. We therefore conclude that we must abstain from issuing an injunction against enforcement of the Texas Abortion Laws.... ◫

Although Weddington and Coffee succeeded in having the district court declare the Texas abortion law unconstitutional, they failed to persuade it to stop the state from enforcing the law. Nor was Wade pleased by the court's ruling. Both sides of *Roe v. Wade* thus appealed the lower court's decision to the U.S. Court of Appeals for the Fifth Circuit, one of eleven (now thirteen) federal appellate courts. In addition, because *Roe* had been decided by a three-judge panel, instead of a single district court judge, as is typical, the rules of the federal judiciary at the time also provided Weddington and Coffee with the opportunity to appeal directly to the U.S. Supreme Court. And so these two young lawyers, with little experience practicing in federal courts and none before the Supreme Court, decided to take their case directly to the highest court. They did so by filing a petition for a writ of *certiorari,* explaining the questions presented in the case and asking the Court to grant review. (A writ of *certiorari* is an order issued by the Court at its discretion to review a decision of a lower federal court or state supreme court. The vast majority of the over six thousand cases annually filed at the Court come as *certiorari* petitions and are denied review. The Court grants review to a few more than one hundred cases a year and does so only if they present "substantial questions of federal law." In those few cases granted review, the parties involved then file briefs, which present their arguments for how they think the questions presented should be decided; later they have an opportunity to argue their positions orally before the justices.)

Roe v. Wade *before the Supreme Court*

Roe v. Wade was granted review on 3 May 1971, near the end of the Supreme Court's term. Because the Court hears oral arguments only every two weeks from the first Monday in October, when its term opens, until the end of April and concludes its annual term at the end of June, *Roe* was scheduled for oral arguments in the next term. Although the Burger Court's eventual ruling would affect the laws in virtually every state, little public attention was paid to *Roe* at the time. The *New York Times* simply reported that the Court "agreed to consider if state anti-abortion laws violate the constitutional rights of pregnant women by denying their right to decide whether or not to have children."

At the time there was no way for Weddington and Coffee to predict how the Court might decide *Roe*. They knew that the high bench had become more conservative with the appointments of Burger and Blackmun. Yet, just one month earlier, in *United States v. Vuitch*,[14] a bare majority had upheld the District of Columbia statute prohibiting abortions unless "necessary for the preservation of the mother's life or health." The District of Columbia statute, unlike the Texas law, was one of the most liberal in the country at the time; it allowed an abortion not only to save the woman's life but, when necessary, to preserve her physical and psychological well-being. In upholding that statute, the Burger Court allowed an increase in the availability of abortions in Washington, D.C. Still, it did not address the question whether women have a constitutional right to obtain abortions. Burger, Harlan, White, and Blackmun joined Black's opinion for the Court. Black held only that the law was not unconstitutionally vague in allowing abortions for "health" reasons. By contrast, the most liberal member of the Court, Douglas, dissented. He thought the law was "void for vagueness" because it was uncertain whether psychological considerations, such as anxiety and the stigma of having an unwanted or illegitimate child, counted as health factors entitling women to have abortions. Douglas's concern was not that the statute allowed too many abortions. Instead, he felt strongly that women had a right to choose whether or not they should terminate their pregnancies and that psychological considerations should be more explicitly included in the statute as a legitimate basis for women's obtaining abortions.

Weddington and Coffee could count on the votes of Douglas, Brennan, and Marshall, given their past voting records. But it remained far from certain that there was a majority on the bench for striking down the Texas law. Black and Stewart had dissented in *Griswold*. Although Harlan and White had concurred in *Griswold*, they were generally conservative on such matters and might not go as far as Weddington and Coffee wanted in *Roe*. Burger and Blackmun had voted to uphold the District of Columbia's abortion law in *Vuitch*, but here *Roe*'s attorneys were asking the Court to strike down a state law. And that ran against their philosophy of self-restraint and professed deference to legislatures.

Weddington and Coffee, moreover, could not have foreseen that Black and Harlan would retire four months later. Black had been a leading liberal on the bench and Harlan one of the Court's more conservative members. But neither looked kindly on claims to a constitutional right to abortion. Nor could Weddington and Coffee have known that at the justices' private conference discussion of *Vuitch,* Black said that he could not go along "with a woman's claim of [a] constitutional right to use her body as she pleases." Burger also had rejected out of hand any "argument that [a] woman has [an] absolute right to decide what happens to her own body."[15]

Without Black and Harlan, the Court was diminished, and Nixon's last two nominees —Powell and Rehnquist—had not been confirmed by the Senate by the time oral arguments in *Roe v. Wade* were heard on 13 December 1971.

Arguing before the High Bench — Round One
Chief Justice Burger opened the Court's oral argument session with the simple announcement that "we will hear arguments in No. 18, *Roe* against *Wade.*"[16] Each side had just thirty minutes to make its arguments and answer questions from the bench. Weddington appeared remarkably calm in her first appearance before the high court. She began by reviewing the lower court's holding, but Burger interrupted to ask whether *Vuitch* had not decided the questions here. No, Weddington explained, the Texas law was more restrictive in permitting abortion only when necessary to save the life of the woman, and doctors were not free to consider the effects of pregnancy on a woman's mental or physical health. *Vuitch,* furthermore, was not binding in Texas, and doctors were threatened with prosecution for performing abortions other than those necessary in saving a woman's life.

Women who sought to terminate unwanted pregnancies had to go to New York, the District of Columbia, or some other state with liberal abortion laws. Women like Jane Roe, who were poor and for whom abortions were not necessary to save their lives, had no real choice. They faced unwanted childbirth or attempting medically unsafe self-abortions, which could result in death. Ironically, moreover, women who performed self-abortions were guilty of no crime, since Texas authorized the prosecution only of doctors or others who performed abortions.

At that point in Weddington's argument, White interrupted to observe that "so far on the merits, you've told us about the important impact of the law, and you made a very eloquent policy argument against it." Adding that "we cannot here be involved simply with matters of policy," White pressed for the constitutional basis for a woman's right to an abortion.

Arguments could be made on the basis of the Ninth Amendment's guarantee of "rights retained by the people," Weddington responded, or on the basis of the Fourteenth Amendment. In concluding her argument, she stressed that if "liberty is meaningful ... that liberty to these women would mean liberty from being forced to continue the unwanted pregnancy."

Jay Floyd, the assistant attorney general of Texas, next stood at the lectern. This controversy is not one for the courts, he argued, pointing out that arguments about freedom of choice are misleading:

> There are situations in which, of course as the Court knows, no remedy is provided. Now I think she makes her choice prior to the time she becomes pregnant. That is the time of the choice. It's like, more or less, the first three or four years of our life we don't remember anything. But, once a child is born, a woman no longer has a choice, and I think pregnancy then terminates that choice. That's when.

But one of the justices shot back, "Maybe she makes her choice when she decides to live in Texas." Laughter almost drowned out Floyd's feeble reply, "There is no restriction on moving."

"What is Texas's interest?" Justice Thurgood Marshall demanded to know, "What is Texas's interest in the statute?" Floyd tried to explain that Texas had "recognized the humanness of the embryo, or the fetus," and had "a compelling interest because of the protection of fetal life." Yet, Justice Potter Stewart interjected, "Texas does not attempt to punish a woman who herself performs an abortion on herself." Floyd conceded that, and then rather ineffectively added:

> And the matter has been brought to my attention: Why not punish for murder, since you are destroying what you—or what has been said to be a human being? I don't know, except that I will say this. As medical science progresses, maybe the law will progress along with it. Maybe at one time it could be possible, I suppose, statutes could be passed. Whether or not that would be constitutional or not, I don't know.

Stewart countered, "We're dealing with the statute as it is. There's no state, is there, that equates abortion with murder? Or is there?" There was none, admitted Floyd. But he hastened to emphasize that although courts had not recognized the unborn as having legal rights, states have legitimate interests in protecting the unborn. As to a woman's choice on abortion, Floyd reiterated, "We feel that this choice is left up to the woman prior to the time she becomes pregnant. This is the time of choice."

The Court's Internal Dynamics

By tradition, the chief justice begins the justices' private conference discussions of cases on which they have heard oral arguments earlier in the week. Each justice then generally speaks and votes in order of seniority on the bench. When the justices initially discussed *Roe* in conference, Burger began by noting that oral arguments had not gone very well. On such a "sensitive issue," he added, perhaps the case should be reargued so that the newly appointed justices, Powell and Rehnquist, could participate and a full Court could reach a decision. On the merits of *Roe,* the chief justice said that the Texas law was "certainly arcane," but he did not deem it unconstitutional. Burger concluded, however, by indicating that he was inclined to void the law for vagueness and thus affirm the lower court's ruling.

As he so often did, Douglas sharply disagreed. The Texas law, he charged, was not merely vague; it also impinged on a woman's right of privacy. Brennan and Stewart agreed, as did Marshall. But White took the opposite view. Although he had concurred in *Griswold,* White could not go along with the argument that women have a constitutional right of privacy that gives them a choice on abortion. White now found unpersuasive the argument that a right of privacy was one of the unenumerated rights "retained by the people" under the Ninth Amendment or protected by the due process clause of the Fourteenth Amendment.

Blackmun, then the newest member of the Court, spoke last: "[I] [d]on't think there's an absolute right to do what you will with [your] body." He added, though, that the Texas statute was poorly drawn and too restrictive. It "doesn't go as far as it should and impinges too far on [Roe's] Ninth Amendment rights."[17] Although tentative about where he stood, Blackmun appeared in the middle, yet inclined toward the view of Douglas, Brennan, Stewart, and Marshall. There thus appeared to be a majority in favor of striking down the Texas law.

After the conference, the chief justice, if he is in the majority, by tradition assigns a justice to write the opinion announcing the Court's decision. At conference, Burger had appeared in the minority. He nonetheless in late December 1971 assigned Blackmun to write the Court's opinion. When Douglas complained, Burger responded that the issues were complex and the conference discussion so diverse "that there were, literally, not enough columns to mark up an accurate reflection of the voting" in his docket book. He "therefore marked down no vote and said this was a case that would have to stand or fall on the writing, when it was done."[18]

Blackmun did not circulate a first draft to the other justices until 18 May 1972. It immediately troubled Douglas and Brennan. It struck down the Texas law, but along the lines advanced at conference by the chief justice. The abortion law was void for vagueness, according to Blackmun's draft, rather than found to be in violation of a woman's constitutional right of privacy, as a majority of the Court had appeared to hold at their conference.

Douglas and Brennan demanded to know why Blackmun failed to address the core issue, "which would make reaching the vagueness issue unnecessary." Blackmun responded that he was "flexible as to results" and had tried his "best to arrive at something which would command a court." With "hope, perhaps forlorn, that we might have a unanimous Court," he explained in a memo to the other justices, "I took the vagueness route."[19]

Still a newcomer in his second year on the high bench, Blackmun was deeply disturbed by the emerging dispute. On the one hand, Burger was his longtime friend and had recommended his appointment to the Court. On the other hand, Blackmun felt more strongly than Burger about Texas's infringement on women's liberty and was attracted to Douglas's position. Torn, he concluded that it might be better to have *Roe* reargued, as Burger and White had suggested. "Although it would prove costly to [him] personally, in the light of energy and hours expended," Blackmun wrote in a memo, "on an issue so sensitive and so emotional as this one, the country deserves the conclusion of a nine-man, not a seven-man court, whatever the ultimate decision may be."[20]

Douglas was shocked at the prospect of two Nixon appointees —Powell and Rehnquist—participating in *Roe;* the result might go the other way. If Blackmun could be persuaded to withdraw his motion for reargument, Douglas calculated that it would fail, for the vote would be 4–3 against reargument. Douglas appealed to Blackmun not to vote for reargument. Instead of complaining about the initial draft opinion, he commended Blackmun for his "yeoman service" and emphasized that he had "a firm 5 and the firm 5 will be behind you" on the opinion. Brennan followed with a similar note.[21]

By tradition, only justices voting to grant oral arguments in specific cases and participating in them may vote on hearing rearguments. But with tensions mounting over *Roe,* Powell broke with tradition. In response to Blackmun's memo, Powell circulated one of his own. He noted that during his first months on the Court, when decisions on rearguments were made, he had held to "the position then, as did Bill Rehnquist, that the other seven Justices were better qualified to make those decisions." Now, however, Powell explained, "The present question arises in a different context. I have been on the Court for more than half a term. It may be that I now have a duty to participate in this decision." He and Rehnquist would vote for a rehearing.[22]

There thus was a majority for carrying *Roe* over for reargument. Douglas was angry, and threatened, "If the vote of the Conference is to reargue, then I will file a statement telling what is happening to us and the tragedy it entails."[23] That would only have intensified tensions, and Douglas was finally persuaded not to publicize his outrage. Instead, he simply dissented from the Court's order for *Roe*'s reargument.

"May It Please the Court" — Round Two

Rearguments in *Roe* were heard on 11 October 1972. Weddington again stood before the high bench to ask it to strike down the Texas abortion law. Since *Vuitch,* she stressed, more than sixteen thousand Texas women had gone to New York City for abortions, and "many other women [were] going to other parts of the country." This time around, however, Weddington's arguments were repeatedly interrupted by questions from the bench about the rights of the unborn.

Justice White bluntly asked, "Would you lose your case if the fetus was a person?" That would require a balancing of the interests of the woman, the unborn, and the state, Weddington replied. But that was not the issue before the Court in *Roe,* she added. The Court had not held, nor did Texas assert here, that a fetus had constitutional rights. The issue, Weddington reminded the justices, involved a conflict between the constitutional rights of women and the regulatory interests of the state. Before a state could claim a compelling interest in prohibiting abortions that would require the Court to balance that interest with the constitutional rights of a woman, the Court would have to establish that the fetus is a "person" under the Fourteenth Amendment or some other part of the Constitution. But the Fourteenth Amendment applies only "to all persons born or naturalized in the United States." For the Court to hold that the amendment also includes protection for the unborn would be an extreme exercise of judicial activism.

White remained obviously troubled by Weddington's argument. Toward the end of her allotted time, he again asked, "That's what's involved in this case? Weighing one life against another?" No, Weddington reiterated.

"Well," queried Stewart, "if it were established that an unborn fetus is a person, with the protection of the Fourteenth Amendment, you would have almost an impossible case here, would you not?" Wedding-

Supreme Court of the United States
Washington, D. C. 20543

CHAMBERS OF
JUSTICE HARRY A. BLACKMUN

November 21, 1972

MEMORANDUM TO THE CONFERENCE

Re: No. 70-18 - Roe v. Wade

     Herewith is a memorandum (1972 fall edition) on the Texas abortion case.

     This has proved for me to be both difficult and elusive. In its present form it contains dictum, but I suspect that in this area some dictum is indicated and not to be avoided.

     You will observe that I have concluded that the end of the first trimester is critical. This is arbitrary, but perhaps any other selected point, such as quickening or viability, is equally arbitrary.

     I have attempted to preserve Vuitch in its entirety. You will recall that the attack on the Vuitch statute was restricted to the issue of vagueness. 402 U.S. at 73. I would dislike to have to undergo another assault on the District of Columbia statute based, this time, on privacy grounds. I, for one, am willing to continue the approval of the Vuitch-type statute on privacy as well as on vagueness. The summary here attempts to do just that. You may not agree.

     I apologize for the rambling character of the memorandum and for its undue length. It has been an interesting assignment. As I stated in conference, the decision, however made, will probably result in the Court's being severely criticized.

Sincerely,

H. A. B.

FIGURE 2.1.

JUSTICE HARRY A. BLACKMUN'S MEMORANDUM IN *ROE*,
21 NOVEMBER 1972 (FROM JUSTICE WILLIAM J. BRENNAN'S PAPERS,
COLLECTIONS OF THE LIBRARY OF CONGRESS).

ton conceded that she then would have a very difficult case. "I'm sure you would," replied Stewart, adding, "So, if you had the same kind of thing, you'd have to say that this would be the equivalent— after the child was born, if the mother thought it bothered her health any having the child around, she could have it killed. Isn't that correct?"

"That's correct," Weddington answered, but further explanation was cut off by Burger. "Could Texas constitutionally," asked the chief justice, "declare that—by statute, that the fetus is a person, for all constitutional purposes, after the third month of gestation?" Weddington firmly countered that question when exhausting her time before the Court: "I do not believe that the state legislature can determine the meaning of the federal Constitution. It is up to this Court to make that determination."

Burger then called Robert C. Flowers, who had replaced Floyd as the assistant attorney general and would now defend the Texas law before the Court. Like Weddington, he faced a steady stream of questions about whether a fetus could be considered a "person" under the Constitution. Flowers conceded that no prior case recognized the fetus as a person and that the Fourteenth Amendment extended protection only to those born or naturalized in the United States.

In response to questioning from White, Flowers also agreed that *Roe* would be lost if the fetus was not recognized as a person. Yet Flowers adamantly insisted that the unborn were entitled to some constitutional protection. His line of argument prompted Marshall and Rehnquist to interrogate him further about whether there was any medical evidence establishing a fetus to be a person at the time of conception. Although he could not supply any, he stated that he knew of no way "that any court or any legislature or any doctor anywhere can say that here is the dividing line. Here is not a life; and here is a life, after conception."

Whether a fetus is a person, Flowers maintained, was an issue for states to decide. That argument again aroused Stewart, who countered from the bench:

Well, if you're right that an unborn fetus is a person, then you can't leave it to the legislature to play fast and loose dealing with that person. In other words, if you're correct, in your basic submission that an unborn fetus is a person, then abortion laws such as that which New York has are grossly unconstitutional, [aren't they]?

But liberal abortion laws, Flowers protested in his remaining minutes at the lectern, allow "the killing of people."

Weddington had only five minutes for her rebuttal. Her time was largely taken up with questions from Burger. He once again returned to whether *Vuitch* had not already settled the issues here. Weddington again reiterated that whether a woman has a right to terminate an unwanted pregnancy was not directly addressed in *Vuitch*. Lower federal courts, moreover, were divided on that question; nine had upheld the constitutionality of liberal abortion laws, and five had not. The issue, Weddington continued to insist, was one that the Court could not avoid. "We are not here to advocate abortion," Weddington concluded in her final statement:

> We do not ask this Court to rule that abortion is good, or desirable in any particular situation. We are here to advocate that the decision as to whether or not a particular woman will continue to carry or will terminate a pregnancy is a decision that should be made by that individual; that, in fact, she has a constitutional right to make that decision for herself; and that the State has shown no interest in interfering with that decision.

The Final Vote and Postconference Deliberations

Following rearguments in *Roe,* there remained a majority for striking down the Texas abortion law. Burger remained tentative about where he stood; he wanted to await circulation of the proposed opinion for the Court. Powell and Rehnquist, who had not originally participated in *Roe,* now split on the merits of the case. Powell tentatively voted to strike down the Texas law; Rehnquist had no doubts about his voting to reverse the lower court and uphold the law. The others stood by their votes cast a year earlier.

Almost another full month passed before Blackmun finished a new draft of his opinion for *Roe.* "It has been an interesting assignment," as he put it while circulating his draft. Notably, the draft, which eventually became the Court's final opinion, struck down the Texas abortion law on the basis of a woman's constitutional right of privacy.

During the rest of November and most of December, Blackmun reworked parts of his draft as other justices responded with comments and suggestions. On 21 December, he circulated the final draft. Douglas, Brennan, Marshall, and Stewart immediately joined. Soon after the Christmas holidays, Powell also agreed and commended Blackmun for his "exceptional scholarship."[24] By mid-January, Burger also finally signed on, though he added a short concurring opinion emphasizing that he did not support "abortion on demand." Rehnquist and White dissented.

Blackmun also prepared and circulated a special statement that he would read from the bench when announcing the Court's decision. He even went so far as to have copies of his statement made available to reporters. Usually, only copies of the Court's opinion are made available. But, as he wrote in a memo to the other justices, he hoped that a simple explanation of the ruling would stop reporters from going "all the way off the deep end." In his statement, Blackmun explained in very simple terms that the Texas abortion law infringed on women's constitutional right of privacy. States could no longer categorically proscribe abortions or make them unnecessarily difficult to obtain. The promotion of maternal care and the preservation of the life of a fetus were not sufficiently "compelling state interests" to justify restrictive abortion laws. During roughly the first trimester (three months) of a pregnancy, the Court ruled, the decision on abortion is that of a woman and her doctor. During the second trimester, states may regulate abortions, but only in ways reasonably related to their interests in safeguarding the health of women. In the third trimester, states' interests in preserving the life of the unborn become compelling, and they may limit or even ban abortions, except when necessary to save a woman's life.

Roe v. Wade, 410 U.S. 113 (1973)

At the outset of his opinion for the Court, Blackmun dealt with whether "Jane Roe" had standing and whether, as Floyd and Flowers had argued, the issue was moot because Roe was not pregnant. Blackmun dismissed that argument out of hand:

> When, as here, pregnancy is a significant fact in the litigation, the normal 266-day human gestation period is so short that the pregnancy will come to term before the usual appellate process is complete. If that termination makes a case moot, pregnancy litigation seldom will survive much beyond the trial stage, and appellate review will be effectively denied. Our law should not be that rigid. Pregnancy often comes more than once to the same woman, and in the general population, if man is to survive, it will always be with us. Pregnancy provides a classic justification for a conclusion of nonmootness. It truly could be "capable of repetition, yet evading review."

Blackmun then turned to the merits of *Roe v. Wade*. In the excerpt reprinted here, note that Blackmun, a former counsel to the Mayo Clinic, canvasses a broad range of medical and sociological literature on abortion; he also surveys the history of restrictions on the availability of abortions, beginning with ancient Greece and running down through the English common law and U.S. state legislation enacted in the nineteenth and twentieth centuries. He aimed to provide historical and medical support for his interpretation of the Constitution and to balance the interests of women against those of the states in regulating and banning abortion. In anticipation of how sharply the Court's ruling would be criticized, Blackmun also devoted a major portion of his opinion to reviewing the development of a constitutional right of privacy and explaining why that right should be extended here to embrace a woman's liberty interests in deciding whether or not to terminate a pregnancy. Still, he did not rely only on historical and medical evidence, together with the Supreme Court's prior rulings, in trying to rationalize the ruling in *Roe*. Notably, his opinion rests on an examination of the language and historical context of the Fourteenth Amendment's guarantee that "all persons born or naturalized in the United States" shall not be deprived by the states of "life, liberty, or property, without due process of law" and "the equal protection of the laws." In this respect, Blackmun advanced a strict construction of the amendment in rejecting the argument that the unborn are constitutionally protected "persons" under the Fourteenth Amendment. The opinion thus weaves together various textual, historical, and contextual approaches to constitutional interpretation and draws on extrajudicial sources found in medicine, sociology, and philosophy.

⚖️ Justice BLACKMUN delivers the opinion of the Court.

The Texas statutes that concern us here make it a crime to "procure an abortion," as therein defined, or to attempt one, except with respect to "an abortion procured or attempted by medical advice for the purpose of saving the life of the mother." Similar statutes are in existence in a majority of the States. . . .

It perhaps is not generally appreciated that the restrictive criminal abortion laws in effect in a majority of States today are of relatively recent vintage. Those laws, generally proscribing abortion or its attempt at any time during pregnancy except when necessary to preserve the pregnant woman's life, are not of ancient or even of common-law origin. Instead, they derive from statutory changes effected, for the most part, in the latter half of the 19th century. . . .

Abortion was practiced in Greek times as well as in the Roman Era. . . . Greek and Roman Law afforded little protection to the unborn. . . .

It is undisputed that at common law, abortion performed *before* "quickening"—the first recognizable movement of the fetus *in utero,* appearing usually from the 16th to the 18th week of pregnancy—was not an indictable offense....

Gradually, in the middle and late 19th century the quickening distinction disappeared from the statutory law of most States and the degree of the offense and the penalties were increased. By the end of the 1950's a large majority of the jurisdictions banned abortion, however and whenever performed, unless done to save or preserve the life of the mother....

It is thus apparent that at common law, at the time of the adoption of our Constitution, and throughout the major portion of the 19th century, abortion was viewed with less disfavor than under most American statutes currently in effect. Phrasing it another way, a woman enjoyed a substantially broader right to terminate a pregnancy than she does in most States today....

The Constitution does not explicitly mention any right of privacy. In a line of decisions, however, going back perhaps as far as *Union Pacific R. Co. v. Botsford,* 141 U.S. 250 (1891), the Court has recognized that a right of personal privacy, or a guarantee of certain areas or zones of privacy, does exist under the Constitution. In varying contexts, the Court or individual Justices have, indeed, found at least the roots of that right in the First Amendment, *Stanley v. Georgia,* 394 U.S. 557 (1969); in the Fourth and Fifth Amendments, *Terry v. Ohio,* 392 U.S. 1 (1968), *Katz v. United States,* 389 U.S. 347 (1967); *Boyd v. United States,* 116 U.S. 616 (1886), see *Olmstead v. United States,* 227 U.S. 438 (1928) (BRANDEIS, J., dissenting); in the penumbras of the Bill of Rights, *Griswold v. Connecticut;* in the Ninth Amendment, *id.* (GOLDBERG, J., concurring); or in the concept of liberty guaranteed by the first section of the Fourteenth Amendment, see *Meyer v. Nebraska,* 262 U.S. 390 (1923). These decisions make it clear that only personal rights that can be deemed "fundamental" or "implicit in the concept of ordered liberty," *Palko v. Connecticut,* [302 U.S. 319] (1937), are included in this guarantee of personal privacy. They also make it clear that the right has some extension to activities relating to marriage, *Loving v. Virginia,* 388 U.S. 1 (1967); procreation, *Skinner v. Oklahoma,* 316 U.S. 535 (1942); contraception, *Eisenstadt v. Baird,* [405 U.S. 438 (1972); family relationships, *Prince v. Massachusetts,* 321 U.S. 158 (1944); and child rearing and education, *Pierce v. Society of Sisters,* 268 U.S. 510 (1925)....

This right of privacy, whether it be founded in the Fourteenth Amendment's concept of personal liberty and restrictions upon state action, as we feel it is, or, as the District Court determined, in the Ninth Amendment's reservation of rights to the people, is broad enough to encompass a woman's decision whether or not to terminate her pregnancy....

We, therefore, conclude that the right of personal privacy includes the abortion decision, but that this right is not unqualified and must be considered against important state interests in regulation....

Where certain "fundamental rights" are involved, the Court has held that regulation limiting these rights may be justified only by a "compelling state interest," and that legislative enactments must be narrowly drawn to express only the legitimate state interests at stake....

The appellee and certain *amici* argue that the fetus is a "person" within the language and meaning of the Fourteenth Amendment. In support of this, they outline at length and in detail the well-known facts of fetal development. If this suggestion of personhood is established, the appellant's case, of course, collapses, for the fetus' right to life would then be guaranteed specifically by the Amendment. The appellant conceded as much on reargument. On the other hand, the appellee conceded on reargument that no case could be cited that holds that a fetus is a person within the meaning of the Fourteenth Amendment.

The Constitution does not define "person" in so many words. Section 1 of the Fourteenth Amendment contains three references to "person." The first, in defining "citizens," speaks of "persons born or naturalized in the United States." The word also appears both in the Due Process Clause and in the Equal Protection Clause. "Person" is used in other places in the Constitution: in the listing of qualifications for Representatives and Senators, Art. I, §2, cl. 2, and §3, cl. 3; in the Apportionment Clause, Art. I, §2, cl. 3; in the Migration and Importation provision, Art. I, §9, cl. 1; in the Emolument Clause, Art. I, §9, cl. 8; in the Electors provisions, Art. II, §1, cl. 2, and the superseded cl. 3; in the provision outlining qualifications for the office of President, Art. II, §9, cl. 5; in the Extradition provisions, Art. IV, §2, cl. 2, and the superseded Fugitive Slave Clause 3; and in the Fifth, Twelfth, and Twenty-second Amendments, as well as in §§2 and 3 of the Fourteenth Amendment. But in nearly all these instances, the use of the word is such that it has application only postnatally. None indicates, with any assurance, that it has any possible prenatal application.

All this, together with our observation, that throughout the major portion of the 19th century prevailing legal abortion practices were far freer than they are today, persuades us that the word "person," as used in the Fourteenth Amendment, does not include the unborn....

This conclusion, however, does not of itself fully answer the contentions raised by Texas, and we pass on to other considerations.

The pregnant woman cannot be isolated in her privacy. She carries an embryo and, later, a fetus, if one accepts the medical definitions of the developing young in the human uterus. The situation therefore is inherently different from marital intimacy, or bedroom possession of obscene material, or marriage, or procreation, or education, with which *Eisenstadt* and *Griswold, Stanley, Loving, Skinner* and *Pierce* and *Meyer* were respectively concerned. As we have intimated above, it is reasonable and appropriate for a State to decide that at some point in time another interest, that of health of the mother or that of potential human life, becomes significantly involved. The woman's privacy is no longer sole, and any right of privacy she possesses must be measured accordingly.

Texas urges that, apart from the Fourteenth Amendment, life begins at conception and is present throughout pregnancy, and that, therefore, the State has a compelling interest in protecting that life from and after conception. We need not resolve that difficult question of when life begins. When those trained in the respective disciplines of medicine, philosophy, and theology are unable to arrive at any consensus, the judiciary, at this point in the development of man's knowledge, is not in a position to speculate as to the answer....

In areas other than criminal abortion, the law has been reluctant to endorse any theory that life, as we recognize it, begins before live birth or to accord legal rights to the unborn except in narrowly defined situations and except when the rights are contingent upon live birth....

In view of all this, we do not agree that, by adopting one theory of life, Texas may override the rights of the pregnant woman that are at stake. We repeat, however, that the State does have an important and legitimate interest in preserving and protecting the health of the pregnant woman, whether she be a resident of the State or a nonresident who seeks medical consultation and treatment there, and that it has still *another* important and legitimate interest in protecting the potentiality of human life. These interests are separate and distinct. Each grows in substantiality as the woman approaches term and, at a point during pregnancy, each becomes "compelling."

With respect to the State's important and legitimate interest in the health of the mother, the "compelling" point, in the light of present medical knowledge, is at approximately the end of the first trimester. This is so because of the now-established medical fact that until the end of the first trimester mortality in abortion may be less than mortality in normal childbirth. It follows that, from and after this point, a State may regulate the abortion procedure to the extent that the regulation reasonably relates to the preservation and protection of maternal health. Examples of permissible state regulation in this area are requirements as to the qualifications of the person who is to perform the abortion; as to the licensure of that person; as to the facility in which the procedure is to be performed, that is, whether it must be a hospital or may be a clinic or some other place of less-than-hospital status; as to the licensing of the facility; and the like.

This means, on the other hand, that, for the period of pregnancy prior to this "compelling" point, the attending physician, in consultation with his patient, is free to determine, without regulation by the State, that, in his medical judgment, the patient's pregnancy should be terminated. If that decision is reached, the judgment may be effectuated by an abortion free of interference by the State.

With respect to the State's important and legitimate interest in potential life, the "compelling" point is at viability. This is so because the fetus then presumably has the capability of meaningful life outside the mother's womb. State regulation protective of fetal life after viability thus has both logical and biological justifications. If the State is interested in protecting fetal life after viability, it may go so far as to proscribe abortion during that period, except when it is necessary to preserve the life or health of the mother.

Measured against these standards, Art. 1196 of the Texas Penal Code . . . sweeps too broadly. The statute makes no distinction between abortions performed early in pregnancy and those performed later, and it limits to a single reason, "saving" the mother's life, the legal justification for the procedure. The statute, therefore, cannot survive the constitutional attack made upon it here. . . .

To summarize and to repeat:

A state criminal abortion statute of the current Texas type, that excepts from criminality only a *life-saving* procedure on behalf of the mother, without regard to pregnancy stage and without recognition of the other interests involved, is violative of the Due Process Clause of the Fourteenth Amendment.

(a) For the stage prior to approximately the end of the first trimester, the abortion decision and its effectuation must be left to the medical judgment of the pregnant woman's attending physician.

(b) For the stage subsequent to approximately the end of the first trimester, the State, in promoting its interest in the health of the mother, may, if it chooses, regulate the abortion procedure in ways that are reasonably related to maternal health.

(c) For the stage subsequent to viability, the State in promoting its interest in the potentiality of human life may, if it chooses, regulate, and even proscribe, abortion except where it is necessary, in appropriate medical judgment, for the preservation of the life or health of the mother. . . .

This holding, we feel, is consistent with the relative weights of the respective interests involved, with the lessons and examples of medical and legal history, with the lenity of the common law, and with the demands of the profound problems of the present day. 🔲

The Concurring Justices

In the 1965 ruling proclaiming a constitutional right of privacy in *Griswold v. Connecticut,* Stewart had dissented and had sharply criticized the majority for inventing that right out of whole constitutional cloth. But in *Roe* he concurred; he now accepted the Court's reading of a substantive right of privacy into the guarantee of the Fourteenth Amendment's due process clause and the finding that the Texas abortion law denied women's constitutionally protected liberty interests in controlling their own bodies. In separate opinions, Chief Justice Burger and Justice Douglas concurred in the Court's decision as well. Each, though, pointed in opposite directions. Burger made clear that he did not support "abortion on demand," whereas Douglas staunchly defended a woman's constitutional right to choose.

The Dissenters

Whereas Stewart came to accept the Court's recognition of a constitutional right of privacy in *Griswold* and its extension in *Roe,* Rehnquist and White rejected the majority's analysis and reasoning for striking down the Texas law. In Rehnquist's dissenting opinion, he marshaled a strict constructionist argument against the Court's extension of the right of privacy and supported his interpretation of the Fourteenth Amendment by drawing on history. Contrary to Blackmun's reading of the text and historical context of the Fourteenth Amendment, Rehnquist concluded that the fact that several states had restrictive abortion laws in

1868, when the Fourteenth Amendment was adopted, is evidence that the amendment was not intended to bar states from regulating abortion. As Rehnquist explained:

> 🔲 If the Court means by the term "privacy" no more than that the claim of a person to be free from unwanted state regulation of consensual transactions may be a form of "liberty" protected by the Fourteenth Amendment, there is no doubt that similar claims have been upheld in our earlier decisions on the basis of that liberty. I agree with the statement of Justice STEWART in his concurring opinion that the "liberty," against deprivation of which without due process the Fourteenth Amendment protects, embraces more than the rights found in the Bill of Rights. But that liberty is not guaranteed absolutely against deprivation, only against deprivation without due process of law. The test traditionally applied in the area of social and economic legislation is whether or not a law such as that challenged has a rational relation to a valid state objective. *Williamson v. Lee Optical Co.,* 348 U.S. 483 (1955).
>
> The Due Process Clause of the Fourteenth Amendment undoubtedly does place a limit, albeit a broad one, on legislative power to enact laws such as this. If the Texas statute were to prohibit an abortion even where the mother's life is in jeopardy, I have little doubt that such a statute would lack a rational relation to a valid state objective under the test stated in *Williamson, supra.* But the Court's sweeping invalidation of any restrictions on abortion during the first trimester is impossible to justify under that standard, and the conscious weighing of competing factors that the Court's opinion apparently substitutes for the established test is far more appropriate to a legislative judgment than to a judicial one....
>
> The fact that a majority of the States reflecting, after all the majority sentiment in those States, have had restrictions on abortions for at least a century is a strong indication, it seems to me, that the asserted right to an abortion is not "so rooted in the traditions and conscience of our people as to be ranked as fundamental." ...
>
> To reach its result, the Court necessarily has had to find within the scope of the Fourteenth Amendment a right that was apparently completely unknown to the drafters of the Amendment. As early as 1921, the first state law dealing directly with abortion was enacted by the Connecticut legislature. By the time of the adoption of the Fourteenth Amendment in 1868, there were at least 36 laws enacted by state or territorial legislatures limiting abortion....
>
> The only conclusion possible from this history is that the drafters did

not intend to have the Fourteenth Amendment withdraw from the States
the power to legislate with respect to this matter. 🔲

Rehnquist thus staked out a position that he would continue to fight for
in the years to come in *Webster v. Reproductive Health Services* (see
chapter 6) and *Planned Parenthood of Southeastern Pennsylvania v. Casey* (see chapter 10).

The Immediate Aftermath

Initial reactions to the Burger Court's ruling in *Roe v. Wade* were intense
and mixed, as they continue to be in the decades following the decision.
The president of Planned Parenthood Federation of America, Dr. Alan
Guttmacher, hailed the ruling as "a wise and courageous stroke for the
right of privacy, and for the protection of a woman's physical and emotional health." Others sharply disagreed. New York's Cardinal Terence
Cooke charged that "the justices have made themselves a 'super-legislature.'" He added: "Whatever their legal rationale, seven men have made
a tragic utilitarian judgment regarding who shall live and who shall
die."[25] Observed Philadelphia's Cardinal John Krol: "Apparently the
Court was trying to straddle the fence and give something to everybody.
Abortion on demand before three months for those who want that,
somewhat more restrictive abortion regulations after three months for
those who want that."[26] Even those who favored the ruling sharply criticized *Roe* for resting on a constitutional right of privacy and attacked
the Court's legal analysis and reliance on scientific and medical evidence
in the opinion.[27] Other court watchers critical of *Roe* took their cue
from Rehnquist's dissenting opinion. For states' rights advocates, the
Court impermissibly imposed its own view on state legislatures. For still
others, the Court had committed a more fundamental sin: It had written
the rights of the unborn out of the Constitution. "In my opinion,"
Utah's Republican Senator Orrin Hatch proclaimed, "this is clearly the
Dred Scott issue of this century."[28]

  Roe v. Wade elevated the issue of abortion to the national political
agenda and invited a larger political struggle in the country. In the following decades, the abortion controversy became transformed. Prochoice and antiabortion groups were mobilized, and state legislatures,
Congress, the president, and the courts faced competing and crosscutting
pressures to respond. At the same time, as the following chapters discuss, the Court and the country changed, leaving *Roe v. Wade* by no
means the final word.

Notes

1. *Roe v. Wade,* 410 U.S. 113 (1973).
2. *New York Times,* 23 January 1973, A1.
3. See, generally, C. Herman Pritchett, *The Roosevelt Court* (New York: Macmillan, 1948).
4. *Baker v. Carr,* 369 U.S. 186 (1962).
5. See, e.g., *Mapp v. Ohio,* 367 U.S. 683 (1961); *Miranda v. Arizona,* 384 U.S. 436 (1966).
6. See *Griswold v. Connecticut,* 381 U.S. 479 (1965); David M. O'Brien, *Privacy, Law, and Public Policy* (New York: Praeger, 1979).
7. See Jeffrey Segal and Harold Spaeth, "Decisional Trends on the Warren and Burger Courts," *Judicature* 73 (1989): 103.
8. Quoted, David M. O'Brien, *Storm Center: The Supreme Court in American Politics,* 2d ed. (New York: Norton, 1990), 125.
9. See Segal and Spaeth, "Decisional Trends."
10. See Richard Funston, *Constitutional Counter-Revolution?* (New York: Wiley, 1977); Leonard Levy, *Against the Law: The Nixon Court and Criminal Justice* (New York: Harper & Row, 1974).
11. For further discussion, see David M. O'Brien, "The Supreme Court from Warren to Burger to Rehnquist," *PS: Political Science and Politics* 20 (1987): 12.
12. Quoted, Lloyd Shearer, "Intelligence Report," *Parade,* 12 January 1983.
13. *Roe v. Wade,* 314 F. Supp. 1217 (1970), quoting *Dombrowski v. Pfister,* 380 U.S. 479 (1965).
14. *United States v. Vuitch,* 402 U.S. 62 (1971).
15. Docket Book, William J. Brennan, Jr., Papers, Box 417, Manuscript Room, Library of Congress.
16. The quotations from oral arguments in this chapter are taken from a recording of the arguments, available at the National Archives and Records Service, and Philip Kurland and Gerhart Casper, eds., *Landmark Briefs and Arguments of the Supreme Court of the United States* (Arlington, Va.: University Publications of America, 1974).
17. Docket Book, Brennan Papers, Box 420A.
18. Memos, Brennan Papers, Box 281.
19. Ibid.
20. Ibid.
21. Ibid.
22. Ibid.
23. Ibid.
24. Ibid.
25. Quoted, *New York Times,* 23 January 1973, A1, A20.
26. Quoted, ibid.
27. See, for example, John Hart Ely, "The Wages of Crying Wolf: A Comment on *Roe v. Wade,*" *Yale Law Journal* 82 (1973): 920.
28. Quoted, Senate Committee on the Judiciary, Subcommittee on the Constitution, *Constitutional Amendments Relating to Abortion: Hearings,* 97th Cong., 1st sess. (1981), 1:90.

CHAPTER 2

Interest Groups Battle over *Roe*

The Supreme Court, as Justice Robert Jackson once said, is "not final because we are infallible, but we are infallible only because we are final."[1] History instructs, though, that the finality of a controversial Supreme Court decision is often transitory indeed. Commanding no sword and controlling no purse, the Court must depend on other branches of government to enforce its rulings. But the executive and legislative branches, and the fifty state governments, are political institutions very much subject to the passions and will of the people, or, more accurately in terms of U.S. politics, to the passions and will of organized interest groups that have the resources to play pressure politics.

Roe was not a resolution of the abortion issue. It only marked the end of one engagement in a prolonged national conflict. In 1983, on the tenth anniversary of the Court's decision, the *Washington Post* summed up its effect:

[*Roe*] has drastically changed the Court's image, fostered wholesale attack on "judicial activism" and mobilized thousands of supporters and opponents of legalized abortion in a debate that has reshaped the political terrain in many states and, at times, has virtually halted the work of Congress. Few court decisions have had a more immediate impact on such a personal aspect of American life.[2]

For many activists on both sides of the abortion issue, the decades-long struggle has been a very warlike experience. Indeed, the rhetoric of war is a prominent feature of abortion politics. "Both Sides in the

Opposite: March for Life demonstration. *Photo:* Prints and Photographs Division, Library of Congress.

Abortion War Dig in for the Battle of the '80s," headlined an article in *USA Today*.[3] "Images Are Weapons on Abortion Battle Field," declared a *New York Times* report.[4] "We have to fight a political guerrilla war, not a fixed battle in Washington, D.C., but hundreds of skirmishes in congressional districts around the country," stated Howard Phillips, founder of the Conservative Caucus.[5]

As a political issue, abortion, with its religious, moral, and ethical overtones, is a particularly sticky wicket. In some ways the politics of abortion is similar to the historic struggle over Prohibition in the early 1900s. In 1919 it was the Anti-Saloon League and various religious groups promoting the "moralist viewpoint" that won the initial struggle with passage of the Eighteenth Amendment to the U.S. Constitution outlawing the manufacture, sale, and transportation of liquor. Anti-Prohibition groups had only one way to reverse that victory: win passage of another constitutional amendment to undo Prohibition. They succeeded at just that with ratification of the Twenty-First Amendment in 1933. Ironically, sixteen years after *Roe,* the Supreme Court in 1989 upheld a number of restrictions on abortion and appeared on the brink of overturning *Roe* (*Webster v. Reproductive Health Services* is discussed in chapter 6).

But the abortion struggle has been unlike the struggle over Prohibition in important ways. There are the obvious differences—the secular interests won the first triumph in abortion, and the religious-moralist position was forced to take the offensive; and the abortion struggle is over a constitutional decision by the Court rather than a constitutional amendment. More important, the interest-group combat over abortion has been played out on a very changed political battlefield—as distinct as modern battlefields are from those of World War I.

Interest Groups and American Politics

Group pressure has always been part of politics in the United States, but the contemporary version is startlingly different from that of even the recent past. The dissimilarity is attributable to a multitude of factors: the dramatic growth of national government's size and responsibility as a result of the Great Society programs of the mid-1960s and the social regulatory explosion of the 1970s; the emergence of television as the primary political medium; the technological advances in mass marketing, computers, and polling techniques that were quickly adopted by politicians and politically active groups; the exponential growth in nationally organized, narrowly focused interest groups, many with associated campaign fund-raising political action committees (PACs); and the broader public awareness of pressure-group politics that followed the national publicity surrounding the civil rights movement.

Writing in the early 1950s, political scientist David B. Truman presaged the development of interest-group pluralism run riot. "Associations," he noted, "come into being or are activated as a consequence of disturbances" that upset an equilibrium that has come to be expected. Disturbances may be caused by sudden discrete events, or *triggers,* or they may be occasioned by the culmination of a gradual series of adjustments that, in total, result in distress in some sector of the population. Through association of like-minded individuals who share the distress, groups seek to "restore a previous equilibrium or to facilitate the establishment of a new one."[6] Groups do not just spring into being in response to disturbances, though, as Truman seemed to imply. Something more is usually needed. That something is leadership: somebody or somebodies with the time, resources, commitment, and charisma to bring people together and to motivate and channel their shared distress into an effective unitary voice.

As society became increasingly complex, the means of dealing with and correcting problems moved out of the hands of private groups, and groups had to seek powerful outside mediators to aid their causes. In the United States, with its religious diversity and its constitutional separation of church and state, religious institutions lack sufficient political clout to undertake the mediator role they played historically and still do play in some countries. And as national power grew at the expense of state power, state and local governments ceased to be the central political organizations in citizens' lives. By the second half of the twentieth century, the national government had become the most powerful organizational structure with the potential authority for mediating competing group demands.

The "universal tendency" of interest groups to resort to government action to supplement their own resources, as Truman pointed out, is cumulative. When one group attains that end, other groups pressure government to recover what they perceive they have lost. In the process, the power of government is inevitably expanded. As its power expands, government is more likely to become the perpetrator of disturbances. And as information about the efficiency of group pressure spreads, those affected by disturbances know more about how to organize and how to play interest-group pressure politics. The result is that government power grows and interest groups become more numerous and effective.

Most of the groups Truman analyzed had interests based in economics—that is, their stake was a pocketbook one. Labor groups seek to

protect their salaries, jobs, and benefits against large, sometimes monop-
olistic, business organizations; professional groups (lawyers and doctors,
for example) seek to restrict entry into their fields or to secure special
government protections; farmers and other agricultural producers seek
government financial assistance in maintaining market prices for their
products. The National Association for the Advancement of Colored
People (NAACP) and various other civil rights groups formed from the
1930s to the 1960s sought something different from government: an end
to discrimination—a goal that would require governmental action to
change attitudes and behavior. The strategies of economic interest
groups are not sufficient to such an end.[7] The marches and placards of
the women suffragettes and the Prohibitionists, or the battle for the public soul in the antislavery movement, are closer historical group-pressure
models.

One new instrument of social change that the civil rights activists encountered was television. The full panoply of the civil rights movement
unfolded in the nation's living rooms on sets tuned in to the sit-ins,
marches, police violence, crowds. Public opinion, measured regularly by
"scientific" polling and reported by the media, swayed against the segre-
gationists, and government gradually responded to the civil rights
groups' demands. The message was clear to others—the Court, Congress, and the president effect social-policy change, and interest groups
can influence their policy outcomes. Other groups emerged following the
civil rights model: the anti–Vietnam war movement, the women's movement, the environmental movement, the consumer movement, the anti-
nuclear-power movement. And in response to all these liberal-policy-
seeking groups, the New Right (later known as the Moral Majority)
joined the antiabortion movement that materialized in response to *Roe*.
And they too adopted the techniques of the civil rights movement.

Interest groups and their tactics are looked at askance. "Americans
distrust interest groups in general," observes political scientist Jeffrey M.
Berry, "but value the organizations that represent them.... Intellectually
we accept the legitimacy of all interest groups; emotionally we separate
them into those we support and those we must view with suspicion."[8] In
other words, Americans approve of pressure when used by groups they
agree with and attack it as unfair when used by other groups. Cultivat-
ing the media, resorting to advocacy advertising, staging demonstrations, framing issues and using rhetoric and symbols advantageously, orchestrating letter-writing and telephone campaigns targeted at public
officials, soliciting funds by direct mail, mounting voter-registration
drives, funneling donations to political candidates, endorsing candidates,
running negative campaigns against candidates, lobbying national and

state legislatures or executive departments, developing litigation strategies, and dozens of other approaches are used by groups on both sides of
nearly every public policy issue. These are neutral means within the political system, available to any and all but not, unfortunately, on an
equal basis.

To adopt any of these means effectively, interest groups need some
combination of the basic resources: money, membership, expertise
and/or information, and reputation.[9] The ability of a group to advance
or protect its interests depends on the abundance of its resources.
Money has the enormous advantage of convertibility, and groups rich in
dollars have a distinct advantage. But a large or intensely committed
membership can compensate for lack of money, as may command of information or expertise that is essential to the political decision-making
process. Moreover, the public perception of a group is as important an
ingredient in its reputation and power as is the reality of other resources.

Interest-group politics requires both an inside and an outside strategy; groups have to play to their own members and prospective members, but also to the larger public and the political decision makers. Often what is useful relative to the former is not useful for persuading the
public or the politicians. For example, it might be productive to stress
impending defeat to motivate the membership, but this might result in
politicians' perceiving the group as losing power and public support.
There are inevitable trade-offs in the pressure politics game, and what
works today may be counterproductive tomorrow. Simply put, interest-
group politics is about the efforts of losers to find a way to become winners and about the effort of winners to protect their gains.

Interest-Group Politics and the Abortion Issue

Many Americans view abortion as murder. To them, *Roe* came as a
"bolt from the blue." In interviews with activists who joined the right-
to-life movement after *Roe*, sociologist Kristin Luker found memories of
the day the decision was announced to be "extraordinarily vivid" ones
of sadness and disbelief.[10] It simply did not seem possible that their
country could stand for a principle so at variance with their beliefs.

That many were taken by surprise by a major Supreme Court decision may seem strange, but it is understandable, given the way abortion
had been treated throughout most of the country's history. Until the
mid-1800s, abortion was a mostly haphazard procedure primarily dependent on folk remedies and midwifery. Early abortion (before quickening—the visible and/or felt movement of the fetus) was not an offense

under early law; indeed, historically it had not been an offense in Christian (including Catholic canon law) or Roman law. Scientific advances that enabled abortion by surgical means (the invention of dilators and curettage in the 1870s) brought on a struggle between "professional" physicians and other practitioners of medicine (such as midwives and herbalists), who were tagged by the professionals as "quacks." Out of that struggle came the first right-to-life movement (1850–90), which was primarily a physician-led effort to claim the practice of abortion as a "regular-doctors-only" field. In a fascinating "ideological sleight of hand" that enabled them to "create and control a moral problem at the same time," physicians of the American Medical Association (founded in 1847) declared that all abortions were murder but that some were necessary, and that only physicians could tell which were necessary.[11]

Responding to pressure from the medical community, by 1910 all but one state had outlawed and criminalized abortion at any stage unless necessary to save the woman's life. Nearly every state left the necessity decision and the procedure itself up to the physician. Gaining that control was an important victory for the fledgling professional medical community in its effort to foreclose nonprofessional competition. After antibiotics were discovered shortly before World War II, abortion became safer, and although accurate statistics are unavailable, it seems clear that abortion was prevalent throughout the first half of this century.

Abortion was not a subject of great public debate, however. The late-nineteenth-century right-to-life movement had successfully "medicalized" abortion, making it subject to discussion between only doctor and patient. No uniform definition of what constituted a "medically necessary" abortion was imposed either within the medical community or from the outside by government. The availability of physician-performed abortions varied according to the individual doctor's beliefs. A woman seeking an abortion could look for another doctor if a doctor refused her request, or she might resort to an illegal abortion. As medical advances in maternity care reduced the hazards of pregnancy, the situations in which abortion was realistically a "medical necessity to save the life of the woman" were drastically reduced. This fact did not noticeably reduce either the demand for or the practice of abortion. But when the primary site for the practice of minor surgical procedures, including abortion, moved from the doctor's office or the home to the hospital following World War II, physician-performed "legal" abortions became increasingly subject to notice by other medical personnel. Renewed debate ensued within the medical community. Doctors were no longer free agents. Hospital boards and peer-review groups, created to protect hospitals from adverse publicity and lawsuits, gained control over permissible therapeutic abortions. Inevitably, group oversight resulted in more restraints, which meant fewer legal, safe abortions were to be had. Supply, as it were, was reduced while demand continued; illegal "back-alley" abortions filled the gap.

Before the late 1950s there was "nothing resembling a political movement aimed at changing abortion laws."[12] By 1959, though, concern within the medical community about its legal exposure under the existing statutes prompted some doctors and lawyers to call for a "liberalization" of the laws in order to reflect better the reality of existing abortion practice. They wanted abortion allowed when necessary for the mental health of the mother, in cases of pregnancy from rape or incest, and in cases of fetal deformity.[13] Then in 1962 public attention was drawn to the abortion issue by media coverage of the discovery that the drug thalidomide could cause fetal abnormalities if a woman took it during pregnancy. Sherri Finkbine, who had taken thalidomide, learned of its dangers and sought a therapeutic abortion. When her case was reported in detail the day before the scheduled abortion was to be performed, wary hospital personnel canceled the procedure.[14] In no time, the story was on the news wires, and the slumbering abortion issue awoke to a public clamor. On one side were those who supported Finkbine's decision not to chance giving birth to a seriously malformed child. On the other side were those who were horrified at her even considering such an option. Under growing public scrutiny, hospitals and doctors caught in the middle became more reluctant to approve and perform abortions.

Because abortion laws at that time were state laws, groups favoring legal abortion pressed state governments for change. Proponents of the status quo fought back. The early battles were battles between the generals: health and legal professionals were the major activists on both sides. For most Americans, the abortion debates of the early 1960s were not sufficiently visible or threatening to move them to action. Such attention as the average citizen paid was limited to responses to news reports of cases like Finkbine's or to horror stories about women maimed or killed during illegal abortion attempts. Public concern was short-lived, and the news media quickly refocused on other issues.

The timing of the reemergence of the abortion debate, however, soon resulted in a broadening of participation on the liberalization side. By the mid-1960s, the women's movement was gathering steam; world overpopulation and zero population growth had become powerful public concerns. "The pill" was making family planning both easier and more comfortably open to public discussion. And the sexual revolution was coming into bloom. Pro-choice advocates now could appeal to a much wider audience. In states where they were active, it is not surprising that state legislators perceived their voice to be that of the majority. By 1967 three states had passed new abortion statutes; by 1973, nearly a third of the states had done so (see table 3.1, p. 75, and the discussion of the status of state abortion laws prior to *Roe* in chapter 3).

With laws decriminalizing abortion on the books, the number of abortions grew exponentially and the distress of opponents grew apace. The experience in California, one of the first states to pass a more permissive abortion law, is instructive. In 1968, the first year under the new law, 5018 abortions were performed; in 1969, 15,952; in 1970, 65,369; and in 1971, 116,749.[15] This represented a 2000 percent increase in just four years. Abortion opponents outside California's medical and legal community began to form groups to fight a situation they found abhorrent.

In New York State, where a liberalized abortion statute passed the legislature in 1970, one antiabortion group formed out of a women's book discussion group. A member recalls: "I don't remember what book we were discussing that day at Diane's house.... But I remember that someone said they had seen something on the TV about the move to legalize abortion. We never felt we were going to be involved.... We thought our legislators would take care of it. But they didn't."[16] Hundreds of similar groups sprang up around the country, but until *Roe* there was little coordination or cooperation among them; indeed, there was probably little if any knowledge of one another's existence.[17] State legislative debates over abortion did not draw much national media notice, and the small brushfires of local opposition smoldered.

Roe, though, commanded national media attention, and abortion opponents nationwide were jarred into realizing that there had been a drastic reversal of what they believed was long-established public policy. The ultimate goal of many was to eliminate all abortions, with the possible exception of those to save the life of the woman. Of course, that had not been the state of affairs before *Roe* or at any time in the nation's history. But that reality had been obscured by the compromise of the late 1800s, which had removed the abortion question from public view. The informal accommodation that enabled the states to restrict abortion in their laws, which appeased abortion opponents while allowing abortion to continue in fact, thereby taking care of the ongoing demand, was no longer a viable solution. Facts about the number and frequency of abortions had suddenly become too well known. The issue had turned into a cause célèbre for groups holding antithetical views. And politicians were left with little hope of satisfying both positions or of keeping the issue at bay.

Following *Roe,* individuals and groups that had participated in the crusade to legalize abortion turned to other concerns: expanding the availability of abortion, fighting discrimination against women in the workplace, promoting day-care and family-planning policy, and simply pursuing their own careers and private concerns. Success bred confidence and complacency in their ranks. Commenting years later on the ground lost by what was commonly referred to by then as the pro-choice position, one leader explained the problem: "It is hard to get people whipped up when the 'law' reflects your perspective."[18] With the highest court in the land behind them, supporters thought they had little to fear. What they could not foresee was that *Roe* came at the end of a period of liberal activism and that just beyond it a conservative backlash would in time affect all three branches of the federal government and many state governments as well.

The Second Right-to-Life Movement

Early Years. — While abortion supporters turned their attention elsewhere, abortion opponents were gearing for action. Only a few avenues were available to accomplish their goal of eliminating abortion. They could use a litigation strategy to get a case to the Supreme Court in an effort to persuade the Court to change its mind; that required new state or national abortion legislation that could be tested in court. They could try to get a constitutional amendment outlawing abortion; that would require agreement from two-thirds of the members of both the House and Senate and three-quarters of the states (see figure 4.1, p. 138, and discussion of the constitutional amendment process in chapter 4). They could try to persuade Congress, the president, or state governments to ignore the Court and work to undercut the new "right to abortion" upheld in *Roe.* They could try to prevent abortions by making it uncomfortable for women seeking them or persuading women not to get abortions. None of these options would be easy to accomplish.

The first imperative was to gain public attention and support for their cause. The antiabortion movement needed to become a power in fact or in the perception of politicians, which meant mounting a public relations campaign requiring money, expertise, and staff.

Immediately following *Roe,* the extent of the antiabortion forces was unknown. It took time for leaders to emerge and develop politically effective organizations. If the membership of the movement was coextensive with the Catholic population, it was large and politically powerful, and could be reached and coordinated locally by neighborhood churches. Moreover, a strong and politically astute national organization existed to represent its interests: the U.S. Catholic Conference, which comprises the nation's Catholic bishops. One clear message from the new-movement politics was that a critical ingredient of successful pressure is a national, preferably Washington, D.C.–based organization, staffed by full-time professionals (experienced lobbyists, lawyers, media and public relations experts). Perhaps recognizing that public opinion generally frowns on any official church role in pressure or electoral politics (at least this was so in the 1970s), the U.S. Catholic Conference provided funding for the creation of the National Committee for a Human Life Amendment. Until other sectors of the antiabortion forces formed similar national organizations, this committee acted as the major national lobbying force on abortion.

The National Committee for a Human Life Amendment wielded considerable weight. During a congressional conference-committee meeting on the question of federal funding of abortions, for instance, the effectiveness of its staff member, Mark Gallagher, was reported in the national press:

> He is an unobtrusive man who makes his unofficial home on Capitol Hill in the office of Representative Henry Hyde ... author of the ban on Federal funding of abortions for low-income women.... His name is Mark Gallagher and he represents the National Committee for a Human Life Amendment.... Every time the Senate conferees make a compromise offer, Mr. Gallagher quietly walks to the conference table to tell a staff aide to the 11 House conferees whether the proposal is acceptable to the bishops. His recommendations invariably are followed.[19]

Gallagher's actions were not unlike those of other powerful lobbyists. With the opening up of congressional meetings to the public in the mid-1970s, the men and women who populate "Gucci Gulch" (the lobby area outside the House and Senate chambers, where spokespersons of interest groups gather to collar members as they enter or leave) were able to move into the committee negotiating and decision-making rooms. The connection of Gallagher to a religious group was not unique. Other politically active pressure groups have equally strong connections to religious organizations. American Israeli Public Affairs Committee (AIPAC), with its strong connection to Jewish religious organizations, is one obvious example. And, like AIPAC, the National Committee for a Human Life Amendment's clout was based to a large extent on the size of the segment of the general population that presumably stood behind its positions. In the mid-1970s it was estimated that 120 of the 435 U.S. House districts had sizable Catholic constituencies, and that 30 percent of the representatives and 13 percent of the senators were Roman Catholics. Precisely how many Catholics in or out of Congress supported Gallagher's goals was unknown, but elected representatives were not apt to underestimate the potential political costs of ignoring his requests.

It was soon apparent, though, that the antiabortion movement's membership was both less than the country's Catholic population and much more. Public opinion polls, which began asking questions on abortion in the late 1960s, reported a split among lay Catholics. Statistics gathered by the Alan Guttmacher Institute showed that a significant proportion of abortions were being sought and obtained by Catholics (see chapter 7 for a discussion of public opinion and the abortion issue). Church members' support for the church-hierarchy-aided lobby effort to ban abortions was by no means universal. Moreover, *Roe* came just as "born again" evangelical Protestantism was gaining ground. Evangelicalism, the dominant religious mode of nineteenth-century America, had lost prominence as a result of the theological liberalism of the 1920s. But by the late 1970s and throughout the Ronald Reagan era of the 1980s, the political force of the evangelical right was soaring. High on its political agenda was outlawing abortion. At the grass-roots level, and soon on the national level, additional and often rival voices could be heard in the chorus for changing abortion policy. This broadening of the base of the antiabortion camp proved to be of mixed value.

On the first anniversary of *Roe,* 23 January 1974, antiabortion groups converged on Washington. Just 6000 strong, they came in chartered buses from cities and towns around the Northeast to show support for a constitutional amendment outlawing abortion proposed by Senator James Buckley (R-New York). "Many demonstrators," according to a news account, "said they had been designated as representatives of local Roman Catholic parishes or schools."[20] They marched carrying signs and then rallied on the Capitol steps to listen to speeches. Compared to the civil rights marches, which drew as many as 250,000, or the anti–Vietnam war marches, which drew, by some counts, as many as 600,000, this first effort of the antiabortion groups was not particularly impressive. But it was a beginning, and in later years the numbers swelled.

Around the nation, smaller groups gathered at state capitols in support of Buckley's proposed amendment. At some of the demonstrations a few abortion supporters gathered to make their viewpoint manifest. At a rally of abortion opponents in Albany, New York, a forty-five-year-old salesman was arrested for tearing up a placard advocating legal abortion, which had been held by two young women. In New York City, members of the National Organization for Women marched in the street with some of their number in chains to represent what they called "Senator Buckley's attempt to enslave women by unwanted childbirth."[21] A group called Catholics for a Free Choice staged a counterdemonstration on the steps of St. Patrick's Cathedral. Each side in the struggle adopted the proven tactics of earlier pressure groups: march to show strength, stage demonstrations, and use creative symbolism to gain attention.

In her study of California abortion activists, Kristin Luker found that new recruits to the antiabortion movement after *Roe* were "predominantly women homemakers without previous experience in political activities."[22] In contrast to the activists who supported abortion, opponents were much less likely to be employed (94 percent of pro-choice women worked; 63 percent of pro-life women did not). In short, the opponents of abortion were not in the workplace and could picket daily at abortion clinics. Available time translated into other important political resources, especially as central organizational structures developed to harness and train antiabortion forces. Orchestrating letter-writing campaigns and phone calls to state and national legislators is easier when volunteers have the time to give. Demonstrations at state capitols that are a car or chartered-bus ride away can be scheduled during workday legislative sessions if an organization's members can come without having to take time off from employment. In other words, the demographic differences between the two sides in the abortion struggle give the advantage in grass-roots lobbying to abortion opponents, and it is an advantage that they have used regularly and effectively.

Differences in organizational style and membership demography of the two sides of the abortion issue have had an enormous effect on their political strategies. More significantly, these differences have determined the contours of much of the debate. To a large extent, the politics of the abortion controversy has been a referendum on the meaning of motherhood and the proper role of women. A transformation has taken place over the past few decades in the composition of the workforce and the composition of the family unit. The once traditional family (working father, mother at home with the kids) is no longer the norm. Economics, advances in birth control, divorce, and the women's movement combined to change that. As a result, two very different constituencies of women emerged. Although the legislative and judicial participants in the abortion debate are by large majorities males, the activists on both sides of the debate are predominantly women. And they approach the abortion question from very different notions about the role of pregnancy in women's lives. In the words of Luker:

> The abortion debate has become a debate among women, women with different values in the social world, different experiences of it, and differ-

ent resources with which to cope with it. How the issue is framed, how people think about it, and, most importantly, where the passions come from are all related to the fact that the battlelines are increasingly drawn (and defended) by women. While on the surface it is the embryo's fate that seems to be at stake, the abortion debate is actually about the meanings of women's lives.... To attribute personhood to the embryo is to make the social statement that pregnancy is valuable and that women should subordinate other parts of their lives to that central aspect of their social and biological selves. Conversely, if the embryo is held to be a fetus, then it becomes socially permissible for women to subordinate their reproductive roles to other roles; particularly in the paid work force.[23]

The demographic and value differences between pro-choice and pro-life activists has affected their choice of symbols, images, and rhetoric. Abortion opponents try to keep the debate focused on the humanness of the fetus and the value of family. Abortion supporters focus on the needs of the woman and the value of individual liberty and choice. The public debate thus emerges as pro-life versus pro-choice; as murder versus individual liberty; as care for the child versus care for the woman; as jars of fetuses versus bloody coat hangers. Not until after *Webster* altered the political landscape of the abortion issue in 1989 and it became clear that capturing the support of the uncommitted middle was key to winning in the abortion struggle did both sides attempt to reconsider and refashion the public presentation of their positions. But by then, the sloganeering had become so integral to the struggle that it was nearly impossible to shed.

At the same time that Washington-based antiabortion lobbyists like Gallagher were pressing Congress to end federal funding of abortions, groups around the country were mounting similar efforts. On 25 November 1975 the National Council of Catholic Bishops adopted a "Pastoral Plan for Pro-Life Activities," calling on all Catholic-related agencies to support a comprehensive pro-life legislative package. The plan urged the faithful to work to elect legislators who would support its goals. Although the plan did not create a nationwide network of pro-life organizations, it did provide an impetus for many local pro-life groups.[24] In New York State, for example, local groups pressed county legislatures to stop financing abortions; in 1978 three counties did. The Suffolk County legislature voted to halt abortion funding and then overrode a veto of that action by the county executive. Fifty pro-life supporters, mostly women, some with their babies in tow, applauded. Following the veto override, the women handed out baskets of long-stemmed roses to

the legislators—a symbolic gesture to signify life that became a trade-
mark of pro-life volunteer lobbyists. Said one spokeswoman of the
group, "Local pro-life people are already working for passage of similar
measures" in other counties.[25] Their aim was to start at the grass roots
and build enough momentum to force the New York State legislature to
change the state's permissive abortion law.

Many pro-life groups sought to affect electoral politics more directly.
On Long Island, New York, a small band of women formed the Right to
Life party. One of their members, Mary Jane Tobin, ran for governor in
1978 and won over 120,000 votes—more than the long-standing Liberal
party and enough to qualify under state law as a regular party with a
place on the ballot in future elections. "We found very early," said
Tobin, "that it's in politics that the big decisions are made. So we decided to run our own candidates." Their success sent shock waves
through the major parties, not because they were a real threat electorally
but because their one and only issue had proved to be so much more
powerful than anyone had thought it would. After the election, Tobin
discussed the Right to Life party's plans to force politicians on major-
party tickets to go on record regarding abortion. Asked whether she really meant everyone, even, say, a local tax assessor, she nodded affirma-
tively. "The issue is overriding," she said. Her campaign manager, Ellen
McCormick, added, "Disqualifying."[26] Their strategy of making opposition to abortion a litmus test for suitability for public office was followed by local- and state-level antiabortion groups around the country.
By 1980 it was a cornerstone of the national-level antiabortion strategy,
and by the end of the 1980s both sides of the abortion controversy were
applying such litmus tests.

On every anniversary following *Roe*, the marchers and demonstrations of abortion opponents returned to the Capitol. By 23 January
1980, the numbers in the March for Life, as the annual event became
known, swelled to 100,000 by organizers' estimates (the official park
police estimated 55,000). In less than seven years the antiabortion forces
had successfully pressed Congress to pass the Hyde Amendment, which
limited federal funding of abortions under Medicaid programs to cases
where pregnancy threatened the woman's life. In 1980 they were march-
ing in celebration of that success and to send a message about their
growing political strength.

A march on the Capitol is an indispensable part of pressure politics
in the United States. It rallies a membership and sends a message about a
group's strength to both opponents and political decision makers. The
critical question following a march is, How many people participated?
The higher the turnout, the more the presumed political power. Not sur-

prisingly, disputes about the number of marchers are legend. Groups tend to exaggerate their numbers and are not receptive to others' revising the numbers downward. For demonstrations in the capital, the U.S. Park Police (for demonstrations on the Mall) or the U.S. Capitol Police (for demonstrations around the Capitol) have the unenviable job of providing estimates. Their estimates are always much debated. In 1969 the park police originally calculated the Vietnam Moratorium Day crowd at 119,000 to 250,000. The figures later were revised upward to 500,000 to 600,000. Back then, the park police adhered to what an official spokesman called "the SWAG system, the scientific wild-ass guess." When rallies were antigovernment, the "guesses" were often low because "it wasn't unusual for politics to intercede."[27] Today there is a slightly more "scientific" method for arriving at the number of people in demonstrations.

During demonstrations the police now take pictures of the crowd from the top of the Washington Monument and from helicopters. They then plot the crowd on a map and a one-acre grid of the area around the Capitol and the Reflecting Pool. Based on the density of the crowd the pictures show, police estimate the number of persons present. For example, in the 28 April 1990 antiabortion rally, the park police estimated one person per five square feet and that twenty-two acres of the fifty-five acres around the Monument were covered with people. This translated into 198,000 people, the official figure. The rally organizers first said 700,000 people, which they later revised to 350,000. The park police, the media, and members of Congress were bombarded with complaints about the too-low official estimate. Senator Gordon Humphrey of New Hampshire and Representatives Robert Dornan of California and Christopher Smith of New Jersey—all outspoken abortion opponents—summoned the head of the park police to a meeting to "prove" the official estimate. The rally-numbers game, Dornan asserted, "is driving public policy. It's driving congressmen."[28] His concern was so great that he proposed using National Guard squadrons overflying in military jets with quality cameras to film demonstrations and thereby enable more "scientific" counts.

Crowd estimates are among the few issues that both sides of the abortion debate agree on. In the 9 April 1989 Washington rally staged by abortion supporters, the official estimate of the crowd was 300,000; rally organizers said 600,000. In the November Mobilize for Women's Lives rally, the official estimate was 150,000; abortion supporters said 300,000. Whatever the rational significance of these numbers, turnout figures have political significance. The political equation compares one side's turnout with the other's and plots the change in numbers of each side's participants over time. The "winners" enjoy added media attention; the "losers" suffer media dismissal. The public's perception of power (thus often the politician's perception as well) is molded in the process. Figure 2.1 presents the official turnout figures for the annual March for Life since 1974. The pro-choice side of the abortion struggle did not get into the march business until the mid-1980s. The turnout figures for its marches are included for the March 1986 Washington rally and for 1989 marches in April and November. From 1974 to 1989 the total estimated number of pro-life participants in sixteen marches was 647,500. The total number of pro-choice participants in three marches was 450,000. It is obvious that these "statistics" could be manipulated in any number of ways to prove the greater strength of either side.

The numbers game drives other aspects of pressure politics as well. How many organizations with how many members each side of an issue can claim is often a key measure in assessing interest-group political power. But it is impossible to determine which side of the abortion struggle is winning the membership numbers game because there is no accurate method for measuring how many members an organization really has or, in organizations that have a broader set of policy concerns, which of its claimed members support its abortion stand. One problem is that organizations have an interest in claiming the maximum membership possible. Even for dues-paying organizations, there is leeway for fudging the numbers—members who do not renew their membership may be carried on the rolls. For non-dues-paying organizations, the problem is greater. Who counts as a member? Anyone who writes or calls the organization? Anyone who voices support for its goals? Anyone who attends a meeting or event sponsored by the group? For single-issue groups, such as the National Abortion Rights Action League and the National Right to Life Committee, it is reasonable to conclude that the total membership embraces the group's positions on abortion. For dozens of broader-based organizations that take a public stand on abortion—from the American Federation of Teachers, the Sierra Club, and the American Association of University Women, who support abortion rights, to the Conservative Caucus, the Roman Catholic church, and the National Christian Action Coalition, who oppose abortion—extrapolating an accurate estimate of members who share the group's stand on abortion is impossible.

The New Right Joins the Struggle. — A little over a year after its founding in 1978 by a Texas minister and Jerry Falwell, a television evangelist, the Moral Majority became a political force to be reckoned with. Working loosely with other religious and conservative groups, in-

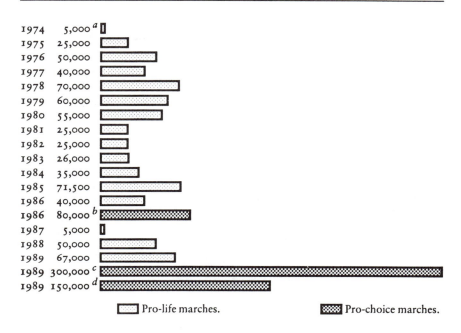

1974	5,000 [a]	
1975	25,000	
1976	50,000	
1977	40,000	
1978	70,000	
1979	60,000	
1980	55,000	
1981	25,000	
1982	25,000	
1983	26,000	
1984	35,000	
1985	71,500	
1986	40,000	
1986	80,000 [b]	
1987	5,000	
1988	50,000	
1989	67,000	
1989	300,000 [c]	
1989	150,000 [d]	

☐ Pro-life marches.   ▩ Pro-choice marches.

FIGURE 2.1

TURNOUTS FOR ABORTION MARCHES, 1974–89

NOTE: Total turnout for the sixteen March for Life rallies (1974–89), 647,500; total turnout for the three abortion rights rallies, 450,000. All turnout figures are based on park police estimates as reported in the *Washington Post* the day after the event.

a. March for Life, 1974–89. Abortion opponents. Low turnout in 1987 explained by bad storm. March for Life rallies have been held since 1973, always on 23 January, the anniversary of *Roe*, in protest of the decision.

b. March for Women's Lives, 1986.

c. 12 April; March for Women's Lives, 1989 (before *Webster* was argued).

d. 12 November; Mobilize for Women's Lives.

cluding many single-issue pro-life groups, the Moral Majority made its power felt in the nation's capital. Candidates who did not support the group's positions found their districts flooded with mail attacking them. Members of Congress were rated on their votes in a new "family rating." Lobbyists alerted members of Congress before votes on issues of concern to the Moral Majority coalition groups, warning that members who failed to vote "right" risked becoming targets of the movement's negative campaigns. "We will create a climate where it's not necessary to lobby in Washington," said one leader of the religious coalition. The grass-roots pressure from congressional districts would make the "appropriate course" of action "obvious."[29] One uncooperative congressman, John Buchanan of Alabama, lost his bid for reelection as a result of a negative campaign by the moral right. Later he commented, "They did a rather thorough job of beating my brains out with Christian love."[30] It did not take long for the message to circulate in the halls of Congress: crossing these groups carried heavy potential costs for members interested in keeping their seats.

On 21 and 22 August 1980, the National Affairs Briefing, billed as a political revival meeting, was held in Dallas, Texas, and attracted thousands of participants. More important in terms of national impact, a crowd of reporters gave it extensive coverage and dubbed it the most important political phenomenon of the year. The theme was "It's time for Christians to crawl out from under the pews."[31] The meeting was a call to political arms, and the attendees, more than a quarter of whom were ministers, were there to learn how to blow the trumpet when they returned home. Various Christian groups on the political right (Moral Majority, Religious Roundtable, Christian Voice, National Christian Action Coalition) and several right-to-life organizations were being molded into a more effective political force.

The delegates to the meeting embraced "a laundry list for the Eighties," as Jerry Falwell called it, and among the top goals was a constitutional amendment to ban abortion. They planned voter-registration drives centered on the churches, church-level laymen's leagues to study candidates and legislation, state and regional training seminars in political tactics, the expansion of an already thriving network of newsletters that "simplify" and "clarify" the issues, a telephone network to bring an avalanche of Christian opinion down on Congress at critical points in the legislative process, and a concerted courting of the media. None of these approaches was new. Organized labor, the Catholic church in its antiabortion crusade, environmental groups, consumer groups, and others had tried them all before; and groups on the other side of the abortion issue had tried them as well. The point was to make the cause impossible to ignore, to become the squeaky wheel that gets the political grease.

With the election to the presidency of Ronald Reagan, who voiced support for most of their goals, the New Right groups hoped that the 1980s would see a religious and moral awakening in the United States that would translate into success for their agenda. In terms of the abortion issue, the evangelical revival became a new and powerful force on the antiabortion side, but the result was not as positive as abortion opponents hoped.

Political scientist E.E. Schattschneider called "the contagiousness of conflict, the elasticity of its scope and the fluidity of the involvement of the people the X factors of politics."[32] In any political conflict, the first people to be involved are those who feel most intensely about the issue and for whom it is most salient. If the issue is an economic one, activists are likely to be those who are most financially disadvantaged by the status quo or those whose pockets will be lined with the most silver if the issue is resolved in their favor (or who will lose the most if it is resolved against them). Economic issues more clearly define potential participants. Only those with a significant financial stake are likely to pay much attention or devote time; the cost to the average tax-paying or product-purchasing citizen is usually too minute to be motivational. In other words, the contagiousness of conflict is limited because the scope of the issue and the number of people interested is limited. Economic issues also offer at least potential grounds for compromising—a little silver in your pocket, a little in mine. For a social policy issue in which the benefits and disadvantages are less tangible or more diffuse, the initial hard-core activists are usually those who feel most ardently about the issue; it is passion, not a financial stake, that motivates. Moreover, the potential participants are the population at large—the "fluidity of the involvement of the people" is a potential tidal wave. Finding acceptable compromises in social-policy issues is also more difficult, especially on issues involving strongly held moral, ethical, or religious beliefs.

Schattschneider also pointed out that losers in a political struggle have a high incentive to expand the scope of the conflict in order to tilt the balance of power in their favor. To do this, they must make their issue more visible and persuade more people that its resolution is critical. But if losers are successful persuaders and new converts are recruited, the ability of the original players to control the issue is weakened. Loss of control is complicated as converts are added who do not feel quite as strongly as the original activists or who have broader agendas. Holding onto a growing constituency often requires expanding the definition of the problem or making modifications in the desired solution. Such compromises can anger those committed to the original agenda and lead to splinter groups, which in turn may undercut the effectiveness of a movement. All efforts to build coalitions of the size necessary to influence national politics risk these pitfalls. As the antiabortion movement expanded to include the New Right activists, it too ran into them.

Buoyed by the 1980 election that brought to the Republicans control of the Senate and White House, the New Right believed it could win all it wanted. Among the pro-life forces, however, this confidence of the New Right immediately caused schisms, which were evident in hearings held by a Senate judiciary subcommittee in early 1981 on proposals to "overturn" *Roe*. Differences in opinion among abortion opponents about how best legally to accomplish the outlawing of abortion erupted openly. That the split contributed to the defeat of antiabortion legislation is acknowledged in the comments of Richard Doerflinger, legislative assistant to the National Conference of Catholic Bishops:

> Senator Helms' effort to link the pro-life effort with various "New Right" concerns [proposals to strip the courts of the power of review over school prayer and antibusing measures, for example] did not prove to be a formula for success. . . . By blurring the issues, Helms prevented unified pro-life support and allowed his opponents to caricature his efforts as an attack upon the separation of powers.[33]

Jesse Helms had chosen a parliamentary strategy that linked the school prayer and abortion issues; he sought to strip the courts of jurisdiction over both. He presented his proposal in a way that forced his colleagues to vote for or against the whole package. Doerflinger explained that the Catholic bishops had not supported Helms's abortion amendment, even though they supported its purpose. This was because "the bishops' conference took no position on school prayer legislation and did not want to get involved in the issue of separation of powers." The New Right's agenda included goals that the Catholic bishops were not prepared to accept. But the New Right was unwilling to focus solely on the abortion issue.

The Senate hearings had another effect on the interest groups involved, as a Planned Parenthood director explained: "People had been worried about the New Right before but they didn't feel personally affected. The hearings were a real plus for us, they galvanized things. They moved abortion from No. 9 on [our] people's agenda to No. 1."[34] The national attention given the hearings highlighted the potential threat to the post-*Roe* status quo. Abortion supporters began to awaken to the possibility that their 1973 victory was not the end of the war. In addition, the public notice given the broader agenda of the New Right galvanized other liberal groups, especially those concerned about civil rights and the protection of the courts. "When you push people's backs to the wall, they fight back," commented a director of the NAACP. "There was too much Jesse Helms, too much New Right."[35] The counterlobbying effort of supporters was strengthened by others who were alarmed by the prospect of a triumphant New Right. The balance of power in the abortion conflict was shifting again.

In 1982 and again in 1983, the Senate voted against antiabortion proposals to amend the U. S. Constitution. Abortion opponents had run into a brick wall on their constitutional-amendment strategy (constitutional amendment proposals are discussed in chapter 4). There was much recrimination within the movement over its failure to achieve congressional passage of a constitutional amendment overturning *Roe*. But leaders in the antiabortion movement had been aware for some time that they did not have the necessary votes. Shortly after the 1980 elections the executive director of the National Committee for a Human Life Amendment presented an analysis to its lobbyists, concluding that although they had picked up ten new supporters in the Republican takeover of the Senate, this brought their total to only forty-eight—three votes short of a majority necessary for passing legislation and nineteen votes short of the two-thirds necessary for a constitutional amendment.[36] They had won the banning of the federal funding of abortion, but support for the next step in Congress was simply not there.

From the start the Reagan administration announced its intent to seek out those who were sympathetic to its conservative agenda (including its opposition to abortion) in appointing judges to the federal bench (chapter 5 provides a full discussion of this strategy and its successes). Abortion opponents shifted their strategy from a constitutional amendment to litigation; again, the civil rights movement provided a model.

In April 1984 Americans United for Life, a legal arm of the antiabortion movement, held a conference in Chicago featuring a dozen scholars and litigators and attended by over 500 clergy, lawyers, law students, physicians, and ordinary citizens. Its aim was to devise a coordinated strategy for developing cases for court challenges to abortion. Legal challenges to *Roe* had thus far not fared well in the Supreme Court. To be sure, the Court had upheld national and state restrictions on public financing of abortion, as well as state-imposed requirements for informed consent and notification of parents of minors. In addition, the margin of support among the justices was dwindling from the original 7–2 in *Roe* to 6–3, and by 1986 this would become 5–4 (see 3.1 , p. 97, for a summary of Supreme Court rulings following *Roe*).

Comparing their meeting to one held in 1931 by Thurgood Marshall

and other NAACP lawyers, participants proposed that they focus on the
advantages and disadvantages of a frontal assault on *Roe* or a siege leading to the erosion and eventual collapse of *Roe*. University of California
at Berkeley Professor of Law John T. Noonan, Jr. (who was later
appointed by Reagan to the federal bench), explained:

> Essentially [the NAACP] strategy was one of gradualism, taking the easi-
> est, most outrageous cases first, dealing with segregation at the graduate
> level, then with segregation at the law school level, piercing the fraud
> that there were separate but equal facilities there and then eventually,
> step by step, getting the judges and the country to see that separate but
> equal was a fraud everywhere. That is the pattern that beckons to this
> movement.[37]

For such a litigation strategy, they needed cases to bring the issue before the courts. One participant suggested that the group should lobby
for state laws that would add new limitations to the availability of abortions, which might have a better chance of surviving judicial review. For
example, states might be persuaded to adopt laws outlawing late-term
abortions or requiring that abortions be performed in hospitals, where
they would be more expensive. Then test cases could be devised to defend such statutes. Their hope was that as the composition of the judicial branch changed with Reagan's appointees, some of the test cases
could be won. As more and more restrictive state abortion laws were
upheld, the breadth of *Roe*'s protection for a woman's right to choose an
abortion could be chipped away. "Reasoning, experience and new facts"
might, as one delegate put it, "open the eyes" of judges and justices who
had supported *Roe*.[38] It had worked for the civil rights groups in school
desegregation cases, and abortion opponents believed it could work for
them as well.

A legal strategy takes time, and some in the antiabortion movement
were losing patience with the political system. Although the movement
had been successful in turning off the federal spigot financing abortions,
this win had little effect on the numbers of abortions performed in the
United States, which remained constant at about 1.5 million a year. For
many activists, stopping abortions, even if it meant stopping only a few,
became the paramount goal. Demonstrations in front of abortion clinics
had been a local strategy of abortion opponents from the start. For the
most part, these were peaceful protests, even though some demonstrators went beyond the law. Perhaps the most famous was Joan Andrews,
a pacifist and longtime protestor for human rights, who ended up spending two and a half years in jail for attempting to disengage a suction ma-

chine used in abortions. Demonstrators, with increasing frequency by the mid-1980s, were resorting to civil disobedience: trespass, interfering with the movement of others, and damaging property. One proponent of the strategy, Joseph Scheidler, a former Benedictine monk, published a book listing ninety-nine ways to close abortion clinics. Included was a suggestion that activists jam a clinic's door locks with glue. Other suggestions were to flood abortion clinics with calls to tie up their phone lines and to track down women who visited abortion clinics by their license-plate numbers or by hiring a private detective (something Scheidler once did himself) and then try to stop them from going through with the abortion. Before long some resorted to more extreme measures—bombing and setting clinics on fire.

✒ The Pro-Life Nonviolent Action Project (PNAP) was one of the earliest to organize antiabortion activists, as the group's founder put it, "to use nonviolent action to protect babies." The PNAP produced flyers and pamphlets and educated other activists in the means of nonviolent protest. At the 1984 National Right to Life party convention in Kansas City, antiabortion activist Scheidler led 100 people to the abortion clinics in the city—they all closed. That event provided the model for the PNAP's subsequent "rescue" attempts. In 1986 and 1987 it asserted that its activities resulted in "shut[ting] down almost the entire abortion industry in Washington during the March for Life; despite our very limited numbers.... And at the National Right to Life Convention [in 1988], we closed down the abortion industry in Denver and New Orleans, but failed in Washington and Arlington."[39] Another activist, Juli Loesch, worked to organize "We Will Stand Up," a series of clinic protests at cities visited by Pope John Paul II on his 1987 tour of the United States.

Antiabortion crusades to block access to clinics captured considerable media attention, but the strategy did not gain national notoriety until, during the summer of 1988 in front of hordes of news crews that had gathered to cover the Democratic presidential convention, Operation Rescue staged its "Siege on Atlanta." The siege was orchestrated by a young evangelical convert, Randall A. Terry. A fellow activist described Terry's efforts: "He organized without distraction for two years to undertake a national action, lasting several days, first in New York and then in Atlanta. He organized it brilliantly and brought in all the pro-life groups."[40] Some 1200 demonstrators converged on Atlanta to blockade the entrances to abortion clinics in the city during the political convention. One measure of the success of the demonstration was the inflow to Operation Rescue's treasury. Before the event the income of the group was about $5000 per month; four months after the event it was in excess of $60,000 per month.[41] Soon the group prepared to expand its blockade tactic, targeting dozens of cities and hundreds of abortion clinics around the nation. By May 1989 Operation Rescue was claiming that it had over 35,000 members in 200 cities and that more than 250 "rescues" had been performed, including the "Holy Week Rescue" staged during March 1989 in Los Angeles, California, where 1278 Operation Rescue protestors were arrested. Many earned the group's special designation of "Prisoner of Christ" for spending thirty days or more behind bars.[42]

Operation Rescue's tactics are self-consciously modeled after the passive-resistance approach of Mahatma Gandhi and Martin Luther King, Jr. The aim is to blockade abortion clinics and prevent those seeking abortion from entering. Demonstrators are coached ahead of time and warned not to push or shove, not to bring posters, and to lie or stand tightly together in a wall of bodies so that no one can pass (see 2.1 , p. 60). As one news account described their actions: "They move in a human sludge, on their knees, not standing, to make confrontation possible."[43] When the police attempt to move them, participants go limp, forcing the officers to carry or drag them away. If arrested, they are supposed to continue their noncooperation by refusing to give their names or pay any fines—a strategy that usually lands them in jail.

Events purposely staged to include civil disobedience offer drama, an aura of danger, and the potential for violence—the perfect ingredients for attracting media attention. Reporters are well aware of their readers' or viewers' fascination with confrontation and violence, and they scurry to cover situations that hold out such promise. What starts as a nonviolent demonstration can easily turn ugly with the addition of counterdemonstrators or the police—antiabortion forces are *not* always nonviolent. Indeed, violence has erupted during a number of Operation Rescue attempts. The civil disobedience approach of Operation Rescue is not a strategy supported by all antiabortion groups; some see in it the potential for creating a public backlash against the whole pro-life movement.[44]

Although he does not criticize those who have bombed clinics, Operation Rescue's Randall Terry recognizes the danger of using violence to advance the pro-life cause: "I believe in the use of force. But, I think to destroy abortion facilities at this time is counterproductive because the American public has an adverse reaction to what it sees as violence."[45] But as long as the rescuers start out and continue to be nonviolent, confrontation may work to their advantage. When television audiences and newspaper readers are presented with pictures of uniformed police dragging off the limp, uncooperative bodies of "average citizens" who do not look anything like hoodlums or criminals, the hope is that the public will be repelled (as it was eventually in the civil rights and antiwar demonstrations) and will move to support the demonstrators and their cause.

Operation Rescuers see themselves as nonviolent, but their opponents have a different view. And they use a different analogy to the civil rights movement to make their point:

> Anti-abortion activists have no more right to stand in the doorways to clinics to block women from entering to choose abortion than Governor Ross Barnett had the right to stand in the doorway of the University of Mississippi to block James Meredith from choosing desegregated education.... Both the segregationists and the blockaders are physically preventing people from exercising their constitutional right.[46]

Terry's rescue strategy soon ran into a legal brick wall. In September 1989 he was convicted for his role in the Siege on Atlanta and sentenced to jail because he refused to pay a $500 fine. (He spent four and a half months behind bars before an anonymous benefactor paid the fine for him.) Subsequently, he faced far more substantial court-imposed fines for other demonstration activities (in one instance, the fine was $50,000). As a result, in February 1990 he announced that his organization was broke and that he was closing its national headquarters. Nevertheless, the civil disobedience strategy of the abortion rescues continued to play a significant role in abortion politics, and Terry was soon back on the picket lines himself.

The Reawakening of the Pro-Choice Movement

As abortion opponents focused their attention on state legislatures with an eye to creating opportunities for court challenges, and on staging raids on abortion clinics, groups on the other side of the issue turned their attention to lobbying state legislatures and mounting counterdemonstrations to protect access to the clinics.

Although many of the groups that actively support abortion, such as the National Abortion Rights Action League, Planned Parenthood Federation of America, National Organization for Women, and American Civil Liberties Union, have state chapters with substantial memberships, their major strength has always been their professionally staffed central organizations. Personnel employed by these and other pro-choice interest groups played a significant role defending legal challenges to *Roe* in the courts, providing facilities where abortions could be obtained, and mounting legal defenses for clinics subjected to demonstrations and

2.1 | Rules for On-Site Participants

I UNDERSTAND the critical importance of Operation Rescue being unified, peaceful, and free of any actions or words that would appear violent or hateful to those watching the event on TV, or reading about it in the paper.

I REALIZE that some of the pro-abortion elements of the media would love to discredit this event (and the entire prolife movement) and focus on a side issue in order to avoid the central issue at hand: murdered children and exploited women.

HENCE, I UNDERSTAND that for the children's sake, this gathering must be orderly and above reproach.

THEREFORE ...

(1) As an invited guest, I will cooperate with the spirit and goals of Operation Rescue, as explained in this pamphlet.

(2) I commit to be peaceful, prayerful, and nonviolent in both word and deed.

(3) Should I be arrested, I will not struggle with police in any way (whether deed or word), but remain polite and passively limp, remembering that mercy triumphs over judgement.

(4) I will listen and follow the instructions of Operation Rescue's leadership and crowd control marshall.

(5) I understand that certain individuals will be appointed to speak to the media, the police, and the women seeking abortion. I will not take it upon myself to yell to anyone, but will continue singing and praying with the main group, as directed.

I SIGN THIS PLEDGE, HAVING SERIOUSLY CONSIDERED WHAT I DO, WITH THE WILL AND DETERMINATION TO PERSEVERE BY THE GRACE OF GOD.

_____

DATE

_____

SIGNATURE

CIRCLE ONLY ONE ITEM

(1) I am prepared to risk arrest in order to rescue children from the violent death of abortion.

(2) I will be present to pray, picket, and show support for this rescue.

SOURCE: Operation Rescue of Central Virginia.

blockades. The groups favoring abortion rights, however, were hampered in developing a grass-roots strategy by the fact that the vast majority of their constituency works full-time. Their members and supporters are better able to donate dollars than time. But, as is usually the case with fund raising, unless there is a sense of crisis, it is difficult to wring donations out of any but the most committed. Without huge war chests to finance more hiring, the central staffs of the pro-choice groups remained too small to spread around fifty states to compensate for unavailable volunteers.

Money and numbers: the stuff of pressure politics. Abortion-rights supporters needed more of both, but to counter the well-honed state-level grass-roots force of abortion opponents, what they needed most was numbers. In 1989 a political consultant to the National Abortion Rights Action League conceded that "the right-to-life forces have a big advantage over us because they've worked the state legislatures for years. Our people haven't thought the action was at the state level.... It's a question of getting our people organized."[47] More critical than organization was the need to awaken their constituency to the threat to *Roe*. For a short time during the pro-life constitutional-amendment heyday in 1982 and 1983, it appeared that the pro-choice side was prepared to counterattack, but as soon as the amendment threat passed, the pro-choicers went back to sleep.

The decision in *Thornburgh v. American College of Obstetricians and Gynecologists* announced in June 1986 served as another wake-up call. The pro-choice count in the Supreme Court slipped to a bare majority. Chief Justice Warren Burger for the first time deserted the *Roe* majority, joining in dissent with Justices William Rehnquist, Byron White, and Sandra Day O'Connor, Reagan's first appointee and the only woman on the Court. Concern about how the Court might rule in *Thornburgh* had prompted abortion rights supporters to stage a demonstration in Washington just before the case was argued to counter the annual march by abortion opponents. The March for Women's Lives on 9 March drew 80,000 participants, double the pro-lifers who had marched that year on the anniversary of *Roe*. "The Religious Right has the ear of the White House," complained one participant who had traveled from Texas. "They will influence the impressionable, and the tide will swing.... I thought it was important to come here to be counted as a defender of women's rights. I'll be paying for this trip for the next six months but I thought it was important to come."[48]

Abortion supporters were jubilant with the size of the turnout. But it was going to take a much greater sense of urgency than that stirred by a near-loss to transform their working-9-to-5 women and college-student partisans from occasional weekend marchers into an effective grass-roots force. As one congressional aide put it, "There is fear of the Right-to-Life Committee, not of the choice groups. They'll have to create that."[49] To gain that reaction on the Hill, the abortion rights side needed to prove it could turn its people out to vote for like-minded candidates. Moreover, it would have to do so again and again, just as the other side had done and would do in the future. Some crisis was needed to energize its constituents.

A suit against a new restrictive antiabortion law passed by the Missouri legislature provided that sense of crisis. In January 1989 the Supreme Court announced that it was accepting the Missouri case, *Webster v. Reproductive Health Services,* for review. There was an upsurge of fear among abortion rights supporters that the Court would overrule *Roe.* "Until the Supreme Court announced the decision to hear the *Webster* case, we had difficulty communicating to pro-choice people that we were at risk," remarked the director of the clinic that challenged the Missouri statute. "Now there is an outpouring of support, something I've never seen since I've been at this agency."[50]

Abortion rights supporters were apprehensive with reason. Between the 5–4 *Thornburgh* decision in June 1986 and the Court's acceptance of *Webster,* dramatic changes had taken place in the composition of the nation's highest bench. In July 1986 Chief Justice Burger had announced his retirement. President Reagan elevated Rehnquist to chief justice and nominated Antonin Scalia to replace Rehnquist as the ninth justice. Then, in June 1987 Justice Lewis F. Powell, Jr., who had cast the key fifth vote for upholding *Roe* in *Thornburgh,* gave notice that he would retire. If the president replaced him with an abortion opponent, the scales would tip and *Roe* might fall. When Reagan nominated Robert H. Bork, warning sirens wailed in pro-choice camps and joyful bells sounded in pro-life quarters. The lobbying and public relations machinery of both sides went into high gear.

If the abortion rights groups had battled Bork alone, it is at least open to question whether they would have succeeded. But, as was true with Helms's 1982–83 constitutional-amendment efforts, the abortion issue was only one of many concerns surrounding Bork's nomination. Bork's voluminous writings on a host of topics provided a public record of his disagreement with the legal basis for a number of the Court's past liberal rulings—issues such as school prayer, affirmative action, and defendants' rights. Equally clear was Bork's sympathy for the broad conservative agenda. Groups concerned with all sorts of issues joined the confirmation battle. A news account describes the lobbying scene:

Almost as soon as Bork's nomination was announced last week, both sides started to write and telephone their members, recruit other groups, bombard editorial writers with information about the Senate's role in the confirmation process and design advertising campaigns and legislative strategies to prevent or assure Bork's elevation to the high court.... At the annual convention of the NAACP yesterday, delegates unanimously passed a resolution criticizing Bork's stands ... and call[ed] for an all-out effort to block confirmation. "We must let our senators know that a vote against Mr. Bork is a prerequisite for our vote in the next election," Coretta Scott King said to loud applause.... The 1.8 million-member National Education Association, the nation's largest teachers union, also voted to fight the nomination. NOW [the National Organization for Women] ... plans to organize rallies against Bork, establish telephone banks to generate mail and telegrams to key senators.... People for the American Way, a liberal lobbying group ... has five or six people working full time on the Bork nomination and about $360,000 in "seed money" to spend on the battle.... Likewise, conservative groups have weighed in ... for "the biggest liberal-conservative battle since the 1984 election." ... The first meetings of conservative leaders to brainstorm and begin to start action were the very next morning.... Concerned Women for America, a 500,000-member conservative group, sent letters yesterday to about 50 area leaders nationwide asking them to activate phone banks and urge members to write their senators.... The American Conservative Union contacted its top 1000 contributors ... asking them to send contributions to support the Bork effort.[51]

When the Senate finally voted against confirmation, pro-choice groups were quick to claim their share of the credit for the defeat. But, by the time the coalition that had fought against Bork was faced with Reagan's third nominee for Powell's seat, Anthony Kennedy, as one participant commented, "We were simply worn out. It just isn't possible to keep the troops at full pitch for that long."[52]

Subsequently, abortion opponents declared George Bush's election as president "a very big feather in the pro-life cap." The director of the Pro-Life Action League commented, "On the first day after his election, George Bush said that while he wouldn't use a litmus test on any one issue for Supreme Court appointments, he would look for conservatives who do not use the court to make new law—and that adds up to people who will overturn *Roe v. Wade*."[53] Norman Ornstein agreed: "By using rhetoric that appealed to the pro-life people, George Bush did mobilize people that might not otherwise have voted for him. He is going to think twice before he acts to alienate that base. I think there is almost no question that in making Supreme Court appointments, abortion will be among the top three questions the White House will ask."[54]

In November 1988 voters in Michigan, Arkansas, and Colorado approved measures to bar the use of state funds for abortion, bringing the number of states that refuse to pay for abortions for the poor to thirty-seven. "Our main strategy is to overturn *Roe v. Wade,* so state referenda are not something we devote a lot of time and energy to," remarked a spokeswoman for the National Right to Life Committee. "But, I think we've made our point by winning all three, one in the South, one in the industrial Midwest and one in the West."[55] That piece of bad news for abortion rights supporters rendered the appearance of *Webster* on the Supreme Court's 1989 docket even more inauspicious. The litigation strategy of abortion opponents was beginning to show results.

Abortion rights groups around the country reacted with alarm. The National Organization for Women, Planned Parenthood Federation of America, National Abortion Rights Action League, American Civil Liberties Union, and a multitude of other concerned groups went to red alert. They needed some dramatic way to prove their strength, and they needed it fast. The Court had scheduled the *Webster* argument for 26 April 1989. There is no way to lobby Supreme Court justices, at least not directly, but as Faye Wattleton, president of the Planned Parenthood Federation of America, pointed out, "The Court is not sequestered on another planet. They do hear the voices of the American people."[56]

One way to let the Court hear is through personal communication. The pro-choice groups mobilized their members and supporters, and an avalanche of letters and phone calls followed. The opposition arranged for the same. Normally, the Court receives about 1000 pieces of mail daily; within weeks the volume reached 40,000. Toni House, the Court's public information officer, cautioned, "I hope they understand this is not a popularity contest. We are not keeping score of who favors abortion and who does not. While people have a right to write to the court I hope they do not expect that the enunciation of their opinion will have any effect on the justices."[57]

There is no official way to lobby Supreme Court justices, but justices, as Wattleton recognized, do not live in a vacuum. In a speech given in 1986, Justice Rehnquist conceded with surprising candor that the justices are indeed affected by "the court of public opinion." Although they "work in an isolated atmosphere," he went on, "the same judges go home at night and read the newspapers or watch the evening news on television. They talk to their family and friends about current events.

Judges, so long as they are relatively normal human beings, can no more escape being influenced by public opinion in the long run than can people working at other jobs."[58]

Pro-abortion groups set about preparations for a march in Washington, hoping that as many as 100,000 would bring the message home to the justices about public support for *Roe*. It was to begin at the Washington Monument and end at the U.S. Supreme Court building. No one believed that even a larger turnout would sway many on the Court. But as Justice Charles Evans Hughes once put it, the Court's credibility could be strained and its authority undermined "if it marched too sharply in one direction while public opinion marched in the other." The abortion rights cause needed five votes; four (Harry Blackmun, William Brennan, Thurgood Marshall, and John Paul Stevens) were fairly certain, four were pretty clearly lost (Rehnquist, Scalia, White, and Kennedy). As Representative Thomas J. Downey (D-New York) pointed out, the show was "all for Sandra Day O'Connor. One signal for one Justice: I hope she gets the message."[59]

On 9 April the march organizers were overwhelmed. An estimated 300,000 people, one of the largest political demonstrations ever held in Washington, "jammed elbow-to-elbow, blowing whistles, beating drums and waving banners" paraded past the Supreme Court for more than four hours. "We've hit middle America," exulted Eleanor Smeal, president of the Fund for the Feminist Majority, "I can't get over it."[60] "This is the reawakening of the silent majority, a sleeping lion that's awakened. We are angry," said Brooklyn District Attorney Elizabeth Holtzman, who joined the marchers.[61] This is a "statement to the political leadership of this country—to President Bush, the Congress of the United States and the Supreme Court—that the women of this country will not go back. There is no turning back for us. . . . We are going to reshape this whole argument to make clear that we are the overwhelming majority," declared Molly Yard, president of the National Organization for Women. Yard hoped the Supreme Court would listen: "They are political creatures and they do understand public opinion. And, I have to believe the Supreme Court doesn't want to tear apart the social fabric of this country."[62]

The abortion rights march was full of the symbols and drama that command media attention. Marchers had been asked to wear white in honor of the suffragettes who had marched for women's rights before them. White coat hangers hung around many necks, symbolic of a self-abortion method used when the procedure was illegal. Signs, T-shirts, and buttons adorned the marchers: *My body, my baby, my business. Keep your laws off my body. Keep Abortion Legal. Stand up for Choice.*

Mothers and daughters and whole families, children included, marched to show that families were important to the pro-choice side too. *Motherhood by Choice* was a popular sign among family marchers. Busloads organized by churches came to prove that there were plenty of religious people who supported abortion rights. There were thousands of the abortion rights regulars, the long-term activists, but there were many more first-time marchers, many who had come on their own, not as a part of any group effort. And big-name celebrities assured even more media attention: Whoopi Goldberg, Jane Fonda, Morgan Fairchild, Glenn Close, Veronica Hamel, Marlo Thomas, Leonard Nimoy, among many others. Barbra Streisand, creator of Hollywood Women's Political Committee, made calls to some members of Congress who were hesitant to join the effort. And there was an abundance of political figures, too, with a notable exception: President Bush was nowhere to be seen. The White House responded, "We have no comment."

On the other side of the Capitol, a few hundred abortion opponents gathered at their "Cemetery of the Innocents," amid 4400 white crosses they had erected near the Reflecting Pool for a prayer vigil. The crosses were intended as symbols of the average number of abortions performed in a day. Some counterdemonstrators dressed as babies in bonnets and bloomers shouted their own slogans at the marchers, but there were no major incidents. On 9 April it was the abortion rights side that commanded the news and numbers. But a few months later, the tables turned again. The Supreme Court made clear that the march had not persuaded the justices. The Court did not use *Webster* to overturn *Roe,* but it did draw back from its past limits on state regulation of the procedure, and the majority sent strong signals that it might be receptive to overturning *Roe* in the near future. But the loss provided a dramatic disturbance of the sort that could reinvigorate the pro-choice forces. "There is no question," said Congresswoman Barbara Boxer, "the Supreme Court awakened a sleeping giant." Even abortion opponents recognized, as Paige Cunningham, a lawyer for Americans United for Life, commented, that "the pro-choice movement is fresh so they're operating with a much greater energy reserve. They've really rallied in light of *Webster*."[63]

After *Webster,* both sides realized they would have to make changes in their approach. The uncommitted or complacent middle seemed to hold the key to winning the abortion struggle. The purple-prose approach of the earlier abortion activists is not likely to capture that middle, a fact that both sides recognize. A National Right to Life Committee spokesman conceded that the abortion rights side was winning in the court of public opinion because they had been better at framing and positioning their message. "We need to focus on specific legislative measures that are clearly in the mainstream," he commented, adding that there is much support for limiting the circumstances under which abortion is allowed.[64] At nearly the same time, the National Abortion Rights Action League concluded that its side was losing in the public opinion race. To the extent that "abortion is thought of as a selfish or irresponsible act, and if our rhetoric looks frivolous or selfish," a professional consultant to the group concluded, we will "lose a lot of the people in the middle."[65] Each side focused on finding ways to talk about its position that would resonate with the public. In the meantime, one thing was certain: The Supreme Court had once again altered the battlefield.

Notes

1. *Brown v. Allen,* 344 U.S. 443, 540 (1953).

2. *Washington Post,* 23 January 1983, A1.

3. *USA Today,* 21 January 1983, 1.

4. *New York Times,* 6 April 1989, B10.

5. Quoted, *Congressional Quarterly Weekly Report,* 6 September 1980, 2629.

6. See David B. Truman, *The Governmental Process* (New York: Knopf, 1951); all quotations from 106-7.

7. Of course, social policy can and often does have an economic component as well. The NAACP was (and still is) as much interested in the economic well-being and advancement of African-Americans as in their social status within the community. Indeed, the two goals are inextricably entwined. But the early stages of the civil rights struggle had to be focused on the moral and legal "rightness" of equality, in much the same way as the abortion struggle focuses on issues of moral and legal "rightness." The abortion struggle, to be sure, has also had a financial component involving the question of government funding of abortions. The muddled complexity of the real politics of policy making resists manageable categorizing, but many social scientists have attempted to map the interest-group policy-making battlefield. For example, Randall B. Ripley and Grace A. Franklin present a six-category map of the national policy-making process based on the nature of the players and the nature of the policy issue. See *Congress, the Bureaucracy and Public Policy,* 5th ed. (Chicago: Dorsey Press, 1990). James Q. Wilson presents a categorizing scheme based on economic winners and losers. See *The Politics of Regulation* (New York: Basic Books, 1980), chap. 10.

8. Jeffrey M. Berry, *The Interest Group Society,* 2d ed. (Glenview, Ill.: Scott, Foresman, 1989), 8.

9. For an excellent discussion of group strategies and resources, see Kay

Lehman Schlozman and John T. Tierney, *Organized Interests and American Democracy* (New York: Harper & Row, 1986), chaps. 5, 7.

10. Kristin Luker, *Abortion and the Politics of Motherhood,* (Berkeley: University of California Press, 1984), 137–44.

11. Ibid. For a more complete history of the first right-to-life effort, see chaps. 1 and 2.

12. Ibid., 41. Luker bases this assertion on a content analysis of all articles written on abortion between 1890 and 1960, as indexed in the *Readers' Guide to Periodical Literature,* the *Index Medicus,* and three large California newspapers.

13. In 1959 the American Law Institute's Model Penal Code proposal included this wording on abortion.

14. Finkbine eventually obtained an abortion in Sweden. See Luker, *Abortion,* 62–65.

15. The figures are from Luker, *Abortion,* 94. See chap. 6 for an analysis of the emergence of the right-to-life movement in California.

16. *New York Times,* 25 November 1978, 28.

17. People join organizations for many reasons. They seek *material benefits* (a sort of, What's in it for me?), *purposive benefits* (I'm doing good and it makes me feel good), and *solidarity benefits* (misery loves company, especially if the prevailing public winds seem to be blowing against me). Abortion activists on both sides of the issue, like most other interest-group activists, join and support organizations that take positions and act on the abortion issue for a combination of these reasons, rarely for one alone. For a discussion of mobilization and organization of interest groups, see Berry, *Interest Group Society,* chap. 3.

18. Quoted, *Newsweek,* 1 May 1989, 31.

19. *New York Times,* 27 November 1977, sec. 4, p. 4.

20. *New York Times,* 23 January 1974, 38.

21. Ibid.

22. Luker, *Abortion,* 145.

23. Ibid., 193–94. Others have studied and remarked on the dramatic differences between pro- and antiabortion supporters. A study by Donald Granberg of the characteristic and attitudinal differences between activists in the National Abortion Rights Action League (NARAL) and the National Right to Life Committee (NRLC) concluded that "NRLC members are far more likely than NARAL members to have been reared in large families, to prefer large families and to have large families. . . . About 70 percent of NRLC members are Roman Catholic—two and one-half times the proportion in the general population; only four percent of NARAL members are Catholic." He also found dramatic differences between the role religion played in activists' lives, with nine out of ten NRLC members declaring it plays a "very important role and that they attend religious services at least once a week"; only one out of five NARAL members made similar assertions. ("The Abortion Activist," *Family Planning Perspectives* 13, no. 4 [1981]: 157–63.) Public opinion polls show similar, though less dramatic, differences between those who voice support for the two sides. (See chapter 7 for an analysis of the demographics of those holding different opinions on abortion.)

24. See John E. Jackson and Maris A. Vinovskis, "Public Opinion, Elec-

tions, and the 'Single Issue' Issue," in *The Abortion Dispute and the American System,* ed. Gilbert Y. Steiner (Washington, D.C.: Brookings Institution, 1983), 72–73.

25. Quoted, *New York Times,* 1 March 1978, B3.

26. Quoted, *New York Times,* 25 November 1978, 28. In 1976 McCormick had run as a pro-life candidate in the Democratic presidential primaries. She did not attract many votes, but she did manage to raise enough funds in twenty states to qualify for federal matching funds.

27. Quoted, *Washington Post,* 4 May 1990, C6.

28. Ibid., C1.

29. James Robinson, quoted, *Congressional Quarterly Weekly Report,* 6 September 1980, 2629.

30. Ibid., 2627.

31. Quoted, ibid., 2630.

32. E.E. Schattschneider, *The Semisovereign People* (Hinsdale, Ill.: Dryden Press, 1960), 1–19.

33. Quoted, *Congressional Quarterly Weekly Report,* 16 October 1982, 2676.

34. Ibid.

35. Ibid., 2677.

36. Ibid., 2676.

37. Quoted, *New York Times,* 2 April 1984, A15.

38. Ibid.

39. Quotes and information on the PNAP from John Cavanaugh-O'Keefe, "Peaceful Presence: Rescue's Roots," *ALL About Issues* (American Life League), March 1989, 19.

40. Quoted, *Time,* 1 May 1989, 28.

41. See Gary Wills, "Evangels of Abortion," *New York Review of Books,* 15 June 1989, 19.

42. *Newsweek,* 1 May 1989, 32.

43. Ibid., 27.

44. One measure of the National Right to Life Committee's disagreement with the civil disobedience approach is that their newsletter never refers to the activities of the most visible of such groups, Operation Rescue.

45. Quoted, *Washington Post,* 6 March 1989, A3.

46. Quoting John H. Henn, legal counsel in suit against Operation Rescue, *National Law Journal,* 13 November 1989, 30.

47. Quoted, *Washington Post,* 22 July 1989, A3.

48. Quoted, *Washington Post,* 10 March 1986, D1.

49. Quoted, *Washington Post,* 22 July 1989, A3.

50. Ibid.

51. *Washington Post,* 7 July 1987, 7.

52. Statement to author by Alan Morrison, chief attorney and director of Public Citizen Litigation Group, one of the participants in the coalition.

53. Quoted, *New York Times,* 11 November 1988, B7.

54. Ibid.

55. Ibid.

56. Quoted, *New York Times,* 6 April 1989, B10.

57. Quoted, *Daily Progress,* Charlottesville, Virginia, 19 April 1989, A3.

58. Quoted in article by R.W. Apple, Jr., *New York Times,* 10 April 1989, B6. The speech was given at the Suffolk University School of Law in Boston.

59. Ibid.

60. Quoted, *Washington Post,* 10 April 1989, A1.

61. Quoted, *USA Today,* 10 April 1989, 3A.

62. Quoted, *New York Times,* 9 April 1989, 28.

63. Quoted, *New York Times,* 15 October 1989, sec. 4, p. 1.

64. Quoted, *Washington Post,* 21 December 1989, A8.

65. Quoted, *New York Times,* 21 July 1989, B2.

CHAPTER 3

The States as Battlegrounds

The battles over abortion in state legislatures increased in number and intensity after *Roe v. Wade.* In the early 1970s state legislatures had confronted growing pressure to liberalize abortion laws. After *Roe,* pro-life and antiabortion campaigns sparked by the Court's ruling sought enactment of the most restrictive abortion laws possible. Like other controversial watershed rulings of the Court,[1] *Roe* left numerous questions unanswered. It afforded ample grounds for state and local governments, pressured by interest groups, to limit the availability of abortion. As more and more restrictive abortion laws emerged in the states, pro-choice groups challenged their constitutionality in the courts. In the process the Supreme Court and the country became further locked in an ongoing political struggle over abortion, which would more sharply define and delimit *Roe*'s mandate, and may ultimately lead to its outright reversal.

Abortion and American Federalism

"It is one of the happy incidents" of American federalism, Justice Louis D. Brandeis observed, "that a single courageous state may, if its citizens choose, serve as a laboratory; and try novel social and economic experiments without risk to the rest of the country."[2] American federalism—the division of political power between the national government and the states—is a unique contribution of the Constitution and reflects an attempt to accommodate the political values of national unity and diversity among the states. The relationship between the national government and the states has changed dramatically and the power of the national government has grown enormously since 1787, when the Con-

Opposite: New York demonstration, "Human Rights for Unborn Humans." *Photo:* Prints and Photographs Division, Library of Congress.

stitution was adopted.³ Yet states remain vital political forums and, as Brandeis noted, decentralized centers for political struggles and social and economic experimentation.

The states, however, are only semisovereign and are not entirely free to legislate as they wish. In Article VI of the Constitution, the supremacy clause provides that "the laws of the United States ... shall be the supreme law of the land." Each state thus may enact its own laws as long as they do not conflict with provisions of the Constitution, congressional legislation, or federal administrative regulations, or with the Supreme Court's interpretations of those sources of federal law. In proclaiming that women have a constitutional right to decide whether to have an abortion, at least in the first trimester, *Roe* invalidated not only the Texas law but also similar restrictive laws in other states. Yet states remained free to enact new abortion laws as long as they did not conflict with the basic ruling in *Roe*.

Roe transformed the political battle over abortion within the states. Before that ruling, pro-choice advocates and interest groups in the late 1960s were pushing for the repeal of state laws proscribing contraceptives and abortion. They had received important support in 1962 when the American Law Institute (ALI) in its Model Penal Code advocated permitting abortion in pregnancies that threatened the physical or mental health of the woman or when there was a risk of birth defects. Three years later the Board of Trustees of the American Medical Association (AMA) endorsed a report adopting the ALI's position on reforming abortion laws in the states. In 1968, Lawrence Lader and others founded the National Association for the Repeal of Abortion Laws and began to push states to reform their abortion laws. In just two years the movement to revise or abandon restrictive abortion laws achieved major victories in four states.⁴ Hawaii became the first state to repeal its law and permit abortions of "nonviable" fetuses as long as the procedures were done in hospitals. Next New York removed all restrictions on abortions performed in the first twenty-four weeks of pregnancy. Alaska and Washington followed with similar laws.

The landscape of state abortion laws was changing when *Roe* came down (see table 3.1). Notably, only Louisiana, New Hampshire, and Pennsylvania prohibited all abortions. Besides the four states, along with the District of Columbia, that permitted early abortions for virtually any reason, thirteen other states allowed abortion to preserve the life of the woman or to protect her mental or physical health. Mississippi permitted abortions also in cases of rape. Still, twenty-nine states made abortion unlawful except when it was necessary to save the life of the woman. Moreover, as Weddington pointed out during her oral arguments in *Roe*,

TABLE 3.1

STATE ABORTION LAWS BEFORE *ROE V. WADE*

Allowed abortions

For any reason (4 states)	To protect the woman's physical and mental health (13 states)	To preserve the woman's life and in cases of rape (1 state)	Only to preserve the woman's life (29 states)	Prohibited all abortions (3 states)
Alaska	Arkansas	Mississippi	Alabama	Louisiana
District of	California		Arizona	New
Columbia	Colorado		Connecticut	Hampshire
Hawaii	Delaware		Idaho	Pennsylvania
New York	Florida		Illinois	
Washington	Georgia		Indiana	
	Kansas		Iowa	
	Maryland		Kentucky	
	New Mexico		Maine	
	North		Massachusetts	
	Carolina		Michigan	
	Oregon		Minnesota	
	South		Missouri	
	Carolina		Montana	
	Virginia		Nebraska	
			Nevada	
			New Jersey	
			North Dakota	
			Ohio	
			Oklahoma	
			Rhode Island	
			South Dakota	
			Tennessee	
			Texas	
			Utah	
			Vermont	
			West Virginia	
			Wisconsin	
			Wyoming	

TABLE 3.2

WOMEN OBTAINING ABORTIONS OUT OF STATE, 1972

State	Percentage	Number	State	Percentage	Number
New Jersey	100.0	22,832	Vermont	81.7	859
Ohio	100.0	16,666	Massachusetts	80.7	14,187
Texas	100.0	16,022	Wisconsin	76.0	2,347
Michigan	100.0	14,626	South Carolina	72.3	2,208
Illinois	100.0	14,091	Florida	70.9	8,246
Missouri	100.0	6,953	Connecticut	69.1	5,757
Indiana	100.0	5,481	Georgia	64.5	4,561
Kentucky	100.0	3,132	Pennsylvania	62.5	14,232
Oklahoma	100.0	2,843	Virginia	60.0	6,707
Iowa	100.0	2,356	Nebraska	56.1	1,008
Minnesota	100.0	2,227	Arkansas	49.0	762
Rhode Island	100.0	1,869	Alabama	45.1	948
Maine	100.0	1,690	Delaware	41.7	914
Nevada	100.0	1,630	Maryland	40.3	6,002
West Virginia	100.0	1,491	North Carolina	30.0	3,539
New Hampshire	100.0	1,483	Colorado	10.6	573
Louisiana	100.0	1,210	Kansas	6.8	311
Utah	100.0	730	New Mexico	5.1	100
Wyoming	100.0	269	District of	2.0	145
Montana	100.0	172	Columbia		
North Dakota	100.0	148	Alaska	.8	9
South Dakota	100.0	116	Oregon	.7	49
Idaho	100.0	20	Hawaii	.3	12
Tennessee	99.8	4,279	Washington	.2	42
Mississippi	93.0	809	California	.1	152
Arizona	90.4	2,590	New York	.0	44
			Total		199,489

SOURCE: Senate Judiciary Committee, Subcommittee on the Constitution, *Hearings on Constitutional Amendments Relating to Abortion*, 97th Cong., 1st sess., 1981.

in the early 1970s many women had to travel outside their states of residence to obtain abortions; and many, like Norma McCorvey, were too poor to do so (see table 3.2, p. 76). Indeed, in twenty-three states, every woman seeking an abortion had to leave her state of residence to obtain one; in only eight states did fewer than 10 percent *not* have to do so.

By altering what abortion regulations were constitutionally permissible, *Roe* ignited a firestorm of debate in state legislatures. Lawmakers and citizens on the pro-choice side of the controversy initially thought that the battle was over and that they had won the war. As Alfred F. Moran, an executive vice-president of Planned Parenthood of New York, recalled, "Most of us really believed that was the end of the controversy. The Supreme Court had spoken, and while some disagreement would remain, the issue had been tried, tested and laid to rest."[5] But Moran and others in pro-choice groups were wrong. Pro-life interest groups dedicated themselves to waging a counteroffensive in the states. In the year immediately following *Roe,* for instance, some 260 abortion-related bills were introduced in state legislatures, and 39 passed. By 1974 another 19 out of 189 bills were enacted.[6] Legislative battles over new, more restrictive abortion laws continued, as did challenges to their constitutionality brought in the courts by individuals and pro-choice groups.[7]

The decentralized structure of American federalism—with fifty state jurisdictions, diverse populations, and distinctive regional political cultures—openly invites competition among political forces. In that structure, federalism affords multiple opportunities for thwarting compliance with, or implementation of, controversial Supreme Court rulings. Moreover, although *Roe* forbids states to deny women the right to seek abortions, it does not require state and local governments to make abortions available, let alone compel public funding or the use of public hospitals for performing abortions. Because *Roe* is silent on the latter, state and local governments moved to deny public funding and the use of public hospitals for abortions, and to restrict access to abortion in other ways.

Under pressure from pro-life groups, local governments passed ordinances restricting the availability of abortion. Some public and private hospitals continued to refuse to perform nontherapeutic abortions. In the year *Roe* came down, about three-fourths of all public and private hospitals around the country performed *no* abortions;[8] three years later, the overwhelming majority of public and private hospitals still refused to perform them.[9] In 1977 the Planned Parenthood Federation of America reported that 80 percent of all public hospitals and 70 percent of private ones had never allowed abortions.[10]

Family-planning clinics increasingly became the primary providers of abortions (see table 5.1, p. 191). In other words, *Roe* did not significantly change the practices of most hospitals with regard to abortion. As political scientist Gerald Rosenberg emphasizes, "A majority of abortions are performed by a minority of providers. That is, the few providers willing to perform abortions on a regular basis perform the vast majority of them."[11]

The hospitals' refusal to perform abortions was reinforced by state and local laws denying public funding and the use of public facilities for abortions. In upholding the policy of St. Louis, Missouri, denying poor women access to nontherapeutic abortions in public hospitals in 1977, the Burger Court noted that in 1975–76 "only about 18 percent of all public hospitals in the country provided abortion services, and in 10 states there were no public hospitals providing such services."[12] In 1980 fifty-nine metropolitan areas provided no facilities for abortion.[13] In rural states such as North and South Dakota, no hospitals and few clinics performed abortions.[14] As a result, a decade after *Roe,* more than 10 percent of the women seeking abortions in twenty-two states still had to travel out of state. In Wyoming and West Virginia, 57 and 47 percent of the women having abortions had them outside their home states. In ten other states (Arizona, Indiana, Iowa, Kentucky, Maryland, Mississippi, Missouri, New Mexico, Oklahoma, and South Dakota), 20 to 36 percent of the women wanting abortions traveled to other states to have them. The percentage ranged from 10 to 19 percent in ten more states (Arkansas, Delaware, Idaho, Louisiana, Maine, New Hampshire, North Dakota, South Carolina, Vermont, and Virginia).[15] Not surprisingly, states like New York and California, which had liberal abortion laws prior to *Roe,* emerged as the largest providers of abortion.

Roe undeniably affected the availability of abortions. States could no longer categorically deny women the right to seek abortions or prosecute doctors who performed abortions in the first trimester. Because abortion per se was no longer illegal, women had access to safe abortions performed by physicians at clinics and some hospitals. Moreover, a smaller percentage of women seeking abortions had to travel out of state to obtain them.[16] Nonetheless, the Burger Court's ruling fell far short of making "abortion available on demand" in every state, and it met with open resistance in various parts of the country.

Resurrecting State and Local Barriers

In the years following *Roe,* most new state abortion laws (for example, laws requiring that abortions be performed by licensed physicians) were in conformity with the Court's ruling. Yet many other state laws sought to restrict the availability of abortions in several ways: by requiring the informed consent of a woman's husband or of a minor child's parents, by forbidding the advertising of abortion services, or by withholding state funds for abortions that were not medically necessary. Ten state legislatures passed laws or resolutions pledging to ban abortion or restrict it severely in anticipation of *Roe*'s eventually being overturned. Fifteen others kept their pre-*Roe* antiabortion laws on the books. Whether they would be enforced if *Roe* were overturned remained unclear.

State and local regulations on abortion fell into five broad categories:

1. States passed health regulations requiring physicians and clinics performing abortions to be licensed and to report to public authorities the number of abortions they performed. Most of these regulations were in conformity with the Burger Court's rulings on abortion; some aimed at erecting procedural obstacles for women seeking abortions.

2. Some states retained their bans on advertising and other activities aimed at promoting abortion services.

3. A number of states imposed viability and postviability regulations, and some even required doctors to try to save the life of an aborted fetus.

4. States discouraged abortions by requiring a woman's "informed consent" or "spousal consent" and, for minors, parental notification or consent or both.

5. A number of states and localities denied public funding and the use of public hospitals for abortions.

Health Regulations: Licensing and Reporting Requirements

During the sixteen years following *Roe*, thirty-eight states adopted new health regulations governing abortion. Most (Alabama, Arkansas, Georgia, Hawaii, Idaho, Indiana, Kentucky, Maine, Maryland, Minnesota, Mississippi, Missouri, Montana, Nebraska, Nevada, New York, North Carolina, South Carolina, Tennessee, Texas, Utah, Virginia, Washington, and Wyoming) required abortions to be performed by licensed physicians and in licensed clinics or hospitals. All but five of those states (Alabama, Maryland, Montana, New York, North Carolina, and Texas) also required performers of abortions to report them to public health authorities, as did five other states (California, Delaware, Illinois, South Dakota, and Wisconsin).

Although these licensing and reporting requirements did not run afoul of *Roe,* other regulations went too far in limiting availability. In spite of *Roe,* six states (Delaware, Florida, Illinois, Iowa, Kansas, and Mississippi) passed laws prohibiting abortion except when necessary to save the life of the woman or in cases of fetal abnormality, rape, or incest. Kentucky enacted a law, which a lower federal court later invalidated, forbidding saline abortions after the first trimester.[17]

Still other states disregarded *Roe* in proscribing all nontherapeutic abortions after the sixteenth week (Delaware), the twentieth week (California and Colorado), the twenty-fourth week (New York), and the twenty-sixth week (Maryland). Despite the fact that such restrictions had been ruled out in *Roe* and subsequent Burger Court opinions,[18] not all states complied. California's attorney general, for one, held that his state's prohibition was constitutional.[19] In doing so, he anticipated that if his ruling were challenged, the Rehnquist Court would uphold California's law. In contrast, Maryland's attorney general ruled that his state's ban on abortions after the twenty-sixth week was unconstitutional. Similar state laws were also invalidated by state and lower federal courts.[20]

Finally, fourteen states (California, Hawaii, Idaho, Indiana, Kansas, Louisiana, Maryland, Minnesota, Missouri, Nevada, New Jersey, South Dakota, Utah, and Virginia) passed laws requiring abortions to be performed only in licensed hospitals or clinics. Some of these laws sought not only to ensure the health and safety of women seeking abortions but also to limit sharply the availability of abortions by outlawing abortion services provided by family-planning clinics. Such restrictive licensing requirements and regulatory constraints on doctors performing abortions reflected the legal-policy strategy of pro-life groups and their supporters in state legislatures and local governments in the 1970s and 1980s. Instead of pushing for legislation that would directly challenge the principle that women have a right to choose an abortion, pro-life groups won many states over to adopting restrictive regulations that would simply cut back on the availability of abortion.

On the tenth anniversary of *Roe*, the Burger Court was still following up on *Roe* with regard to restrictive state and local licensing and hospitalization requirements. In 1983 the Court handed down a trio of rulings aimed at further clarifying *Roe*'s mandate. In *Planned Parenthood Association of Kansas City, Missouri v. Ashcroft,* a bare majority of the justices struck down a new restriction adopted by Missouri's legislature that required all abortions after the twelfth week to be performed in licensed hospitals. By a 6–3 vote in *City of Akron v. Akron Center for Reproductive Health,* the Court invalidated a city ordinance that aimed at closing abortion clinics by forbidding abortions in all but licensed hospitals. At the same time, in *Simopoulos v. Virginia,* the Court upheld Virginia's statute requiring mandatory hospitalization of women who have abortions in the second trimester of their pregnancies.

The Court tried to find a pragmatic solution to the widening schism in the states between pro-life and pro-choice groups and to delineate how far states might go in restricting the availability of abortion. Still, on the criteria set forth in those three 1983 rulings, the hospitalization requirements in California, Hawaii, Idaho, Indiana, Kansas, Louisiana, Minnesota, New Jersey, South Dakota, and Utah appeared unconstitutional. Yet they remained the law, though they went unenforced. Only Hawaii's attorney general declared that the state's hospitalization requirement was unenforceable during the first trimester.

State Regulations on Advertising and Promotion

Before *Roe,* states not only proscribed abortions but banned advertisements and other activities promoting abortion, even abortion services in other states. Two years after *Roe,* in an important ruling on the First Amendment guarantee of freedom of speech and press, the Burger Court held, in *Bigelow v. Virginia,* that the First Amendment extends constitutional protection to advertisements for abortion services and clinics.

Jeffrey C. Bigelow, managing editor of the *Virginia Weekly* (Charlottesville) had been charged, tried, and convicted for violating a state law that made it a misdemeanor to encourage or prompt the procuring of an abortion. In 1971 Bigelow had published the following advertisement for an abortion clinic in New York:

> UNWANTED PREGNANCY
> LET US HELP YOU
> Abortions are now legal in New York.
> There are no residency requirements.
> FOR IMMEDIATE PLACEMENT IN
> ACCREDITED HOSPITALS AND
> CLINICS AT LOW COST
> Contact
> WOMEN'S PAVILION
> 515 Madison Avenue
> New York, N.Y. 10022
> or call any time
> (212) 371-6670 or (212) 371-6650
> AVAILABLE 7 DAYS A WEEK
> STRICTLY CONFIDENTIAL. We
> will make all arrangements for you
> and help you with information and
> counselling.

After hearing Bigelow's appeal, the Burger Court, by a 7–2 vote (Justices William Rehnquist and Byron White dissenting), overturned Virginia's law as a violation of the First Amendment. Writing for the majority, Justice Harry Blackmun observed:

> 🔲 Viewed in its entirety, the advertisement conveyed information of potential interest and value to a diverse audience—not only to readers possibly in need of the services offered, but also to those with a general curiosity about, or genuine interest in, the subject matter or the law of another State and its development, and to readers seeking reform in Virginia....
>
> Advertising, like all public expression, may be subject to reasonable regulations that serve a legitimate public interest. To the extent that commercial activity is subject to regulation, the relationship of speech to that activity may be one factor, among others, to be considered in weighing the First Amendment interest against the governmental interest alleged. Advertising is not thereby stripped of all First Amendment protection. The relationship of speech to the marketplace of products or of services does not make it valueless in the marketplace of ideas....
>
> If ... this statute were upheld ... Virginia might exert the power sought here over a wide variety of national publications or interstate newspapers carrying advertisements similar to the one that appeared in Bigelow's newspaper or containing articles on the general subject matter to which the advertisement referred. Other States might do the same. The burdens thereby imposed on publications would impair, perhaps severely, their proper functioning. We know from experience that "liberty of the press is in peril as soon as the government tries to compel what is to go into a newspaper." 🔲

Subsequently, in *Carey v. Population Services International* (1977), the Burger Court extended its ruling in *Bigelow* to strike down New York's law forbidding the advertising and sale of contraceptives to minors.

Despite *Bigelow* and *Carey*, sixteen states—including Virginia—retained laws making it a misdemeanor to write, compose, or publish advertisements of any medicine or means for facilitating a miscarriage or an abortion. Notably, though, several of those laws (in Arizona, California, Connecticut, and North Dakota) were struck down by state and federal courts before *Bigelow* and were not enforced.[21] The remaining statutes in other states (Colorado, Florida, Maryland, Massachusetts, Michigan, Minnesota, Mississippi, Montana, Nevada, Oklahoma, and Wyoming) were thought to fail to comply with the ruling in *Bige-low*.

Viability, Postviability, and Fetal Protection

One legal-policy strategy pursued by antiabortion groups for limiting the availability of abortions and adopted by several states was that of requiring physicians to try to save the life of an aborted fetus or to use abortion methods likely to preserve fetal life. Three years after *Roe*, the Burger Court responded by striking down Missouri's "fetal-protection statute," which required doctors to use any means available to preserve fetal life.

The Missouri statute registered the intense opposition of pro-life groups to *Roe* and illustrates how such groups repeatedly sought to undercut the Court's abortion rulings by pressuring state legislatures to enact restrictive abortion laws. Along with the legislatures of Louisiana, Pennsylvania, and Utah, moreover, Missouri's legislature remained one of the most hostile in the country toward the Court's rulings. Indeed, challenges to Missouri's restrictive abortion laws reached the Court on four occasions from 1973, when *Roe* came down, to *Webster v. Reproductive Health Services* (discussed in chapter 6).[22]

Within months of *Roe*, the Burger Court affirmed a lower federal court's striking down of Missouri's 1969 abortion law, which prohibited virtually all abortions. That invalidation drew a quick response from Missouri's General Assembly. A little over a year later, in June 1974, it passed a comprehensive statute regulating abortion during all stages of pregnancy. The new law included a statutory definition of fetal viability; it set forth reporting and record-keeping requirements for doctors performing abortions; it mandated that women give informed and written consent, that married women obtain spousal consent, and that an unwed minor obtain parental consent. In addition, Missouri required physicians "to preserve the life and health of the fetus"; failure to do so was defined as the crime of manslaughter, and physicians were made liable for monetary damages as well.

Three days after the Missouri legislature's 1974 abortion act was signed into law by Governor John Danforth, Planned Parenthood of Central Missouri and several doctors filed a suit challenging the law's constitutionality. Subsequently, a three-judge federal district court upheld the new restrictions other than the fetal-protection requirement. This requirement was deemed "unconstitutionally overbroad" because it applied to all stages of a pregnancy and required doctors to protect the life not only of postviability fetuses but also of fetuses aborted prior to viability. The ruling was immediately appealed by Planned Parenthood to the Supreme Court.

In *Planned Parenthood of Central Missouri v. Danforth,* the Burger Court upheld Missouri's reporting and record-keeping requirements, as well as its provision for the woman's informed consent. But by a 5–4 vote, the justices affirmed the lower court's invalidation of the state's fetal-protection requirement. The majority agreed that that requirement was "unconstitutionally overly broad" in failing to distinguish between nonviable and viable fetuses. Writing for the Court, Blackmun also reversed the district court's upholding of Missouri's statutory definition of fetal viability. In his words, "It is not the proper function of the legislature or the courts to place viability, which is essentially a medical concept, at a specific point in the gestation period." Because fetal viability varies with each pregnancy, Blackmun reasoned, "the determination of whether a particular fetus is viable is, and must be, a matter for the judgment of the attending physician."

Although the Burger Court overturned Missouri's fetal-protection requirement and legislative definition of fetal viability in *Danforth,* Blackmun's opinion for the Court was narrowly tailored. Unanswered was the question whether states might impose fetal-protection requirements on doctors who abort fetuses deemed to be viable. Three years later the Court confronted that question. By a 6–3 vote in *Colautti v. Franklin,* the justices overturned Pennsylvania's 1974 Abortion Control Act. As in Missouri, Pennsylvania's legislature had passed a fetal-protection law a little more than a year after *Roe.* Unlike Missouri's governor, however, Pennsylvania's governor vetoed the bill because he deemed it unconstitutional under *Roe.* But pro-life forces persisted and persuaded the state legislature to override the veto. When a challenge to Pennsylvania's law finally reached the Supreme Court in 1979, a majority underscored that fetal-protection statutes must clearly specify whether the doctor's paramount duty is to the health of the woman or whether the doctor must balance possible health risks to her against the odds of a viable fetus's survival. And as with Missouri's fetal-protection statute in *Danforth,* the Court declared Pennsylvania's law unconstitutionally vague in *Colautti.*

Despite *Danforth* and *Colautti,* several states—including Pennsylvania and Arizona, Arkansas, Illinois, Minnesota, North Dakota, Oklahoma, Utah, and Wyoming—left their statutes intact after the Court's rulings. Unenforced, the statutes registered many states' continuing defiance of the Court's attempt to draw a line between permissible and impermissible restrictions and constraints on the availability of abortion.

Consent and Notification Laws

Another strategy aimed at limiting the number of abortions was to require the pregnant woman's written "informed consent" or "spousal consent" or both as well as parental notification and consent for minors seeking abortions. Such requirements vary widely from state to state (see table 3.3, p. 86). In 1989 thirteen states and the District of Columbia had no consent requirements of any kind, and consent laws in fourteen states were unenforced.

In handing down *Danforth* in 1976, the Burger Court upheld the Missouri requirement that the doctor obtain the written consent of the woman after informing her of the dangers of abortion and discussing alternative possibilities. That ruling was viewed by antiabortion groups as signaling the permissibility of even more stringent informed-consent laws. Two years after *Danforth,* the city council in Akron, Ohio, enacted an ordinance requiring doctors to tell women seeking abortions that, among numerous other "facts," a fetus is human life from the moment of conception. Doctors also had to describe in detail fetal development at each stage of a pregnancy, along with fetal development of sensitivity to pain, brain and heart functions, and other physical responses. In addition, they were required to inform the women that a fetus may be viable at twenty-two weeks of age and that abortion is a major surgical procedure that may result in severe physical and psychological problems.

Akron's 1978 informed-consent ordinance was one of the most rigorous pieces of abortion legislation in the country. Pro-choice groups and abortion clinics in the city were outraged and were committed to fighting its enforcement in the courts. Four major medical organizations joined the Akron Center for Reproductive Health in attacking the ordinance and asking the Supreme Court to overturn it. The 234,000-member American Medical Association, the 23,000-member American College of Obstetricians and Gynecologists, the 24,000-member American Academy of Pediatrics, and the 17,000-member Nurses Association of the Obstetrical College joined in asking the Court to draw a clear line on how far states and localities could go in regulating doctor-patient relations and in attempting to discourage women from seeking abortions.

Pro-life defenders of Akron's ordinance argued that the informed-consent requirements were within the parameters of the ruling in *Danforth* and were simply aimed at curtailing "abortion on demand." The Reagan administration also came to the defense of the ordinance, but on federalist grounds. Endorsing the spirit but not the specifics of Akron's informed-consent requirements, Solicitor General Rex Lee argued that it was time to "call a halt" to judicial supervision of state and local abortion laws.

In contrast, James Breen, president-elect of the American College of Obstetricians and Gynecologists, charged that Akron's informed-consent requirements would force physicians to practice "bad medicine" by

TABLE 3.3

STATES RESTRICTING ABORTIONS BY REQUIRING
NOTIFICATION OR CONSENT, 1989

Allowed abortions

No restrictions (16 states)	Parental notification required for minors (12 states)	Parental consent required for minors (14 states)	Spousal notification (in addition to laws for minors) required (8 states)
Connecticut	Arkansas[a]	Alaska	Colorado
District of Columbia	California[a,b]	Alabama[a]	Florida[a]
Iowa	Georgia[a,b]	Arizona[a]	Kentucky[a]
Hawaii	Idaho[b]	Indiana[a]	Montana[b]
Kansas	Illinois[a,b]	Louisiana[a]	South Carolina[b]
Michigan	Maine[b]	Mississippi[a,b]	South Dakota[b]
New Hampshire	Maryland	Missouri[a]	Utah
New Jersey	Minnesota[a,b]	New Mexico[a,b]	Washington[a]
New Mexico[b]	Nebraska[a]	North Dakota[a]	
New York[a,b]	Nevada[a,b]	Pennsylvania	
North Carolina	Ohio[a,b]	Tennessee[a]	
Oklahoma	West Virginia[a]	Wyoming[a]	
Oregon			
Texas			
Vermont			
Virginia			
Wisconsin			

a. Courts may grant exceptions.   *b.* Law not enforced.

mandating that they tell prospective patients "facts" that he contended were either "untrue, irrelevant, or misleading." Breen pointed out, for instance, that there was "no scientific or medical evidence" to support the claim that fetuses may live outside the womb at twenty-two weeks. Nor was it correct to describe abortion as a "major surgical procedure"; the medical profession considered it to be safer than normal childbirth and a "relatively minor" and "remarkably safe" procedure. Akron's checklist of "horrors" flew "in the face of good medical judgment" and would leave especially young women with misleading and potentially psychologically damaging impressions. In sum, opponents of Akron's informed-consent law insisted that the requirements interfered with a doctor's giving the best care to each patient and unconstitutionally interfered with a woman's right "to consult with her physician freely and privately."

Seven years after *Danforth*, in *City of Akron v. Akron Center for Reproductive Health*, the Burger Court struck down Akron's informed-consent requirements. Six members of the Court held that the requirements unduly restricted a woman's right to obtain an abortion and impermissibly interfered with the physician-patient relationship. States could require informed consent but could not prescribe in exacting detail what doctors must tell their patients about abortion.

Justices Sandra Day O'Connor, Rehnquist, and White dissented from the majority's ruling in *City of Akron v. Akron Center for Reproductive Health*. In her first consideration of the abortion issue since joining the Court in 1981, O'Connor took the position that Akron's requirements did not "unduly burden" women seeking abortions. Moreover, she proposed that the Court abandon *Roe*'s trimester approach to controversies over restrictive abortion laws in favor of an "unduly burdensome" standard:

> The "unduly burdensome" standard is particularly appropriate in the abortion context because of the *nature* and *scope* of the right that is involved. The privacy right involved in the abortion context "cannot be said to be absolute." Rather, the *Roe* right is intended to protect against state action "drastically limiting the availability and safety of the desired service," ... or against "official interference" and "coercive restraint" imposed on the abortion decision.... That a state regulation may "inhibit" abortions to some degree does not require that we find that the regulation is invalid.

O'Connor's dissent was significant in both challenging *Roe* and proposing a new standard for the Court's review of state restrictions on the availability of abortion. And her joining Rehnquist and White—who had dissented in *Roe*—was viewed by pro-life forces as a hopeful sign that the Court might change course as the composition of the bench changed further. Notably, though unenforced in many states, informed-consent requirements remained in place in fifteen states (Delaware, Florida, Idaho, Illinois, Iowa, Kentucky, Pennsylvania, Rhode Island, South Carolina, South Dakota, Tennessee, Utah, Virginia, Washington, and Wisconsin).

No less controversial were state laws requiring spousal consent. These laws were also adopted as a way of curbing access to abortion. They presented an issue that the Court had not addressed in *Roe*. But three years after *Roe,* the Burger Court struck down Missouri's requirement that the spouse of a woman seeking an abortion during the first twelve weeks of a pregnancy sign a consent form. Writing for the Court in *Planned Parenthood of Central Missouri v. Danforth,* Blackmun observed that "we cannot hold that the State has the constitutional authority to give the spouse unilaterally the ability to prohibit the wife from terminating her pregnancy, when the State itself lacks that right." "Ideally," he added:

> the decision to terminate a pregnancy should be one concurred in by both the wife and her husband. No marriage may be viewed as harmonious or successful if the marriage partners are fundamentally divided on so important and vital an issue. But it is difficult to believe that the goal of fostering mutuality and trust in a marriage ... will be achieved by giving the husband a veto power exercisable for any reason whatsoever or for no reason at all.... The obvious fact is that when the wife and the husband disagree on this decision, the view of only one of the two marriage partners can prevail. Inasmuch as it is the woman who physically bears the child and who is the more directly and immediately affected by the pregnancy, as between the two, the balance weighs in her favor.

More than a decade after the ruling in *Danforth,* nine states (Colorado, Florida, Kentucky, Montana, Rhode Island, South Carolina, South Dakota, Utah, and Washington) maintained their spousal-consent requirements on the books. However, the Court stood its ground and declined to reconsider its line-drawing in this area of the abortion controversy. In 1988, for instance, the Rehnquist Court unanimously declined to hear an appeal from a twenty-three-year-old Indiana toy store manager, Erin A. Conn, who had sought a court order preventing his estranged nineteen-year-old wife from having an abortion. Conn's attorney had argued that *Danforth* had left lower courts with the option of deciding on a case-by-case basis how to balance the competing interests of husbands and wives. Whether or not that was so, the Court was in no mood to renew and return to the controversy over spousal-consent laws.

Even more problematic and contentious for the Court were challenges to state and local laws requiring parental notification or consent or both for minors who seek abortions. Parental-notification and parental-consent requirements were two of the initial and primary ways that pro-life groups sought to limit the availability of abortion immediately after *Roe.* Even some supporters of a woman's right to choose an abortion often agreed that limitations ought to be imposed on minors seeking abortions. Moreover, for pro-choice legislators in many state houses, voting for parental-notification and parental-consent requirements represented a political compromise aimed at placating constituents on both sides of the troublesome issue. By so voting, legislators could assert that they were against "abortion on demand" but also against more restrictive laws that would infringe on a woman's fundamental right to choose an abortion.

Massachusetts was one of the first states to enact a parental-consent law. Less than two years after *Roe,* its legislature passed over the governor's veto a statute purporting "to protect unborn children and maternal health within present constitutional limitations" imposed by the Court. Unmarried women under eighteen years of age were required to obtain the consent of both parents before obtaining an abortion. But the statute was ambiguous in also appearing to provide that if one or both parents refused consent, a minor could obtain consent by appearing before a judge and obtaining a court order for an abortion.

The day after the Massachusetts parental-consent law went into effect, 30 October 1974, Dr. William Baird (who headed a nonprofit abortion counseling service known as the Parents Aid Society), four pregnant minors, and several other doctors filed a lawsuit challenging its constitutionality. Asserting that the law enabled a "parental veto" of a minor's decision to seek an abortion and violated the Fourteenth Amendment's guarantees of due process and equal protection of the laws, they asked for an injunction against its enforcement.

A divided three-judge federal district court subsequently invalidated the Massachusetts law for infringing on the constitutional rights of minors and denying them equal protection of the laws. Two members of the panel, moreover, went so far as to construe the Massachusetts law as giving parents a right to veto a minor daughter's decision to seek an abortion. Although it was far from clear whether Massachusetts had indeed conferred a right of "parental veto" in its statute, the majority held that such a parental right would violate the constitutional rights of unwed minors. In the words of the lower court, "even if it be found that parents may have rights of a Constitutional dimension vis-à-vis their child that are separate from the child's, we would find that in the present area the individual rights of the minor outweigh the rights of the parents, and must be protected."

When the district court's construction and invalidation of the Massachusetts parental-consent law was appealed to the Burger Court in *Bellotti v. Baird,* the justices held that the lower court should have abstained from deciding the case because the law had not yet been construed by a state court to determine whether the parental-consent requirement indeed amounted to giving parents a veto over a daughter's decision to seek an abortion. Although vacating the lower court's decision, however, Blackmun's opinion for the Court indicated that states may require minors to obtain parental consent but must provide an alternative "judicial bypass" procedure for procuring a court's authorization for a minor's abortion if parental consent is denied or if the minor does not want to obtain parental consent.

The ruling in *Bellotti* left the states somewhat uncertain about how far they could go in requiring parental notification and consent for minors wanting to terminate their pregnancies. Five years later the Burger Court sought in *H.L. v. Matheson* to clarify some of the confusion. *Matheson* presented a challenge to the constitutionality of a state *notification* requirement, and the justices split 6–3 when upholding Utah's requirement that the physician notify parents, "if possible," prior to performing an abortion on their minor daughter when (1) the girl is living with and dependent on her parents; (2) she has not been emancipated by marriage; and (3) she makes no claim or showing as to her maturity. The Burger Court in essence drew a line that invalidated state laws that required parental consent and provided no alternatives for minors seeking abortions and upheld those that gave minors the option of obtaining judicial consent, or provided a so-called judicial bypass of parental consent.

In 1983, by a 6–3 vote in *City of Akron v. Akron Center for Reproductive Health,* the Burger Court reaffirmed its distinction between permissible and impermissible parental notification and consent laws. In that case the Court struck down an ordinance that required minors to obtain parental consent before obtaining an abortion but that failed to provide minors with a "judicial bypass" option. The Court then upheld, in *Planned Parenthood Association of Kansas City, Missouri v. Ashcroft,* Missouri's requirement that the doctor receive parental consent *or* the consent of a juvenile court judge before performing an abortion on a minor.

Despite *City of Akron* and *Ashcroft,* several states (Colorado, Maine, Maryland, Rhode Island, South Carolina, and Utah) continued to fail to provide for a "judicial bypass" in their parental-notification statutes. Another eleven states required parental consent, but among those only Massachusetts failed to authorize its courts to make some exceptions for minors seeking abortions. In twenty-one states parental notification was required, though in all but ten (Arkansas, Colorado, Florida, Kentucky, Maryland, Nebraska, Rhode Island, Utah, Washington, and West Virginia) the laws were unenforced. Still, in 1989, fifteen states imposed no restrictions on minors seeking abortions.

The line drawn on parental notification and consent laws during the Burger Court years was basically reaffirmed by the Rehnquist Court, though it moved in 1990 to give states greater leeway in toughening parental-notification requirements. When reviewing another, more stringent parental-notification law adopted by Akron in *Ohio v. Akron Center for Reproductive Health,* the Court, in an opinion written by Justice Anthony Kennedy, upheld the city's ordinance requiring a minor to notify at least one parent before having an abortion because it also provided the option of a "judicial bypass." With O'Connor casting the key vote in a companion case, *Hodgson v. Minnesota,* however, a bare majority struck down a section of a Minnesota law requiring, without a "judicial bypass," a minor to notify and obtain the consent of both parents before having an abortion. On that issue, O'Connor joined Justices William Brennan, Blackmun, Thurgood Marshall, and John Stevens in holding that obtaining the consent of both parents is unduly burdensome for a minor whose parents are divorced and might reside in different states. But O'Connor also joined Chief Justice Rehnquist and Justices Antonin Scalia, Kennedy, and White to form a majority in *Hodgson* for upholding the requirement that a minor notify her parents before obtaining an abortion. Minnesota's parental-notification statute, however, provided for a "judicial bypass." And, in separate opinions, Kennedy argued that a "judicial bypass" option was constitutionally unnecessary, whereas Stevens maintained that the state's notification law should have been deemed unconstitutional even if it had a "judicial bypass" provision.

Public Funding and the Use of Public Facilities

One of the most direct and effective state and local government strategies for curbing the availability of abortions after *Roe* was simply to deny public funding and/or the use of public hospitals and facilities for abortions. Four years after *Roe,* the Burger Court squarely confronted the first challenges to such restrictive abortion laws. In three cases decided in 1977, the Burger Court split 6–3 when upholding those restrictions, with Brennan, Blackmun, and Marshall dissenting.

In the leading case, *Maher v. Roe,* the Burger Court basically established that although *Roe* recognized that women have a fundamental liberty interest and constitutional right to decide whether to have an abortion, state and local governments are not obligated to provide funding for indigent women seeking to exercise that right. *Maher* upheld Connecticut's refusal to reimburse Medicaid recipients for the cost of an abortion unless a doctor certified that the abortion was medically or psychiatrically necessary. A companion case, *Beal v. Doe,* held that states participating in the federal Medicaid program do not have to fund nontherapeutic abortions for poor women. Finally, *Poelker v. Doe* upheld the St. Louis, Missouri, policy of denying indigent pregnant women access to nontherapeutic abortions in the city's public hospitals.

Maher v. Roe originated with two indigent women, known as Susan Roe and Mary Poe, suing Edward Maher, the commissioner of the Connecticut Department of Social Services. They challenged the constitutionality of the state's regulation prohibiting the funding of abortions that are not medically necessary and contended that the state's funding for the expenses of childbirth, but not abortions, violated the Fourteenth Amendment's equal protection clause. The state, however, interpreted Title XIX of the Social Security Act, which established the Medicaid program under which participating states may provide federally funded medical assistance to needy persons, as forbidding the funding of nontherapeutic abortions. Roe, an unmarried mother of three children, was unable to obtain an abortion because her doctor refused to certify that an abortion was medically necessary. Poe, a sixteen-year-old high school junior, had an abortion, but because she failed to obtain a certificate of medical necessity, the Department of Social Services refused to reimburse the hospital for her $244 hospital bill.

A federal district court rejected Connecticut's interpretation of Title XIX when deciding that the Medicaid program not only allowed but required funding of nontherapeutic abortions. The district court then overturned Connecticut's regulation forbidding the funding of nontherapeutic abortions. On appeal, the Court of Appeals for the Second Circuit ruled that the program permitted but did not require funding of abortions and remanded the case to the district court. And Maher promptly appealed that ruling to the Supreme Court.

Writing for the Court in *Maher,* Justice Powell reasoned:

⬚ The Constitution imposes no obligation on the States to pay the pregnancy-related medical expenses of indigent women, or indeed to pay any of the medical expenses of indigents. But when a State decides to alleviate some of the hardships of poverty by providing medical care, the manner in which it dispenses benefits is subject to constitutional limitations. Appellees' claim is that Connecticut must accord equal treatment to both abortion and childbirth, and may not evidence a policy preference by funding only the medical expenses incident to childbirth. This challenge to the classifications established by the Connecticut regulation presents a question arising under the Equal Protection Clause of the Fourteenth Amendment. . . .

The Connecticut regulation before us is different in kind from the laws invalidated in our previous abortion decisions. The Connecticut regulation places no obstacles—absolute or otherwise—in the pregnant woman's path to an abortion. An indigent woman who desires an abortion suffers no disadvantage as a consequence of Connecticut's decision to fund childbirth; she continues as before to be dependent on private sources for the service she desires. The State may have made childbirth a more attractive alternative, thereby influencing the woman's decision, but it has imposed no restriction on access to abortions that was not already there. The indigency that may make it difficult—and in some cases, perhaps, impossible—for some women to have abortions is neither created nor in any way affected by the Connecticut regulation. We conclude that the Connecticut regulation does not impinge upon the fundamental right recognized in *Roe*. 🔊

In a dissenting opinion joined by Blackmun and Marshall, Brennan took strong exception to the majority's ruling and reasoning in *Maher*. In particular, he sharply criticized the majority's dismissal of the seriousness of the obstacle that Connecticut had placed in front of indigent women seeking abortions. In his words:

🔊 A distressing insensitivity to the plight of impoverished pregnant women is inherent in the Court's analysis. The stark reality for too many, not just "some," indigent women is that indigency makes access to competent licensed physicians not merely "difficult" but "impossible." As a practical matter, many indigent women will feel they have no choice but to carry their pregnancies to term because the State will pay for the associated medical services, even though they would have chosen to have abortions if the State had also provided funds for that procedure. This disparity in funding by the State clearly operates to coerce indigent pregnant women to bear children they would not otherwise choose to have, and just as clearly, this coercion can only operate upon the poor, who are uniquely the victims of this form of financial pressure.... 🖾

Subsequently, the Burger Court reaffirmed *Maher* when upholding congressional restrictions on federal funding of abortions (see ⎡5.1⎤, p. 162). And as further examined in chapter 6, the Rehnquist Court upheld Missouri's 1986 ban on the use of public hospitals, facilities, and employees for nontherapeutic abortions in *Webster v. Reproductive Health Services*.

Notably, for more than a decade the Court legitimated state and local government policies denying public funding and the use of public hospitals for nontherapeutic abortions. Yet in 1989 there remained no restrictions on public funding for indigent women seeking abortions in thirteen states, including the large and populous states of California and New York. Four other states (Idaho, Minnesota, Pennsylvania, and Wyoming) allow public financing of abortions in cases of rape, incest, and when necessary to save a woman's life. Still, the overwhelming majority of states (thirty-one) did pass laws denying funding for indigent women seeking abortions, except when medically necessary to save their lives (see table 3.4).

Struggles in Constitutional Politics between the Supreme Court and the States

American federalism diffuses political conflict and makes state and local governments more directly accountable to and reflective of the views of the people who participate in the electoral process. As long as states abide by the limitations imposed on their powers by the Constitution, congressional legislation, and the Supreme Court's interpretation and application of federal law, they are free to experiment with new kinds of regulations, and to maintain and reinforce particular cultural values and regional differences among the states. The price of preserving diversity in the states, of course, comes at the cost of nationally uniform laws. As a result, political change and legal reform are also often slow and piecemeal and result in overlapping and, occasionally, crosscutting and conflicting laws. Yet the process of reforming law and public policy in state and local governments involves public education and places a premium on building political consensus in the states and the nation.

When handing down *Roe*, the Burger Court did more than radically restructure the legal landscape of state and local abortion laws. It transformed the political struggle over abortion that was emerging in the

TABLE 3.4

PUBLIC FINANCING FOR ABORTIONS FOR INDIGENT WOMEN,
1989

Allowed abortions

Without restrictions (13 states)	In cases of rape, incest, or to save the woman's life (6 states)	To save the woman's life (31 states)	
Alaska	Idaho	Alabama	Montana
California	Iowa[a]	Arizona	Nebraska
Connecticut	Minnesota	Arkansas	Nevada
Hawaii	Pennsylvania	Colorado	New Hampshire
Massachusetts	Virginia[b]	Delaware	New Mexico
New Jersey	Wyoming	Florida	North Dakota
New York		Georgia	Ohio
North Carolina		Illinois	Oklahoma
Oregon		Indiana	Rhode Island
Vermont		Kansas	South Carolina
Virginia		Kentucky	South Dakota
Washington		Louisiana	Tennessee
West Virginia		Maine	Texas
District of		Michigan	Utah
Columbia		Mississippi	Wisconsin
		Missouri	

a. Funding was available in cases of rape or incest, where a woman's health was gravely threatened, and in order to save a woman's life.

b. Funding was available in cases of rape, incest, and severe fetal abnormality.

country. *Roe* and the ensuing political controversy over abortion thus brought out the inherent tensions in American federalism and the inevitability of conflict and struggles for political power in a governmental system that tries to combine the ideals of national uniformity and diversity among the states.

The political struggles in the states over adopting restrictive abortion laws after *Roe* further underscore that the Supreme Court is virtually powerless to resolve, or lay to rest, major political controversies at a single stroke. Instead, the Court and the country became locked into a colloquy carried out in litigation and challenges to the constitutionality of state and local laws. In the process the Court answered many of the questions left unanswered by *Roe* and more sharply clarified its basic holding in *Roe*. The constitutional law giving women the right to choose abortion in turn became more complex and finely tuned as the Court struck down spousal-consent laws and bans on the advertising of abortion services, for example, while upholding state and local laws denying public funding or the use of public hospitals and facilities for abortions (see 3.1 for a summary of the Supreme Court's rulings on state and local abortion laws).

Throughout the 1970s and most of the 1980s the Burger Court essentially stood its ground. But, as discussed in later chapters, with the Court's changing composition in the late 1980s and 1990s, states increasingly enacted more restrictive abortion laws as speculation mounted that the Rehnquist Court might further restrict, if not reverse, *Roe*. The struggles in constitutional law and politics between the Court and the states, Congress, the president, and conflicting interests among the populace were destined to continue.

| | 3.1 | Major Post-*Roe* Rulings on State and Local Abortion Laws |

Case	Vote	Ruling
Doe v. Bolton, 410 U.S. 179 (1973)	7–2	A companion case decided with *Roe.* It extended *Roe* in holding that just as states may not criminalize abortions,

they may not make abortions unreasonably difficult to obtain. *Doe* struck down state requirements that abortions be performed in licensed hospitals, that abortions be approved beforehand by a hospital committee, and that two physicians concur in the abortion decision.

Case	Vote	Ruling
Bigelow v. Virginia, 421 U.S. 809 (1975)	7–2	Held that states may not proscribe newspaper advertisements for abortions and abortion-related services.

Case	Vote	Ruling
Bellotti v. Baird, 428 U.S. 132 (1976)	9–0	Ruled that although states may require minors to obtain parental consent, the states must provide an alternative judi-

cial procedure for procuring authorization of a minor's abortion if parental consent is denied or the minor does not want to seek it.

Case	Vote	Ruling
Planned Parenthood of Central Missouri v. Danforth, 428 U.S. 552 (1976)	5–4	Ruled that informed-consent statutes requiring the doctor to obtain the written consent of the woman after informing her of the dangers of abortion and possible alternatives are permissible if the

requirements are related to maternal health and are not overbearing. The requirements must also be narrowly drawn so as not to interfere unduly with the physician-patient relationship. In addition, the Court upheld requiring doctors to provide information to states on each abortion performed, as long as the reporting requirements relate to maternal health, remain confidential, and are not overbearing. The Court, however, struck down "fetal-protection statutes" that pertain only to previable fetuses and require doctors to use available means to save the lives of fetuses. Finally, the Court held that "it is not the proper function of the legislature or the courts to place viability, which is essentially a medical concept, at a specific point in the gestation period. The time at which viability is achieved may vary with each pregnancy, and the determination of whether a particular fetus is viable is, and must be, a matter for the judgment of the attending physician."

Carey v. Population   7–2   Held that prohibitions on sales and ad-
Services Interna-   vertisements of contraceptives for mi-
tional,   nors are unconstitutional.
431 U.S. 678 (1977)

Beal v. Doe,   6–3   Held that nothing in the language or his-
432 U.S. 438 (1977)   tory of Title XIX of the Social Security
                                 Act required the funding of nonthera-
peutic abortions as a condition of a state's participating in the Medicaid program established under the act. The Court indicated that Title
XIX leaves states free to include coverage for nontherapeutic abortions
if they choose to do so, but also that they can refuse to fund unnecessary medical services.

Maher v. Roe,   6–3   Upheld Connecticut's refusal to reim-
432 U.S. 464 (1977)   burse Medicaid recipients for abortion
                                expenses except where the attending
                                physician certifies that an abortion is
                                medically or psychiatrically necessary.

Poelker v. Doe,   6–3   Upheld the policy of the city of St. Louis,
432 U.S. 59 (1977)   Missouri, to deny indigent pregnant
                                women access to nontherapeutic abor-
                                tions in *public* hospitals.

Colautti v. Franklin, 6–3   Struck down a fetal-protection statute
439 U.S. 379 (1979)   that applied to viable fetuses and held
                                that state statutes must precisely set
forth the standards for determining viability. In addition, the Court
noted that fetal-protection laws must specify whether the doctor's paramount duty is to the patient or whether the doctor must balance the
possible danger to the patient against the increased odds of fetal survival.

H.L. v. Matheson,   6–3   Upheld a Utah statute requiring the phy-
450 U.S. 398 (1981)   sician to notify the parents, "if pos-
                                sible," before performing an abortion on
their minor daughter (1) when the girl is living with and dependent on
her parents, (2) when she is not emancipated by marriage or otherwise,
and (3) when she has made no claim or showing as to her maturity or
as to her relationship with her parents.

City of Akron v.   6–3   Struck down five sections of a city ordi-
Akron Center for Re-   nance for unduly restricting a woman's
productive Health,   right to obtain an abortion. The sections
462 U.S. 416 (1983)   provided that (1) after the first trimester
                                of a pregnancy, an abortion must be per-

formed in a hospital; (2) there be notification of consent by parents before an abortion is performed on an unmarried minor; (3) the attending
physician make certain specified statements to the patient so that the
patient's consent for an abortion would amount to "informed consent"; (4) there be a 24-hour waiting period between the time the patient signs the consent form and when the abortion is performed; and
(5) fetal remains be disposed of in a "humane and sanitary manner."

Planned Parenthood   6–3   Invalidated Missouri's second-trimester
Association of Kan-   hospitalization requirement, but a bare
sas City v. Ashcroft,   majority struck down the state's require-
462 U.S. 476 (1983)   ment that, after twelve weeks of preg-
                                nancy, the abortion be performed in a
hospital and (voting 5–4) *upheld* three other sections of Missouri's law.
They required (1) pathological reports for each abortion performed, (2)
the presence of a second doctor during abortions performed after viability, and (3) that a minor obtain parental consent or consent from a
juvenile court before obtaining an abortion.

Simopoulos v.   8–1   Upheld Virginia's mandatory hospitaliza-
Virginia   tion requirement for abortions per-
462 U.S. 506 (1983)   formed in the second trimester.

Thornburgh v. Ameri- 5–4   Struck down a Pennsylvania law requir-
can College of Obste-   ing (1) women to be advised of medical
tricians & Gynecologists,   assistance and that the natural father is
476 U.S. 747 (1986)   responsible for child support; (2) physi-
                                cians to inform women of the detrimen-
tal effects and risks of abortion; (3) doctors to report all abortions to
the state; (4) a higher degree of care in postviability abortions in an attempt to save the life of the fetus; and (5) the presence of a second physician during the performance of all abortions.

Webster v. Repro-   5–4   Upheld the constitutionality of Mis-
ductive Health Serv-   souri's 1986 restrictive abortion law: (1)
ices,   decreeing that life begins at conception
492 U.S. 490 (1989)   and that "unborn children have protect-
                                able interest in life, health, and well-be-
ing"; (2) requiring a physician, before performing an abortion on a
woman believed to be 20 or more weeks pregnant, to test the fetus's
"gestational age, weight, and lung maturity"; (3) prohibiting public
employees and facilities from being used to perform an abortion not
necessary to save the woman's life; and (4) making it unlawful to use
public funds, employees, and facilities for the purpose of "encouraging
or counseling" a woman to have an abortion except when her life is endangered.

Hodgson v. Minne-   5–4   Without a judicial bypass option, the
sota,   state's requirement that a minor notify
497 U.S. 417 (1990)   both parents before obtaining an abor-
                            tion was made unconstitutional. On that
issue, O'Connor joined Brennan, Blackmun, Marshall, and Stevens. But
she also joined Chief Justice Rehnquist and Justices Scalia, Kennedy,
and White in upholding the constitutionality of the parental-consent
law. In separate opinions, Stevens contended that the law was unconstitutional even without the judicial bypass option, and Kennedy said
that the judicial bypass option was constitutionally unnecessary.

Ohio v. Akron   6–3   Writing for the Court, Kennedy upheld
Center for Repro-   the Ohio law that (1) requires a minor
ductive Health,   to notify at least one parent before ob-
497 U.S. 502 (1990)   taining an abortion, and (2) also pro-
                            vides for a judicial bypass option.

Notes

1. See David O'Brien, *Storm Center: The Supreme Court in American Politics*, 3d ed. (New York: Norton, 1993), chap. 6; Gerald Rosenberg, *The Hollow Hope: Can Courts Bring About Social Change?* (Chicago: University of Chicago Press, 1991).

2. *New State Ice Co. v. Liebmann*, 285 U.S. 262 (1932) (Brandeis, J., dis. op.).

3. See, e.g., David O'Brien, "Federalism as a Metaphor in the Constitutional Politics of Public Administration," *Public Administration Review* 49 (1989): 411.

4. See Lawrence Lader, *Abortion II: Making the Revolution* (Boston: Beacon Press, 1973).

5. Quoted, Nadine Brozan, *New York Times*, 15 January 1983, A17.

6. Judith Blake, "The Supreme Court's Abortion Decisions and Public Opinion in the United States," *Population and Development Review* 3 (1977): 46.

7. See Eva Rubin, *Abortion, Politics, and the Court* (Westport, Conn.: Greenwood Press, 1982), 126–36.

8. This discussion draws on Rosenberg, *The Hollow Hope*, 189–93.

9. Quoted, Rubin, *Abortions, Politics, and the Court*, 154.

10. See Stanley Henshaw, "Induced Abortion: A Worldwide Perspective," *Family Planning Perspectives* 17 (1986): 250.

11. Rosenberg, *The Hollow Hope*, 193.

12. *Poelker v. Doe*, 432 U.S. 59 (1977).

13. See Stanley Henshaw, J. Forrest, E. Sullivan, and C. Tietze, "Abortion Services in the United States, 1979 and 1980," *Family Planning Perspectives* (1982): 5.

14. See, e.g., Alan Guttmacher Institute, *Abortion 1974–1975: Need and Services in the United States, Each State and Metropolitan Area* (New York: Planned Parenthood Federation of America, 1976); Susan B. Hansen, "State Implementation of Supreme Court Decisions: Abortion Rates Since *Roe v. Wade,*" *Journal of Politics* 42 (1980): 372.

15. See Rosenberg, *The Hollow Hope*, 192.

16. For a different view of the impact of the Court's ruling in *Roe*, see ibid., 192–201.

17. See *Wolfe v. Schroering*, 541 F.2d 523 (6th Cir., 1976).

18. See *Planned Parenthood of Central Missouri v. Danforth*, 428 U.S. 32 (1976).

19. 62 *Ops. of Atty. Gen.* 3 (1977).

20. See, e.g., *People v. Norton*, 507 P.2d 862 (1973) (striking down Colorado's prohibition of aborting fetuses more than sixteen weeks old).

21. See, e.g., *State v. New York Times*, 20 Ariz. App. 183, 511 P.2d 196 (Ariz. Ct. App. 1973); *People v. Orser*, 31 Cal. App. 3d 528, 107 Cal. Reptr. 458 (Cal. Ct. App. 1973); *Leigh v. Olson*, 487 F. Supp. 1340 (1980).

22. See *Danforth v. Rodgers*, 414 U.S. 1065 (1973); *Planned Parenthood of Central Missouri v. Danforth*, 428 U.S. 552 (1976); *Planned Parenthood Association of Kansas City, Missouri, Inc. v. Ashcroft*, 462 U.S. 476 (1983); *Webster v. Reproductive Health Services*, 109 S.Ct. 3040 (1989).

Cemetery
of the
Innocents

4,100 Children have died
in abortion chambers
each day, day after day,
since 1973.
4,100 crosses stand here,
a silent memorial.

"A plea by the American Coalition for Life"

CHAPTER 4

A Reluctant Congress Faces the Abortion Issue

"Millions of American women feel more secure and more free today as the result of yesterday's Supreme Court ruling in the cases of *Roe against Wade* and *Doe against Bolton,*" declared Bella Abzug, New York's flamboyant Democratic feminist, on the floor of the House of Representatives one January day in 1973.[1] By contrast, Senator James B. Allen (D-Alabama) told his colleagues, "I believe this decision is bad logic, bad law and bad morals.... The Supreme Court is up to its old failing of permissiveness and of taking over the legislative functions of the Congress and State legislatures. First it outlaws the death penalty for criminals and then it permits it to be imposed on unborn babies."[2] There was surprisingly little other immediate congressional comment, perhaps because members were more intent on eulogizing former President Lyndon Baines Johnson, but congressional silence on the abortion issue did not last long.

By the end of 1973 nearly 10 percent of the representatives had signed on as cosponsors of antiabortion legislation or proposed constitutional amendments aimed at undoing *Roe*.[3] Virtually every possible legislative response was introduced in Congress that year by members who opposed the Court's decision: (1) constitutional amendments that would extend due process protection under the Fifth and Fourteenth amendments to the fetus "from the moment of conception"; (2) constitutional amendments returning power to the states to regulate abortion; (3) bills that would define the word *person* as used in the Fourteenth Amendment to include fetuses; (4) bills incorporating various restrictions on the federal funding of abortion services; and (5) bills containing so-called conscience-clause provisions aimed at protecting medical personnel from

Opposite: Mock cemetery erected near the Capitol by the American Coalition for Life, 8 April 1989. *Photo:* Reuters/Bettmann Newsphotos.

having to participate in abortions. Few of these proposals made any headway in 1973, but they and their progeny would consume many thousands of hours of congressional time in the years to come.

The Court's ruling came at a time when the country was facing a "crisis in confidence" after the Vietnam war and amid the growing Watergate scandal. The changing national political climate affected the strategies of the interest groups that organized to attack or defend *Roe*. The political climate also was a principal factor in how the abortion issue played out in Congress. Other important factors were changes in election laws, in congressional budget procedures, and in a number of congressional practices.

The Birth of the Modern Congress

In the early 1970s Congress underwent a wrenching series of procedural changes that dramatically altered the behavior of its members and the manner in which Congress conducts its business. The net effect of the changes, often referred to as the "subcommittee bill of rights," was a decentralization of institutional power and responsibility. Instead of twenty or so committee chairs in each chamber exercising nearly arbitrary control over legislative procedure and business, power was shared among more than a hundred subcommittee chairs. Coordination and cooperation, both prerequisite to arriving at the majority consensus constitutionally required for the passage of laws, was made far more difficult to achieve. Two other major "reforms" soon compounded the decentralization of congressional power in critical and unforeseen ways: the Federal Election Campaign Act of 1974 and the Budget Impoundment and Control Act of 1974. The potential for conflict was increased as well—a potential repeatedly realized as Congress struggled with the abortion issue during the decades following *Roe*.

The decentralization of congressional power and the unintended consequences of the 1974 election and budget reform acts have enormously expanded the likelihood of delay built into the Constitution's blueprint for government. And, they have had other effects. To understand the abortion drama as it has unfolded on Capitol Hill, it is necessary first to look at how these procedural and legal changes both structured and limited the actions of the players in and out of Congress.

Election Reform and Unintended Consequences

Passage of major legislation in Congress frequently requires a crisis or scandal to create a sense of urgency. The scandals surrounding the

Nixon reelection campaign and the Watergate break-in and a number of instances of malfeasance by members of Congress heightened the realization that corrective measures were needed to placate a public whose tolerance had ebbed.[4] Predictably, Congress responded by passing a law.

Like all laws, the Federal Election Campaign Act of 1974[5] was born of bargaining and compromise. Like most laws, it was not necessarily the most rational solution to a problem. Instead, it was the best that Congress could pass. Its primary intent was to lessen the effect, or at least the appearance of the effect, of big money on campaigns and to eliminate the possibility that a few rich backers could control elected officials. Public funding and spending limits for elections were to accomplish these ends for presidential campaigns. The law also set spending limits on congressional campaigns but did not provide for their public funding.[6] In the absence of a provision for public funding, the spending limits were subsequently ruled unconstitutional by the Supreme Court and hence were never enforced.[7] What was left was a cap on contributions from any single source to a congressional campaign. By forcing candidates to seek more donors, the legislation aimed at ensuring that no donor, no matter how wealthy or powerful, could *buy* any candidate. As campaigns have become more costly, the donation limits have forced candidates to cast their fund-raising nets ever wider and to devote much more time and energy to money gathering.

One of the accommodations made by Congress was a provision that allows a political action committee (a PAC was defined as any organized group of fifty or more persons that donates to at least five political candidates) to give from the pooled donations of its membership more than a person could give when acting alone: a $5000 donation per candidate compared with $1000 by an individual. Candidates have found PAC financing irresistible.[8] Another accommodation in the law allowed political parties to donate up to $25,000 to a candidate's campaign; the hope was that the higher limits would enhance the role of parties in elections and, more important, that the enhanced role would translate into cooperation and teamwork in the legislative process. The logic: If members of Congress are dependent on the continued support of party campaign funds for reelection, the parties would have both a carrot and a stick to bring about loyalty. Things have not turned out that way.

Other developments in the larger political environment have complicated the election process and undercut the goals of the 1974 reform law. In the mid-1970s the national government appeared to many citizens to be the problem. One 1974 congressional candidate said of the situation: "There was a ground swell of public animosity toward the federal government growing around me."[9] Perceiving this mood, candidates for national offices began running against the Washington establishment. They increasingly chose to stand alone with little more than a label connection to party affiliation. As the campaign slogan of Connecticut's former Senator Lowell Weicker put it, "I'm nobody's man but yours!"

Individual congressional campaign organizations also came to rely on computers, television, polling, and mass communication techniques to "sell" the candidate and on paid campaign consultants to manage the sales campaign. The traditional party functions of recruitment and selection of candidates and running volunteer-staffed campaigns became largely obsolete.[10] But technology and consultants are enormously expensive. The average cost of a House race in 1974 was approximately $61,000; by 1992 it was over $300,000—with many candidates spending more than a million dollars. The average cost of a Senate race in 1974 was approximately $450,000; by 1992 it was nearly $3 million.[11] Members of Congress turned to PACs for more and more funds. And with incumbent reelection rates close to 100 percent, long-term relationships are inevitably built up between PACs or interest groups that give substantial amounts and the receiving members of Congress. Without the parties' funding function, no buffer stands between candidates and the money suppliers.

Organized groups use an array of techniques for getting congressional attention and cooperation besides the obvious campaign contributions and delivery of votes from their memberships. Mass-mail blitzes, often computer generated, give rise to floods of letters into congressional offices. Large and small staged events draw attention to interest-group causes, and the media multiply the effect by pressing members of Congress for their reactions. Thousands of privately financed polls, carefully structured to assure the appearance of mass support for particular sides of issues, are paraded past senators and representatives. A host of lobbyists representing every conceivable interest that could want to get something, keep something, or protect something from government ply their trade on Capitol Hill. Sophisticated tracking of every congressional vote was aided by the introduction in 1973 of electronic-teller voting in the House, and interest groups were quick to press their allies therein to insist on recorded votes so that scorekeeping would be easier.[12] If one interest group tries a new tactic and it appears advantageous, others immediately adopt and adapt it. Dozens of groups on both sides of the abortion issue have at one time or another applied all these tactics and have enjoyed varying degrees of success.

As a result of these developments, members of Congress are skittish about offending anyone. Because any action is bound to displease some group, decision avoidance (at least the avoidance of decisions for which they could be held accountable) is a favored counterstrategy. But over time sympathetic remarks and symbolic actions that do not really further a group's cause become inadequate returns from the member-of-Congress half of the relationship. More explicit action is demanded as a quid pro quo, such as introducing a bill, getting committee action on a bill, becoming a regular standard-bearer for the cause on the floor and in the media, pressing a bill into law or convincingly pressing toward that end, voting regularly for desiderata of the interest group, with its ever-increasing expectation of 100 percent support, and interceding in behalf of the interest group when other government actors (usually bureaucrats) are causing it problems. Not surprisingly, the big and powerful contributors usually get the most servicing.

Besides "constituents" who give money, there are "constituents" who give votes, and "constituents" who can give "visibility" of both the harmful and helpful variety. None of these so-called constituents has to live in or even near a member's district or state to count. In other words, there does not have to be a voter-member relationship for a group or individual to get a representative's attention and "service." A group with a large membership, especially if spread throughout many members' districts (e.g., construction workers, the elderly, or savings-and-loan institutions) or a group with an intensely committed membership willing to make regular and repeated public waves that garner media attention (e.g., pro-lifers brandishing jars containing aborted fetuses or pro-choicers waving metal coat hangers) can be as effective as a group with huge financial resources.

In this era of media-orchestrated negative campaigning and image politics, to offend large or committed groups can be political suicide, even if few of their adherents reside in a member of Congress's district or state. Regarding the abortion issue, even members from overwhelmingly liberal or conservative districts are often leery about taking a public stand that might provoke either side or provide ammunition for a negative campaign attack. In contrast, when the tide of public sympathy appears to be moving to one side of the abortion issue, some members choose to go with the flow.

The 1974 election reforms, rising public expectations for governmental responses to social problems, the growth in numbers and sophistication of organized interest groups, and the fragmentation of power within Congress have created a very different and more contentious congressional policy-making process. In addition, another development—the country's mounting deficit—has caused the legislative process to become even more fractious.

Budget Reform and Deficit Politics

The 1974 reform of the congressional budget process was another element that affected congressional responses to the abortion controversy. As with election reform, the results turned out to be not quite what had been intended. The impetus for reform was President Richard Nixon's refusal to spend the funds appropriated for a number of social programs and highway building projects. Democrats in Congress were outraged. Determined to check a seemingly imperial president and to protect its own power over budget matters, Congress passed the Budget Impoundment and Control Act of 1974.[13] The act set up an elaborate process, with deadlines for action on budget matters and new budget committees in each house responsible for managing the process.

The earlier congressional appropriations process had been characterized by political scientist Charles Lindblom as "incrementalism," or the "politics of muddling through."[14] Each year the president submitted a budget to Congress that essentially accepted the previous year's budget as a baseline, adjusted most accounts upward to reflect inflation, tinkered at the margins with spending for existing programs, and proposed funding a few new programs. Congress would then add a bit to the increases here, cut a bit from the increases there (though rarely did the cuts go below the previous year's baseline), and accept or reject new programs. All this was done with thirteen separate appropriations bills. Accordingly, the compromise and bargaining essential to hammering out a bill that could win majority support in both houses under these conditions went on in thirteen arenas; each contained and focused on specific programs, such as education or energy. Most differences of opinion were over who got how much more, and whether some new interest won a slice of the federal pie.

Had the 1974 changes in the congressional budget process been carried out in more auspicious circumstances, the only difference might have been a greater assertion of congressional power. But inflation, high interest rates, high unemployment, and a galloping trade deficit overtook the economy, and the era of deficit politics arrived. The incrementalism of the past was no longer possible, and Congress was faced with voting for sizable tax increases, cutting funding, and saying no. To sidestep that predicament, it resorted to deficit financing. Because the politics of deficit financing is particularly contentious, Congress tended to postpone action on its appropriations bills as long as possible. As the start of the new fiscal year (1 October) approached, Congress would bundle all the unpassed bills—in some years as many as ten of the thirteen regular appropriations bills were handled this way—into one huge omnibus appropriations bill. Sometimes Congress passed temporary funding bills (called omnibus continuing resolutions) to give itself a few more days or weeks to work out spending compromises for the year. These monster appropriations bills were as much as a foot thick, and few members had any clear idea what precisely was included in them.

Following *Roe,* members of Congress and groups who passionately believed that the Court was morally wrong were at a distinct political disadvantage. To overcome the tyranny of the status quo, abortion opponents had to jog the political system into action. The changes in Congress brought about by the decentralization of power, the changes in the election process, and the deficit provided unique opportunities. Deficit politics, election politics, and abortion politics were destined to be entwined. Moreover, the tensions arising in divided party control of the executive and legislative branches were exacerbated by confrontational politics within and between the two houses of Congress. Accommodation, comity, and compromise, which are essential to the development of a majority coalition in large legislative bodies, became less likely and sometimes impossible to achieve.

Congressional Politics and the Abortion Issue

For those in Congress strongly opposed to *Roe,* their colleagues' reluctance to deal with the issue was frustrating. Between 1973 and 1976, a few days of hearings were held by a subcommittee in each house, but no legislative action resulted. Abortion opponents were soon able to claim one victory, though. When Senator James Buckley (R-New York) noticed that the *Congressional Record* indexed abortion under the general category "Birth Control," he requested that the subject be given its own listing. Commenting on his success, Buckley stated, "This correction is important. We are not dealing with a trivial semantic distinction, but a fundamental conceptual error that would be all the worse if it appeared to have the Government's official seal of approval."[15]

The first major congressional legislation dealing with abortion, a ban on spending federal Medicaid funds on abortion, passed in 1976. In the ensuing years similar bans were placed on a number of other federally funded programs, such as medical coverage of Department of Defense personnel, federal employee health benefits, and family-planning services. Efforts to pass a constitutional amendment banning or limiting abortions failed, but not from want of trying.

During a filibuster in 1985 aimed at stopping an abortion amendment barring funding of abortions for inmates in federal prisons, Senator Howard Metzenbaum (D-Ohio) noted that the Senate had considered

"431 abortion proposals in the last nine years."[16] Most failed to pass, but many did make it into law (4.1, pp. 112–13, provides a chronology of major legislation concerning abortion passed from 1973 to 1989). Nevertheless, the influence of the abortion issue on congressional procedure and policy cannot be measured by numbers of laws passed alone.

A congressional staffer described her experience in promoting comprehensive energy legislation in 1977–78 as being like "swimming in a kettle of spaghetti. You get tangled up in controversy no matter which way you turn."[17] Dealing with the abortion issue in Congress proved to be the same sort of experience, only worse: The controversy had a way of spilling over and becoming entangled in an array of utterly unrelated issues like congressional pay raises and civil rights legislation. The abortion issue, in short, had a major effect on how Congress behaved and what it produced.

The Saga of the Hyde Amendment

Politics is said to be the art of the possible. A constitutional amendment to undo *Roe* was not a very realistic immediate prospect for abortion opponents. The far more promising approach was to try to reduce the availability of abortion.

One result of *Roe* was that poor women could qualify for federal funds under Medicaid to cover the costs of abortions. The number of legal abortions increased dramatically after 1973, and a large proportion were paid for by the federal government. In 1973 itself, approximately 270,000 abortions were federally funded at a cost of $45 to $50 million (see table 4.1). Eliminating or restricting *publicly funded* abortions became an initial goal of abortion opponents in Congress.

Congress's rules regarding legislative policy decisions require that a bill authorizing a policy or program must pass *before* a bill to fund the program may be passed. The purpose of the sequence is "to ensure that substantive and financial issues are subject to separate and independent analysis."[18] The two-step arrangement, however, is only as effective as Congress chooses to make it. Political and practical realities have often prompted Congress to pass appropriations bills without first passing authorization bills and to allow amendments to appropriations bills that effectively make policy. Because appropriations bills must pass each year or no funds can be spent, they are especially attractive targets for members who have not been successful at accomplishing their policy goals in the authorization process.

In 1974, for example, Representative Angelo D. Roncallo (R-New York) offered an amendment on the floor of the House to the Labor–Health, Education, and Welfare (HEW) appropriations bill:

TABLE 4.1

ABORTION RATES BEFORE AND AFTER *ROE,*

1970–78

Year	Number of abortions reported to Centers for Disease Control	Number of abortions reported to Alan Guttmacher Institute
1970	193,500	NA
1971	485,800	NA
1972	586,800	NA
1973	615,800	744,600
1974	763,500	898,600
1975	854,900	1,034,200
1976	988,300	1,179,300
1977	1,079,400	1,316,700
1978	1,157,800	1,409,600

SOURCE: Senate Committee on the Judiciary, Subcommittee on the Constitution, *Hearings on Constitutional Amendments Related to Abortion,* 97th Cong., 1st sess., 1981, 2 (Appendix): 105. Reprint of Christopher Tietze, "Induced Abortion: A World Review" (1981).

No part of the funds appropriated under this Act shall be used in any manner directly or indirectly to pay for abortions or abortion referral services, abortifacient drugs or devices, the promotion or encouragement of abortion, or the support of research designed to develop methods of abortion, or to force any State, school or school district or any other recipient of Federal funds to provide abortions or health or disability insurance abortion benefits. As used in this section, abortion means the intentional destruction of unborn human life, which life begins at the moment of fertilization.[19]

A point of order was immediately raised, challenging the amendment on "the ground that this is legislation in an appropriations bill and it requires the imposition of new duties upon members of the executive branch ... in order to determine when life begins."[20] The protracted late-night debate that followed showed the danger of giving the opposition an opportunity to recast the debate to its advantage—a lesson that abortion opponents quickly learned. The phrasing of Roncallo's amendment could be interpreted to prohibit birth-control methods like the pill and the intrauterine device (IUD). Though some abortion opponents,

4.1 Major Legislation on Abortion Passed by the U.S. Congress, 1970–89

Family Planning Services and Population Research Act of 1970 — Barred the use of funds for programs in which abortion is a method of family planning.

Health Program Extension Act of 1973 — Barred judges or public officials from ordering recipients of federal funds to perform abortions or to make facilities available for such procedures if doing so was contrary to a recipient's religious beliefs or moral convictions. Also barred discrimination against personnel for participation or lack of participation in abortions.

Legal Services Corporation Act of 1974 — Barred lawyers in federally funded legal-aid programs from providing legal assistance for procuring a "nontherapeutic abortion." Also barred legal aid in proceedings to compel an individual or institution to perform an abortion, assist in an abortion, or provide facilities for an abortion.

Public Health Service Act of 1977 Amendments — Required the secretary of the Department of Health, Education, and Welfare to conduct a study to determine whether medical, nursing, or osteopathic schools denied admission or otherwise discriminated against any applicant because of the applicant's reluctance or willingness to counsel, suggest, recommend, assist, or in any way participate in the performance of abortions contrary to the applicant's religious beliefs or moral convictions.

Pregnancy Disability Amendment of 1977 to Title VII of 1964 Civil Rights Act — Provided that employers were not required to pay for health insurance benefits for abortion except to save the woman's life, but did not preclude employers from providing abortion benefits.

Public Health Service Act, 1979 Amendments — Barred recipients of federal funds from denying admission or otherwise discriminating against any applicant for training or study because of the applicant's reluctance or willingness to counsel, suggest, recommend, assist, or participate in performing abortions or sterilizations contrary to or consistent with the applicant's religious beliefs or moral convictions.

Budget Reconciliation Act of 1981 — Title IX (Health Services and

Facilities) allowed grants or payments only to programs or projects that do not provide abortions, abortion counseling, or referral, or subcontract with or make payments to any person providing such services, except counseling *for a pregnant adolescent* if the adolescent and her parents or guardians request such referral.

Adolescent Family Life Act of 1981 — Prohibited funding for organizations involved in abortions but allowed religious organizations to receive funds to promote self-discipline as a form of birth control.

Appropriations Bills

Department of Health, Education, and Welfare — Since 1 October 1976 appropriations bills for the Department of Health, Education, and Welfare (later, Health and Human Services) have contained provisions barring the use of Medicaid funds for most abortions. The 1976 amendment barred funding for abortion except to save the woman's life. In subsequent years funding also was allowed for abortion in cases of rape or incest or when two doctors determined that the woman would suffer serious, long-lasting physical problems if the pregnancy were carried to term. In June 1981 the ban was tightened again to cover funding only for abortions to save the woman's life. That restriction remains in effect.

Foreign Assistance and Related Programs — Since 1979 no foreign aid funds appropriated under the bill could be used for abortions or for lobbying for abortion. Included in the ban was aid to the United Nations Fund for Population Activities (specifically targeting aid to China) and the International Planned Parenthood Federation.

District of Columbia — Since 1981 federal funding for abortions has been barred in the district except to save the woman's life or in cases of rape or incest promptly reported to law enforcement or public health officials. In 1985 Congress eliminated the exception for rape and incest, and in 1988 it prohibited the district from using its own funds to pay for abortions as well.

Department of Defense — Since 1982 no funds under this act could be used for abortion except to save the woman's life. This meant that military personnel could not get abortions at military hospitals.

Second Continuing Appropriations Resolution of 1984 — Prohibited the use of federal employee health benefits to pay for abortion except when the woman's life was imperiled.

particularly those whose objections were based on strict acceptance of
Catholic church teachings on contraception, opposed all except natural
family-planning methods, the number of representatives prepared to go
this far was well short of a majority. By focusing on the consequences of
this potential result, opponents were able to split the antiabortion forces
and defeat the amendment by a vote of 247–123.[21] The remarks of Representative Abzug are illustrative:

> We should be aware of the consequences of approving such a blunder-
> buss restriction. A young girl or any woman who is raped could be de-
> nied anticonception drug treatment under this amendment. Family plan-
> ning would be prohibited. The morning-after pill would be proscribed.
> Five to eight million women who use the intrauterine device as a contra-
> ceptive would be denied access to this method of birth control. . . . This
> issue is being used in an improper way at a late hour of night, 10:15 P.M.
> It is being used to inflame all of us here, to make Members feel that un-
> less they vote for this word "abortion" as it happens to appear in this
> amendment, somehow or other their political lives will be affected.

Just how critical to its defeat the recasting of Roncallo's amendment
as one against family planning was is evident from the fact that this vote
was the first and last time the abortion rights supporters in the House
won on an antiabortion funding amendment until after the *Webster* decision in 1989. In the words of David R. Obey (D-Wisconsin), "I believe
as a Catholic, and I believe as a person who is opposed to abortion personally, that the best way that we can discourage abortion is to promote
family planning. This amendment discourages family planning, and we
ought to vote it down."

Supporters of Roncallo's amendment attempted to counter by charging gross exaggeration and by focusing the issue as a proabortion versus
antiabortion vote. For example, Representative Lawrence J. Hogan (R-
Maryland) argued that "there has been so much misinformation spread
about what this amendment does and does not do that I must speak. The
only thing this amendment does is to prohibit spending money under
this bill for abortion. Period. . . . It only prohibits those drugs which are
abortifacient, which by its very definition means something that causes
an abortion. So if you are opposed to abortion, you will support the
Roncallo amendment and if you are in favor of it, you will vote against
it."

Hogan's assurances were immediately called into question by Representative William R. Roy (D-Kansas):

I do feel, as the only obstetrician and gynecologist in the House, that I should give my interpretation of the term "abortifacient drugs or devices." Certainly the intrauterine device acts by not allowing the fertilized egg to implant.... By the same token the recognized birth control pills, which are most commonly used, at times act by not permitting the fertilized ovum to implant.... By any reasonable interpretation of the language of this amendment we are knocking out $287 million for present ongoing programs of family planning. I do not think the House wishes to do that.

Roy's interpretation added credence to abortion rights supporters not only because he could claim medical expertise but because he identified himself as opposed to the federal funding of abortions, and thus could not be dismissed as a biased partisan. Recognizing inevitable defeat, abortion opponents attempted to amend the amendment by striking everything but the first phrase, thereby simply prohibiting the expenditure of funds under the act to pay directly or indirectly for abortions. When the only other doctor in the House, Representative Tim Lee Carter (R-Kentucky), declared that the revised amendment would prevent an operation to save the life of a mother, it was clear that compromise would prove impossible.

"I will be damned," exclaimed Obey, "if I, a male legislator, will vote to prohibit a woman from having a therapeutic abortion necessary to save her life by any action I take tonight." Without an explicit exception for saving the life of the woman, the antiabortion forces were not able to persuade a majority. Although they had not "won" in their first major attack on *Roe,* the experience taught them a good deal about what might be politically possible in the future.

The connection between congressional behavior, interest-group pressure, and election politics is evident throughout this first major abortion debate following *Roe.* Some members addressed the connections explicitly, as did Representative Robert Giaimo (D-Connecticut):

I know of the great lobby and the great pressures which are being put on Members in this entire area of the right to life.... This is a mischievous amendment, designed to try to terrify us into doing what we really know to be wrong.... Take the popular cause, or the safe cause, and vote for this amendment, or do what is right and stand up and vote down this amendment, and give the lie to what so many citizens in this Nation are saying about us, that we as a Congress do not have the courage to do what is necessary and what is right.

Although abortion opponents were not successful in persuading a majority in the House to support a funding ban, they did not come away empty-handed. They had forced a recorded vote: 370 representatives were now "on the record" on abortion, which gave the antiabortion groups a measure of their support as well as the names of those who had voted against them—targets for future lobbying activity. Perhaps the best evidence of their subsequent lobbying success is the fact that from 1975 until 1989 the House regularly and repeatedly voted by large margins in favor of proposals to prohibit the federal funding of abortions.

Senate debate on prohibiting the federal funding of abortions for the poor did not occur until two months after the House defeat of Roncallo's amendment. It was immediately clear that the antiabortion forces had learned from that defeat. The amendment introduced by Senator Dewey F. Bartlett (R-Oklahoma) specifically provided for an exception "to save the life of the mother," and there were no references to abortifacient drugs. This left those who opposed funding restrictions with a more difficult task: Simply raising the specters of outlawed birth-control pills or of a woman's dying would not work. Without the "cover" of such outcomes, a senator could less easily explain a "no" vote to the antiabortion forces. Declaring allegiance to both sides was also made more vexatious.

The Senate's abortion opponents won by a vote of 50–34. Their victory, too, was aided by taking advantage of an opportunity to recast the debate. The strategy was to embrace the rhetoric of individual rights, one of the central defenses of abortion supporters. As Senator John O. Pastore (D-Rhode Island) put it, "There are many people in this country who pay money and pay their taxes and they have a very strong feeling against [abortions]. Why should their money be used and abused in this fashion?"[22] The "right" to choose *not* to participate in the funding of abortions became a regular counter to the right-to-choose arguments of abortion supporters in subsequent debates.

Although the antiabortion forces could claim a victory in the Senate, ultimately their cause was lost in 1974 as a result of conference committee compromises over the differences between the House and Senate Labor–HEW appropriations bills. It took two more years of perseverance for the antiabortion advocates to "win" their no-federal-funding-of-abortions crusade in Congress.

After 1974 the two chambers switched sides on the abortion issue: The House voted regularly to restrict abortion funding; the Senate not to do so. Seven Democrats and one Republican who had voted for funding restrictions in 1974 changed their minds in 1975, accounting in part for the reversal. Other votes against the Bartlett Amendment came from senators who were not present for the 1974 vote, and from two freshmen who reversed the position of their predecessors (see table 4.2).

TABLE 4.2

SENATE VOTES ON BARTLETT AMENDMENT,

1974 AND 1975

	1974		1975	
Party	*Members voting for funding restrictions*	*Members voting against funding restrictions*	*Members voting for funding restrictions*	*Members voting against funding restrictions*
Republican	22	14	19	16
Democratic	28	20	17	38
Total	50	34	36	54

SOURCE: Adapted from *Congressional Quarterly Almanac,* 94th Cong., 1st sess., 1975, 594.

Often presented as a *"Republicans against"* versus *"Democrats for"* issue because of each party's presidential platforms, the abortion controversy in Congress is decidedly more complex. Throughout the 1970s and 1980s, the battles in the Senate were fought with Republicans as the admirals on both sides. Abortion opponents such as Jesse Helms (R-North Carolina), Orrin Hatch (R-Utah), and Bartlett faced abortion rights supporters Edward Brooke (R-Massachusetts), Robert Packwood (R-Oregon), and Lowell Weicker (R-Connecticut). Although Democrats joined on both sides, they tended to leave it to the Republicans to beat up on one another. In the House, which has had a large Democratic majority since 1973, both Republicans and Democrats have spoken on the floor in favor of restricting federal funding and regularly voted to do so.[23] Even women members of Congress have split over the issue, with little regard for official party lines. For example, in 1977 six of the eighteen women representatives voted the antiabortion position on funding restrictions: three Democrats (Lindy Boggs of Louisiana, Marilyn Lloyd of Tennessee, and Mary Rose Oakar of Ohio) and three Republicans (Margaret Heckler of Massachusetts, Marjorie Holt of Maryland, and Virginia Smith of Nebraska).[24] Supporting abortion rights were both Republicans and Democrats, including Millicent Fenwick of New Jersey and Elizabeth Holtzman of New York.

The 1976 Funding-Ban Rider

By 1976, the bicentennial of the Declaration of Independence and the first presidential election year since *Roe,* the antiabortion forces were significantly more visible and vocal. That year they prevailed upon the House to attach a rider banning the use of funds to pay for or to promote abortions for any reason. (The ban became known as the Hyde Amendment, after Henry Hyde [R-Illinois], its principal sponsor in the House.) They did not prevail in the Senate. The two bills contained many other differences as well. Before a bill can be sent to the president for signing into law, it must be enacted by both houses in identical form. When bills passed by both the House and Senate are not identical, the leadership of each chamber appoints members to a conference committee that attempts to hammer out the differences. (Of course, the vigor with which individual conferees defend the position of their chamber depends in part on their own personal preferences.) Conferees do not have the last word, however; the bill they settle on must be voted on by the full membership of both houses.

The conference committee appointed to deal with the two versions of the Labor–HEW appropriations bill settled all matters at issue except abortion funding; conferees clung tenaciously to their respective chamber's point of view. Frustrated, the committee reported the bills back to both chambers with the one matter unresolved. Each chamber voted repeatedly to sustain its position.

A second conference committee was formed. After weeks of wrangling, a proposal put forward by Representative Silvio O. Conte (R-Massachusetts) was finally accepted; it limited funding except "where the life of the mother would be endangered if the fetus were carried to term." Timing and deadlines were pivotal in bringing about agreement. With elections less than two months away, patience was growing thin, and it was clear that abortion opponents were prepared to stick to their guns and thereby keep their colleagues from campaigning. Obstinacy might not have won their colleagues' hearts, but it worked to win their votes. Committee members filed out of the conference room to the applause of antiabortion demonstrators. There was no doubt which side had triumphed.

Abortion supporters, meanwhile, were doing what interest groups often do when they lose in Congress: preparing to go to court. Once again, a court provided a more sympathetic ear. Almost immediately following the funding-ban's passage, U.S. District Court Judge John Dooling enjoined its enforcement while his court considered constitutional and other challenges raised by the ban's opponents.[25] A battle just won in the legislature appeared on the verge of being lost in the judicial branch. But it was not just in the courts that antiabortion forces would see their victory diminished: Executive branch interpretation of the ban proved to be another stumbling block.

Although the language of the Conte compromise appeared clear on its face, there was ample "wiggle room" for HEW, which had responsibility for implementing the abortion funding restrictions if the court lifted its injunction. How much danger for a pregnant woman would render abortion permissible? As is often the case, the conference committee had used a less legal and less visible forum for clarifying the restrictions. It filed a report to accompany the bill explaining its understanding of the law. Few members of either chamber have the time or inclination to read committee reports, which are typically written by committee staff. As a result, the effect of a law may be greatly expanded or limited by that means. Although a committee report is not legally binding (at least no court has yet said so), it is accorded great weight by the bureaucrats who enforce laws and by the courts that interpret congressional intent.

The conference committee report on the abortion funding restrictions contained language that limited abortion funding to cases where the woman's life was "clearly endangered by disease" and barred the use of abortion funds for "the emotional or social convenience" of the woman.[26] "Clearly endangered" set up a more strict review than the statutory "endangered," but still left some room for interpretation. During floor debate, Conte had stated that some psychological factors could constitute sufficient danger to the life of the woman to warrant abortion funding. Another "clarification" in the report stated that federal funding for the treatment of rape or incest victims was not prohibited, though no such exception appeared in the law. This left the bureaucrats at HEW to decide how much emotional suffering would be necessary to overcome the report-language funding restriction and to meet Conte's floor-language exception and whether to stick to the letter of the law or allow the exception for rape and incest included in the report language. Abortion opponent Hyde later charged that "the position of the House was torpedoed and sabotaged by the people who really run the country, the regulators, the bureaucrats."[27]

The 1977 Funding-Ban Riders

Reelection campaign pressures on members on both sides of the abortion issue in 1976 overcame the commitments of some to their earlier positions. The next year there was no election to worry about, but the divisive abortion issue kept Congress in session well into December. Again there was a deadline; this time the collective desire to adjourn for the holidays was the critical catalyst for compromise. During 1977 there were twenty-five roll-call votes (eleven in the House; fourteen in the Senate) and numerous voice votes on abortion-related matters. The Labor–HEW appropriations bill was held hostage to the abortion issue, with Congress forced to pass several temporary continuing resolutions to keep the two departments in operation. Lengthy debate in both houses was peppered with hot exchanges over nearly every word and comma in the proposed legislation.

The House Appropriations Committee reported the Labor–HEW bill with an amendment identical to the 1976 Conte compromise. When abortion supporters successfully challenged the amendment as substantive legislation in an appropriations bill—because a federal official would have to make a qualitative determination about whether the woman's life was really endangered—Hyde offered his unqualified ban on all funding. On 17 June 1977 the House passed the Hyde alternative 201–155.[28] Three days later the Supreme Court ruled that states and cities do not have to spend public funds for abortions of an elective or nontherapeutic nature.[29] The opinions handed down did not answer the question of the constitutionality of the federal funding ban but did send a very promising message to its supporters. Further clues to the permissibility of funding restrictions came with an order of the Court to District Judge Dooling that he lift his injunction on implementation of the Hyde Amendment. Lifting the injunction meant that HEW regulations barring the use of Medicaid funds for abortion would go into effect on 4 August 1977. This development gave a sense of urgency to abortion supporters and a sense of renewed hope to abortion opponents.

The Senate debated the Labor–HEW appropriations bill on 29 June 1977. There were sixteen roll-call votes on riders involving restrictions on funding for busing, affirmative action programs, and abortion attached to it. Congressional rules against substantive legislation in appropriations bills were clearly being flouted. Debate on the no-abortion-funding rider consumed almost an entire day, during which only one Democrat spoke out against it. Most of the debate was between Republicans, as it had been on earlier such occasions. Abortion supporters were losing ground in the Senate, although the House-proposed absolute ban remained far short of commanding a majority.

The Senate's votes on amendments to restrict abortion funding are illustrative of the vexing politics of congressional coalition building. Helms's amendment to restrict the federal funding of abortions except in cases where the woman's life was endangered was defeated by a vote of

33–65. Immediately thereafter the Senate approved by a vote of 56–42 a funding restriction that provided exceptions when the life of the woman was endangered, in cases that were "medically necessary," and in cases of rape or incest. Although this wording was considerably less restrictive than that of the House's 1977 bill or Helms's amendment, the vote represented movement toward the abortion opponents' camp. In fact, eighteen senators—three Republicans and fifteen Democrats—shifted from their 1976 opposition to bans on abortion funding. Among them were a number of prominent liberals and some of the most powerful leaders in the Senate: Edmund Muskie (D-Maine), Edward Kennedy (D-Massachusetts), Sam Nunn (D-Georgia), Hubert Humphrey (D-Minnesota), Patrick Leahy (D-Vermont), Howard Baker (R-Tennessee), Lawton Chiles (D-Florida), and Frank Church (D-Idaho). Only one senator moved in the opposite direction: voting against a ban in 1977 after having voted for a ban in 1976. (The excerpts in 4.2 illustrate the heightened conflict occasioned by the politics of the abortion issue in Congress.)

Once again the Labor–HEW appropriations bills went to a conference committee. And once again the abortion funding issue prevented a compromise before the start of the new fiscal year. House conferees were united in sticking to a funding ban for all abortions except those to save the life of the woman. Senate conferees could not even reach agreement among themselves; seven of the thirteen voted against Packwood's effort to eliminate the ban altogether, and four voted against the "medically necessary" exception. Movement toward resolution of the bills' differences was almost imperceptible. Should the wording be "severe *or* long-lasting physical illnesses" or "severe *and* long-lasting physical illnesses?" Should a provision be added to require that two doctors certify that an abortion is absolutely necessary to protect the woman's health? Should the "medical-procedures" exception that allowed for medical treatment for rape and incest victims be limited to "forced rape," to eliminate the possibility of an abortion's being available to any underage teenager who wanted one? Should a requirement that rape be "reported to a law enforcement agency" be added? Should the wording be "promptly reported" or just "reported"?

Throughout the bargaining, Senate conferees were on the defensive against the House conferees and other Senate conferees who did not share their views on abortion rights. Each Conference Committee concession made in modifying the Senate language was met by an unbending House. In regard to the Senate's limitation of the health exception to cases of severe *and* long-lasting physical illnesses, Hyde charged that the language would result in "trading a human life for a kidney."[30] When the Conference Committee report with this language was voted on in the

4.2 Excerpts from Senate Debate on Abortion Funding Rider, 29 June 1977

Senator Jake Garn: I want to know about my rights as a taxpayer and those of millions of people around this country who ... do not believe their money should be taken involuntarily to fund something they feel is a heinous crime.... I am deeply disappointed ... and frankly resent the sarcasm, the innuendos, and the laughter that was caused by some of [Senator Percy's] statements deriding some of our positions.... I believe in my views, too, Senator, as passionately as you do. I disagree with you. But you have a right to your opinions, and the millions of others around this country have the same right to our moral decisions, and the right to debate them on the floor without deriding those positions ... or making the galleries laugh about them.

Senator Packwood: I am curious if the Senator from Utah [Garn] is suggesting that anyone in this country who is morally opposed to some government expenditure does not have to pay taxes. There were millions who were genuinely opposed to the Vietnam war, but we made them pay taxes.... I hope the Senator is not seriously suggesting that we will henceforth adopt the standard of personal morality for payment of taxes.... Is that what the Senator is suggesting?

Senator Garn: Obviously not; I expected the Senator to come back with that.... This is one that is rather more deeply felt than other issues.... Obviously there are some issues that my tax money is taken for, things that I do not support. But I hardly feel as strongly about it as I do about the taking of human life.

Senator Packwood: Is the standard, therefore, how personally deeply a taxpayer feels about the issue? ...

Senator Helms: I think I have never been quite so intrigued with arguments presented on this floor as I have this afternoon.... They [Senators Percy and Packwood] dragged out all the clichés, carefully avoiding the bottom line.... They do not want to confront the inevitable basic question, the only one that really matters ... the deliberate termination of an innocent human life.... So instead they talk about the population explosion, and they offer the remedy of killing human beings who have never had the right even to be born.... I can draw only one conclusion, that you consider that it is cheaper to kill unborn children than it is to let them be born....

· · ·

Senator Birch Bayh: I would suggest after we have disposed of this issue, that my distinguished colleague [referring to Senator Hatch] ... ask his staff to research and see the remarkable similarity between people who oppose the right of a mother to choose abortions and the votes of those same individuals who vote against increased Head Start programs, increased money for food and medical assistance for children, ... and increased money for rat control so you can keep the babies who are born from being bitten by rats.

Senator Hatch: I would like to say to my distinguished colleague that there is a remarkable similarity between many of those who believe in abortion and who are spending us into bankruptcy.

Senator Bayh: If you spend money to inoculate kids to prevent disease, that is getting bankrupt?

Senator Hatch: Nobody ever accused me of that. But let us not use those kinds of arguments when we know what the liberals have done to this country. They have wrecked it.

Senator Bayh: I only brought this up because, I say to my colleague, he said nobody on this floor would be unwilling to spend $200 to save a life. The fact is there are some who are unwilling to spend money to supply the ingredients of life to children who are born under conditions over which they have no control.... We are going to separate out a certain group of Americans, a minority of Americans, those on the low end of the economic scale, those who do not have the financial resources to exercise the constitutional right which the Supreme Court says they have.... Who are we kidding? We are not going to stop poor women from trying to have abortions. What we are going to do is ... put them on a kitchen table with a butcher knife or a bed in the back room with a hanger.... What we are doing is really not stopping abortions. We are taking them out of the medically safe atmosphere.... The Supreme Court has just told us there are other sources [for funding]. But as Justice Brennan pointed out in his very logical dissent, where are they? ... Let us not wait for some white rabbit to pop out of a hat and suddenly bring a bundle of cash into the dusty living room of a poor family with no money for an abortion, because it is not going to be there.... Old Anatole France said: "The law in its majestic equity forbids the rich as well as the poor to sleep under bridges, to beg in the streets, and to steal bread." I think that pretty well sums it up....

SOURCE: Excerpted from *Congressional Record, Senate,* 95th Cong., 1st sess., 1977, 21480–96.

House, it was defeated by a vote of 193–172. When the "forced rape promptly reported to a law enforcement agency or public health service" language was proposed by the Conference Committee, the House voted that down as well. When the "two-doctor" compromise was proposed by the Conference Committee, Hyde quipped, "I never knew an abortionist who did not have a partner,"[31] and urged defeat. As Hyde saw it,

> Yesterday I took only 2 minutes and I was low-keyed and attempted to be moderate. . . because I know that [is] the scenario that is devoutly desired for the pro-life congressmen. . . . I just do not choose to do so today because the immoderate subject of killing prenatal young does not lend itself to moderate discourse. . . . What am I supposed to do, abandon prenatal life because the Senate wants to change the existing law? The citizens of Dachau and Buchenwald, when they visited the furnaces and ovens of the prison camps cringed and shuddered and said, "We didn't know." . . . We know that unborn life is human life.

By 7 December 1977 the House members had had enough of battling and voted 181–167 to accept what they had agreed upon thus far and to go home. The final compromise provided that

> none of the funds provided for in this act shall be used to perform abortions except where the life of the mother would be endangered if the fetus were carried to term, when so determined by two physicians; or except for such medical procedures necessary for the victims of rape or incest, when such rape or incest has been reported promptly to a law enforcement agency or public health service; or except in those instances where severe and long-lasting physical health damage to the mother would result if the pregnancy were carried to term.[32]

Just how shaky the truce was became evident as the Senate prepared to vote on the language the House had accepted. Brooke's comments in floor debate underscore the lack of trust between the houses at that point:

> The House acted upon [the latest compromise language] this morning and rejected it. They held the bill at the desk and there were many consultations back and forth. Finally, a proposal was made that the House would include only—and I say only—one change in the language as sent by the Senate to the House. That one change is this: The words were "when so determined by two physicians." . . . It is my understanding

that the debate and the vote in the House were based upon those additional words, and those additional words only. As I now read the language that came back from the House to the Senate, and which we are now acting upon I see an additional change, I do not know whether it was due to inadvertence or whether it was deliberate.[33]

Brooke was referring to the elimination of a colon! The colon appeared after the words "None of the funds provided in this act shall be used to perform abortions." The worry was that the absence of that punctuation mark might enable HEW to allow only the medical procedure known as a D and C (dilatation and curettage)—a procedure that is useful only if done promptly—and not to provide federal funding for abortions for rape and incest victims. Brooke continued:

One might wonder why I raise this question. We have been back and forth with the House on many occasions with respect to one word and now with respect to punctuation marks. I want to make it crystal clear, and I want to make it certain for the record, as to what was intended by the Senate and, as I understand, what was intended by the House by their vote—because no other change was referred to in that debate—is that we are talking about medical procedures being abortions. There is no doubt in my mind that medical procedures are abortions, and when that colon was placed in there and it [the text] went on after "abortions," the antecedent of course would have been "abortions."

Brooke went on word by word making clear precisely what "Congress" meant in the amendment. There was to be "no doubt" left in "[HEW Secretary Joseph] Califano's mind as to what we intend." To be certain the clarifications were understood as "the official word," Brooke staged a colloquy with Warren Magnuson (D-Washington), whose comments as chair of the Senate Appropriations Committee would have more sway at HEW because his committee had jurisdiction over that department. It was a tactic that was not without detractors. John Stennis (D-Mississippi) commented, "I know the Senator from Massachusetts is a splendid fine lawyer. I do not see how we can go on with the practice of trying to read into our own language certain interpretations that we expect the courts to follow or we expect the Secretary of the Department of HEW to follow. . . . I do not accept the idea that a Member of this body can get up on the floor as an individual and read in interpretations."

Brooke was undaunted. Although he knew that courts and administrators are not bound by congressional debate, he also knew that both often paid close attention when members used that forum to expound on statutory language. Because Califano had made his personal opposition to abortion a matter of public record, Brooke saw added reason to limit the administrator's options.

Magnuson agreed and then made a gesture at smoothing relations with his colleagues on the other side of the abortion issue. It was a gesture reflecting the need for ongoing civil interaction in a body whose members must deal with one another on hundreds of issues over many years—especially because today's opponent may be tomorrow's collaborator on some other issue. The interchange between abortion opponents and supporters after five months of heated jousting underscores congressional recognition of the importance of healing wounds.

> *Senator Magnuson:* I have been around this place for a long time ... I have had more conferences on [abortion] than anything I can think of.... But the Senators have been very, very helpful in helping the Senate arrive at some kind of resolution with the House, and I deeply appreciate it.
>
> *Senator Richard Schweiker (R-Pennsylvania):* My position is well known, I strongly support the anti-abortion language in the Labor–HEW conference report of last year.... I shall vote against this pending proposal because I cannot support language allowing the use of taxpayers' funds to pay for abortions.... However, while I disagree with the chairman and the ranking Republican members of the subcommittee, I respect their beliefs and their efforts to reach agreement with the House.

Then Magnuson noticed Senator S.I. "Sam" Hayakawa (D-California), a well-known semanticist. "I must say," commented Magnuson, with perhaps the only humor evident in the long days of abortion discussions, "that we were very remiss in all these discussions between the House and Senate on the question of what 'prompt' means or whether 'grave' is serious, or 'serious' is grave. At no time did we call upon the expert advice of the Senator from California. I am sorry about that because he might have cleared up a lot of the fog for us on what the words actually mean." With a bit of well-directed sarcasm, Hayakawa responded: "The distinguished Senator from Washington does me too much credit altogether. My learned colleagues in the Senate have been dealing with words for a longer time than I have been.... No one knows better how to use words for their own purposes or broaden them for their own purposes or make them vague for their own purposes. They are all better at that than I am. Maybe after I have been a Member of this body for a number of years, I shall be as adept as they are." Amid laughter, the Senate recessed.

When the final vote was taken on the issue later that day, only a few senators were present. No recorded vote was asked for or taken. The compromise reached with so much agony in 1977 held for one more year, although not without another protracted fight in both houses.

Abortion opponents were not happy with the 1977 compromise language, but William Cox, executive director of the National Committee for a Human Life Amendment, said, "The most important aspect of this entire thing is that the pro-life movement established itself as a major political force in this Congress. We'll come back much wiser and better prepared to get a narrower provision in 1978."[34] If it had not been for election and budget politics, his prediction might well have been accurate.

The 1978 Funding-Ban Rider

In an effort to avoid a rerun of the 1977 fight, House Majority Leader Jim Wright (D-Texas) implored the House in 1978 to accept the existing compromise language. "Last year there were 28 separate votes on this single subject," he lamented:

> It took 6 months of the time of the Congress.... Some $60 billion or more in Federal programs were delayed. The language that finally was agreed to last year undoubtedly falls short in the view of many people.... But I do not know any reason to expect that, if we were to delay and debate and consume precious time of this House ... on this subject, we could come to anything basically different from this. The Committee personnel in both House and Senate are the same. The people who will have to make the linguistic decision are the same.... Therefore, I suggest ... that the Members might wish to accept this amendment now.... Heaven knows we heard enough oratory last year on those 11 separate occasions when we debated rules, debated amendments, and debated conference reports.[35]

Sentiment to contain the issue ran high, and members on the floor quickly agreed to limit debate to one hour, with speakers allotted two minutes each until the hour ran out. Two minutes is about enough time to identify where one stands and urge others to join that position—not enough time to say much of any substance. Rules of the House and Senate, however, enable members to add to what they actually said on the floor in the *Congressional Record*.[36] What is added does not influence colleagues but has important other uses. Copies of what looks like floor debate can be mailed out as evidence of a member's commitment. Some members were anxious to "go on the record" as proof to constituents and interest groups that they were indeed pro or con. Some, like Representative George Miller (D-California), inserted expositions that would have taken twenty to thirty minutes to deliver live. Others seemed more interested in avoiding the unpleasantness of another fruitless debate. Even some of those who had supported the Hyde Amendment in the past simply joined Wright in urging this approach to a hot potato in an election year. Representative George Mahone (D-Texas) pleaded: "Whether we are right or left, whether we are pro-abortion or anti-abortion, as a practical matter compromise is necessary in a legislative body. It should accept the inevitable. It should seek to do the attainable. This is something we can do."

The call for an "ethics of responsibility"[37] ran headlong into those who saw abortion as a moral issue not susceptible to compromise. Edward J. Derwinski (R-Illinois) pointed out that "last year's so-called compromise" was "a last-minute adjustment that caught many Members away and it has not been properly administered by HEW." John Rousselot (R-California) added that "many Members of the House did not really know the full impact of what they were voting for in the conference report" and that sixty members were not present for its passage. Because the vote had been 181–167, sixty members obviously could have tipped the balance against the compromise—after all, the House had voted repeatedly and overwhelmingly for the Hyde Amendment (even with no exception for the life of the woman) in the past. James Oberstar (D-Minnesota) saw change in the air: "This is an election year. The other body has its ear a little closer to the ground this year.... I think if we stand firm, ... the other body might just get the message that we mean business and maybe they will be ready to settle early on our terms in favor of the unborn."

Hyde went to bat for his amendment: "I do not feel guilty about the delay we had in this House in resolving this because I ask: How many lives were saved during this delay?" Then Obey made a last-ditch plea that spared neither side:

Two Members have referred to the fast way last year's language was drawn.... Every newspaper in the country knew that we were trying to find almost on an hourly basis, compromise language and *certainly no one was surprised by the effort, unless they wanted to be and unless they wanted to miss the vote. I suspect there were some people who did....* In the next to the last broadcast before retiring, Eric Sevareid observed that one of the requirements of American citizens in this modern age ought to be to retain the courage of one's doubts as well as one's convictions in this world of dangerously passionate certainties. I can think of no advice that applies more strongly to this issue today. I honestly do not know what amendment can be drafted that would put this question to rest for all time....

Most reasonable people do not want to increase the back-room back-alley abortions, that the committee language will lead to.... Many right-to-life groups will not be satisfied with this language. The Civil Liberties Union [ACLU] certainly will not be satisfied with this language.

I can remember one Wisconsin Women's group that produced a newsletter with the following sentence: "We have a problem, and his name is Dave Obey." That was because I would not oppose all prohibitions against abortions. So I know what kind of unfair pressure Members have from certain women's groups on one side, and I certainly know of the lies and selective truths peddled by Mr. Gallagher [chief lobbyist for the National Committee for a Human Life Amendment] and some other people who agree with him.

But this is a reasonable compromise. This is supposed to be a reasonable place.... I think every Member here knows that this language would pass if Members voted the same way, when the [voting] lights go on as they talk in the privacy of their offices and in the cloakrooms before the [voting] machine is turned on. [Emphasis added.]

Compromise was not in the cards. The recorded vote demanded by Obey proved he was right. His colleagues were not ready to go public, at least not so close to an election. Wright's efforts went down by a vote of 212–198. Representative Patricia Schroeder (D-Colorado) later commented that some members had voted against the leadership's compromise because they thought "that another long fight with the Senate could be avoided since Senator Brooke might be less active than he was in 1977 in leading the Senate fight against restrictions" because he was up for reelection in a heavily Catholic state.[38] That assumption proved wrong (although Brooke's leadership in the fight carried heavy political costs when, at least in part as a result of attacks funded by antiabortion forces, he lost his reelection bid).

Senate debate in 1978 was a shortened rerun of the debate a year earlier, with few members in attendance, a fact bemoaned by Majority Leader Robert C. Byrd (D-West Virginia): "We have five Senators on the floor. This is the HEW appropriations bill, the second largest appropriations bill. . . . We cannot get Senators to the floor to call up their amendments . . . We just cannot get anywhere."[39]

Technically, a quorum (fifty-one senators) is required for the Senate to conduct business. As with so many rules in our political system, informal means have been fashioned to enable flexibility of action. Both houses avoid the quorum rule by simply assuming that a quorum is present unless a member suggests its absence. This means, of course, that any member, at any time, can force the attendance of colleagues or prevent the chamber from continuing in session by requesting a quorum call. Mostly, the shared advantage of all members in not having to be present on the floor means that members cooperatively wink at the quorum rule. Calling for a quorum is an available tactic for delay, however; if a majority does not appear, the chamber is forced to recess.[40]

Another obstacle to getting things accomplished on the floor of the Senate is the existence of the filibuster and its cloture rule. A senator is allowed to talk as long as he or she wishes or is able (filibustering) unless sixty senators vote to end debate (cloture). One way around the problem is unanimous agreement on a time limit for debate. But unanimous consent means just that, and it is difficult to achieve.

When Byrd failed to get a unanimous-consent agreement on the Labor–HEW appropriations bill, he resorted to a countertactic: consideration of another political "hot potato," extension of the time for ratification of the Equal Rights Amendment.[41] He explained the move:

It was because we have not been able to . . . get on with the work of the Senate. I have indicated more than once that if we do not get time agreements, then we are going to get some of those bills that apparently, some Senators do not want up, and because they do not want them up, they are attempting to . . . delay the work so that come October 14 there will not be any time left to take those measures up. . . . So what I did was, of course, make the motion to proceed to ERA. That seems to be the great scare around here. . . . I have sought in good faith to get time agreements. . . . If there is going to be foot dragging on this bill . . . that cuts two ways.

Magnuson complained: "You two [Byrd and Minority Leader Howard Baker (R-Tennessee)] can argue about ERA later. . . . let me go on with my poor old HEW bill. . . . I feel like a hostage." Byrd agreed, only half in jest, that Magnuson was a "put-upon hostage" who had been subjected to "cruel and unusual punishment." The leadership was losing patience with continued disputatiousness over abortion riders.

Byrd's tactic worked. He got debate-time agreements on the various proposed amendments—funding bans on forced school busing, on the enforcement of restrictions on prayer in public schools, and on abortions. Action on the Equal Rights Amendment was set aside. Later that day the Senate addressed the abortion funding proposals. Hatch offered an amendment to restrict funding to abortions necessary to save the life of the woman. Brooke asked for more permissive language than that included in the 1977 legislation. Brooke's plea was more tactical than substantive: The Senate could not simply adopt last year's compromise language "to satisfy those who believe that doing so at this stage may avoid another lengthy battle." The House would likely view such action not as an end to the struggle but as a sign of weakening in the Senate's determination to protect poor women and as a starting point, a beginning, for extracting further compromises from the Senate. Brooke carried the day; the Senate rejected Hatch's amendment by a vote of 55–30.

Again the Labor–HEW appropriations bill headed for conference and again abortion was the sticking point. When it was sent back to the two houses with no compromise reached, the House rejected the Senate position. The Senate gave a bit, substituting the 1977 compromise language for its more permissive amendment. The reality of budget politics provided the "cover" for House members nervous about not appearing committed enough to the goals of the abortion opponents. If the House did not accept the 1977 compromise language, the Department of Labor and the Department of Health, Education, and Welfare would have to be funded under a continuing resolution and that would mean the 1977 compromise language would rule. It was a lose-lose situation and as Representative Obey pointed out, failure to act on the 1978 bill meant that HEW would be able to "squirrel out from" other important limitations and directions in the new law. Members were eager to take home to their campaigns proof of their fiscal responsibility, especially in light of the 6 June 1978 passage in California of Proposition 13—a ballot initiative that limited increases in local property taxes. The Labor–HEW bill had funding cuts aimed at saving close to $60 billion. To throw away the whole bill over language dealing with restrictions on funding abortions was simply not good politics. Election politics, budget politics, and frustration won out. The House passed the 1977 compromise language.

The apparent loss for abortion opponents was balanced by gains in 1978. New restrictions were added over federal funding of abortion in programs under the Peace Corps and Department of Defense budgets.[42] Proponents of a sweeping expansion of working women's rights, called the "Motherhood Bill," wanted to do away with employment discrimi-

nation on the basis of pregnancy by requiring disability and health insurance plans to cover pregnant workers, and ran squarely into the abortion issue. The price of passage was a provision exempting insurance
coverage for abortions. "The cold fact," said one representative, "is that
whatever the procedure we utilize, this House is not going to approve a
bill without the abortion provision in it."[43] "If this legislation which can
be considered nothing but 'pro-life' must be amended by those who oppose abortion," said another member, "no bill which comes before the
House ... can be insured of freedom of such an amendment."[44] Indeed,
more than a decade passed before abortion supporters had another
"win" on the question of federal funding. And 1978 was also the last
year that Congress was able to pass most of its funding bills as individual appropriations bills. Deficit politics and the era of the omnibus appropriations bills were just around the corner.

Omnibus Continuing Resolutions and Abortion

When abortion was elevated to the national political agenda in 1973, it
had to compete with a number of other pressing policy issues, prime
among them inflation, unemployment, and energy. In 1973 the first oil
shortage orchestrated by the Organization of Petroleum Exporting
Countries (OPEC) brought a dramatic increase in the cost of oil and gas-
oline that slowed recovery from the 1970–71 recession. But this first oil
crisis was shortlived; and although there were still plenty of problems to
occupy Congress as the seventies wore on, the press of fiscal crisis was
absent (or at least mostly ignored). By 1979 fiscal and energy problems
were again in the forefront. When the shah of Iran was overthrown, the
new regime, under the Ayatollah Khomeini, staged another worldwide
oil shortage that sent prices skyrocketing. Soon inflation and interest
rates were in the double digits and unemployment was drastically rising.
Congressional efforts to deal with the annual appropriations bills fell
apart.

By late September 1979, just days before the new fiscal year, Congress had passed only three of the thirteen regular appropriations bills.
This forced passage of two temporary bills, which bundled the ten
unpassed appropriations bills into one huge temporary omnibus bill
(omnibus continuing resolution) to fund federal programs while Congress continued to debate what to do. Passage of these omnibus bills was
enormously complicated by the interaction of two unrelated but equally
volatile issues: abortion and congressional pay raises.

Members had not had a pay raise since February 1977, when they hiked their salaries from $44,600 to $57,500. In 1979 a cost-of-living increase of 5.5 percent (which members had denied themselves in 1978, an election year) plus a 7 percent increase for 1979 would go into effect automatically unless they voted against their own pocketbooks. The effect on voters of the $7400 increment, however, was predictable and gave pause to the legislators. The leadership drafted a compromise: a 5.5 percent raise in a proposal attached to the omnibus funding bill. When an amendment to delete the pay raise was offered, a recorded vote was demanded. But instead of voting by electronic teller cards that identify who voted which way, members simply stood to be counted. Seventy-two voted against the raise; 155 voted to accept it.[45] Seemingly set to rest, the issue was destined to become hopelessly entangled with abortion funding.

The Senate made two changes in the bill—both guaranteed to create a major conflict with the House. The first eliminated the pay increase; the second added an amendment on abortion. By a 55–36 vote the Senate adopted language prohibiting funding for abortions unless performed to save the life of the woman, or in cases of promptly reported rape or incest, or if two doctors certified that continued pregnancy would cause the woman severe physical harm. It was not an attempt to return to no restrictions on federal funding of abortions—political reality made that too long a shot. Rather, it was another holding action, an effort to keep the status quo of the 1977 and 1978 compromise language.

A conference committee failed to resolve the abortion issue. The new fiscal year would start in just two days and still ten of the thirteen appropriations bills had not been passed. The House decided to play "hard ball." It voted to accept the omnibus funding bill with the pay-raise amendment and with its own abortion language. *Then it voted to recess for ten days*—an action that was unconstitutional. Article 1 Section 5 of the Constitution provides that "neither house, during the session of Congress, shall, without the consent of the other, adjourn for more than three days." The Constitution is not self-enforcing, though, and it did not provide a brake on the House. The House was counting on the Senate to behave with more responsibility than the House itself had exhibited. After all, if the Senate did not pass the omnibus funding bill, the government would come to a standstill.

The House plan backfired. The Senate closed ranks and refused to pass the omnibus funding bill. Arizona's Republican Senator Barry Goldwater railed:

The real scoundrel in this act, the dog in the manger, is the House of

Representatives.... Never at any time in our history that I can remember has this country been so bereft of leadership in every part of the government and now we have to add Congress. We have to add the House of Representatives.... Here we are on a Saturday sitting on our duffs doing nothing because the House of Representatives has taken it onto themselves to quit, to put their tail between their legs ... and wander off home.[46]

So direct and public a dressing-down is extremely rare, but the reality of the legislative process soon forced the two houses to resume cooperative, if strained, relations.

A compromise was reached: The 5.5 percent pay raise went into effect. The House gave up its opposition to funding abortions for rape and incest victims. The Senate finally gave up on funding abortions to protect the woman's physical health after voting repeatedly, by large margins, to stick to its guns. In the end the House won most of what it wanted. Congress was never able to pass the regular Labor–HEW appropriations bill, and so from 1 October 1979 to 1 October 1980 a second and third continuing resolution were required to keep the departments in operation. Under the second continuing resolution the Senate succeeded in reinstating the physical-health exception. It was a short-lived accomplishment.

In 1979 the abortion issue spilled over into and complicated the passage of a number of other bills. President Carter's effort to create a Department of Education was held up for months when the issue was used by opponents of the new department as a means to undercut liberal support for the authorization bill. Reauthorization of the family-planning and sudden-infant-death-syndrome programs came close to failing over the abortion issue. Abortion opponent Robert K. Dornan (R-California) charged that funding restrictions were being circumvented by federally funded agencies that referred clients to abortion clinics. "There is no evidence that a single abortion has been performed with [these] funds," charged the bill's sponsor, Representative Paul Rogers (D-Florida). "A vote for this bill is a vote against abortion. [Family planning] is the only national program which will actually prevent the condition which could lead to a request for abortion."[47] The bill passed but not without some fancy parliamentary maneuvering. Restrictions over District of Columbia funds prohibited the expenditure of federal money on abortions except to save the life of the woman or in cases of rape or incest. Only after a protracted Senate fight did the House agree to drop its original prohibition against the district's expenditure of its own local funds on abortions. Congress was unable to pass the foreign aid appropriations bill because of a number of controversial issues, including abortion. All told, abortion held up six appropriations bills and two authorization bills, as well as the omnibus continuing resolutions. The antiabortion movement was flexing its muscles.

During 1979 "the House continually teetered on the brink of chaos, and occasionally fell over." The reasons: "the lack of party discipline in the House, the breakdown of the power of the committee chairmen and party leaders, an increasing militancy on the part of younger Republicans and the ability of many Democrats to be re-elected without help from their party or their president."[48] The unintended consequences of election reform, the efforts to "democratize" the distribution of power within Congress, the frustration of deficit politics as it played out under the new congressional budget process—all combined to place an enormous strain on the collegial decision-making process of the legislative body. The additional complication of abortion politics made chaos inevitable.

On 30 June 1980, the Supreme Court upheld the Hyde Amendment restrictions on federal funding of abortions (see 5.1, p. 162, for two justices' opinions).[49] The decision took away what little wind remained in the abortion supporters' congressional sails on the funding issue. Only the question of fairness remained, and this proved insufficiently persuasive for members to go out on a politically dangerous limb. Senator Brooke had lost his 1978 reelection bid, his colleagues believed, due to antiabortion forces. Those forces had already announced their "hit list" for 1980, and few members wanted their names added to it.

Following Reagan's election as president and the Republican takeover of the Senate in 1981, the war in Congress against the federal funding of abortions came to an end. As the *Washington Post* noted, "The Republican Senate rolled over its moderate leadership ... and approved the strongest anti-abortion provisions Congress has ever passed."[50] The language prohibited the federal funding of abortions in all cases except those in which the life of the woman was at risk.

Interestingly, the 1981 battle surrounded an effort by Senate Appropriations Committee Chair Mark Hatfield (R-Oregon) to "clean up" the congressional budget process. In their new leadership role after more than two decades of minority status, top Republicans hoped to set a precedent by enforcing the rule against legislation riders on appropriations bills. "We cannot tolerate the kind of excess baggage and encumbrances that have been placed on the appropriations process in recent years," Hatfield warned. His aim was to separate the process from debilitating debates on abortion, busing, school prayer, and other subjects that had prevented orderly consideration of spending bills. Debate over these questions was to be returned to the authorization process, where it belonged. A strong abortion opponent, Hatfield now had the responsibility of shepherding the annual appropriations bills through the Senate. (The majority party in each house controls the committee and subcommittee chairmanships, as well as the principal leadership posts, and organizes and schedules the work load.)

For members who opposed abortion the strategic importance of the "must-pass" status and the media attention given critical appropriations bills were too valuable to give up. Hatfield tried to portray as a necessary "institutional reform" the stripping of all extraneous amendments from the supplemental appropriations bill that would provide funds to operate the government through the end of the 1981 fiscal year.[51] But Helms, not about to allow members to hide behind such cover, made it clear that abortion opponents would be watching and counting: "Now we are not talking about a procedural question here. This vote will be seen as a vote on the substance of the issue. . . . This is a substantive question as to whether we believe it is right or is it wrong to take money forcibly from taxpayers who cannot and will not condone the deliberate termination of innocent human life using their money. . . . Let them vote in the knowledge that this is not a procedural vote."[52]

No doubt sensing that they were about to lose the political war over abortion funding, abortion supporters lashed back. Weicker thundered, "We are not running this country by divine commandment or instructions from Mount Sinai."[53] Packwood countered Helms's not-so-subtle threat: "There is growing in this country a Cotton Mather mentality that is trying to impose upon this country a Cotton Mather morality. And I had hoped we quit burning witches 300 years ago, but apparently not."[54] In the end, by a vote of 52–43 that "criss-crossed ideological as well as party lines,"[55] the Senate turned down stripping the abortion rider from the bill. From 1981 on, federal funding of abortions was outlawed except to save the life of the woman. Federally funded abortions fell from close to 300,000 in 1977 to 84 by 1988.

The politics of the abortion controversy had changed. For those who could afford to pay, the constitutional "right" to abortion remained in place; for those who could not, the constitutional "right" was beyond reach. Organized groups that supported abortion were now the politically disadvantaged, in part because they were unable to mobilize their forces. The backbone of their constituency—younger, educated, professional women—did not yet feel threatened. Poor women who did feel threatened were not organized to exercise what political clout they might have had. Abortion opponents, meanwhile, were emboldened by events, the most notable of which was the election to the presidency of

Ronald Reagan, who had made his opposition to abortion clear and who had pressed for and won an antiabortion plank in the Republican platform. In addition, several senators on the "hit list" had been defeated and a Republican majority sat in the Senate in 1980. It was time to win the battle that could have won the war: passage of a constitutional amendment outlawing abortion.

Constitutional Amendments and Abortion in the 1980s

Article V of the U.S. Constitution lays out the amending procedure. It is a two-stage process that requires gathering a supermajority for first proposing and then ratifying an amendment (see figure 4.1, p. 138).

Only twenty-seven amendments have been added to the Constitution. Of those, the first ten, known as the Bill of Rights, were proposed by the first Congress and ratified by three-quarters of the states within three years of the Constitution's signing. Three of the amendments—the Thirteenth (outlawing slavery), Fourteenth (providing for due process and equal protection by the states to all citizens), and Fifteenth (providing that the right to vote cannot be denied because of race or color) —were passed following the Civil War. Most of the remaining thirteen amendments deal with procedural changes, such as the popular election of senators (the Seventeenth) and the order of succession in the event of the death of the president (the Twenty-fifth), or with the enfranchisement of new voters (the Nineteenth, extending the vote for women; the Twenty-sixth, extending the vote to eighteen-year-olds). And the Twenty-seventh, ratified in 1992, limits Congress's power to raise its members' salaries while in session.

Amending the Constitution is not easy and has rarely been accomplished (though it has often been tried) for substantive policy issues like abortion. One exception is that of the Prohibition Amendment proposed by Congress in 1917 and ratified by three-quarters of the state legislatures by 1919. Although it was repealed by the Twenty-first Amendment in 1933, it represented a successful campaign by a conservative, morally and religiously based citizen coalition to create a constitutional mandate supporting their position.

The Committee Hearing Stage

To have a constitutional amendment considered by the two houses of Congress, abortion opponents first needed to get both judiciary committees to hold hearings to consider proposed amendments. Congressional

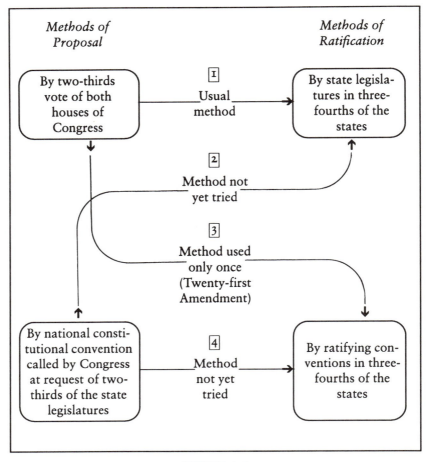

FIGURE 4.1
U.S. CONSTITUTIONAL AMENDMENT PROCESS

expert Walter Oleszek explains that this is not really a rule but a political necessity:

> Above all, hearings are important because members of Congress believe them to be important. The decision to hold hearings is a critical point in the life of a bill. Seldom is a measure considered on the floor without first being the subject of hearings. The sanctity of the committee stage is based on the assumption that the experts—the committee members —carefully scrutinize a proposal, and hearings provide a demonstrable record of that scrutiny.[56]

But the congressional process does not fit the assumption, as Oleszek notes.

Hearings are used for a number of reasons: to establish congressional concern about a subject (symbolic action); to buy time and/or to allow passions to cool (a sort of public-catharsis function); to gain support for a position (subject publicity); to provide a public platform for an ambitious committee chair (career publicity); to provide public "evidence" to support a predetermined position (stacking the deck); or simply to fulfill the institutional need to get past the hearing stage (procedural necessity). Sometimes hearings actually serve the professed purpose: to gather information from experts to enable Congress to fashion better legislation. Abortion opponents needed hearings to overcome the regular objections to their efforts to add constitutional amendment proposals on the floor; it was a procedural necessity.

The 1980 election gave control of the Senate and hence the assigning of committee and subcommittee chairs to the Republicans. A chair enjoys a range of powers in regard to the hiring of staff, the scheduling of the committee agenda (including which bills will be considered and voted upon), and the allocation of committee funds. To get a hearing scheduled, committee members have to get either the chair's approval or a majority vote of the committee membership to overrule the chair's objections. During the 1970s the chairs of the House and Senate judiciary committees had blocked action on abortion amendments by simply refusing to schedule hearings or by preventing full committee consideration of the measures in the few instances when subcommittees did hold hearings. But abortion opponents now had new opportunities.

The House remained under Democratic control. Judiciary Committee Chair Peter W. Rodino (D-New Jersey) filled vacancies with three liberals,[57] and thereby was able to preclude hearings on proposed constitutional amendments on abortion from being held.[58] In the Senate the chair of the Judiciary Committee passed from Kennedy, a vocal supporter of the pro-choice position, to Strom Thurmond (R-South Carolina), a vocal supporter of the pro-life position. Thurmond added three like-minded Republicans (Jeremiah Denton from Alabama, Charles Grassley from Iowa, and John P. East from North Carolina) to the committee.

East scheduled hearings before the judiciary subcommittee that he chaired—the Subcommittee on Separation of Powers—for 22 April 1981 on a proposal by his senior colleague from North Carolina, Helms, to overturn *Roe* by statute rather than the constitutional amendment process. The Helms bill stated that human life begins at conception and that fetuses are legal "persons." Its effect would be to bring fetuses under the

protection of the Fourteenth Amendment, which obliges states to provide
due process and equal protection to all "persons." It also prohibited federal courts from hearing cases challenging new state abortion statutes. If
the bill passed both houses, there was little doubt that Reagan would sign
it. It was, Helms thought, the approach with the best odds of achieving
the central goal of abortion opponents: outlawing all abortions.

On the first day of the hearings, five doctors testified that human life
begins at conception. East barred the Democratic members' counsel
from asking questions of the witnesses and refused to schedule witnesses
selected by the Democrats. It was a clear effort to stack the hearings,
and although the strategy is used often, it did not work for East. Abortion was too salient an issue: The media paid close attention, and positions were intensely held. Abortion supporters packed the hearing room,
and in a move tailored to the media, three women from the Women's
Liberation Zap Action Brigade interrupted testimony by jumping up on
their chairs, unfurling banners, and shouting, "A woman's life is a human life. Stop the hearings!" The protest helped to persuade East to allow other sides to be heard. The perception of fairness is every bit as
much a political necessity as having a hearing.

The political desirability of gaining credit with the powerful antiabortion groups made it inevitable that other solutions would have to be
given an airing as well. In 1981 at least eighteen proposed constitutional
amendments were introduced, each with a list of cosponsors. Many constitutional experts and many members of Congress believed Helms's bill
to be unconstitutional. Six former U.S. attorneys general from Republican and Democratic administrations jointly told the subcommittee that
it was unconstitutional because Congress could not amend the Constitution by merely passing a law—which is what changing the meaning of
the word *person* in the Fourteenth Amendment would do.[59] Twelve constitutional law professors representing a range of views on the abortion
issue stated in writing that they considered the bill to be unconstitutional. Another group of twelve constitutional law professors came to
the opposite conclusion. Both sides were playing the "my team is as big
as your team" numbers game.

Concern over constitutionality and political tactics prompted Senator
Hatch to draft his own proposed constitutional amendment. Hatch was
chairman of a judiciary subcommittee (the Subcommittee on the Constitution) that had equal claim to jurisdiction over the issue. He was thus
in a position to advance his proposal over competing proposals (most of
which simply outlawed abortion completely or did so with an exception
to save the life of the woman). He wanted to avoid the controversy surrounding the prohibition of abortion by returning the issue to legisla-

tures—the pre-*Roe* situation. Although a more politically realistic approach, its effect, ironically, was to divide the antiabortion forces.

Following the vote in the East subcommittee to support the Helms bill, Hatch scheduled hearings on his and a number of other constitutional amendment proposals before his subcommittee. The National Conference of Catholic Bishops endorsed the Hatch proposal, as did the National Right to Life Committee and the National Pro-Life Political Action Committee. But other groups, like March for Life and the Life Amendment Political Action Committee, declared it "a sellout of the principles that have motivated the pro-life movement from its beginning."[60] The depth of the schism within the movement is evident in the following excerpts from testimony before Hatch's subcommittee:

> The Right to Life Movement is now split almost 50–50 on the Hatch Amendment. This split will not continue. When knowledge of the defects of the Hatch Amendment spreads, most of the Right to Life Movement is going to oppose [it].[61]
>
> In political terms, the Hatch Amendment is going nowhere.... Its proponents, including Senator Hatch himself, are sincere. But the Amendment is a sham.... It is time for all of us to reflect on the fact that abortion presents an inescapable choice as to whether life is a gift of God or of the State. The choice is clear. Life is a gift of God. And there can be no compromise on abortion.[62]

Dozens of people on both sides of the abortion issue testified during nine days of hearings in October, November, and December. Doctors pro and con. Clergy pro and con. Law professors, psychiatrists, social workers, members of the House, all pro and con. The record covers over 2000 pages. Within an hour of the last words of the last witness, the subcommittee took less than fifteen minutes to vote 4–0 to report Hatch's proposal favorably to the full Judiciary Committee.

On 10 March 1982 the Judiciary Committee voted 10–7 to endorse the Hatch amendment proposal. Democrats Joseph Biden (Maryland) and Dennis DeConcini (Arizona) plus Republicans Hatch, Thurmond, Alan Simpson (Wyoming), Paul Laxalt (Nevada), Robert Dole (Kansas), East, Grassley, and Denton outnumbered Democrats Kennedy, Byrd, Leahy, Max Baucus (Wyoming), and Metzenbaum plus Republicans Arlen Specter (Pennsylvania) and Charles Mathias (Maryland). It was the first such full-committee endorsement. Dr. J.C. Wilke, president of the National Right to Life Committee, called it "a major victory." President of Planned Parenthood Faye Wattleton saw it "as part of a broader agenda of repression by extremists, by those who are attempting to define morality and to enact laws that reflect their narrow interpretation of what is moral."[63]

The abortion issue moved on to the Senate floor.

The Floor Debate Stage

By 1982 deficit politics was driving the congressional process. And by the start of the new fiscal year, 1 October, none of the regular appropriations bills had passed. Congress approved three temporary continuing appropriations resolutions and then a final omnibus appropriations resolution funding seven departments and various agencies.[64] As the costs of government escalated and resistance to raising taxes grew apace, Congress repeatedly increased the debt ceiling. Without an increase in 1982, the nation's ability to borrow would have ended on 30 September and the government would have been out of money. Congressional leadership prepared to bring a debt-ceiling bill to the floor in both houses.

Floor procedure in the House is far more structured than in the Senate. Control over scheduling legislation for floor action in the House is in the hands of the majority leadership and the Rules Committee. Following committee hearings, consideration, and a vote to recommend passage, a bill is sent to the Rules Committee, the so-called traffic cop of the House. The Rules Committee structures the limits on and conditions for debate of the bill on the floor. One thing Rules can do is to limit the number and subjects of amendments that can be offered. Another is to limit debate time prior to action. Still another is to delay granting a "rule" to a bill, thereby preventing floor action altogether.

The powerful Rules Committee most often cooperates with the majority leadership (which has a good deal of control over who will serve on the committee) to expedite floor action and to avoid controversies that the leadership wants avoided. An increase in the debt ceiling is controversial legislation that must pass; it cannot be bottled up in Rules. But the Rules Committee and the leadership can contain the controversy by granting a "closed" rule (no amendments allowed) or a "modified" rule (a limited number of specified amendments allowed). By this means the House was able in 1982 to get its debt-ceiling bill passed in short order. It was different in the Senate.

Conservatives in the Republican-controlled Senate, who had been held back by the priority given the economic agenda during Reagan's first year in office, were champing at the bit to get their social legislation to the floor for debate. In June, Helms announced his intention to attach his "fetus-is-a-person" proposal as an amendment to the debt-ceiling bill. In effect, he was withholding his consent for the consideration of the debt bill under unanimous-consent procedures, the only way the Senate limits debate and the introduction of amendments to bills.

Marathon talk combined with various parliamentary maneuvers to delay or prevent action on a bill—filibustering—in the past was typically a tactic of southern Democrats to delay civil rights measures.[65] Since the electoral and internal congressional reforms of the 1970s and in the era of conservative Republican presidents facing a more liberal Democratic-controlled Congress, filibustering has been practiced by individuals of all political stripes, and its incidence has increased.[66] Helms is often accused of being the king of filibustering; in 1982 he ran into another king of the same kind, Packwood.

The Senate Budget Committee staffers coined *Packwooding* to describe the addition of nongermane measures to their spending bills. Packwood's reaction was reported to be "That doesn't bother me. Everyone here regards it as legitimate to use the rules. All I did was take the budget process and achieve what I wanted."[67] Soon Packwood was filibustering to stop Helms from "Packwooding" his abortion amendment to the debt-ceiling bill.

Senate Majority Leader Baker tried and failed all summer to negotiate a time-limit agreement for debate and vote on the abortion amendment. On 16 August he was forced to bring the bill to the floor for action. Helms immediately moved to amend the bill. His amendment: "At the end thereof, add the following: TITLE II." No one, least of all Packwood, was fooled by the cryptic wording, which gave no clue to the substance of the amendment. "We are about to enter into apparently a rather lengthy discussion on the subject of abortion amendments," Packwood said. "I think it clear that we are going to need lengthy discussion on this subject ... so I wish to have a chance to read the Senate the *History of Abortion in America* by Dr. James C. Mohr."[68]

Packwood began reading. After several hours a second standard-bearer, Baucus, took over by reading excerpts from testimony given by various constitutional scholars at the Separation of Powers Subcommittee hearings on the Helms bill. Their materials were at least germane to the issue at hand; past filibusterers on occasion had resorted to cookbooks, the Bible, telephone books, and the like.

Deficit politics forced a change in the nature of filibusters, however. The debt-ceiling bill was not like the civil rights legislation, which had taken years to pass over filibuster efforts.[69] The debt-ceiling bill had to pass by a certain date. Congress had not acted on other critical money bills needed in order for government to continue functioning. Moreover, 1982 was an election year, and dozens of other senators wanted to attach amendments to the debt-ceiling bill. The megamoney bills (temporary continuing resolutions, omnibus appropriations bills, supplemental appropriations, reconciliation resolutions, and the debt-ceiling bills) had become the engines pulling long trains of coupled programs. And the debt-ceiling bill was one of the last trains that would leave Congress Station before the 1982 elections. If members did not get their pet projects on the train, the projects would not be passed. There were 1400 proposed amendments, including a $1 billion jobs program and expanded unemployment benefits to address recession problems (in 1982 the nation was in the midst of a significant recession); a sugar-price-support program; and hundreds of local public works projects, the critical "pork" incumbents believed they must take back to their districts for reelection credits.

The situation made Packwood's filibuster both more powerful and more threatening. In the past the leadership had often kept the Senate in session around the clock trying to wear the filibusterers out and, unless there were many, the strategy worked. In the 1980s, though, with filibusters threatening to hold critical money legislation hostage, the leadership had to compromise. That enabled filibusterers to pursue their strategy successfully, with far less effort.

Throughout the filibuster on the Helms amendment to the debt-ceiling bill, only about four to five hours a day was actually devoted to filibustering; the remainder was given over to other matters at the leadership's request. From the beginning Packwood, Baucus, and Weicker focused on the effect the Helms amendment would have on the federal judiciary in stripping it of its "constitutional jurisdiction." It was a clear effort to provide a "cover" for colleagues to vote against Helms. Until the filibuster was resolved, action on the debt-ceiling bill could not proceed. Packwood was determined to filibuster until he was sure that the result would protect the constitutional right to abortion the Supreme Court had found in *Roe*.

After its summer recess the Senate defeated a cloture motion introduced by Baker 41–47, nineteen votes short of the sixty needed to break the filibuster. Subsequent cloture efforts also failed, but the numbers willing to support Baker's motion steadily increased as the deadline for the debt-ceiling bill approached. Packwood had alternative strategies in reserve should he lose on cloture. If cloture is invoked, a hundred-hour limit is placed on further debate. Packwood had filed over 600 amendments to the debt-ceiling bill to prolong debate. With this trump in hand, he was in a stronger position to bargain for what he wanted: to strip the Helms amendment from the debt-ceiling bill.

Over the summer recess, a group of Senate staffers had met with lobbyists for abortion-support groups to devise parliamentary tactics for the showdown with Helms and Hatch, who had added his constitutional-amendment proposal as a rider to the debt-ceiling bill as well. Their concern was that if the Hatch proposal were voted on first and defeated (as they expected it would be because their counts showed that it was short of the necessary two-thirds to pass), then the pressure from the right-to-life groups on senators a few weeks before election might be enough to garner the simple majority that the Helms proposal needed to pass. If the Helms proposal were voted on first, they thought it could be defeated on the grounds that so many prominent legal experts considered it unconstitutional. Then they could still hold the line on Hatch.

The strategists' worries about pressure on senators were well founded. The American Life Lobby mounted a campaign to "win over" nineteen senators who had voted in 1981 against federal funding for abortion, but who also had opposed Helms in his first effort to end Packwood's filibuster. On the other side, abortion supporters were energized by the growing power and gains of abortion opponents. The National Organization for Women set up "reproductive rights" phone banks to generate calls and visits to senators. The National Abortion Rights Action League and the Planned Parenthood Federation mobilized their members to call and write, and in addition Planned Parenthood ran full-page advertisements in New York and Washington, D.C., papers (those read most widely by incumbents).[70]

On 8 September President Reagan entered the picture, ostensibly because of an open letter from the National Right to Life Committee: "When addressing pro-lifers, you speak the unvarnished, enduring truths that someday will make the unborn safe. But when talking with the entire American public, these fundamental truths are ignored or carefully sidestepped. Why? One can tiptoe around principles only so long."[71] Reagan wrote to nine "wavering" Republican senators urging them to support cloture, and called six senators from Air Force One. His persuasive powers did not carry the day.

On 15 September Packwood won. First, Hatch made a surprise announcement that he was withdrawing his constitutional amendment because there was insufficient time to debate it fairly. The majority leader had promised to schedule the amendment for floor debate in February 1983. That left the Helms amendment. Following a failed third try to invoke cloture (50–44, ten votes short), the Senate voted 47–46 to table Helms's proposal, in effect stripping it from the debt-ceiling bill. The parties split: eighteen Republicans and twenty-nine Democrats voted against Helms; thirty-three Republicans and thirteen Democrats voted to support him.

Each side claimed that it had won. "The pro-life movement is rolling," exulted Helms. He believed that the right-to-life groups would show their muscle in the November elections by defeating senators who had voted to table his amendment. Abortion proponents meanwhile were encouraged by the growing evidence of their own grass-roots support and by having stopped the antiabortion proposals.

The Constitutional Amendment Stands Alone

When Congress returned in 1983, Senate Majority Leader Baker delivered on his promise to Hatch by scheduling floor consideration of a constitutional amendment dealing with abortion. The antiabortion forces within Congress had come up with an alternative wording for their constitutional amendment. As proposed by Thomas F. Eagleton (D-Missouri), it contained just the first ten words of the Hatch amendment: "A right to abortion is not secured by this Constitution." The effect of this would be to overturn *Roe* and return abortion to regulation by the states. Hatch acceded to the change.

To many of the antiabortion groups who wanted an outright ban on abortion, the newly proposed amendment was even less appealing than Hatch's original proposal. For one thing, fifteen states, including many of the most populous,[72] and Washington, D.C., were paying for abortions for the poor from their own funds. North Carolina, home to two of the major antiabortion activists in Congress—Senator Helms and Senator East—was among them. Thus, even if the Eagleton amendment passed, many more abortions would still be performed than in the pre-*Roe* days.

When on 28 June 1983 the Senate voted 49 for the amendment, 50 against (eighteen votes short of the two-thirds constitutionally required for passage), Helms charged that a tactical error had been made by the amendment's supporters in bringing it up without the necessary votes for passage. Hatch responded that it was time for members to take a public stand, and that regrettably there simply was not support in Congress for outlawing abortion. Proof of the senators' wish to be done with the issue was the manner in which the "debate" had proceeded: thirty-two senators trooped in one at a time to deliver a speech on the issue to a virtually empty chamber.

As Hatfield took his turn addressing the empty chairs of the chamber, there seemed to be recognition of the inevitability of the constitutional amendment's defeat. "On either side of the [abortion] question," he began,

> the ardent protagonist seems more frequently compelled by thoughtless passion and even vindictiveness than by sensitive reason. Such fervor and fury are understandable, for this issue touches on the most personal of beliefs and affects in the most intimate way the lives of women.

An issue marked by such intensity and divisiveness invites public neutrality on the part of the politicians, quite candidly; it usually seems pragmatically imprudent to become strongly and unapologetically committed on either side of this controversy.... The reason why it has become so difficult and even perilous to discuss the issue of abortion is because of the growing realization by women that they have inner gifts to express, and roles in society to explore, that have previously been disregarded and resisted by society—or more specifically by men.... Many women today believe deeply that their worth is defined in ways that far transcend their ability to bear children.... They reject the notion that the only normal, worthy, and respectable role they should play is that of being a mother. Rather, that is an option that can be chosen and embraced, if desired, rather than arbitrarily imposed by society's expectations. I believe they are right.[73]

Hatfield's answer to enabling women's choice was not abortion but "society's obligations" to provide support—psychological, medical, nutritional, and financial—for those caught in unwanted pregnancies. He wholeheartedly embraced "planned parenthood," as well as an "uncompromising commitment to sex education and family planning services." His commitment was not shared by many of his fellow abortion opponents. The religious teachings of perhaps the most powerful component of the antiabortion faction, the Catholic church, remained unalterably counter to Hatfield's suggestions, as does the thinking of a large proportion of the fundamentalist Christian groups.

The antiabortion camp, like most interest groups, proved far more heterogeneous than it often appears. Hatfield hoped that the return of the abortion issue to the states and direct citizen participation would bring about a national moral consensus on the issue. Many of his antiabortion colleagues had little interest in chancing the "moral consensus" that might emerge. What if the opinion polls were right and the public was not supportive of their position? The antiabortion political coalition fell apart over its differing goals.

Abortion as a Weapon in Other Congressional Wars

After 1983 both sides of the abortion controversy in Congress were at a standoff. There appeared to be a "gentlemen's agreement" to accept the language that restricted federal funding of abortions to cases in which the woman's life was endangered and to avoid the issue of a constitutional amendment. The truce was repeatedly breached by one side or the other, however. In 1986, for example, Weicker managed to get his Senate appropriations subcommittee to add an exception to the funding ban to allow payment for abortions in cases of rape and incest. Though he lost at the full committee level, he was able to "trade" dropping the rape and incest exception for the elimination of school prayer and antibusing riders and an agreement from Helms not to seek to delete or otherwise restrict $145 million provided in a bill for family-planning programs.

Following the defeat of the Equal Rights Amendment on 30 June 1982,[74] Congress attempted to bring it back to life by reproposing it. In 1971 (two years before *Roe*) the original ERA had passed the House 354–24. In 1983 ERA was defeated 278–147 (six votes short of the two-thirds vote necessary for proposing a constitutional amendment). Abortion was the major difference. Antiabortion groups argued that if ERA were passed, abortion funding bans might be considered sex discrimination and thus unconstitutional. In an effort to avoid controversy, the House leadership brought the ERA proposal to the floor under a limited rule that prevented floor amendments. The strategy backfired. Without an amendment specifically to exempt abortion from ERA's reach, support for its passage could not be gathered.

One of the most contentious abortion-related battles surrounded Congress's effort to overturn a Supreme Court interpretation of requirements of Title IX of the 1972 Education Act Amendments, which barred discrimination on the basis of sex.[75] Grove City College, a four-year liberal arts college in Pennsylvania, refused to fill out federal forms to prove compliance with antidiscrimination regulations. The college took the position that because it did not receive any direct federal aid (though many of its students received federally funded student aid to pay for their college costs), it did not have to comply with the federal requirements. In a court challenge to the college, the Supreme Court ruled that the aid received by students counted as federal aid under the law, but that only the financial aid program was covered by the antidiscrimination provision of Title IX. The implications of the case went far beyond sex discrimination; three other major laws used the same approach to barring discrimination in federally aided programs: the Civil Rights Act of 1964 (race, color, national origin), the Rehabilitation Act of 1973 (handicapped), and the 1975 Age Discrimination Act (elderly). An effort to amend the laws to make clear congressional intent that these laws prohibit discrimination in an entire institution even if only a portion of it receives federal aid was quickly mounted. The clarifying amendment passed the House by an overwhelming margin (375–32) in 1984, only to be stalled in the Senate when the Reagan administration attacked it as "too vague." In 1985 the amendment became entangled in abortion politics.

On 26 February 1985 the U.S. Catholic Conference told Congress that the clarifying legislation could force Catholic teaching hospitals to perform abortions or lose some of the federal assistance they were receiving. In the ensuing lobbying battle the Catholic Conference was pitted against Planned Parenthood and the American Civil Liberties Union, and members of Congress were caught in the middle. One political ramification of the issue was the strained relationship between the Catholic church and the Congressional Black Caucus. To many of the groups affected by the Court's interpretation of the antidiscrimination requirements, the abortion issue appeared as a red herring to scare off support for civil rights enforcement. The congressional fix was stalled until 1988, when the abortion issue was finally resolved by an amendment that stated, "Nothing in this title shall be construed to require or prohibit any person or public or private entity to provide or pay for any benefit or service, including facilities, related to abortion. Nothing in this section shall be construed to permit a penalty to be imposed on any person because such person has received any benefit or service related to legal abortion." Reacting to the demonstrated power of the antiabortion forces, Senator Metzenbaum commented: "The right-to-life groups are not to be underestimated in these halls."[76] By 1988 the power of the pro-choice side had grown considerably, but this did not mean that the other side's influence in Congress had waned.

As the 1980s progressed, President Reagan's involvement in congressional abortion battles became more pronounced. Repeated presidential veto threats tempered the emerging strength of the pro-choice side within Congress and added important clout to the pro-life forces. When Congress failed to add a restriction to the District of Columbia funding bill forbidding the district from using its own locally raised tax funds on abortion services, Reagan threatened to veto the bill. Congress gave in, adding the restriction the president (and a large majority of the House) wanted.

The abortion issue affected congressional behavior and was itself affected by behavioral changes within Congress. The advantage of each side waxed and waned in the years after *Roe* as competing issues emerged, as membership in Congress changed, as the perception or reality of the abortion interest groups' power changed, and as other actors in the governmental system—in particular the executive and judicial branches—acted on the issue.

Abortion supporters in and out of Congress played mostly a defen-

sive game. Their trump card was always the Supreme Court's rulings upholding the constitutional right to abortion enunciated in *Roe*. The goal
of abortion opponents was to overtrump their adversaries by destroying
Roe. Though abortion opponents were able to make significant progress
in getting Congress to stop federal funding of abortions, it seemed clear
that their ultimate goal—eliminating *Roe*—was not going to be accomplished through congressional action.

Notes

1. *Congressional Record, House,* 93d Cong., 1st sess., 23 January 1973,
179.

2. *Congressional Record, Senate,* 93d Cong., 1st sess., 23 January 1973,
1862.

3. Robert Packwood, "The Rise and Fall of the Right-to-Life Movement in
Congress," in *Abortion, Medicine, and the Law,* ed. J. Douglas Butler and David F. Walbert (New York: Facts on File Publications, 1986), 5.

4. For example, in 1970 Representative John Dowdy (D-Texas) was in-
dicted by a grand jury for allegedly accepting a bribe to intervene in a federal
investigation of the Monarch Construction Company; Senator Joseph D.
Tydings (D-Maryland) was accused of conflict of interest for allegedly intervening with the Agency for International Development to help a Florida company
obtain a $7 million loan guarantee; and Senator George Murphy (R-California)
admitted to receiving a $20,000-a-year retainer from a private corporation.

5. Federal Election Campaign Act of 1974, P.L. 93-443.

6. Limits were set at $70,000 per candidate for House elections; $150,000
or 12 cents for each person of voting age in the state, whichever was greater,
for Senate elections. In part, resistance to public funding for congressional campaigns was economic; it would cost a great deal to fund almost 500 races every
two years. Moreover, many members were less than keen about the idea of providing funds for potential challengers.

7. Several provisions of the Federal Election Campaign Act were constitutionally challenged (*Buckley v. Valeo,* 426 U.S. 1 [1976]). The Supreme Court
ruled certain provisions unconstitutional, among them the composition of the
Federal Election Commission (which included several members appointed by
Congress); the limit on the amount an individual could contribute to his/her
own campaign; the campaign expenditure limits for congressional campaigns;
and the limits on independent expenditures of groups or individuals not associated with a candidate. The limits on contributions by PACs and on contributions by individuals to the campaigns of others were upheld. Congress amended
the 1974 act to bring it into line with the Court's decision, reconstituting the
FEC to allow for presidential appointment of all its members, eliminating the
limit on candidates' contributions to their own campaigns, and eliminating the
spending limit on congressional races (P.L. 94-283).

8. In 1974 there were 608 PACs, which contributed $12.8 million to
congressional campaigns, accounting for some 17 percent of the funds raised.
By 1992 there were 4195 PACs, which contributed $161 million, accounting

for some 32 percent of the funds raised. For an overview of the growth and role of PACs, see Roger Davidson and Walter J. Oleszek, *Congress and Its Members,* 3d ed. (Washington, D.C.: CQ Press, 1990).

9. Barbara Hinkson Craig, *Chadha: The Story of an Epic Constitutional Struggle* (Berkeley: University of California Press, 1990), 45, quoting Representative Elliott Levitas (D-Georgia).

10. The cause and result of the disintegration of the parties in the 1970s and 1980s has been commented on by many. See, for example, James L. Sundquist, *The Decline and Resurgence of Congress* (Washington, D.C.: Brookings Institution, 1981); Everett Carll Ladd, *Where Have All the Voters Gone? The Fracturing of America's Political Parties,* 2d ed. (New York: Norton, 1982).

11. These figures understate the actual cost of winning a seat in a competitive race; Senate races can exceed $10 million, and House seats usually cost a half million. See Davidson and Oleszek, *Congress and Its Members,* 64–65.

12. In 1960 there were 93 recorded votes in the House and 207 in the Senate; in 1980, 604 in the House and 531 in the Senate. Tabulations of recorded votes from 1947 to 1980 show how significant was the increase in numbers of recorded votes during the 1970s. As Congress became entangled in deficit politics in the 1980s and moved to huge omnibus funding bills, the number of recorded votes dipped a bit but still remained consistently higher than in the 1950s and 1960s. See Norman J. Ornstein, Thomas E. Mann, Michael J. Malbin, and John F. Bibby, *Vital Statistics on Congress, 1989–90* (Washington, D.C.: American Enterprise Institute, 1989).

13. P.L. 93–344.

14. Charles Edward Lindblom, *The Intelligence of Democracy: Decision Making through Mutual Adjustment* (New York: Free Press, 1965).

15. *Congressional Record, Senate,* 94th Cong., 1st sess., 1975, 4859.

16. *Congressional Quarterly Almanac,* 99th Cong., 1st sess., 1985, 349.

17. Quoted, Barbara Hinkson Craig, *The Legislative Veto: Congressional Control of Regulation* (Boulder, Colo.: Westview Press, 1983), 124.

18. Walter J. Oleszek, *Congressional Procedures and the Policy Process,* 3d ed. (Washington, D.C.: CQ Press, 1989), 51.

19. *Congressional Record, House,* 27 June 1974, 21687.

20. All quotations from the floor debate on the Roncallo amendment, *Congressional Record, House,* 27 June 1974, 21687–95.

21. *Congressional Quarterly Almanac,* 93d Cong., 2d sess., 1974, 76-H. The party division of the vote: Republicans, 70–98; Democrats, 53–149 (northern Democrats, 35–96; southern Democrats, 18–53). Both parties and both the northern and often more conservative southern Democrats voted by a large majority to defeat the amendment. And both parties had significant numbers voting the other way. Party membership does not provide much of a clue to the voting on this issue at this time.

22. *Congressional Record, Senate,* 17 September 1974, 31453.

23. See note 21. A few other examples. In 1977, on a 201–155 vote to adopt the Hyde Amendment prohibiting funding of all abortions, the party split was Republicans 98 to prohibit, 21 against; Democrats 103 to prohibit, 134 against (northern Democrats 65–97; southern Democrats 38–37). In 1978, on Representative Stokes's amendment to delete language prohibiting use of funds for abortion (in other words, a yes vote would allow funding of abortions), the

vote was 122–287 to reject. The party split was Republicans 19 to allow funding, 124 against; Democrats 103 to allow funding, 163 against (northern Democrats 87 to allow, 97 against; southern Democrats 16 to allow, 66 against. Although in each vote a larger percentage of Republicans than Democrats voted against abortion funding, it is also true that in each case a majority or near-majority of Democrats voted against abortion funding as well, and this has been the case repeatedly in the House on abortion funding votes since 1975.

24. *Congressional Quarterly Almanac,* 95th Cong., 1st sess., 1977, 301.

25. *McRae v. Califano,* 421 F. Supp. 533.

26. Conference Committee Report of the House Appropriations Committee, No. 94-1555.

27. *Congressional Quarterly Almanac,* 95th Cong., 2d sess., 1978, 110.

28. See note 23 for party division on this vote.

29. *Beal v. Doe,* 432 U.S. 438, a Pennsylvania case; *Maher v. Roe,* 432 U.S. 464, a Connecticut case; and *Poelker v. Doe,* 432 U.S. 519, a St. Louis, Missouri, case.

30. *Congressional Quarterly Almanac,* 95th Cong., 2d sess., 1978, 105.

31. *Congressional Quarterly Almanac,* 95th Cong., 1st sess., 1977, 313.

32. *Congressional Record, Senate,* 95th Congress, 1st sess., 1977, 38691.

33. All excerpts from the Senate debate on 7 December 1977, ibid., 38692–97.

34. *Congressional Quarterly Almanac,* 95th Cong., 1st sess., 1977, 296.

35. All excerpts from the House debate, *Congressional Record, House,* 95th Cong., 2d sess., 1978, 17266–74.

36. After the *Congressional Record* printed a speech by a representative supposedly given by him on the floor of the House two days following his death, the House altered its practice regarding publication of remarks in the *Record.* Thenceforward a bullet (a solid black dot) would precede material not actually said on the floor. Members are still allowed to revise and extend their remarks by inserting pages of undelivered text. This makes it difficult to tell what other members (assuming any were present) actually heard. What looks on paper like the give-and-take of real debate can be misleading; only when a time limit was imposed and that piece of information is included in the *Record* can one differentiate the probable spoken from the later additions.

37. Robert Dahl explains the ethics of responsibility: "Lying between the simple extremes of unprincipled politics and rigid morality is a domain of action that has been called an ethics of responsibility.... Acting according to the ethics of responsibility, a political leader cannot enjoy the luxury of rejecting an imperfect compromise, even a highly imperfect compromise, so long as that compromise represents the best possible alternative presented by the world as it happens to be. Irresponsibility, in this view, consists not in making concessions, but in making unnecessary concessions, not in making imperfect bargains, but in failing to make the best possible bargains, not in adhering strictly to principles, but in holding rigidly to one principle at the excessive cost to other principles." *Democracy in the United States: Promise and Performance,* 3d ed. (Chicago: Rand McNally, 1976), 78.

38. *Congressional Quarterly Almanac,* 95th Cong., 2d sess., 1978, 110.

39. All excerpts from the Senate debate on 27 September 1978, *Congressional Record, Senate,* 95th Cong., 2d sess., 1978, 31867–75, 31916–18.

40. There is another use of quorum calls in the Senate: to allow for a pause in the conduct of business so the leadership and/or members can work out accommodations privately (off the record). Oleszek calls this sort of quorum call a *"positive* delay as opposed to a *negative* delay." When a quorum call is used as a positive delay, members are not expected to come to the floor; rather, a clerk simply drones slowly through the list of senators until the quorum call is dispensed with by unanimous consent. Effectively, this is the equivalent of a recess.

"Live" quorum calls result when a member makes clear that he or she intends to object to any unanimous consent motion to end the call—this is a tactical delay and as such requires attendance to get a majority or the Senate will be forced into adjournment for the day. Senators can tell which kind of quorum call is going on by the number of bells that ring throughout the Capitol and Senate office buildings. See Oleszek, *Congressional Procedures and the Policy Process,* 206–7.

41. The Equal Rights Amendment had been sent to the states for ratification in 1972, with a provision requiring that it must be ratified within seven years. The requisite three-quarters of the states had not ratified it by 1978, and with only one more year to go, Congress was being pressed by women's groups to extend the deadline.

42. In the previous fiscal year more than 26,000 abortions had been performed in military hospitals or funded for military personnel and employees.

43. *Congressional Quarterly Almanac,* 95th Cong., 2d sess., 1978, 598, quoting Representative Ronald Sarasin (R-Connecticut).

44. Ibid., 599, quoting Representative Ted Weiss (D-New York).

45. *Congressional Quarterly Almanac,* 96th Cong., 1st sess., 1979, 276.

46. Ibid., 277.

47. Ibid., 611.

48. Ibid., 14.

49. *Harris v. McRae,* 448 U.S. 297.

50. "Toughest Curbs on Abortion Funds Voted by Senate," *Washington Post,* 22 May 1981, A1.

51. Supplemental appropriations bills were another wrinkle in the congressional deficit-politics process. With increasing regularity, Congress had to resort to adding funds part way through the year in order to keep government programs functioning. This inability to forecast the amount needed for a single year (or unwillingness to admit up front the full cost) brought charges that the United States is becoming another "Banana Republic"—a comparison to Latin American countries that have to rebudget several times during the year, usually because of galloping inflation and inability to predict spending needs.

52. *Congressional Record, Senate,* 97th Cong., 1st sess., 21 May 1981, 10684.

53. Ibid.

54. Ibid.

55. *Washington Post,* 22 May 1981, A6.

56. Oleszek, *Congressional Procedures and the Policy Process,* 99.

57. Recruitment to committees in Congress is a complicated process in which new members indicate their preferences to special committees of each party responsible for assigning members to committees. As with most proce-

dures in Congress, a lot of politicking goes on behind the scenes, with leadership attempting to get "appropriate" talent (read, those with "appropriate political positions on the issues" or for some of the more powerful committees like Appropriations, with the "appropriate" party or personal loyalty) on important committees and members trying to maneuver themselves onto the best committees. Committee chairs can have a significant influence on who from their party will be given vacant spots. Rodino clearly used his influence to protect the liberal bent of the House Judiciary Committee. Thurmond clearly used his influence to enhance the conservative bent of the Senate Judiciary Committee.

58. Seven days of hearings had been held in 1976 (consuming 1089 pages of testimony in the printed hearing record) by the Subcommittee on Civil and Constitutional Rights of the House Judiciary Committee on proposed constitutional amendments on abortion. The chairman of the subcommittee at that time was Don Edwards (D-California), a vocal abortion supporter, a circumstance that would lead to the conclusion that the hearings were of the delay-and-allow-passions-to-cool variety. No action was ever taken by the full committee on the subject. In a 1981 op-ed piece in the *Washington Post,* Minority Leader Robert H. Michel chastised his colleagues, saying antiabortion proposals had "languished in House subcommittees for years because the House majority simply doesn't want to see the issue dealt with openly." Abortion opponent Hyde went further, charging that the committees "are structured to kill this bill. We're not going to mess around with a subcommittee." His intent was to try the discharge petition route (getting the signatures of 218 representatives, a majority of the House). He was not successful in this effort. (*Congressional Quarterly Weekly Report,* 28 February 1981, 385–87.) In addition, Senate hearings had been held in 1974 and 1975, but no action had followed these either.

59. The six former attorneys general—Herbert Brownell, Nicholas Katzenbach, Ramsey Clark, Elliot Richardson, William Saxbe, and Benjamin Civiletti—signed a letter to the committee stating: "Our views about the correctness of the Supreme Court's 1973 abortion decision vary widely, but all of us are agreed that Congress has no Constitutional authority ... to overturn that decision by enacting a statute redefining such terms as 'person' or 'human life.' ... We thus regard [such provisions] as an attempt to exercise unconstitutional power and a dangerous circumvention of the avenues that the Constitution itself provides for reversing Supreme Court interpretations of the Constitution." Letter reprinted in *Congressional Record, Senate,* 97th Cong., 2d sess., 16 August 1982, 21185.

60. *Congressional Quarterly Weekly Report,* 19 December 1981, 2526.

61. Senate Judiciary Subcommittee on the Constitution, *Hearings, Constitutional Amendments Relating to Abortion,* 97th Cong., 1st sess., 5, 14, 19 October; 4, 5, 12, 16 November; 7, 16 December, 1981. Testimony of Robert L. Sassone, 1229.

62. Ibid., testimony of American Life Lobby, 1239.

63. *New York Times,* 11 March 1982, B9.

64. In 1981 stopgap funding was required for programs covered by five regular appropriations bills; in 1980 six regular appropriations bills never cleared. On 23 November 1981 thousands of federal workers were sent home for the

day when Reagan vetoed a stopgap continuing resolution. On 21 December 1981, with the government again on the brink of shutdown (technically the government was "out of money" from Friday, 17 December to Tuesday, 21 December), Reagan signed a continuing resolution to fund programs under the six regular appropriations bills that never passed. The struggle between the Republican president and the divided-party-controlled Congress was escalating with the use of presidential vetoes to force modifications in congressional spending plans. By 1990 this struggle over money bills and deficit politics degenerated into a ludicrous budget process lampooned in the press—"Bring in the Clowns."

65. Senator Strom Thurmond of South Carolina holds the individual record for filibustering for his twenty-four hours of nonstop talking against the 1957 civil rights bill. For more information on the role and history of filibustering, see Oleszek, *Congressional Procedures and the Policy Process,* 220–30.

66. Former senator Thomas Eagleton (D-Missouri) commented in 1986 that there had been many more filibusters in the seventeen years he had served in the Senate than in the 120 years before he got there. Ibid., 221.

67. *Congressional Quarterly Weekly Report,* 11 September 1982, 2241.

68. *Congressional Record, Senate,* 97th Cong., 2d sess., 16 August 1982, 21185.

69. When a filibuster cannot be stopped by cloture, the leadership can end the deadlock by withdrawing the bill in question from the floor, thus effectively tabling the issue until a later date. In the case of substantive authorizations like civil rights or child care or clean air legislation, if the bill does not pass, the government will go on. With debt-ceiling bills and omnibus appropriations bills, however, the leadership has no alternative. The bill must pass. Filibusters must be stopped, or dealt with, and when the sides are as far apart as the abortion camps it is exceedingly difficult to find acceptable compromises.

70. One showed a couple in bed with a "senator" between them. It was captioned, "The decision to have a baby could soon be between you, your husband and your senator." *New York Times,* 15 August 1982, 22E.

71. Quoted in *Congressional Quarterly Weekly Report,* 4 September 1982, 2202.

72. California, Colorado, Connecticut, Hawaii, Maryland, Massachusetts, New Jersey, New York, North Carolina, Oregon, Pennsylvania, Washington, and West Virginia.

74. Quoted in *Congressional Record, Senate,* 98th Cong., 1st sess., 27 June 1983, pp. S9089–92.

74. Congress had provided that ERA must be ratified by the states within seven years. When that deadline loomed (in 1979), Congress agreed to extend it by three more years. By the second deadline the amendment was still three states short of the thirty-eight necessary for ratification.

75. *Grove City College v. Bell,* 465 U.S. 555 (1984).

76. *Congressional Quarterly Almanac,* 100th Cong., 2d sess., 1988, 65. See pp. 63–68 for a summary of the legislative history in response to the *Grove City* case.

CHAPTER 5

Abortion and Presidential Politics

Presidents and presidential candidates in the 1970s, whether Republicans or Democrats, generally flip-flopped on the issue of abortion, which increasingly divided the country. In contrast, Ronald Reagan boldly spearheaded the cause of overturning *Roe* and championed the forces that elevated abortion to the national political agenda. In the second decade following *Roe,* the abortion controversy was thus infused into presidential politics. Moreover, the Reagan administration not only fundamentally changed the national debate over abortion but set the stage for how the controversy will play out in the 1990s.

Ambivalence and the "Crisis in Confidence": The Nixon and Ford Presidencies

Unlike Reagan, conservative Republican President Richard M. Nixon asserted no presidential leadership in the emergent battle over abortion, or even in opposing the Burger Court's ruling in *Roe.* To be sure, when *Roe* came down, Nixon was in the middle of his own political troubles, which would eventually drive him from the White House. In January 1973 the trial of the "Watergate" burglars was just beginning, and Congress was moving toward holding hearings on the administration's obstruction of justice and cover-up of the break-in. Just six months earlier, before the 1972 presidential election, five men had broken into and were arrested in the Democratic National Committee's headquarters in the

Opposite: President Reagan at a press conference, 1981. *Photo:* Prints and Photographs Division, Library of Congress.

Watergate Hotel in Washington, D.C. One, James W. McCord, Jr., was the security director of Nixon's Committee to Re-Elect the President. Two other men, E. Howard Hunt, Jr., and Gordon Liddy, also connected with the White House and Nixon's campaign team, were linked to the burglars as well. As the highly publicized trial proceeded in the spring of 1973, a Senate committee discovered that the break-in had been part of a larger White House program of political espionage directed at anti-Vietnam war protesters and that Nixon had been involved in its cover-up. A little over a year later, amid growing public outcry at further revelations of the administration's illegal activities, the House Judiciary Committee approved three articles of impeachment. Nixon was forced to resign on 9 August 1974, and Vice President Gerald R. Ford assumed the presidency.

Although largely preoccupied with his troubles at home and abroad over the Vietnam war, Nixon had publicly opposed abortion shortly before his reelection bid. Pro-choice groups and liberal women's organizations had mobilized in the late 1960s and early 1970s to liberalize state abortion laws. In the process, they had also gradually elevated abortion and other women's rights issues to the national political agenda by forcing presidential candidates to stake out their positions. Abortion had not been an issue in the 1968 presidential election, but it was emerging as a volatile campaign issue by 1972.

Nixon's major pronouncement on abortion came before *Roe,* when he reversed a federal regulation making abortions more available in hospitals on military bases. In ordering that "the policy on abortions at American military bases in the United States be made to correspond with the laws of the States where those bases are located,"[1] Nixon, arguably, attempted to avoid the controversy and leave the battle over abortion to state legislatures. He nonetheless expressed "personal" opposition to abortion:

> From personal and religious beliefs I consider abortion an unacceptable form of population control. Further, unrestricted abortion policies, or abortion on demand, I cannot square with my personal belief in the sanctity of human life—including the life of the yet unborn. For, surely, the unborn have rights also, recognized in law, recognized even in principles expounded by the United Nations.[2]

In this respect Nixon distanced his administration from that of his Democratic predecessor. LBJ had aggressively promoted the use of contraceptives, among other birth-control measures, and family-planning services under Medicaid as part of his "War on Poverty."[3]

Nixon's 1972 unsuccessful Democratic opponent George McGovern also declined to make abortion a major campaign issue. Other issues—the Vietnam war, the economic recession, the busing of children to achieve school desegregation, and "crime control"—continued to dominate electoral politics. When pressed on his views, McGovern sided with pro-choice and liberal women's organizations. Yet when criticized, he backpedaled: "In my judgment abortion is a private matter which should be decided by a pregnant woman and her doctor. Once the decision has been made, laws should [not] stand in the way of its implementation. I do believe, however, that abortion is a matter to be left to the state governments."[4] Six months later, McGovern moved even closer to Nixon's own defense of states' power over abortion. In response to criticism that he favored eliminating "all restrictions on abortion," McGovern countered, "That is a lie, and my critics know it is a lie. The states have sole jurisdiction over abortion. I have never advocated federal action to repeal those laws, and if I were elected President, I would take no such action."[5]

By the 1976 election abortion loomed somewhat larger in presidential politics. That in part was due, of course, to the 1973 decision in *Roe* and the opposition it immediately sparked, but there were other reasons. In the years immediately following *Roe*, abortion became one of the most frequently performed surgical procedures in the country, with approximately 1.5 million abortions performed each year; more than one-fifth of all pregnancies ended in abortions in 1975.[6] Under Medicaid, $45 million in federal funds was spent on approximately 300,000 abortions for women on welfare. In addition, in July 1976, just as presidential campaigns were hitting high gear, the Burger Court further fanned the controversy by striking down Missouri's requirements that a woman obtain spousal or parental consent before having an abortion.[7]

President Ford faced an uphill fight in his unsuccessful race to hold onto the presidency. His efforts to restore public confidence in government after Watergate and Nixon's resignation were undermined by his unconditional pardoning of Nixon for any and all criminal activities. Besides not having a electoral mandate of his own, Ford was more moderate than Nixon and the right wing of the Republican party, which was led by California's Governor Ronald Reagan and Arizona's U.S. Senator Barry Goldwater. Finally, Ford's 1975 appointment of Justice John Paul Stevens—a relatively unknown federal appellate court judge—instead of either a woman or a prominent conservative like Robert H. Bork disappointed both women and hard-line conservatives.[8]

Ford cautiously and rather ambivalently opposed *Roe*. He lamented the Court's having "gone too far" and declared that states should have the power to decide whether and how to restrict abortions. (His wife, Betty, publicly supported the right of women to have abortions.) And he opposed any constitutional amendment that would limit or overturn *Roe*.[9] Moreover, unlike Reagan's Department of Justice, Ford's filed no *amici curiae* ("friends of the court") briefs in cases challenging restrictive post-*Roe* state abortion laws and gave virtually no public support to antiabortion forces. As a result of his fence-straddling, both sides of the abortion controversy criticized Ford.

From the outset of the 1976 presidential primary season, candidates of both parties confronted crosscutting pressures from groups favoring or opposing legalized abortion. Congressional failure to respond to *Roe* had led the National Conference of Catholic Bishops to call for the formation of "pro-life" groups in all 435 congressional districts to work to influence the 1976 election. Although public opinion polls indicated that only a minority of all voters considered abortion a major factor in the presidential election and American Catholics appeared sharply split on the permissibility of abortion, neither Ford nor his Democratic opponent in the election for the presidency, Jimmy Carter, could ignore the growing prominence of abortion in the election.

On the campaign trail Carter and Ford were repeatedly asked to define their positions on abortion. A deeply religious southern Baptist and governor of Georgia, Carter personally opposed abortion and federal funding for abortions, but he also opposed any constitutional amendment to overturn *Roe*. That was the position of the Democratic party in its 1976 platform, which held that "it is undesirable to amend the U.S. Constitution to overturn the Supreme Court decision [on abortion]." As the election neared, though, Carter moderated his opposition to a constitutional amendment. In August, after six Catholic bishops had met with Carter, the chairman of the National Conference of Catholic Bishops (Archbishop Joseph Bernardin) announced that Carter agreed not to oppose those fighting for such an amendment. Carter later explained that he disliked the language used in the platform, even though his own people had drafted it. According to Carter, the platform implied a moral judgment (which he said he did not share) on those seeking a constitutional amendment that would reverse the Court's ruling.

Ford also sent mixed signals when confronting demands to take a strong stand on abortion. Like Carter two months before election day, Ford met with members of the National Conference of Catholic Bishops and then issued a public letter expressing his opposition to abortion:

One of the most controversial issues of our time and one in which we share a keen interest is the question of abortion. I have grave concern over the serious moral questions raised by this issue. Each new life is a miracle of creation. To interfere with that creative process is a most serious act.

In my view, the Government has a very special role in this regard. Specifically, the Government has a responsibility to protect life—and indeed to provide legal guarantees for the weak and unprotected.

It is within this context that I have consistently opposed the 1973 decision of the Supreme Court. As President, I am sworn to uphold the laws of the land and I intend to carry out this responsibility. In my personal view, however, this court decision was unwise. I said then and I repeat today—abortion on demand is wrong.

Since 1973 I have viewed as the most practical means of rectifying the situation created by the Court's action a Constitutional amendment that would restore to each State the authority to enact abortion statutes which fit the concerns and views of its own citizens. This approach is entirely in keeping with the system of Federalism devised by the founders of our Nation. As Minority Leader of the House of Representatives, I cosponsored an amendment which would restore this authority to the States, and I have consistently supported that position since that time.

My position has been based on three fundamental convictions:

• I am against abortion on demand.

• The people of every State should have the Constitutional right to control abortion.

• There is a need to recognize and provide for exceptional cases. . . .[10]

A little over two weeks later, however, Ford vetoed the 1977 appropriations bill. That legislation contained the so-called Hyde Amendment, which forbade under the Medicaid program federal funding of nontherapeutic abortions. Ford declared that he was forced to veto the bill because it was nearly $4 billion over his budget request, and that Congress had presented him with the "dilemma of offending the voting groups who benefit by these government programs or offending those primarily concerned with certain restrictions embodied in the bill." He reasserted support for "the restrictions on the use of federal funds for abortion" and rested his objection to the appropriations bill "purely and simply on the issue of fiscal integrity." Many opponents of abortion were unsatisfied. Congress subsequently overrode his veto, enacting the Hyde Amendment by a vote in the House of Representatives of 312–93 and in the Senate of 67–15; the Burger Court later upheld the amendment (see 5.1).

| 5.1 | Supreme Court Upholds Ban on Federal Funding of Abortions in *Harris v. McRae*, 448 U.S. 297 (1980) |

⚖ Justice STEWART delivered the opinion of the Court.

Since September 1976, Congress has prohibited—either by an amendment to the annual appropriations bill for the Department of Health, Education, and Welfare or by joint resolution—the use of any federal funds to reimburse the cost of abortions under the Medicaid program except under certain specified circumstances. This funding restriction is commonly known as the "Hyde Amendment," after its original congressional sponsor, Representative Hyde. . . .

The constitutional underpinning of [*Roe v.*] *Wade* was a recognition that the "liberty" protected by the Due Process Clause of the Fourteenth Amendment includes not only the freedoms explicitly mentioned in the Bill of Rights, but also a freedom of personal choice in certain matters of marriage and family life. This implicit constitutional liberty, the Court in *Wade* held, includes the freedom of a woman to decide whether to terminate a pregnancy.

But the Court in *Wade* also recognized that a State has legitimate interests during a pregnancy in both ensuring the health of the mother and protecting potential human life. . . .

The remaining question then is whether the Hyde Amendment is rationally related to a legitimate governmental objective. It is the Government's position that the Hyde Amendment bears a rational relationship to its legitimate interest in protecting the potential life of the fetus. We agree ...

Where, as here, the Congress has neither invaded a substantive constitutional right or freedom, nor enacted legislation that purposefully operates to the detriment of a suspect class, the only requirement of equal protection is that congressional action be rationally related to a legitimate governmental interest. The Hyde Amendment satisfies that standard. It is not the mission of this Court or any other to decide whether the balance of competing interests reflected in the Hyde Amendment is wise social policy. If that were our mission, not every Justice who has subscribed to the judgment of the Court today could have done so. But we cannot, in the name of the Constitution overturn duly enacted statutes simply "because they may be unwise, improvident, or out of harmony with a particular school of thought." . . .

Justice MARSHALL, dissenting.

Three years ago, in *Maher v. Roe,* the Court upheld a state program that excluded nontherapeutic abortions from a welfare program that generally subsidized the medical expenses incidental to pregnancy and childbirth. At that time, I expressed my fear "that the Court's decisions will be an invitation to public officials, already under extraordinary pressure from well-financed and carefully orchestrated lobbying campaigns, to approve more such restrictions" on governmental funding for abortion.

That fear has proved justified. . . . The Court's opinion studiously avoids recognizing the undeniable fact that for women eligible for Medicaid—poor women—denial of a Medicaid-funded abortion is equivalent to denial of legal abortion altogether. By definition, these women do not have the money to pay for an abortion themselves. If abortion is medically necessary and a funded abortion is unavailable, they must resort to back-alley butchers, attempt to induce an abortion themselves by crude and dangerous methods, or suffer the serious medical consequences of attempting to carry the fetus to term. Because legal abortion is not a realistic option for such women, the predictable result of the Hyde Amendment will be a significant increase in the number of poor women who will die or suffer significant health damage because of an inability to procure necessary medical services. . . .

[In separate opinions, Justice WHITE concurred and Justices BRENNAN, BLACKMUN, and STEVENS dissented.] ▨

Ford's loss of the presidency was due to the interplay of many factors, of which abortion had been one of the most visible and volatile. For voters, abortion was coming to symbolize a wide range of other issues. As Robert Teeter, director of research in Ford's campaign committee, observed, a large portion of the electorate "are conservative in life-style rather than in an ideological sense ... and they are afraid of radical social patterns."[11] The observation was not lost on Carter as he moved into the White House, or on Reagan, who would capitalize on abortion in his 1980 challenge to Carter for the presidency.

Abortion and the Carter Years

President Carter did little either to legitimize the ruling in *Roe* or to overturn it. Like Ford, he consistently proclaimed personal opposition to abortion and federal funding of abortions. But he also sent mixed signals. His administration, for instance, largely stayed out of the annual appropriations fight in Congress over reenacting the Hyde Amendment, which forbade federal funding of abortions under Medicaid, except for women who had been raped or whose lives were endangered by their pregnancies.

Carter sent mixed signals as well in his selection of political advisers and appointees. On the one hand, he named a strong pro-choice advocate, Midge Costanza, as a senior White House aide and supported passage of the Equal Rights Amendment. On the other hand, he named Joseph Califano, a Catholic opposed to abortion, as his Secretary of Health, Education, and Welfare (HEW). That appointment stirred controversy in the Senate when at his confirmation hearings Califano opposed federal funding of abortions. Still, Califano did little as HEW secretary to further fan the fires of the abortion controversy.[12]

The issue of federal funding for abortions was where the Carter administration basically drew the line, taking a middle-of-the-road anti-abortion stand that satisfied neither side of the abortion controversy. In 1977, when the Burger Court upheld states' refusals to fund non-therapeutic abortions under Medicaid, Carter applauded the decision at a press conference. Later, his solicitor general, Wade McCree, filed a brief and defended before the Court the Hyde Amendment's restriction on federal funding of abortions in *Harris v. McRae* (see 5.1, p. 162).

Toward the end of his presidency and less than a month before his unsuccessful bid for reelection, Carter summarized his administration's stand on abortion. Resting on the distinction that he and Califano drew between their private opposition to abortion and their responsibilities as public officeholders to respect the law, Carter refused to assert any presidential leadership on the matter. He put it in a kind of political doublespeak during a 1980 town meeting:

> I am not in favor of abortions, and as President I have done everything I could to minimize the use of abortion in this country. When I was inaugurated I took an oath to uphold the laws of this country and the Constitution of our country, so when the Supreme Court makes a ruling concerning abortion or concerning anything, it's my duty, regardless of my personal beliefs, to carry out the laws of this land.
>
> You know what the Supreme Court ruling is on abortion. I have taken a firm position against the use of Federal funds to pay for abortions, because people feel so deeply and emotionally about this subject, on both sides. But it doesn't seem right to me for the Federal Government to collect taxes from those who have deep religious feelings against abortion and use that same tax money to finance abortions.
>
> I don't want to mislead the rest of the audience. I don't see the need for a constitutional amendment on the subject. I believe that what the Supreme Court has ruled is adequate for our country.
>
> So, my personal beliefs are deeply against the use of abortions. I will oppose the use of Federal funds to finance abortions. But, as President, I have to uphold the law the way Congress passes it and the way the Supreme Court interprets our Constitution.[13]

By 1980 both sides of the abortion controversy demanded more. With the exception of Ronald Reagan, however, presidential aspirants in both parties generally tried to downplay the abortion controversy. On the Republican side, for example, when challenging Reagan for his party's presidential nomination, George Bush stood about where Carter did on abortion. Bush opposed both federal funding of abortions and a constitutional amendment that would overturn *Roe.*

Within the Democratic party, pro-choice forces were more active than they had been at the 1976 convention and secured language in the 1980 platform strongly supporting abortion (see 5.2). The new platform expressly acknowledged that "a woman has a right to choose whether and when to have a child." Carter had opposed that language but yielded in a compromise that enabled his advisers to defeat narrowly an even stronger pro-choice proposal made by feminist-writer Gloria Steinem. Steinem had called for language supporting federal funding of abortions through Medicaid, which was contrary to the position of the Carter administration.

5.2 Abortion and Party Platforms, 1980, 1984, 1988, and 1992

Republican Party   *Democratic Party*

1980

There can be no doubt that the question of abortion, despite the complex nature of its various issues, is ultimately concerned with equality of rights under the law. While we recognize differing views on this question among Americans in general—and in our own Party—we affirm our support of a constitutional amendment to restore protection of the right to life for unborn children. We also support the Congressional efforts to restrict the use of taxpayers' dollars for abortion.

We protest the Supreme Court's intrusion into the family structure through its denial of the parents' obligation and right to guide their minor children.

We fully recognize the religious and ethical concerns which many Americans have about abortion. We also recognize the belief of many Americans that a woman has a right to choose whether and when to have a child.

The Democratic Party supports the 1973 Supreme Court decision on abortion rights as the law of the land and opposes any constitutional amendment to restrict or overturn that decision.

1984

The unborn child has a fundamental individual right to life which cannot be infringed. We therefore reaffirm our support for a human life amendment to the Constitution, and we endorse legislation to make clear that the Fourteenth Amendment's protections apply to unborn children. We oppose the use of public revenues for abor-

The Democratic Party recognizes reproductive freedom as a fundamental human right. We therefore oppose government interference in the reproductive decisions of Americans, especially government interference which denies poor Americans their right to privacy by funding or advocating one or a limited number of reproductive choices only. We

tion and will eliminate funding for organizations which advocate or support abortions. We commend the efforts of those individuals and religious and private organizations that are providing positive alternatives to abortion by meeting the physical, emotional, and financial needs of pregnant women and offering adoption services where needed.

We applaud President Reagan's fine record of judicial appointments, and we reaffirm our support for the appointment of judges at all levels of the judiciary who respect traditional family values and the sanctity of innocent human life.

fully recognize the religious and ethical concerns which many Americans have about abortion. But we also recognize the belief of many Americans that a woman has a right to choose whether and when to have a child. The Democratic Party supports the 1973 Supreme Court decision on abortion rights as the law of the land and opposes any constitutional amendment to restrict or overturn that decision. We deplore violence and harassment against health providers and women seeking services, and will work to end such acts. We support a continuing federal interest in developing strong local family planning and family life education programs and medical research aimed at reducing the need for abortion.

1988

That the unborn child has a fundamental individual right to life which cannot be infringed. We therefore reaffirm our support for a human life amendment to the Constitution, and we endorse legislation to make clear that the Fourteenth Amendment's protections apply to unborn children.

We oppose the use of public revenues for abortion and will eliminate funding for organizations which advocate or support abortions. We commend the efforts of those individuals and religious and private organizations that are providing positive alternatives to abortion by meeting

We further believe that ... the fundamental right of reproductive choice should be guaranteed regardless of ability to pay. . . .

the physical, emotional, and financial needs of pregnant women and offering adoption services where needed.

We applaud President Reagan's fine record of judicial appointments, and we reaffirm our support for the appointment of judges at all levels of the judiciary who respect traditional family values and the sanctity of innocent human life.

1992

We believe the unborn child has a fundamental individual right to life that cannot be infringed. We therefore reaffirm our support for a human life amendment to the Constitution, and we endorse legislation to make clear that the 14th Amendment's protections apply to unborn children. We oppose using public revenues for abortion and will not fund organizations that advocate it. We commend those who provide alternatives to abortion by meeting the needs of mothers and offering adoption services. We reaffirm our support for appointment of judges who respect traditional family values and the sanctity of innocent human life.

Democrats stand behind the right of every woman to choose, consistent with *Roe v. Wade,* regardless of ability to pay, and support a national law to protect that right. It is a fundamental constitutional liberty that individual Americans—not government—can best take responsibility for making the most difficult and intensely personal decisions regarding reproduction.

What changed in the 1980 presidential primaries and election was Reagan's early and aggressive championing of the antiabortion cause. Whereas virtually all other presidential contenders equivocated on abortion Reagan took a hard-line pro-life position. He alone energetically attacked the legitimacy of the Supreme Court's rulings and charged that they were "an abuse of power as bad as the transgressions of Watergate and the bribery on Capitol Hill."[14] Reagan endorsed a constitutional amendment to reverse *Roe,* promised to appoint to the federal bench judges opposed to abortion, and vowed to prohibit the use of federal funds for abortion except when necessary to save the life of the woman. With Reagan's landslide election and his administration's politically symbolic and strategically aggressive attack on *Roe,* the abortion controversy was irrevocably a part of presidential politics.

Abortion and the Reagan Revolution

Ronald Reagan worked major changes in the national debate over abortion in five ways. First, his antiabortion rhetoric effectively erased the distinction between private and public morality. He not only distinguished his position from those of Nixon, Ford, and Carter but also vigorously appealed to the growing antiabortion movement. Reagan gave presidential legitimacy to the legal enforcement of the antiabortion movement's moral views. Second, his administration supported a constitutional amendment and other congressional legislation aimed at reversing *Roe.* Third, and in many ways most important, Reagan's Department of Justice scrutinized potential appointees to the federal bench, screening out those deemed supportive of the pro-choice side of the abortion controversy. Fourth, during Reagan's second term his solicitor general, Charles Fried, aggressively pressed the Supreme Court to abandon *Roe.* Fifth, the administration enacted regulations that restricted the availability of abortions.

Reagan's Rhetoric

No president before Reagan so passionately and consistently championed the antiabortion cause. Nor did groups on the opposite side have anyone as prominent as the president to defend their position publicly. By the end of the Reagan era, the legitimacy given to the antiabortion movement had effectively put pro-choice advocates on the defensive. As the only public official elected nationwide, the president is positioned as no other politician to mold public opinion through daily media coverage, news conferences, public statements, proclamations, and other activities. And Reagan strategically used rhetoric and those opportunities in advocacy.

Reagan's rhetoric reinforced the hard-line antiabortion planks in his party's platforms. Although he initially disappointed some pro-life supporters by selecting George Bush as his vice president (Bush had opposed any constitutional amendment on abortion), he consistently reassured them and frustrated pro-choice and women's rights advocates within the party.

Reagan's denouncements of the Court's abortion rulings were stronger than any of his predecessors'. In 1983, when the Burger Court by a 6–3 vote struck down several restrictions on abortion, Reagan publicly lamented the Court's continued course and called for congressional action.[15] His language was typically impassioned and moralistic, particularly in comparing the battle over abortion to that over slavery. In this respect, Reagan abandoned his otherwise staunch defense of "states' rights," further distancing himself from Nixon's and Ford's calls for simply returning to the pre-*Roe* days when states could ban or permit abortion. In remarks to the annual convention of National Religious Broadcasters in 1984, for instance, Reagan made a spiritual appeal for a constitutional amendment that would not only reverse *Roe* but take the matter completely out of the hands of the states.[16] His "sermon" rivaled even those of Jerry Falwell, the leader of the 1980s' Moral Majority (see 5.3).

The antiabortion movement also received Reagan's presidential imprimatur during his annual State of the Union addresses and other messages delivered to Congress before national television. In his 1988 address, for instance, he repeated familiar themes, along with the mistaken and misleading assertion that "medical evidence confirms the unborn child is a living human being entitled to life, liberty and the pursuit of happiness."[17] In other messages to Congress calling for "legislation prohibiting the use of all Federal funds to finance, promote, encourage or otherwise support abortion," Reagan's rhetoric was even bolder. "Abortion is the taking of human life," he proclaimed in 1986, "and it debases the underpinnings of our country."[18]

At annual "March for Life" rallies, which grew in number throughout the 1980s, Reagan praised antiabortion protesters through a telephonic loudspeaker hookup. The protesters, including those associated with Operation Rescue, were heartened by Reagan's language. In his 1985 remarks, for instance, he renewed his promise "to work with all of those—in the Congress and out—who believe, as I do, that abortion is taking the life of a living human being; that the right to abortion is

5.3 President Reagan's Remarks at Annual Convention of National Religious Broadcasters, 30 January 1984

Let's begin at the beginning. God is the center of our lives; the human family stands at the center of society; and our greatest hope for the future is in the faces of our children....

God's most blessed gift to His family is the gift of life. He sent us the Prince of Peace as a babe in a manger. I've said that we must be cautious in claiming God is on our side. I think the real question we must answer is, are we on His side?

I know what I'm about to say now is controversial, but I have to say it. This nation cannot continue turning a blind eye and a deaf ear to the taking of some 4000 unborn children's lives every day. That's one every 21 seconds. One every 21 seconds.

We cannot pretend that America is preserving her first and highest ideal, the belief that each life is sacred, when we've permitted the deaths of 15 million helpless innocents since the Roe versus Wade decision—15 million children who will never laugh, never sing, never know the joy of human love, will never strive to heal the sick, feed the poor, or make peace among nations....

This nation fought a terrible war so that black Americans would be guaranteed their God-given rights. Abraham Lincoln recognized that we could not survive as a free land when some could decide whether others should be free or slaves. Well, today another question begs to be asked: How can we survive as a free nation when some decide that others are not fit to live and should be done away with?

I believe no challenge is more important to the character of America than restoring the right to life of all human beings. Without that right, no other rights have meaning.

"Suffer the little children to come unto me, and forbid them not, for such is the kingdom of God."

SOURCE: Ronald Reagan, *Public Papers of the Presidents of the United States, 1984*, book 1 (Washington, D.C.: Government Printing Office, 1986), 119.

not secured by the Constitution; and the state has a compelling interest in protecting the life of each person before birth."[19]

Of Constitutional Amendments and Congressional Legislation

Reagan's record in pushing Congress to enact a constitutional amendment and other legislation limiting the availability of abortion failed to match what his antiabortion rhetoric had promised. When Reagan took office, many in the antiabortion movement expected swift presidential action to end legalized abortion, particularly in light of his landslide victory, which had a "coattails effect" for Republicans running for Congress. For the first time in decades, the GOP regained control of the Senate. Yet during Reagan's first year in office, when his administration achieved its major legislative accomplishments, the White House staff concentrated on securing his economic agenda, cutting taxes and federal spending, and deregulating business and industry.[20] Abortion and other social–civil rights issues were relegated to the back burner.

In the 1982 midterm congressional elections, twenty-six Republicans in the House of Representatives were defeated. Reagan lost the working majority of Republicans and conservative Democrats in Congress that he had pulled together in the first half of his first term and never recovered that early edge. Although Reagan repeatedly asked Congress to enact a constitutional amendment and other pro-life legislation, he was not able to forge the necessary majorities on Capitol Hill.

Reagan's primary legislative successes came in his first term, when as part of his budget reduction package Congress was persuaded to cut by almost one-quarter funding for family planning under Title X of the Public Health Service Act of 1970.[21] Reagan also supported passage in 1981 of the Adolescent Family Life Act, authorizing the funding of religious and other organizations involved in counseling teenagers about sexual affairs and "strong family values," along with prohibiting funding of abortions or family-planning services for adolescents.

In Reagan's second term the prospects for attaining major antiabortion action in Congress grew less likely. With the midterm elections in 1986, the GOP lost control of the Senate. Reagan continued to call on Congress to "come together in a spirit of understanding" and to find "positive solutions to the tragedy of abortion,"[22] but White House lobbyists did not urge Congress to pass major antiabortion legislation. In short, Reagan failed to generate sufficient congressional backing for a constitutional amendment overturning *Roe*. A House subcommittee defeated a 1985 proposal to ban abortion counseling by federally funded organizations, and Congress defeated the president's efforts to repeal, among other legislation, Title X of the Public Health Service Act.

Packing the Federal Bench

Unable to move Congress to pass a constitutional amendment or any other significant antiabortion legislation, the Reagan administration employed a more indirect strategy (and one that would have a long-term impact not only on legalized abortion but also on other social and civil rights issues), namely, achieving the administration's legal-policy reforms through the appointment of federal judges. "In many areas—abortion, crime, pornography, and others," Reagan observed in 1986, "—progress will take place when the federal judiciary is made up of judges who believe in law and order and a strict interpretation of the Constitution."[23]

Behind the Republican party's platform promises and the campaign rhetoric, the Reagan administration nurtured a more coherent and ambitious agenda for legal reform through judicial appointments than had any previous administration. As Attorney General Edwin Meese III put it, the administration aimed "to institutionalize the Reagan revolution so it can't be set aside no matter what happens in future presidential elections."[24]

Selection of federal judges, of course, is always political, and each administration weighs differently political patronage, professional considerations, and its own legal-policy goals when recruiting judicial nominees. All administrations favor party faithfuls when recruiting judges, and the Reagan administration was no exception (97 percent of Reagan appointees came from the Republican party). But Reagan's Department of Justice put into place the most rigorous and decidedly ideological screening process ever.

Four other factors figured in the department's pursuit of its substantive agenda through judicial appointments. First, there was a greater appreciation than in prior administrations for the significance of the expanding number of judgeships and the changing role of courts in U.S. politics. Bruce Fein, the former associate deputy attorney general who helped set up Reagan's judicial selection process, observed, "The judiciary is a primary player in the formulation of public policy," and hence "it would be silly for an administration not to try to affect the direction of legal policy" when filling vacancies on the federal bench.[25]

Second, the judges appointed by previous Republican administrations were viewed as disappointing. Quite simply, those administrations failed to take judgeships seriously. They let political patronage and professional considerations overshadow their own legal-policy goals in judicial selection. As a result, the judicial trend in the 1960s and 1970s was perceived to go in a liberal-to-moderate direction; the Supreme Court led the way, even though no justice had been appointed by a Democratic president since 1967.

Third, Carter's "affirmative action" program for selecting judges inspired a reaction. Carter forged historic changes in the federal bench by seeking a more "representative judiciary" through the recruitment of blacks, women, and other minorities. Reagan's Justice Department saw that program as sacrificing "judicial merit" for the political symbolism of a more "representative" federal bench.[26]

Fourth, Reagan's Justice Department became more aggressive in his second term in defining and pushing its agenda in litigation, arguments before the Supreme Court, and selection of judicial nominees. This reflected changes in the staffing of the department during Reagan's two terms, along with a reaction to the administration's deteriorating relationship with Congress. During Reagan's first term, under Attorney General William French Smith, the department basically sought to establish what it was *against*. It wanted to overturn the Court's expansive protection of the rights of the accused, especially its enforcement of the exclusionary rule (requiring that evidence obtained illegally by police be excluded at trial) and *Miranda* warnings (informing suspects of their constitutional rights to remain silent and to consult a lawyer). And it opposed judicial decisions permitting abortions and affirmative action as well as those requiring a rigid separation of church and state. In contrast, in Reagan's second term, under Attorney General Meese the department aimed to establish broadly what Reagan justice stood *for*. Nothing symbolized this more (or captured wider public attention) than Meese's call for a "return to a jurisprudence of original intention," and Judge Robert Bork's defense of that view during his Supreme Court confirmation hearings.[27]

"The Reagan administration," in the words of Stephen Markman, who was an assistant attorney general at the time, "has in place what is probably the most thorough and comprehensive system for recruiting and screening federal judicial candidates of any administration ever. This Administration has, moreover, attempted to assert the President's prerogatives over judicial selection more consistently than many of its predecessors."[28] Democrats and even moderate Republican senators contended that Reagan had imposed an "ideological litmus test" on the selection of federal judges. Yet even the sharpest critics had to concede Reagan's prerogative to pursue his legal-policy goals through judicial selection. What disturbed them most, perhaps, was that the administration proved so successful in winning Senate confirmation of its nominees.

Central to Reagan's success in reorienting the federal bench was the reorganization of the judicial selection process within the Justice Department. Primary responsibility shifted and became a larger staff operation, subject to greater White House supervision. The attorney general no longer had total responsibility or solely relied on his deputy attorney general for assistance. Instead, the assistant attorney general for the Office of Legal Policy was put in charge of screening candidates. The White House Judicial Selection Committee was created to decide whom the president should nominate. In addition, a rigorous screening process for potential nominees was introduced. The committee considered candidates only after they had undergone day-long interviews with department officials. In selecting some 300 judges, Markman estimated, "over 1000 individuals [were] interviewed." And the interviews took place after candidates' records—containing speeches, articles, and opinions—had already been compared with hundreds of others in the department's computer data bank. The department's interviews of potential judicial nominees were unprecedented and controversial. Carter's attorney general, Griffin Bell, for one, lamented that they "politicized the process badly. I don't believe that you should ask a judge his views [on specific issues] because he is likely to have to rule on that."[29]

No less controversial were some of the questions asked of candidates for judgeships. Some who made it to the bench and others who didn't told of being asked about their views on abortion, affirmative action, and criminal justice. National Public Radio correspondent Nina Totenberg reported that several contenders said "they were asked directly about their views on abortion." "One female state court judge said she was asked repeatedly how she would rule on an abortion case if it came before her." Another observed, "I guess most of us have accepted that we're not going to get these judgeships unless we're willing to commit to a particular position, which we think would be improper."[30]

Two well-publicized candidates turned down for judgeships were Judith Whittaker and Andrew Frey. Whittaker, associate general counsel of Hallmark Cards, was first in her law school class and was highly rated by the American Bar Association (ABA). Yet the Justice Department refused to nominate her because she once supported the Equal Rights Amendment and was viewed as antibusiness and pro-abortion. Frey was a deputy solicitor general within the Reagan administration, but New Right senators John East (R-North Carolina) and Jeremiah Denton (R-Alabama) pressed him for his views on abortion, religion, school desegregation, and affirmative action. Subsequently, they discovered that he had made donations to Planned Parenthood and the National Coalition to Ban Handguns. Along with Utah's Republican Senator Orrin Hatch and ten others, they prevailed on the department to withdraw his nomination.

Justice Department officials denied having a "litmus test"; in the words of Reagan's White House counsel, Fred Fielding, "No one factor was considered." Candidates, they explained, were asked about past rulings and hypothetical cases—dealing, admittedly, with heated issues like abortion—but that was to "see how they think through a case" and where they stood on the role of the courts. Others in the administration defended the screening process on the ground that "a president who fails to scrutinize the legal philosophy of federal judicial nominees courts frustration of his own policy agenda."[31]

For Reagan, as for any president, the main obstacle to appointing his desired judges was the Senate's power to reject nominees. Yet the Senate rarely posed a major threat. That the Senate does not usually reject the president's nominees is a function of the level of judgeships, fluctuations in presidential strength, the chairman of the Senate Judiciary Committee, and the composition of the Senate. There are few institutional incentives for the Senate to do more than pass on the vast majority of judicial nominees. Supreme Court nominees are the exception; one out of four Supreme Court nominees has historically been rejected or forced to withdraw from consideration. Lower-court judges, though more numerous, are routinely approved by the Judiciary Committee and confirmed by the Senate without debate, due to the norms of political patronage and senatorial courtesy—historically the home-state senator of a candidate for lower-court appointment may exercise a veto over potential nominees. It costs senators to battle with colleagues and gains them little or nothing with their constituents. Besides, the chair of the Judiciary Committee is especially powerful in determining when nominees have hearings, and usually whether they may face opposition and how much. Whether the Senate "rubber stamps" or challenges nominees largely depends on whether the chair is of the president's party (which turns on whose party holds a Senate majority), and on how willing the chair is to push the president's nominees. These factors certainly weighed in Reagan's winning confirmation for his judges when the Republicans were in the majority, just as they did in the processing of judicial appointments when the Democrats regained control of the Senate after the 1986 elections.

During the first six years of Reagan's presidency, the chair of the Judiciary Committee, South Carolina's Senator Strom Thurmond, proved an influential ally. Under Thurmond, most nominees were quickly approved. In comparison with the committee under Massachusetts's Democratic Senator Edward Kennedy (1979–80), which passed on appellate court nominees after an average of sixty-six days and district court nominees after fifty-five days, the committee under Thurmond referred nominees to the full Senate within twenty days of nomination.[32] There was little or no independent inquiry into their backgrounds and only brief hearings before a subcommittee of one or two senators.

The importance of Thurmond's chairmanship and a Republican-controlled Senate was even clearer after Democrats regained a senatorial majority and Joseph Biden (D-Delaware) became chair of the Judiciary Committee in 1987. The committee was no longer disposed to pass quickly on Reagan's nominees. Democrats immediately sought to ensure their power on the committee by reducing its size from eighteen to fourteen, thereby excluding North Carolina's Senator Jesse Helms. Biden also created a four-member panel, headed by Vermont's Democratic Senator Patrick Leahy, to screen nominees and acquired additional investigatory staff. The administration in turn was slow to fill vacancies and named fewer controversial conservatives. Officials in the Justice Department perceived that the kinds of conservatives who had been approved by Thurmond's committee were not as likely to win confirmation, and hence not always worth the trouble of nominating.

The most dramatic consequence of the change in the Senate came with the rejection of Supreme Court nominee Bork, a leading conservative intellectual identified with the legal policies of the Justice Department and the New Right. In 1986 Reagan again made judgeships an issue of campaign politics. When campaigning for Republicans in ten Senate races, including five in the South, he asked voters to elect Republicans so that his judicial nominees would continue to win Senate confirmation. But all ten races were lost to Democrats. The conservative Southern Democrats elected in these races won to a large extent because they received 90 percent of the black vote in their states, and hence they were especially not inclined to be counted as allies in a confirmation battle raising the issue of race and civil rights. Along with six moderate Republicans, they cast the crucial votes defeating Bork's confirmation.

The striking feature about Reagan's lower-court judges is that they are predominantly young, white, upper-middle-class males, with prior judicial or prosecutorial experience, and reputations for legal conservatism established on the bench, in law schools, or in politics. Simply put, the oldest president appointed some of the youngest judges in our history. This registered the department's strategy for ensuring the president's judicial legacy: picking those who will ostensibly stay on the bench longer. Reagan, as earlier noted, appointed few blacks (5) and women (29) out of a total of 382 judicial appointees—more appointees than any other president in this century.

Beyond the demographic changes in the federal judiciary brought about in the Reagan era, the Justice Department's legal-policy goals and rigorous screening of judicial nominees generated controversy over whether the courts were being packed with those who would forge a counterrevolution and "rewrite the Constitution." It is still too soon to draw firm conclusions about the final record of Reagan's lower-court judges, but there is no doubt that they will continue to make a difference. Studies of judicial behavior generally find that judicial ideology appears significant in less than one case out of six; partisan considerations—such as the party affiliation of judges—account for only a smaller fraction of all rulings.[33] That is because appellate court decisions are overwhelmingly unanimous. Differences between Reagan judges and those appointed by other presidents may thus prove narrower or wider than expected, vary according to areas of law, and develop more or less sharply over time and with future changes in the composition and direction of the entire federal judiciary.

In a study of abortion cases in the lower federal courts and the voting behavior of federal district court judges appointed by LBJ, Nixon, Carter, and Reagan, political scientists C.K. Rowland and Steve Alumbaugh found that "Reagan appointees were much more resistant to abortion rights than were the appointees of his predecessors, including the appointees of fellow Republican Richard Nixon. Likewise, President Carter's appointees were much more supportive of abortion claims than were the appointees of other presidents."[34]

Although hugely successful in appointing close to half of all judges in the lower federal courts, Reagan failed to turn the Supreme Court completely around or, by the end of his presidency at least, to win a majority over to his positions on abortion and other hotly contested issues. Reagan's opportunity to turn the Court around, however, didn't come until near the end of his presidency, when Justice Lewis F. Powell, Jr., stepped down on 28 June 1987. It was an opportunity lost; the administration suffered its major setback. Judge Bork, the first nominee for Powell's seat, was defeated after an extraordinary and bitter confirmation battle. The second, Judge Douglas H. Ginsburg, was forced to withdraw from consideration after controversies over his personal affairs led the New Right to turn against him. Judge Anthony M. Kennedy, the third nominee, won confirmation easily because of his reputation for open-mindedness and distance from the administration's hard-line legal-policy positions. Although many members of the administration were disappointed by Reagan's final nominee, who seemed not to be the kind of justice that officials in the Justice Department hoped would "lock in the Reagan Revolution," Reagan's appointees, when joined by those of his successor, forged a solid conservative majority and shifted the Court's direction on abortion and much else (as further discussed in chapters 6 and 10).

Reagan's first appointee—Justice Sandra Day O'Connor—was chosen more for symbolic than for ideological reasons. During the 1980 election Reagan had promised to name the first woman to the Court.

Less than a year later, in May 1981, Justice Potter Stewart privately told the president that he would retire after twenty-three years on the bench at the end of the term. An Eisenhower appointee, Stewart had a reputation as "a swing voter" because he occasionally cast the key vote when siding with the Burger Court's conservative members in cases involving affirmative action and the death penalty and with the liberals on abortion and obscenity. A two-month search for his successor concluded with a woman Reagan said shared his view "that the role of the courts is to interpret the law, not to enact new law by judicial fiat."

Not widely known in legal circles at the time of her nomination, O'Connor had risen through the ranks of Republican politics in her home state of Arizona. She had served as an assistant attorney general and as a member of the state legislature, as well as on a municipal court, before former Democratic Governor Bruce Babbitt appointed her to a state appellate court. Her nomination was endorsed by both senators from Arizona and supported, privately, by Chief Justice Warren E. Burger (who had met her years earlier) and by Justice Rehnquist (a classmate at Stanford Law School). Even the president of the National Organization for Women, Eleanor Smeal, proclaimed her nomination "a major victory for women's rights."

O'Connor's confirmation hearings (the first ever to be televised, and carried by the Public Broadcasting System) generated only minor controversy. The Moral Majority and the National Right to Life Committee, among others, attacked her once it was discovered that as a state legislator she had supported a "family-planning" bill that would have repealed existing state statutes prohibiting abortions. During the Judiciary Committee's hearings, Republican Senators Charles E. Grassley and Roger W. Jepsen (both from Iowa) tried to extract information on how she might vote on such issues, but O'Connor, as had all earlier nominees, refused to be drawn out, saying little more than that she would uphold and apply settled law.[35] Her reticence and her vague answers to other questions disturbed some in the Justice Department, but the Senate voted overwhelmingly (99–0) for confirmation.[36]

Five years later, in June 1986, Chief Justice Burger announced that he would step down, and Reagan shrewdly maximized the opportunity to fill the Court's center chair. The elevation of Rehnquist from associate to chief justice, and the appointment of Judge Antonin Scalia to his seat, could not have been more politically symbolic or strategic. Both men were not just sympathetic to the administration's legal-policy goals, they could claim to be intellectual architects of its agenda. Through their writings and judicial opinions, they had largely defined the administration's positions on separation of powers, federalism, and the role of the judiciary in balancing competing claims between majority rule and minority rights. The White House knew that Rehnquist would prove controversial because of his long-standing, often extremely conservative views, but naming him chief justice would symbolize Reagan's judicial legacy. And Rehnquist's elevation as a sitting justice made it virtually impossible for the Senate to deny confirmation.

Rehnquist's nomination as the sixteenth chief justice thus brought on a battle. Massachusetts's Democratic Senator Kennedy led the attack, as he had when Rehnquist was first named to the Court, calling him "too extreme on race, too extreme on women's rights, too extreme on freedom of speech, too extreme on separation of church and state, too extreme to be Chief Justice." The confirmation hearings, Utah's Republican Senator Orrin Hatch countered, threatened to become a "Rehnquisition."

The Judiciary Committee's televised hearings proved to be less of an enlightenment than an occasion for speeches. Rehnquist was repeatedly asked about prior judicial opinions, but refused to discuss them or how he might handle major issues in the future, saying correctly that to do so would impinge on judicial independence. About all that the committee accomplished was a reassertion of its power to consider judicial philosophy when confirming appointees, no less than the president does when nominating them. Rehnquist was approved by the committee, with five Democrats voting against him and two joining Republicans in a 13–5 vote. The Senate subsequently confirmed him by a vote of 65–33, based on Southern Democrats voting with Republicans and two Republicans siding with thirty-one Democrats in opposition.

In contrast to the intense scrutiny of Rehnquist, the Judiciary Committee staff spent little time on Scalia. His hearings were quick and amicable. The differences are reflected in the committee's final reports on each: Rehnquist's runs to 114 pages, Scalia's to 76 words. Scalia was confirmed by a vote of 98–0, after barely five minutes of debate.

Next to Rehnquist and Bork, no other jurist was closer than Scalia to Reagan's Justice Department. In the 1970s, Scalia had been connected with many persons who would assume positions of power in the Reagan administration. After graduating from Harvard Law School, he practiced for six years before joining the University of Virginia Law School. Then, in 1971–72 he took a one-year leave of absence to work as general counsel in the Nixon administration. Two years later he was tapped by Ford's attorney general, Edward H. Levi, to head the Office of Legal Counsel in the Justice Department. When Ford left office, Levi returned to the University of Chicago Law School and persuaded Scalia to come along.

In 1982 Reagan placed Scalia on the appellate court in Washington, where Scalia continued to make his mark. He developed a trenchant judicial philosophy based on a limited view of freedom of expression and a deep antagonism toward affirmative action, abortion, and the "liberal jurisprudence" that undergirded many of the Warren and Burger Courts' rulings. In addition, he has been a forceful proponent of broad presidential power, a rigid separation of powers, and limited governmental intervention into an economy based on free-market capitalism.

The 1987 battle over Reagan's nominations of Bork and Ginsburg was extraordinary. Instead of becoming the 104th justice, they became the twenty-seventh and twenty-eighth nominees to be rejected or forced to withdraw because of Senate opposition. Bork was opposed by the widest margin ever (58–42). The battle underscores the extent to which judgeships were perceived as symbols and a way to ensure Reagan's legacy, and how intense the fighting over abortion had become by the late 1980s.

The battle had been virtually assured by Reagan's selection of Bork to take the place of Justice Powell. Powell had been not just the pivotal vote on the Court; he had repeatedly cast the crucial vote in cases rejecting the administration's positions on abortion, affirmative action, the death penalty, and some other issues. With his departure, the balance on the Court would decidedly shift. Over more moderate Republicans and conservative jurists, the president chose one of the most outspoken critics of the Warren and Burger Courts. He did so despite the Democrats' having regained control of the Senate in 1986, which foreordained a battle over any nominee closely aligned with the New Right. In addition, Reagan made clear that Bork's confirmation was top priority in the final days of his administration. This appeared to be one of the most visible ways of reasserting presidential strength, badly damaged by the Iran-*contra* affair, which involved members of the administration secretly and illegally selling arms to Iran in exchange for money to support the Nicaraguan *contras*.

The administration underestimated the opposition. Yet Bork had been passed over three times before, by Ford in 1975 and by Reagan in 1981 and 1986. Shortly after Scalia's appointment, the White House had rumored that the next nominee to the Court would be Bork, then a judge sitting on Court of Appeals for the District of Columbia Circuit. Liberal groups therefore had had ample time to study Bork's record and were prepared to take up arms against him.

Senator Kennedy immediately denounced Bork, and more than eighty-three organizations followed. Calling him "unfit" to serve on the high bench, the American Civil Liberties Union (ACLU) abandoned its practice of not opposing nominees. The ACLU had only once before taken such a position; it had opposed Rehnquist's nomination in 1971 but had taken no position on his elevation to chief justice. Women's groups assailed Bork for his sharp criticisms of *Roe*. In 1981, a year before Reagan put him on the appellate bench, when testifying before Congress, Bork had taken the position "that *Roe v. Wade* is, itself, an unconstitutional decision, a serious and wholly unjustifiable judicial usurpation of state legislative authority."[37] Bork had also criticized the 1965 landmark ruling on privacy in *Griswold v. Connecticut.*

New Right organizations were no less active, though they were initially discouraged by White House Chief of Staff Howard Baker from strident support. Over the objections of Meese and others in the Justice Department, the White House advanced the strategy of recasting Bork's conservative record in order to make opponents appear shrill and partisan. In a speech on 29 July, the president equated his nominee with Powell, despite Bork's past attacks on Powell's opinions. A 70-page White House briefing book was prepared, followed by a 240-page report released by the Justice Department, aimed at portraying Bork as a "mainstream" jurist.

The publicity was extraordinary. Numerous reports analyzing Bork's record were distributed to editorial boards around the country. The staff of the Democrat controlled Judiciary Committee issued its own seventy-two-page study refuting the administration's "centrist" depiction of Bork. Bork was a bonanza for political consultants and fund raisers. People for the American Way launched a $2 million media campaign opposing the nomination, and the National Conservative Political Action Committee (NCPAC) committed over $1 million to lobbying for confirmation.

What had far greater impact, however, was Bork's own role in the pre-confirmation fray and in the confirmation proceedings. Even before the hearings began, Bork took the unusual step of granting an unprecedented number of newspaper interviews. As did Louis Brandeis in 1911, Bork faced charges of being a "radical," but Brandeis and all earlier nominees let their records speak for themselves. Bork sought to explain, clarify, and amend his twenty-five-year record as a Yale Law School professor, a solicitor general, and a judge. That break with tradition gave the appearance of a public relations campaign.

During his five days of nationally televised testimony before the Judiciary Committee, Bork continued the appearance of trying to refashion himself into a moderate, even "centrist," jurist. A key consideration thus became, in Senator Patrick Leahy's words, one of "confirmation conversion"—whether Bork was "born again." Besides deserting much of his past record, Bork's lengthy explanations were unprecedented in other ways. Since 1925, when Harlan F. Stone first appeared as a witness during his confirmation hearings, down to Reagan's previous appointees, all nominees had refused to talk about their views on specific cases, let alone discuss how they might vote on issues likely to come before the Court. But Bork gave unusual assurances on how he might vote if confirmed.

By the time Bork finished his thirty hours of testifying, he had contradicted much of what he had stood for and for which he had been nominated. Noting the "considerable difference between what Judge Bork has written and what he has testified he will do if confirmed," Republican Senator Arlen Specter (Pennsylvania) observed: "I think that what many of us are looking for is some assurance of where you are." Even Bork seemed troubled and sought to assure the Senate that "it really would be preposterous to say things I said to you and then get on the Court and do the opposite. I would be disgraced in history."

Bork's testimony weighed far more than that of the 110 witnesses assembled for and against him in the following two weeks. To be sure, they contributed to the atmosphere of campaign politics that surrounded the hearings. For the first time a former president, Gerald Ford, introduced a nominee to the committee. Carter sent a letter expressing his opposition. Theretofore no justices—especially sitting justices—had come out as allies of a president or his nominee, yet retired Chief Justice Burger testified and Justices John Paul Stevens and Byron White publicly endorsed Bork.

In spite of the publicity and pressure-group activities, the hearings were remarkably illuminating, particularly Bork's exchanges with the senators. They focused on the nature of the Constitution: Is it "the Founders' Constitution," as implied in Meese's call for "a jurisprudence of original intention" and defended by Bork? Or is the Constitution a "living document," one that amendments and the Court's rulings have made more democratic and to afford greater protection for civil rights?[38] Put this way, the hearings came closer than any before to a national debate. They were, in the words of the chair of the Judiciary Committee, Senator Biden, "a referendum on the past progress of the Supreme Court and a referendum on the future."

The fundamental issue remained, after all, the constitutional views shared by Bork and the Reagan administration. That is what had already sown divisions with the legal establishment over some lower-court judges and broke open with the battle over Bork. It was reflected in the ABA's rating of Bork as "well qualified" (one third of its committee opposed that rating) and in the broad opposition to his appointment in the legal profession: 1925 law professors (40 percent of the academic legal profession) signed letters opposing Bork, more than six times the number (300) that had opposed Nixon's ill-fated nomination of G. Harrold Carswell.

What captured attention at the end of three weeks of hearings, however, were public opinion polls. A *Washington Post*/ABC News poll found that 52 percent of the public opposed confirmation. An *Atlanta Constitution* poll in twelve southern states found that 51 percent of its respondents were against Bork, including white conservatives. Bork and his supporters, not surprisingly, decried the influence of public opinion on the outcome. But to attribute Bork's defeat entirely to public opinion polls is wrong. Most senators and their staffs spent an entire summer examining Bork's record, reputation, and judicial philosophy. The committee's hearings were more exhaustive than, perhaps, any before. It is no less wrong solely to credit or blame the pressure of civil rights groups for Bork's defeat. There was also a campaign for Bork by the New Right. That is why some senators delayed the Senate's final vote for two weeks, over the objections of Majority Leader Robert Byrd (D-West Virginia) and Minority Leader Robert Dole (R-Kansas), so that more money could be raised and certain senators targeted with letter-writing campaigns from the right.

The publicity and pressure-group activities, to be sure, figured in the outcome. Within a couple of days of the Judiciary Committee's vote, seven conservative southern Democrats, led by Louisiana's Senator J. Bennett Johnston, announced their opposition. This, along with similar announcements by Senators Specter and Dennis DeConcini (D-Arizona) prodded the two remaining Democrats on the committee, Senators Byrd and Howell Heflin (D-Alabama), to abandon their view that the committee ought not make any recommendation to the full Senate. As a result, the vote was 9–5 against confirmation.

Ultimately, Bork was defeated because of his views and association with the Justice Department's and the New Right's legal-policy goals. That was what the debate over the Constitution during the committee's hearings was about. It is what turned conservative southern Democrats and six moderate Republicans against him in the final vote on the Senate floor.

The defeat was a major setback for the Justice Department and the administration. Bork and Meese and others in the department were bitter and blamed White House staff for mismanagement and not pushing hard enough for confirmation. They were also vindictive and persuaded Reagan to nominate Judge Ginsburg, rather than Ninth Circuit Court of Appeals Judge Anthony M. Kennedy, a less controversial conservative.

In its haste to find a suitable successor to Bork, however, the Justice Department had failed to investigate Ginsburg's background fully. Within ten days after his nomination, Ginsburg was forced to withdraw amid disclosures about his personal life and growing concerns about both his ethical conduct as an attorney in the Justice Department and his lack of judicial experience. A few days later Reagan nominated Judge Kennedy for the seat that had been vacated by Justice Powell almost five months earlier.

The nomination of Kennedy met with immediate and generally bipartisan praise. New Right senators and supporters remained disappointed (and initially considered a challenge), but the Democrat controlled Senate was in no mood for another battle. And this was reflected in the confirmation hearings in mid-December. They were reminiscent of most in the past: few reporters showed up, none of the commercial television networks broadcast them (as they had Bork's), and only PBS, C-SPAN, and CNN offered coverage.

At the Judiciary Committee's hearings, Kennedy's testimony was reserved and straightforward. When pressed on heated issues, such as abortion, by Senators Hatch, Grassley, and Gordon Humphrey (R-New Hampshire), he declared that he had "no fixed view." Kennedy also clearly distanced himself from some of Bork's controversial positions. For instance, he accepted the constitutional status of a right of privacy and expressly rejected the view that "a jurisprudence of original intention" provides a sure guide for constitutional interpretation. The latter, in Kennedy's words, is a "necessary starting point" rather than a "methodology," and "doesn't tell us how to decide a case." Although such responses troubled New Right senators, the Judiciary Committee unanimously recommended confirmation.

Kennedy's confirmation occasioned little reaction except from groups like the National Organization for Women, which predicted that Kennedy would vote to overturn *Roe*. Kennedy was defended as a nonconfrontational conservative, but he further reinforced the conservative majority that Reagan had forged on the Rehnquist Court.

Reagan's Crusade before the Burger and Rehnquist Courts

As Reagan incrementally changed the composition and direction of the federal judiciary through his appointments, his Department of Justice grew ever more energetic in asking the justices to overrule *Roe*. The increasing aggressiveness of that effort to win the Court over to the president's position became evident in a series of cases in which it filed *amicus* briefs supporting restrictive state and local laws enacted after *Roe*. (An *amicus* ["friend"] brief was originally intended to bring before a court arguments and data not in the main briefs, but such briefs have become vehicles of advocacy for those seeking to influence a court directly.)

In the early 1980s, even after the appointments of Justices Stevens
and O'Connor, the Burger Court continued to reaffirm *Roe*. In 1983 in
City of Akron v. Akron Center for Reproductive Health,[39] for example,
the Court struck down several restrictions imposed on women seeking
abortions, including requirements that they sign "informed consent"
forms and wait at least twenty-four hours before having an abortion,
along with requiring doctors to perform abortions after the first trimester only in a hospital and to dispose of fetal remains "in a humane and
sanitary way."

In *City of Akron*, Reagan's first solicitor general, Rex Lee, asked the
justices to reconsider *Roe* but stopped short of urging its reversal. That
angered some New Right conservatives who wanted a more vigorous assault on *Roe*. Still, only O'Connor, joined by Rehnquist and White, appeared sympathetic to that. In her dissenting opinion, O'Connor suggested a willingness to reconsider, if not overturn, *Roe*. Powell, however,
countered that the majority would not yield to pressure from within or
from outside the Court. *Roe* "was considered with special care" and
"joined by the Chief Justice and six other Justices," he emphasized.
"Since *Roe* was decided," Powell added, "the Court repeatedly and consistently has accepted and applied the basic principle that a woman has
a fundamental right to make the highly personal choice whether or not
to terminate her pregnancy." In two companion cases handed down
with *City of Akron*, though, the justices split 5–4 (with Powell casting
the crucial fifth vote) in upholding a Missouri law requiring pathology
reports for all abortions, the presence of a second physician during abortions performed after viability, and parental consent for minors seeking
abortions; and sustaining the constitutionality of a Virginia statute mandating that second-trimester abortions be performed in licensed outpatient clinics.[40]

Three years later, in 1986, the administration renewed its attack on
Roe. This time, Reagan's second solicitor general, Harvard Law School
Professor Charles Fried, dared to do what his predecessor had refused to
do: He questioned the Court's wisdom and urged that *Roe* be overturned. In support of Pennsylvania Governor Richard Thornburgh's
appeal of a circuit court ruling, striking down a state law limiting the
availability of abortions, Fried filed an extraordinary *amicus curiae*
brief. There, he boldly proclaimed "the textual, doctrinal and historical
basis for *Roe v. Wade* is so far flawed and . . . a source of such instability in the law that this Court should reconsider that decision and on reconsideration abandon it."

The Burger Court still remained in no mood to reconsider *Roe* and again rebuffed the Reagan administration when handing down its 1986 ruling in *Thornburgh v. American College of Obstetricians*. A majority of the Court, moreover, appeared impatient with the administration's persistence in trying to undo *Roe*. When announcing the decision from the bench, Justice Harry Blackmun exclaimed, "We reaffirm *once again* the general principles of *Roe*." However, Chief Justice Burger broke with *Roe*'s supporters in *Thornburgh*, joining Justices O'Connor, Rehnquist, and Byron White in dissent, and indicated that *Roe* should be "reexamined."

The 5–4 split in *Thornburgh* further escalated speculation about how another Reagan appointee might affect the Court and *Roe*, and that uncertainty contributed to the bitter battle over the nomination of Judge Bork. Despite Bork's defeat, by the final days of the Reagan administration, the Rehnquist Court appeared to be moving closer to reconsidering, and possibly overturning, *Roe*. Indeed, a few weeks before the Senate confirmed Justice Kennedy, the justices split 4–4 in an abortion case, thereby affirming by an equally divided Court a lower court's ruling that struck down a law requiring parental notification for teenagers seeking abortions.[41] Subsequently, during the summer of 1988 Assistant Attorney General William Bradford Reynolds and others in Reagan's Department of Justice talked Missouri's attorney general, William Webster, into appealing an appellate court's invalidation of that state's restrictions on abortions. Webster's legal strategy was to defend Missouri's law as "nothing more than regulat[ing] abortions within the parameters allowed by *Roe v. Wade*." But he was persuaded to repeat word for word in his brief filed before the Court the language Fried had used in his *Thornburgh* brief demanding *Roe*'s reversal. And Fried again asked the Rehnquist Court to abandon *Roe*.[42] *Webster v. Reproductive Health Services* thus became the Reagan administration's parting shot at *Roe* and the Court (see chapter 6).

Changing the Law Through Regulatory Reform

Besides those in the Justice Department, Reagan brought into office others who publicly opposed abortion and worked to reform administrative regulations relating to abortion. Faced with a Congress that would not go along with him on sharply restricting the availability of abortion, the administration combined strategies of packing the federal bench and adopting restrictive abortion regulations (which would be challenged in the federal courts before Reagan judges) and thereby enabled the president to achieve much of what he had failed to persuade Congress to do.

One of Reagan's most controversial antiabortion advocates and appointees, outside the Justice Department, was Dr. C. Everett Koop. When nominated in 1981 to become surgeon general and director of the U.S. Public Health Service, Koop immediately sparked opposition from pro-choice and women's rights groups over his outspoken attacks on not only abortion but also the use of contraceptives.[43] That was precisely the kind of controversy and publicity that the Reagan administration invited and that reassured those in the antiabortion movement. Throughout his tenure, Koop courted controversy as a highly visible and outspoken champion of the antiabortion movement. When leaving office in 1989, he further stirred controversy by announcing that he would withhold from publication a long-awaited medical report that had concluded that there was little scientific evidence that abortion causes women significant physical or psychological harm.[44]

No less controversial was Reagan's secretary of Health and Human Services (HHS), Dr. Otis R. Bowen. In Reagan's first term, Bowen worked with "movement conservatives" in Congress to revise the Public Health Service Act in order to ban under its provisions funding for abortion and counseling on abortion. Defeated in that attempt and increasingly frustrated, Bowen grew bolder in the president's second term. He vigorously defended the Adolescent Family Life Act's authorizations of funds for religious organizations and restrictions on abortion funding and counseling over objections that they ran afoul of the First Amendment's establishment clause. And he successfully appealed a federal district court's holding that the act was unconstitutional because it had "the primary effect of advancing religion." In *Bowen v. Kendrick* a bare majority of the Rehnquist Court reversed the lower court and upheld the act.[45]

In 1985 Bowen sided with those in Congress who wanted to put an end to all funding for organizations that provided counseling and abortion services under Title X of the Public Health Services Act. Congress, however, reached an impasse and, unable to agree, annually passed appropriations bills for HHS that forbade funding for organizations that performed abortions but permitted federally funded family-planning organizations to offer counseling on abortion. Two years later, Bowen and the Reagan administration finally decided on an end run around Congress. He would simply issue new administrative regulations reinterpreting the HHS act so as to bar funding for organizations that performed or provided counseling on abortions. Statutes usually authorize administrative agencies to promulgate regulations implementing congressional goals embodied in legislation. Such authorization gives agencies and the executive branch enormous power to make law. Bowen, along with others in the Justice Department, also bet that when the regulations were challenged, the Rehnquist Court would uphold them.

"Abortion has no place in the Title X family planning program," proclaimed Bowen in August 1987 when announcing his proposed changes.[46] Since 1970 Congress had authorized the secretary of HHS to promulgate regulations and to make grants to public and private organizations engaged in family-planning projects. And for almost two decades organizations like the Planned Parenthood Federation of America had received grants under Title X. Even in Reagan's first four years, when HHS issued new, slightly more restrictive guidelines, grantees could still give women "non-directive[e] counseling" and abortion "referral[s] on request." Bowen's new regulations stopped that. Under the regulations, finally enacted in 1988, several controversial restrictions were imposed on organizations receiving funding under Title X. First, the regulations specified that a "Title X project may not provide counseling concerning the use of abortion as a method of family planning or provide referral for abortion as a method of family planning." Second, grant recipients were barred from engaging in activities that "encourage, promote or advance abortion as a method of family planning." Forbidden activities included lobbying for legislation that would increase the availability of abortion, developing or disseminating materials advocating abortion as a method of family planning, providing speakers to promote abortion, using legal action to make abortion available, and paying dues to any group that advocates abortion. Finally, the regulations required organizations that engaged in family planning and received federal funding to be organized so that they are "physically and financially separate" from the proscribed abortion activities.

The proposed regulations were immediately attacked as unconstitutional by members of Congress and leaders of pro-choice and women's rights groups. In protest, 33 senators and 101 representatives sent letters to Reagan. Senator Kennedy, for one, charged that "the administration seeks to accomplish by executive fiat what it has failed to achieve through the legislative process."[47] The American Civil Liberties Union's Reproductive Freedom Project issued a report attacking the regulations for turning "the Title X program from one giving neutral medical services to a major vehicle for an ideological message against abortion."[48] Not surprisingly, 8 senators and 106 House members wrote Bowen in support of the regulations. Likewise, leaders of antiabortion organizations applauded the move. Under the old regulations, the legislative director of the National Right to Life Committee, Douglas Johnson, observed, "there [was] a *de facto* merger of abortion mills and Title X facilities."[49]

In the political struggle over abortion, the stakes were raised by HHS's revised regulations. For one thing, in the mid-1980s HHS annually received about $145 million in its appropriations for the Title X program. HHS awarded about ninety grants each year to organizations like the Planned Parenthood Federation of America, the nation's largest family-planning organization, and those grantees served approximately 4.3 million women at 3900 clinics throughout the country. The overwhelming majority (an estimated 80 percent) of the women were poor, with family incomes *below* 150 percent of the federal poverty level, and nearly a third were teenagers.[50] But that was not all there was to the regulations.

In spite of almost eight years of antiabortion rhetoric, Reagan had accomplished little in curbing abortion until the promise of the HHS's revised regulations. During his eight years in office, to be sure, the ban on Medicaid funds for abortions continued and his administration extended that ban to apply to foreign health-care organizations[51] and encouraged Congress to forbid the use of public funds to finance abortions in the District of Columbia. Even so, when Reagan took office, roughly three pregnancies in ten ended in abortion and approximately 1.5 million abortions were performed each year. When Reagan left the presidency, that had not changed. Although the number of abortions annually performed remained about the same throughout the 1980s, they were increasingly provided by family-planning and abortion clinics, not public hospitals (see table 5.1).[52] *Roe* had created a market for abortion clinics, as political scientist Gerald Rosenberg argues, in eliminating most illegal abortions by making abortions legal (and safer and more readily available).[53] Abortions performed in clinics are considerably less expensive than those performed in hospitals, and clinics make abortions available to women in rural areas and areas where public hospitals refuse to perform nontherapeutic abortions. Notably, by the time the Reagan administration revised its HHS regulations, 87 percent of all abortions were performed in clinics. In short, by denying funding to organizations and clinics that offer counseling on or perform abortions, the administration aimed to put them out of business, or at least significantly reduce their number (and the number of abortions).

Although Reagan's record fell far short of his rhetoric, the abortion controversy in the 1990s bears the marks of his legacy. Reagan's attention to abortion and his rhetoric intensified the battle over abortion and gave legitimacy to the antiabortion movement. Through his judicial appointments, he went a long way toward achieving in the courts what he was unable to persuade Congress to do. As president, Reagan certainly turned the tide in the political struggle over abortion. The Rehnquist

TABLE 5.1

ABORTIONS AND ABORTION FACILITIES, SELECTED YEARS,
1973–85

Year	Number of abortions	Hospitals		Nonhospital facilities	
		Number	Percentage of all abortions performed	Number	Percentage of all abortions performed
1973	744,600	1,281	52	346	48
1975	1,034,200	1,629	40	769	60
1977	1,316,700	1,654	30	1,055	70
1979	1,497,700	1,526	23	1,208	77
1980	1,553,900	1,504	22	1,254	78
1982	1,573,900	1,405	18	1,503	83
1985	1,588,600	1,191	13	1,489	87

SOURCE: From data reported in Gerald Rosenberg, *The Hollow Hope* (Chicago: University of Chicago Press, 1991), 180, 197.

Court underscored this shift with its rulings in *Webster v. Reproductive Health Services* (which is discussed in the next chapter) and *Rust v. Sullivan,* which upheld the administration's controversial HHS restrictions on federally funded family-planning organizations and clinics (and which is further discussed in chapter 10).

In Reagan's Shadow: The Bush Presidency

George Bush changed his tune when running for the presidency in 1988. When fighting Reagan for the Republican party's nomination in 1980, he had opposed a constitutional amendment on abortion; now he called for the "criminalization of abortion." "Once the illegality [of abortion] is established," the vice president argued on the road to the White House, "then we can come to grips with the penalty side, and of course there's got to be some penalties to enforce the law, whatever they may be."[54] Doctors who perform abortions, not women who have them, Bush later declared, should suffer criminal penalties, as in the days before *Roe.*

As president, Bush stood in the long shadow cast by Reagan. His administration basically pursued the same strategies and tactics as those of Reagan's administration. Bush also copied his predecessor's strong anti-abortion rhetoric. "After years of sober and serious reflection on the issue," Bush told a March for Life rally, "I think the Supreme Court's decision in *Roe v. Wade* was wrong and should be overturned. I think America needs a human life [constitutional] amendment ... [and] I promise the president hears you now and stands with you in a cause that must be won."[55]

Bush's administration pressed Congress for a constitutional amendment on abortion no more forcefully than did Reagan's. Instead, Bush maintained administrative restrictions on abortion and looked to the federal courts to limit further the availability of abortion and to the Rehnquist Court to reverse *Roe*. In 1989 his secretary of HHS, Dr. Louis W. Sullivan, extended the Reagan administration's controversial ban on federal scientists' conducting research using fetal tissue transplants. Sullivan defended that action on the ground that "permitting the human fetal research at issue will increase the incidence of abortion across the country."[56] Bush also vetoed appropriations bills in 1990 for restoring funding for abortions for poor women in the District of Columbia made pregnant by rape or incest.

In the courts Bush's Justice Department continued along the course set by Reagan's department. Indeed, Bush brought back Reagan's solicitor general, Charles Fried, to present his administration's position on overturning *Roe* in *Webster v. Reproductive Health Services*. The tide had turned and the stage was set for the Rehnquist Court's initial confrontation with the abortion controversy.

Notes

1. Richard Nixon, "Statement about Policy on Abortions at Military Base Hospitals in the United States" (3 April 1971), *Public Papers of the Presidents of the United States, 1971* (Washington, D.C.: Government Printing Office, 1972), 127.

2. Ibid.

3. See Joseph Califano, *Governing America* (New York: Simon & Schuster, 1981), 52–53.

4. George McGovern, "Interview Statement" (7 January 1972), *Congressional Quarterly Weekly Report*, 2 September 1972, 2222.

5. George McGovern, "Speech at Fremont, Nebraska" (6 May 1972), ibid.

6. See Edward Weinstock et al., "Abortion Needs and Services in the United States, 1974–1975," *Family Planning Perspectives*, March-April 1976, 58.

7. See *Planned Parenthood of Central Missouri v. Danforth*, 428 U.S. 552 (1976), which is further discussed in chapter 3.

8. For a further discussion of Ford's appointment of Stevens, see David M. O'Brien, "The Politics of Professionalism: President Gerald R. Ford's Appointment of John Paul Stevens," *Presidential Studies Quarterly* 21 (1991): 103–27.

9. See *Congressional Quarterly Weekly Report*, 14 February 1976, 316–17.

10. Gerald Ford, *Public Papers of the Presidents of the United States, 1976–1977* (Washington, D.C.: Government Printing Office, 1979), 3: 768.

11. Quoted, *New York Times,* 21 September 1976.

12. For Califano's reflections on the abortion controversy and the Carter administration, see Califano, *Governing America,* 51–73.

13. James ("Jimmy") Carter, "Remarks and Questions and Answers at Townmeeting" (15 October 1980), *Public Papers of the Presidents of the United States, 1980–1981,* book 3 (Washington, D.C.: Government Printing Office, 1982), 2256. See also Carter's remarks at news conference (17 February 1978), *Public Papers of Presidents of the United States, 1978,* book 1 (Washington, D.C.: Government Printing Office, 1979), 362.

14. For further discussion, see *Congressional Quarterly Weekly Report,* 15 March 1980, 733–34; ibid., 9 August 1980, 2263.

15. See Ronald Reagan, "Statement on the United States Supreme Court Decision on Abortion" (16 June 1983), *Public Papers of the Presidents of the United States, 1983,* book 1 (Washington, D.C.: Government Printing Office, 1984), 876.

16. Ronald Reagan, "Remarks at the Annual Convention of the National Religious Broadcasters" (30 January 1984), *Public Papers of the Presidents of the United States, 1984,* book 1 (Washington, D.C.: Government Printing Office, 1986), 119.

17. Ronald Reagan, "State of the Union Address" (25 January 1988), *Congressional Quarterly Weekly Report,* 30 January 1988, 220, 222.

18. Ronald Reagan, "Message to Congress on America's Agenda for the Future," (6 February 1986), *Public Papers of the Presidents of the United States, 1986,* book 1 (Washington, D.C.: Government Printing Office, 1988), 157.

19. Ronald Reagan, "Remarks to Participants in the 1985 March for Life Rally," (22 January 1985), *Public Papers of the Presidents of the United States, 1985,* book 1 (Washington, D.C.: Government Printing Office, 1988), 62.

20. For further discussion, see Charles O. Jones, "Ronald Reagan and the U.S. Congress: Visible Hand Politics," in *The Reagan Legacy,* ed. Jones (Chatham, N.J.: Chatham House, 1988), 30.

21. See "Special Report: Alternatives to Abortion," *Congressional Quarterly Weekly Report,* 17 November 1984, 2949.

22. Ronald Reagan, "1984 State of the Union Address," quoted, ibid.

23. Ronald Reagan, "Message to the National Convention of the Knights of Columbus" (5 August 1986), quoted, David M. O'Brien, "The Reagan Judges: His Most Enduring Legacy?" in *The Reagan Legacy,* ed. Charles O. Jones (Chatham, N.J.: Chatham House, 1988), 60.

24. Quoted, David M. O'Brien, "Meese's Agenda for Ensuring the Reagan Legacy," *Los Angeles Times,* 28 September 1986, Opinion sec., 1.

25. Quoted, David M. O'Brien, *Judicial Roulette: The Report of the Twentieth Century Fund Task Force on the Appointment of Federal Judges* (New York: Twentieth Century Fund/Priority Press, 1988).

26. For studies of Carter's and Reagan's judicial appointments, see Larry Berkson and Susan Carbon, *The United States Circuit Judge Nominating Commission* (Chicago: American Judicature Society, 1980); Elliot Slotnick, "Lowering the Bench or Raising It Higher? Affirmative Action during the Carter Administration," *Yale Law and Policy Review* 1 (1983): 270; Sheldon Goldman,

"Reaganizing the Judiciary: The First Term Appointments," *Judicature* 68 (1985): 315.

27. See Edwin Meese, "The Attorney General's View of the Supreme Court: Toward a Jurisprudence of Original Intention," in "Law & Public Affairs, Special Issue," ed. Charles Wise and David O'Brien, *Public Administration Review* 45 (1985): 701.

28. Quoted, O'Brien, *Judicial Roulette*.

29. Based on interviews quoted and discussed, ibid.

30. Quoted, Senate Committee on the Judiciary, *Confirmation Hearings on Federal Appointments,* 95th Cong., 1st sess., 1986, pt. 2, 430.

31. Based on author's interviews; discussed in O'Brien, *Judicial Roulette*.

32. Based on data supplied to the author by the Senate Judiciary Committee and further discussed in O'Brien, *Judicial Roulette*.

33. See Donald Songer, "Consensual and Nonconsensual Decisions in Unanimous Opinions of the United States Courts of Appeals," *American Journal of Political Science* 26 (1982): 238; Sheldon Goldman, "Voting Behavior on the United States Courts of Appeals Revisited," *American Political Science Review* 60 (1975): 491.

34. Steve Alumbaugh and C.K. Rowland, "The Links between Platform-based Appointment Criteria and Trial Judges' Abortion Judgments," *Judicature* 74 (1990): 153.

35. See Senate Committee on the Judiciary, *Hearings on the Nomination of Judge Sandra Day O'Connor of Arizona to Serve as an Associate Justice of the Supreme Court of the United States,* 97th Cong., 1st sess., 1981, 57–58.

36. For a critical discussion of Justice O'Connor's confirmation hearings, see Grover Rees III, "Questions for Supreme Court Nominees at Confirmation Hearings: Excluding the Constitution," *Georgia Law Review* 17 (1983): 913. (In Reagan's second term Rees served in the Justice Department and oversaw the judicial selection process, before becoming a territorial judge.)

37. See "Who Is Bork?" *Congressional Quarterly Weekly Report,* 12 September 1987, 2164; Ethan Bronner, *Battle for Justice: How the Bork Nomination Shook America* (New York: Norton, 1989).

38. For further discussion, see Meese, "The Attorney General's View of the Supreme Court," 701; William H. Rehnquist, "The Notion of a Living Constitution," in *Views from the Bench: The Judiciary and Constitutional Politics,* ed. Mark Cannon and David O'Brien (Chatham, N.J.: Chatham House, 1985), 127; Robert Bork, "Tradition and Morality in Constitutional Law," ibid., 166.

39. *City of Akron v. Akron Center for Reproductive Health,* 462 U.S. 416 (1983); further discussed in chapters 3 and 6.

40. *Thornburgh v. American College of Obstetricians and Gynecologists,* 476 U.S. 747 (1986); further discussed in chapters 3 and 6.

41. *Hartigan v. Zbaraz,* 484 U.S. 171 (1987).

42. For further discussion of Fried's role as solicitor general in attacking *Roe,* see chapter 6; Charles Fried, *Order and Law: Arguing the Reagan Revolution—A First Hand Account* (New York: Simon & Schuster, 1991).

43. See "Senate Confirms Koop as Surgeon General," *Congressional Quarterly Weekly Report,* 21 November 1981, 2290.

44. See M. Specter, "Koop Won't Issue Report on Abortion," *Washington Post,* 10 January 1989, A1.

45. *Bowen v. Kendrick,* 487 U.S. 589 (1988).

46. Quoted, "Abortion Rules Complicate Family Planning Fight," *Congressional Quarterly Weekly Report,* 19 September 1987, 2241.

47. Quoted, "Senate Labor Oks Family-Planning Legislation, *Congressional Quarterly Weekly Report,* 14 November 1987, 2821.

48. Quoted, "Abortion Rules Complicate Family Planning Fight," 2241.

49. Ibid.

50. Ibid.

51. In 1991 the Rehnquist Court denied review to a lower court's ruling upholding the Reagan administration's 1984 restriction on federal funding of organizations that counsel on or provide abortion services abroad, in *Planned Parenthood Federation of America v. Agency for International Development,* 111 S.Ct. 335 (1991).

52. See Alan Guttmacher Institute, *Abortion 1974–1975: Need and Services in the United States, Each State and Metropolitan Area* (New York: Planned Parenthood Federation of America, 1976); Alan Guttmacher Institute, *Abortion and the Poor* (New York, 1979); Stanley Henshaw, J. Forrest, and J. Vort, "Abortion Services in the United States," *Family Planning Perspectives* 19 (1987): 63.

53. See Gerald Rosenberg, *The Hollow Hope* (Chicago: University of Chicago Press, 1991), 195.

54. Quoted, Lynn Paltrow, "A Matter of Choice," *National Law Journal,* 7 November 1988, 13.

55. Quoted, "Bush Cites Abortion 'Tragedy' in Call to 67,000 Protesters," *Washington Post,* 24 January 1989, A1.

56. Quoted, "Fetal-Tissue Research Ban Formally Extended," *Washington Post,* 3 November 1989.

The Tide Turns: The Rehnquist Court and *Webster v. Reproductive Health Services*

B y the end of the Reagan era, the Rehnquist Court loomed large in the legal and political struggles over abortion. Fifteen years after *Roe,* the Court appeared poised to reconsider, and possibly to overturn, that landmark ruling. In those years (as discussed in the previous chapter), the composition of the Court had changed dramatically. Shortly before the Senate confirmed Kennedy, moreover, the justices had split 4–4 on an appeal of a lower court ruling striking down a law requiring parental notification for teenagers seeking abortions. The justices thereby affirmed (by an equally divided Court) the ruling by the lower court, underscoring the growing division and shifting direction of the Rehnquist Court.[1]

Because only four justices must agree to grant a case review, Reagan's Department of Justice confidently bet that the high bench would be receptive to cases challenging *Roe. Roe*'s two dissenters—Rehnquist and Byron White—were now reinforced by three Reagan appointees. After the unsuccessful 1987 battle to win Senate confirmation of Bork, the Justice Department also wanted to get back at the senators and women's groups that had defeated their nominee. Persuading the Court to overturn *Roe* would constitute the crowning achievement in the department's war against liberal-judicial activism.

During the summer of 1988 Assistant Attorney General William Bradford Reynolds and others in the department encouraged Missouri's attorney general, William Webster, to seize an opportunity afforded by a federal appellate court's invalidation of that state's 1986 restrictions

Opposite: The Rehnquist Court in 1989. *Seated, left to right:* Justices Thurgood Marshall, William J. Brennan, Jr., Chief Justice William Rehnquist, Justices Byron White, Harry A. Blackmun. *Standing, left to right:* Justices Antonin Scalia, John Paul Stevens, Sandra Day O'Connor, Anthony Kennedy. *Photo:* National Geographic Society/Supreme Court Historical Society.

on abortions. Webster's legal strategy was to defend Missouri's law as simply "within the parameters allowed by *Roe v. Wade*," but he was also persuaded to repeat verbatim in his brief filed before the Court the language of the Reagan administration in its earlier brief in *Thornburgh v. American College of Obstetricians and Gynecologists*,[2] calling for the reversal of *Roe*.

At issue in *Webster v. Reproductive Health Services* was the constitutionality of four provisions of the Missouri law: (1) decreeing that life begins at conception and that "unborn children have protectable interests in life, health, and well-being"; (2) requiring the physician, before performing an abortion on a woman believed to be twenty or more weeks pregnant, to test the fetus's "gestational age, weight, and lung maturity"; (3) prohibiting public employees and facilities from being used to perform an abortion unnecessary to save the woman's life; and (4) making it unlawful to use public funds, employees, and hospitals for the purpose of "encouraging or counseling" a woman to have an abortion, except when her life is in danger.

Even more was at stake in *Webster*, however. Beyond the constitutionality of the Missouri law and the Reagan administration's systematic attack on *Roe*, *Webster* registered both changes in the Court and how the larger political struggle in the country over abortion had been transformed since *Roe*. Not only the Court but the country had changed. Groups on both sides of the abortion controversy were greater in number, more diverse yet better organized, and much more attuned to the politically strategic uses of litigation and the courts. When *Webster* came down on 3 July 1989, the Court split 5–4 on upholding the Missouri law. Although Rehnquist's opinion fell short of overturning *Roe*, a clear majority was inclined to cut back sharply, if not completely to abandon, *Roe*. The tide in constitutional law and politics was turning again.

The Missouri Law and a "Test Case" for Overturning Roe

Although Missouri's state legislators had been debating how restrictively to regulate abortions ever since *Roe*, the 1986 abortion law was the product of intense lobbying by two tireless anti-*Roe* activists: a thirty-three-year-old lawyer, Andrew Puzder, and a thirty-one-year-old former seminarian, Samuel Lee. When the Burger Court struck down the Texas abortion law in *Roe*, it also summarily—that is, without hearing oral arguments and handing down a written opinion—struck down a similar Missouri statute that made abortion a crime except when the woman's life was at stake.[3] The question for the state legislature, then, became not whether to restrict abortion but in what ways and how far that body could go after *Roe*.

Missouri enacted new abortion regulations in 1974 that required women to give written consent to their abortions and, if married, to have spousal consent for elective abortions during the first twelve weeks of pregnancy. Doctors were also required to "preserve the life and health of the fetus," regardless of the stage at which it was aborted, and certain record-keeping requirements were imposed as well. When that post-*Roe* law was challenged, the Burger Court upheld the woman's consent and the record-keeping requirements in *Planned Parenthood of Central Missouri v. Danforth*.[4] But it struck down as too restrictive both the spousal-consent provision (along with a parental-consent requirement for minors seeking abortions) and the stipulation that doctors preserve the life of the aborted fetus.

Missouri again passed new legislation on abortion in 1979. This time the state required (1) that an abortion after twelve weeks of pregnancy be performed in a hospital; (2) a pathology report on each abortion; (3) the presence of a second physician during abortions performed on women whose fetuses were viable; and (4) that minors seeking abortions secure parental or, alternatively, judicial consent.

When faced with a challenge to the Missouri 1979 abortion law in *Planned Parenthood Association of Kansas City, Missouri, Inc. v. Ashcroft*,[5] the Burger Court struck down the second-trimester hospitalization requirement but upheld all of the law's other provisions. That result and the changing composition of the bench signaled that the Court was moving in the direction of upholding more restrictive abortion laws.

In the 1980s Andrew Puzder was no newcomer to the abortion controversy in Missouri. He did not fully realize, however, that circumstances were conspiring to work in favor of the kind of attack on *Roe* that he envisioned. Puzder had first read the Court's opinions in *Roe* and other abortion cases while a student at Washington University Law School in St. Louis. He was appalled—and immediately converted to the antiabortion movement. What especially angered him was that the Court denied that life begins at conception. For him, that was the fundamental issue, and Missouri's enactment of successive restrictions on abortion after *Roe* missed the mark. Missouri's laws requiring spousal or parental consent and denying public funding for abortions simply did not go far enough.

Puzder believed that, along with setting those kinds of restrictions on abortion, Missouri should declare that "life begins at conception" and thereby directly challenge what he regarded as the primary flaw in *Roe*. He initially failed to interest many antiabortion activists in lobbying the Missouri legislature. They believed that a bill declaring "life begins at conception" would come under attack for writing into law a particular religious view and thereby violating the First Amendment's guarantee of religious freedom.

Puzder's luck changed in 1983 when Samuel Lee took his proposal seriously. At the time Lee was in jail for having participated in a sit-in at an abortion clinic, and Puzder was giving him free legal advice. They decided to work together for enactment of a law declaring that "life begins at conception." Upon Lee's release from jail, he became a coauthor of a bill embodying Putzer's phrase and its principal lobbyist.

Lee encountered the same resistance that Puzder had faced, but the two men persisted. In late 1985 they teamed up with Louis deFeo, a lobbyist for the Missouri Catholic Conference, who had been working on a proposed bill that would ban state funding for abortion and prohibit public hospitals from counseling women about abortion and from performing abortions, except when medically necessary. Puzder, Lee, and deFeo drafted a comprehensive and very tough new abortion bill, which State Senator John Schneider agreed to champion. The state chapter of Planned Parenthood doggedly fought its passage for three months, but on 23 April 1986 it was passed overwhelmingly by both chambers (see 6.1, pp. 202–3).[6]

Reproductive Health Services (a nonprofit clinic), the Planned Parenthood Federation of America, and five public health care providers immediately filed a class-action suit in a federal district court. They sought a declaratory judgment striking down provisions in the law as unconstitutional and an injunction against their enforcement. The case was heard by Chief Judge Scott O. Wright, a sixty-six-year-old appointee of President Jimmy Carter.

Almost one year later, on 30 April 1987, Wright overturned the principal provisions of Missouri's most recent (but never enforced) abortion law, including its preamble declaring that the life of each human being begins at conception and that the unborn have protectable interests in life, health, and well-being. He also held invalid the provisions (1) requiring all post-fifteen-week abortions to be performed in hospitals, for being unrelated to the state's interests in maternal health; (2) requiring doctors to conduct tests to determine whether fetuses are viable; and (3) prohibiting the expenditure of public funds for abortions, the use of public facilities for the purpose of performing abortions, and public em-

ployees from counseling women to have abortions unless necessary to
save their lives.[7]

Missouri Attorney General William Webster promptly appealed
Wright's decision to the U.S. Court of Appeals for the Eighth Circuit,
where Chief Judge Donald Lay (an appointee of Lyndon Johnson) and
Theodore McMillan and Richard Arnold (Carter appointees) affirmed
the ruling in all respects but one. Writing for the court, Lay held that the
lower court went too far in invalidating the section of the law denying
public funding for abortions not necessary to save the life of the woman.
That restriction, Lay reasoned, was permissible, given the Burger Court's
upholding similar public-funding restrictions in *Maher v. Roe*[8] and *Harris v. McRae.*[9] Lay nonetheless reaffirmed that "the Supreme Court [had]
unequivocally [held] that states cannot constitutionally impose such burdensome obstacles to what is at bottom a right *to decide* whether to terminate a pregnancy."[10]

Despite two defeats in the lower federal courts, Webster was optimis-
tic that Missouri would prevail before the Rehnquist Court. *Ashcroft* had
upheld several of Missouri's abortion restrictions and, although the 1986
abortion law was tougher, the composition of the Court had significantly
changed since that ruling had been handed down three years earlier. Besides, the Reagan administration agreed to take the lead in calling for
Roe's reversal. *Webster,* then, would be a major test of whether *Roe*
could withstand the passage of time. Not surprisingly, when *Webster*
was granted review and oral arguments were scheduled for 26 April
1989, the national debate over abortion intensified.

Pro-choice groups had been more or less quiescent in the years following *Roe* because they relied on the federal judiciary to continue to
support *Roe*'s basic holding. But as the antiabortion drumbeat grew and
the makeup of the federal bench was steadily transformed, they were
awakening to altered circumstances. The National Organization for
Women and Planned Parenthood Federation of America organized the
March for Women's Equality/Women's Lives, an April 1989 event in
Washington, D.C. But more important than that and other demonstrations in the battle over *Webster* were the strategic efforts of pro-choice
groups to orchestrate a major defense of *Roe*. In contrast to the antiabortion forces, they decided to pull together and try to retake the offensive. What had seemed impossible in the years immediately following
Roe, namely, that that decision would not stand, now did not seem such
a remote eventuality. Although pro-choice groups had lost a few cases
before the Court and seen support for *Roe* among the justices wane in
the 1980s (see 3.1, pp. 97–100), they had failed until *Webster* to confront squarely the prospect that *Roe* itself might be discarded.

| 6.1 | The Missouri 1986 Abortion Law, Excerpts (Missouri Annotated Statutes, Sections 1.205, 188.010-220) |

Section 1.205

1. The general assembly of this state finds that: (1) The life of each human being begins at conception; (2) Unborn children have protectable interests in life, health, and well-being; (3) The natural parents of unborn children have protectable interests in the life, health, and well-being of their unborn child.

2. Effective January 1, 1988, the laws of this state shall be interpreted and construed to acknowledge on behalf of the unborn child at every stage of development, all the rights, privileges, and immunities available to other persons, citizens, and residents of this state, subject only to the Constitution of the United States, and decisional interpretations thereof by the United States Supreme Court and specific provisions to the contrary in the statutes and constitution of this state.

3. As used in this section, the term "unborn children" or "unborn child" shall include all unborn child or children or the offspring of human beings from the moment of conception until birth at every stage of biological development....

Section 188.025

Every abortion performed at sixteen weeks gestational age or later shall be performed in a hospital....

Section 188.029

Before a physician performs an abortion on a woman he has reason to believe is carrying an unborn child of twenty or more weeks gestational age, the physician shall first determine if the unborn child is viable by using and exercising that degree of care, skill, and proficiency commonly exercised by the ordinarily skillful, careful, and prudent physician engaged in similar practice under the same or similar conditions. In making this determination of viability, the physician shall perform or cause to be performed such medical examinations and tests as are necessary to make a finding of the gestational age, weight, and lung maturity of the unborn child and shall enter such findings and determination of viability in the medical record of the mother. . . .

Section *188.205*

It shall be unlawful for any public funds to be expended for the purpose of performing or assisting an abortion, not necessary to save the life of the mother, or for the of encouraging or counseling a woman to have an abortion not necessary to save her life.

Section *188.210*

It shall be unlawful for any public employee within the scope of his employment to perform or assist an abortion, not necessary to save the life of the mother. It shall be unlawful for a doctor, nurse or other health care personnel, a social worker, a counselor or persons of similar occupation who is a public employee within the scope of his public employment to encourage or counsel a woman to have an abortion not necessary to save her life.

Section *188.215*

It shall be unlawful for any public facility to be used for the purpose of performing or assisting an abortion not necessary to save the life of the mother or for the purpose of encouraging or counseling a woman to have an abortion not necessary to save her life.

The Planned Parenthood Federation of America, a party in *Webster,* and the American Civil Liberties Union, which acted as cocounsel, immediately hired an *amici* brief coordinator, Kathryn Kolbert. An otherwise solo practitioner who formerly had worked for the Women's Law Project, Kolbert later described her job as "air traffic controller" for the growing number of groups that felt threatened by the possible reversal of *Roe.*

In contrast, despite their becoming more numerous, vocal, and better organized throughout the 1980s, antiabortion groups failed to coordinate their assault on *Roe.* They had, however, an influential ally: the Reagan and Bush administrations' Department of Justice. And lists of groups filing briefs, along with summaries of their arguments, informally circulated among the groups. "But no one was told not to do anything," recalls the counsel for the National Right to Life Committee, James Bopp. Nor, adds Bopp, was there "any attempt to get drafts together and merge and purge."[11]

The Politics of Interest-Group Litigation

The politics of interest-group litigation and how it had changed since *Roe v. Wade* was registered in the record number of *amici curiae* briefs filed in *Webster.* Together, seventy-eight *amici* briefs were filed in *Webster,* representing a broad range of interests, thousands of individuals, more than 300 organizations, and various coalitions forged over conflicting interpretations of law, history, science, and medicine. The total was twenty more than that filed in the previous Court record holder, *Regents of the University of California v. Bakke,*[12] the only slightly less controversial 1978 reverse-discrimination case in which 120 organizations joined in fifty-eight *amici* briefs.

The Battle of the Briefs—The Attack on *Roe*

When *Roe* had been argued almost twenty years earlier, only six *amici* briefs were filed in defense of the Texas law and in opposition to extending privacy to protect a woman's decision with regard to abortion. In contrast, in addition to an *amici* brief filed by Reagan's former solicitor general, Charles Fried, for the Bush administration, *Webster* was supported by forty-six others (see table 6.1). Among them were briefs for the Knights of Columbus, Catholics for Life, the National Legal Foundation, the Catholic League for Religious and Civil Rights, the Association for Public Justice, and the American Association of Pro Life Obstetricians and Gynecologists. Another was submitted for 250 state

TABLE 6.1

FILERS OF *AMICUS CURIAE* BRIEFS IN SUPPORT OF APPEL-
LANTS, WILLIAM L. WEBSTER, ATTORNEY GENERAL
OF THE STATE OF MISSOURI

6 United States Senators and 50 U.S. Representatives

9 United States Senators and 45 U.S. Representatives

127 Members of the Missouri General Assembly

260 State Legislators

Alabama Lawyers for Unborn Children

American Academy of Medical Ethics

American Association of Pro Life Obstetricians and Gynecologists

American Association of Pro-Life Pediatricians

American Baptist Friends of Life

American Collegians for Life

American Family Association

American Life League

Association for Public Justice

Attorneys General of Arizona, Idaho, Louisiana, Pennsylvania, and Wisconsin

Baptists for Life

Birthright

Catholic Health Association of the United States

Catholic Lawyers Guild of the Archdiocese of Boston

Catholic League for Religious and Civil Rights

Catholics United for Life

Center for Judicial Studies

Certain Members of the General Assembly of the Commonwealth of Pennsylvania

Christian Action Council

Christian Advocates Serving Evangelism

Christian Life Commission of the Southern Baptist Convention

Covenant House and Good Counsel

Doctors for Life

Elliot Institute for Social Sciences Research

Family Research Council of America

Feminists for Life of America

Focus on the Family

Free Speech Advocates

Holy Orthodox Church

Human Life International

International Right to Life Federation

Knights of Columbus

Lawyers for Life

Let Me Live

Lutheran Church–Missouri Synod

Lutherans for Life

Missouri Catholic Conference

Missouri Citizens for Life

Missouri Doctors for Life

Missouri Nurses for Life

Moravians for Life

National Association of Evangelicals

National Association of Pro-Life Nurses

National Legal Foundation

National Organization of Episcopalians for Life

National Right to Life Committee

New England Christian Action Council

Presbyterians Pro-Life

Right to Life Advocates

Right to Life League of Southern California

Rutherford Institute and the Rutherford Institutes of Alabama, Arkansas, California, Colorado, Connecticut, Florida, Georgia, Kentucky, Michigan, Minnesota, Montana, Nebraska, Ohio, Pennsylvania, Tennessee, Texas, Virginia, and West Virginia

Southern Baptists for Life

Southern Center for Law and Ethics

Southwest Life and Law Center

Task Force of United Methodists on Abortion and Sexuality

United Church of Christ Friends for Life

United States Catholic Conference

United States Government

Value of Life Committee

Austin Vaughn and Crusade for Life

Women Exploited by Abortion of Greater Kansas City

legislators, and two more for members of Congress asking that *Roe* be overturned.

Although the groups and organizations supporting *Webster* were not quite as well organized as those supporting *Roe,* they presented virtually every kind of argument against the bases and sources that had been relied on by Justice Blackmun in *Roe.* Some attacked the value of precedent and stressed their view of the proper role of the Court; others urged that the Court return the regulation of abortion to state and local governments.

Pro Life Obstetricians and Gynecologists, for instance, asserted that medical science now acknowledged that life begins at conception. Catholic lawyers argued that *Roe*'s trimester approach denied the human dignity of the unborn and violated "natural law." The National Right to Life Committee—one of the largest and most influential antiabortion groups in the country— focused on the Court's standards for reviewing the Missouri law and urged the justices to uphold its provisions. The 250 state legislators urged the Court to return power to the states to regulate abortion fully and to protect the unborn.

As the abortion controversy intensified in the late 1980s, members of Congress became as divided as their constituents on both tactical and substantive responses to *Roe.* Opponents of *Roe* were also forced to clarify their stands in reaction to the crosscutting pressures. In 1985, for instance, when the Burger Court was considering a challenge to the Pennsylvania abortion law and the Reagan administration first pressed for reconsideration of *Roe* in *Thornburgh v. American College of Obstetricians and Gynecologists,* thirteen senators and sixty-nine representatives had joined a brief advocating *Roe*'s reversal but stopped short of asking the Court to declare that "life begins at conception" or that fetuses are constitutionally protected persons under the Fourteenth Amendment. For the Court to take that position, even some leading conservatives like Utah's Republican Senator Orrin Hatch conceded, would be the same kind of "judicial activism" that many lamented in *Roe. Roe* had taken the abortion question, for a time at least, out of the hands of Congress and state legislatures; so too would a ruling assigning constitutionally protected personhood to the unborn. By 1989 Hatch and some other conservatives in Congress were taking the position that the Fourteenth Amendment admitted no such construction.

By the time the Rehnquist Court considered *Webster,* then, members of Congress were split on whether to ask the Court (1) to return the abortion controversy to the states by simply overruling *Roe* in deference to principles of federalism, or (2) to go further than overruling *Roe* and assign constitutional personhood to the unborn. Notably, only nine senators and forty-five representatives, including Georgia's Newt Gingrich, joined in a brief that pressed the Court in the latter direction. Six senators and fifty representatives joined in a brief filed by the Center for Judicial Studies that asserted the principles of federalism.[13] Table 6.2 lists senators signing 1985 and 1989 antiabortion briefs, and shows some position changes.

TABLE 6.2
SENATORS SIGNING ANTIABORTION BRIEFS, 1985 AND 1989

Senators	*1985 Brief*[a]	*1989 Brief*[b]	*1989 Brief*[c]
J. Abdnor (R-South Dakota)	☒		
W. Armstrong (R-Colorado)		☒	
C. Bond (R-Missouri)		☒	
D. Coats (R-Indiana)			☒
A. D'Amato (R-New York)			☒
J. Danforth (R-Missouri)			☒
D. Durenberger (R-Minnesota)	☒		
J. Garn (R-Utah)		☒	
P. Gramm (R-Texas)	☒		
C. Grassley (R-Iowa)	☒		
O. Hatch (R-Utah)	☒		
M. Hatfield (R-Oregon)	☒		
J. Helms (R-North Carolina)			☒
G. Humphrey (R-New Hampshire)	☒		☒
B. Kasten (R-Wisconsin)	☒		
T. Lott (R-Mississippi)			☒
J. McClure (R-Idaho)	☒		
M. McConnell (R-Kentucky)		☒	
C. Mack (R-Florida)			☒
D. Nickles (R-Oklahoma)	☒		☒
H. Reid (D-Nevada)			☒
S. Symms (R-Idaho)	☒	☒	
S. Thurmond (R-South Carolina)	☒	☒	

a. Unborn are persons in some respects.
b. Let states decide.
c. Unborn are persons.

Excerpts of representative arguments from the antiabortion *amici* briefs filed in *Webster* follow here:

American Association of Pro Life Obstetricians and Gynecologists and the American Association of Pro-Life Pediatricians —

Medical science affirms that human life begins at conception. This is the traditional understanding of American medicine since at least the early nineteenth century. The unborn child who is adversely affected by alcohol in the first month of pregnancy is the same child who suffers intellectual disabilities at four years. Since the time of the *Roe* Court's pronouncements about the potentiality of human life, a new medical discipline has emerged: fetology. This science treats the unborn child as a distinct patient....

Medical technology for the child *in utero* has advanced greatly, developing surgery and treatment for previously untreatable conditions. Medical technology also has moved the line of viability earlier in the pregnancy. In *Roe,* the Court found that "[v]iability is usually placed at about seven months (28 weeks) but may occur earlier, even at 24 weeks." Viability may now occur as early as twenty-two weeks, with substantial potential of viability at twenty-four weeks. Missouri may take into account these tremendous advances in medical science and technology and regulate to protect those fetuses who may survive the abortion procedure....

Catholic Lawyers Guild of the Archdiocese of Boston —

The trimester approach provided in *Roe v. Wade,* and relied upon by the court of appeals, does not provide a conceptually accurate or workable framework for analyzing either society's or women's interests regarding abortion. The trimester approach is premised on the existence of determinate and definable "stages" of fetal life development which have been invalidated by advances in medical technologies. In addition, the concept of trimesters or life "stages" is itself inherently arbitrary, because fetal development progresses in a continuum and because neither medicine, philosophy, nor law otherwise attribute identifiable, distinguishable or qualitative significance to any particular "stages" of fetal development.

The determination that life has variant comparative values at different stages of fetal development, that variant comparative values may be allocated to life according to temporal criteria, and that innocent life may be deliberately terminated at an early stage of temporal development violates principles of Natural Law. In this regard, the authority of Natural Law is supreme, the character of life is unalienable, and the nature of the privacy interests implicated are necessarily qualified. . . .

The Honorable Christopher H. Smith, the Honorable Alan B. Mollohan, the Honorable John C. Danforth, and other United States Senators —

The doctrines of *Roe* have caused great instability and unpredictability in the law, such that reversal is necessary to restore an appropriate balance. Reversal of *Roe* would also be consistent with past willingness to admit error. This Court has corrected decisions which, like *Roe,* have misinterpreted the "liberty" clause of the Fourteenth Amendment to place an undue strait-jacket on legislative authority. And it has renounced the role of "super-legislature," sitting in judgment on the wisdom of state statutes. . . .

National Right to Life Committee —

The necessary first step in the judicial review of the Missouri statutes at issue herein is to determine the appropriate standard of review. Without resolution of this threshold issue, the Court will be uncertain what constitutional analysis to employ, whether a low level of scrutiny, strict scrutiny, or some intermediate standard. . . .

The Court should confront directly the necessary threshold issue of the standard of review. In doing so, the Court should be guided by the analysis of *Bowers v. Hardwick,* 478 U.S. 186 (1986) (which upheld Georgia's sodomy law over claims to constitutionally protected privacy interests in what consenting adults do in their bedrooms), and find that there is no constitutional right to abortion. Thus, the standard of review to be employed herein should be the rational basis test. An attempt to establish an intermediate standard of review would also result in undesirable results. The only lasting resolution of the matter is to overrule *Roe* completely and allow the states to resolve the matter through the mechanisms of the democratic process.

Knights of Columbus —

As a practical matter, *Roe*'s analytical framework is flawed beyond repair because it rests on "viability"—the point at which an unborn child can survive outside of the womb with artificial aid—to determine when a state may protect the life of "the developing young in the human uterus." As Justice O'Connor has pointed out, because viability is almost solely defined by ever-progressing technology, it is a constantly moving point that cannot be a neutral and stable basis for long-term constitutional adjudication.

More fundamentally, viability is an invalid benchmark for construing the meaning of "person" in the Fourteenth Amendment because it has nothing to do with attributes of personhood, or a particularized state of being, but only the state of medical technology. Viability's true utility lies in its insight that a viable infant is certainly a person and that only limitations on technology prevent all unborn children from being viable. If a "viable" unborn child is a person, then so are all unborn children, viable or not....

[T]his Court's understanding of the word "person" has been flexible enough to hold business corporations to be Fourteenth Amendment "persons." If the word can extend the fundamental protections of law to "beings" that are mere legal constructs, no rule of interpretation or principle of law can justify excluding unborn human beings....

Certain State Legislators —

The Court's historical excursus [in Roe] was seriously flawed and failed to take into account the medical and technological context in which the law of abortion evolved. As this brief attempts to demonstrate, both the English common law, as received by the American states, and the anti-abortion statutes enacted by state legislatures in the nineteenth century, sought to protect unborn human life to the extent that contemporary medical science could establish the existence of that life. This evidence undermines the foundations of Roe and suggests that abortion has never been regarded as a "right" in English or American law. Accordingly, abortion cannot be considered a "fundamental right" under the Constitution....

Center for Judicial Studies and Certain (56) Members of Congress —

The Center for Judicial Studies ... is the only educational and public policy organization in the United States that focuses exclusively on the problem of judicial activism.... The Center seeks to confine the power of the federal judiciary to the bounds envisioned by the Framers of the Constitution and of the Fourteenth Amendment. Individual Amici are members of the Congress of the United States. They are concerned about the fact that *Roe v. Wade* has expanded federal judicial powers into areas that are within the rightful legislative domain of Congress and the states. This expansion has adversely affected the constitutional allocation of powers between the judicial and legislative branches and between the states and the federal government. It has effectively prevented both the Congress and the states from implementing sound legislative solutions to abortion issues. . . .

Catholics United for Life, National Organization of Episcopalians for Life, Presbyterians Pro-Life, American Baptist Friends of Life, Baptists for Life, Southern Baptists for Life, Lutherans for Life, Moravians for Life, United Church of Christ Friends for Life, Task Force of United Methodists on Abortion and Sexuality, and the Christian Action Council —

Contrary to *Roe,* history, science, logic, law, and justice all weigh in favor of including unborn children within the protection of the fourteenth amendment. The framers of that amendment clearly drew no distinction between "persons" and biological "human beings." Science demonstrates that each individual member of the human race begins life at the moment of fertilization. Logic supports no essential distinction between human beings on the basis of their dwelling inside or outside the maternal womb, or on the basis of their status as "viable" or "nonviable" individuals. Legal consistency supports the rejection of distinctions, in matters of basic rights, between born and unborn children, as well as between "viable" and "nonviable" unborn children. Finally, the intrinsic sanctity of every human life compels the rejections of any arbitrary exclusion of unborn children from entitlement to the most basic of human rights. . . .

On the Rebound and in Defense of *Roe*

Central to the *amici* strategy of pro-choice groups was the structuring of briefs so as to counter systematically every argument marshaled in the briefs of the antiabortion forces. Distinguished scientists were recruited as signatories to a brief rebutting the contention that medical science could establish that "life begins at conception." Another brief, signed by 281 historians, took to task the Justice Department's assertion that when the Fourteenth Amendment was adopted (1868), abortion had not been considered a fundamental right. The department had cited James Mohr's leading historical work, *Abortion in America: The Origins and Evolution of National Policy,* but Mohr objected to the Department of Justice's selective citation of his work and joined the historians' brief.[14] Other briefs tried to drive home the import of preserving the liberty of women to control their bodies and reproductive organs; presented data on abortion rates, illegal and legal, before and after *Roe,* as well as comparative national data; and detailed the impact that the recriminalizing of abortion would have on minority women. (The groups filing pro-choice briefs in defense of *Roe* in the case of *Webster* are listed in table 6.3, pp. 214–18.)

Excerpts of representative arguments from the pro-choice *amici* briefs filed in defense of *Roe* in the case of *Webster* follow here:

167 Distinguished Scientists and Physicians, Including 11 Nobel Laureates —

Amici have observed that appellants and some *amici* urging that *Roe v. Wade* be overruled have purported to ground their arguments, in part, upon alleged scientific "truth." For example, appellants characterize the proposition that life begins at conception as a "biological fact," comparable to the "truth" that the "Earth still moves around the sun." Other *amici* aligned with appellants have asserted that subsequent advancements in science since *Roe v. Wade* was decided have rendered the decision obsolete.

There is no scientific consensus that a human life begins at conception, at a given stage of fetal development, or at birth. The question of "when life begins" cannot be answered by reference to scientific principles like those with which we predict planetary movement. The answer to that question will depend on each individual's social, religious, philosophical, ethical and moral beliefs and values.

Science can, however, provide answers to certain concrete questions regarding prenatal development that have arisen in the controversy over abortion and *Roe v. Wade....*

The earliest point of viability has remained virtually unchanged at approximately 24 weeks of gestation since 1973, and there is no reason to believe that a change is either imminent or inevitable. The reason that viability has not been pushed significantly back toward the point of conception is that critical organs, particularly lungs and kidneys, do not mature before that time. Progress in science, therefore, has not made obsolete the trimester framework based on viability articulated in *Roe v. Wade.* The trimester framework, moreover, corresponds with another aspect of fetal development—the chronology of human brain development. Not until after 28 weeks of gestation does the fetus attain sufficient neocortical complexity to exhibit those sentient capacities that are present in full-term newborns. In lay terms, the capacity for the human thought process as we know it cannot exist until sometime after 28 weeks of gestation.

This Court's decision in *Roe v. Wade* is as well grounded in "biological justifications" today as in 1973, and the basic chronology of human development recognized in the Court's opinion remains accurate. Accordingly, the Court should reject arguments for overruling the decision because of alleged inconsistency with scientific advancement or "truth."

Bioethicists for Privacy —

The abortion cases are not just about abortion, but about the very basis of what it means to be a free person in a free society. If the state can make reproductive decisions on behalf of any individual, what decision is it precluded from making? If legislatures are allowed to impose without restraint value judgments that deeply and directly affect individual citizens, what is left of personal freedom? Without the right of privacy, what constitutional principle would prevent states from reimposing restrictions on contraceptive distribution and use, since unfertilized ova constitute *potential* human life? ...

281 American Historians —

Abortion was not uncommon in colonial America. Herbal abortifacients were widely known, and cookbooks and women's diaries of the era contained recipes for medicines. Recent studies of the work of midwives in the 1700s report cases in which the midwives provided women abortifacient compounds. More significantly, these cases are described as routine and are unaccompanied by any particular disapproval....

Through the nineteenth century and well into the twentieth, abortion remained a widely accepted popular practice, despite increasing vigorous efforts to prohibit it after 1860. Changing patterns of abortion practice and attitudes towards it can only be understood against a more general background of dramatic change in American economic and family life. During the period between ratification of the Constitution and adoption of the Civil War Amendments, Americans moved to cities and increasingly worked for wages. In 1787, the average white American woman bore seven children; by the later 1870s, the average was down to fewer than 5; by 1900 it was 3.56.

For most of the nineteenth century, abortion was highly visible. "Be-

TABLE 6.3

FILERS OF *AMICUS CURIAE* BRIEFS IN SUPPORT OF
APPELLEES, REPRODUCTIVE HEALTH SERVICES

25 United States Senators and 111 United States Representatives
167 Distinguished Scientists and Physicians, Including 11 Nobel Laureates
281 American Historians
608 State Legislators from 32 States
(2887) Women Who Have Had Abortions and (627) Friends
80% Majority Campaign
A Group of American Law Professors
A Woman's Place
Abortion Rights Council
Abortion Rights Mobilization
Abuse and Rape Crisis Center
ActionAIDS
Agudath Israel of America
AIDS Education Task Force
Alan Guttmacher Institute
Albuquerque Monthly Meeting of Religious Society of Friends
Alliance Against Women's Oppression
All-Peoples Congress
American Academy of Child and Adolescent Psychiatry
American Academy of Pediatrics
American Association of University Women

American Civil Liberties Union
American College of Obstetricians and Gynecologists
American College of Preventive Medicine
American Federation of State, County and Municipal Employees
American Fertility Society
American Friends Service Committee
American Humanist Association
American Indian Health Care Association
American Jewish Congress
American Library Association and Freedom to Read Foundation
American Medical Association
American Medical Women's Association
American Nurses Association
American Psychiatric Association
American Psychological Association
American Public Health Association
American Society of Human Genetics
American Veterans Committee
Americans for Democratic Action
Americans for Religious Liberty

Americans United for Separation of Church and State
Anti-Defamation League of B'nai B'rith
Arizona Attorneys Action Council
Asian American Legal Defense and Education Fund
Association of Latino Attorneys
Association of Reproductive Health Professionals
Association of Sex Educators and Therapists
Attorneys General of the States of California, Colorado, Massachusetts, New York, Texas, Vermont, and West Virginia
Beverly Hills Bar Association
Bioethicists for Privacy
Black Women's Agenda
Board of Homeland Ministries—United Church of Christ
Boston Women's Health Book Collective
Bridge Partnership Project, RCAR of Illinois
Brooklyn Pro-Choice Network
Brooklyn Women's Martial Arts
Brooklyn YWCA
Bronx National Organization for Women
Buffalo Lawyers for Choice

TABLE 6.3 — *Continued*

California Alliance Concerned with School Age Children

California National Organization for Women

California Physicians for Choice

California Republicans for Choice

California Women Lawyers

Canadian Women's Organizations

Cathedral Church of St. John the Divine

Catholics for a Free Choice

Cedar Rapids Clinic for Women

Center for Constitutional Rights

Center for Law and Social Justice

Center for Population Options

Center for Women Policy Studies

Centre County Women's Resource Center

Centre de Sante des Femmes

Chairman of the Yale University Department of Epidemiology and Public Health

Chicago Catholic Women

Child Care Law Center

Chinatown History Project

CHOICE

Choice Network of Tarrant County, Texas

Choices Women's Medical Center

City of New York

Coalition of 100 Black Women of D.C.

Coalition of Labor Union Women

Columbia Law Women's Association

Columbia-Greene Rape Crisis Center

Comision Femenil Mexicana Nacional

Commission on Social Action of Reformed Judaism

Committee for Hispanic Children and Families

Committee of Interns and Residents

Committee of Women of Color, Presbyterian Church (USA)

Committee on Civil Rights, Medicine and Law of the Association of the Bar of the City of New York

Committee on Sex and Law of the Association of the Bar of the City of New York

Committee on Women's Rights of the New York County Lawyers' Association

Committee to Defend Reproductive Rights

Commonwealth of Massachusetts, Department of Public Health

Communications Workers of America, Local 1180

Connecticut Women's Educational and Legal Fund

D.C. Feminists Against Pornography

D.C. Rape Crisis Center

Dean of the Columbia University School of Public Health

Dean of the University of California, Berkeley School of Public Health

Dean of the University of Washington School of Public Health and Community Medicine

Disabled in Action of Metropolitan New York

District 65, UAW, Technical, Office, and Professional Division

District Attorney of Kings County, New York

Education Committee of 100 Black Men of Los Angeles

Episcopal Diocese of Massachusetts— Women in Crisis Committee

Episcopal Diocese of New York

Episcopal Women's Caucus

Equal Rights Advocates

Federally Employed Women

Federation of Feminist Women's Health Centers

Federation of Reconstructionist Congregations and Havurot

Feminist Health Center of Portsmouth

(*Continued* ...)

TABLE 6.3 — *Continued*

Feminist Institute
Feminist Women's
  Health Center
Ferre Institute
Fox Valley Reproductive
  Health Care Center
Fresno Free College
  Foundation
Fund for New
  Leadership
Gay Men's Health Crisis
Gay and Lesbian
  Democrats of America
General Board of
  Church and Society
  —The United
  Methodist Church
Harvard Women's Law
  Association
Hawaii Women Lawyers
Hawaii Women Lawyers
  Foundation
Hispanic Health Council
Human Rights Cam-
  paign Fund
Illinois Women's Agenda
Institute of Women
  Today
International Center for
  Research on Women
International Women's
  Health Organizations
Institute for Community
  Research
Institute for Women's
  Policy Research
International Agency for
  Minority Artist Affairs
Jesse Smith Noyes
  Foundation
Jewish Labor Committee
Judicial Consent for
  Minors Referral Panel
Judson Memorial
  Church

Juvenile Law Center
Junior League of
  Brooklyn
Lambda Legal Defense
  and Education Fund
Latinos Contra SIDA
Lawyers Club of San
  Diego
Lawyers for Reproduc-
  tive Rights
League of Women
  Voters of Missouri
League of Women
  Voters of the United
  States
Los Angeles Feminist
  Women's Health
  Center
Los Angeles Gay and
  Lesbian Scientists
Metro D.C. Coalition
  for Choice
Mexican American Legal
  Defense and Education
  Fund
Mexican American
  Women's National As-
  sociation
Michigan Republicans
  for Choice
Minority Prison Project
Missouri Women's Net-
  work
Mobilization for Youth
  Health Services
Ms. Foundation for
  Women
My Sister's Place
NA'MAT
The Nation Institute
National Abortion
  Rights Action League
National Action Forum
  for Midlife and Older
  Women

National Assembly of
  Religious Women
National Association of
  Nurse Practitioners in
  Reproductive Health
National Association of
  Public Hospitals
National Association of
  Socialist Workers
National Association of
  Women Lawyers
National Black Women's
  Health Project
National Center for
  Lesbian Rights
National Conference of
  Black Lawyers
National Coalition
  Against Domestic Vio-
  lence
National Coalition of
  American Nuns
National Committee to
  Free Sharon Kowalski
National Conference of
  Women's Bar Associa-
  tions
National Council for
  Research on Women
National Council of
  Jewish Women
National Council of
  Negro Women
National Education As-
  sociation
National Family Plan-
  ning and Reproductive
  Health Association
National Federation of
  Business and Profes-
  sional Women's Clubs
National Federation of
  Temple Sisterhoods
National Gay & Lesbian
  Task Force

TABLE 6.3 — *Continued*

National Gay Rights Advocates
National Institute for Women of Color
National Jewish Community Relations Advisory Council
National Latina Health Organization
National Lawyers Guild
National Minority AIDS Council
National Organization for Women
National Organization of Legal Services Workers
National Rainbow Coalition, New York State Chapter
National Society of Genetic Counselors
National Urban League
National Women's Abuse Prevention Project
National Women's Conference Committee
National Women's Health Network
National Women's Law Center
National Women's Political Caucus
National Women's Political Caucus, New York State Chapter
National Women's Studies Association
National Writers Union
Native American Community Board
New Directions for Women
New Hampshire Women's Lobby

New Jewish Agenda
The Newspaper Guild
New York Asian Women's Center
New York Gray Panthers
New York Pro-Choice Coalition
New York State Coalition Against Domestic Violence
New York State Coalition on Women's Legal Issues
New York State Republican Family Committee
New York University Law Women
New York Women Against Rape
New York Women in Criminal Justice
North American Federation of Temple Youth
North Carolina Association of Women Attorneys
North Carolina Equity
Northwest Women's Law Center
NOW Legal Defense and Education Fund
Nurses' Association of the American College of Obstetricians and Gynecologists
Oakhurst Presbyterian Church
Organizacion Nacional De La Salud De La Mujer Latina
Organization of Asian Women
Organization of Pan-Asian American Women

People for the American Way
Permanent Commission on the Status of Hartford Women
Planned Parenthood of Atlanta Area
Population-Balance
Population Communication
The Presbyterian Church (U.S.A.)
Project AWARE
Project Choice: AIDS Education for Co-dependent Women of Color
Public Employee Department, AFL-CIO
Puerto Rican Committee Against Repression
Puerto Rican Legal Defense and Education Fund
Queen's Bench of the San Francisco Bay Area
Radical Women
Rainbow Lobby
Religious Coalition for Abortion Rights
Rockland Family Shelter
St. Louis Catholics for Choice and 30 Other Religious Organizations
San Francisco Women Lawyers Alliance
San Francisco Women's Centers/Women's Building
San Jose–South Bay Chapter, National Organization for Women

(*Continued* ...)

TABLE 6.3 — *Continued*

Santa Barbara Women's Political Committee
Santa Fe Health Education Project
Sex Information and Education Counsel of the United States
Sierra Club
Society for Adolescent Medicine
Staff at Domestic Violence Center of Chester County, Pennsylvania
Stop Abuse for Everyone
Students and Youth Against Racism
Toledo Women's Bar Association
Tucson Women's Commission
Union of American Hebrew Congregations
Unitarian Universalist Association
Unitarian Universalists Women's Association
United Church of Christ Coordinating Center for Women
United Church of Christ Office of Church in Society
United Electrical, Radio and Machine Workers of America
United Labor Action
United Probation Officers Association
Urban League of Greater Hartford
Voters for Choice/ Friends of Family Planning
Washington Ethical Action Center for the American Ethical Union

Washington Women United
Wider Opportunities for Women
Women in Ministry— Garrett Evangelical Seminary
Women in Mission and Ministry—Episcopal Church U.S.A.
Women Employed
Women for Racial and Economic Equality
Women in Film
Women In Spirit of Colorado Task Force
Women of All Red Nations, Minnesota
Women of All Red Nations, North Dakota
Women of Color Partnership Program of the Religious Coalition for Abortion Rights
Womancare Clinic
Women's Action Alliance
Women's Agenda
Women's AIDS Prevention Project
Women's Bar Association of Illinois
Women's Bar Association of Massachusetts
Women's Bar Association of the State of New York
Women's Center of the University of Connecticut
Women's City Club of New York
Women's Equal Rights Legal Defense and Education Fund

Women's Equity Action League
Women's Equity Affiliates
Women's International Resource Exchange
Women's International League for Peace and Freedom
Women's Law Association of the Washington College of Law of the American University
Women's Law Center
Women's Law Project
Women's Lawyers' Association of Los Angeles
Women's League for Conservative Judaism
Women's Legal Defense Fund
Women's Medical Fund
Women's Project
Women's Rights Coalition
Women's Studies Program, Hunter College
World Population Society
Worldwatch Institute
Workers World Party
Yale Journal of Law and Feminism
YWCA of Greater Pittsburgh
YWCA of the Hartford Region
YWCA of the National Capitol Area
YWCA of the U.S.A.
Zero Population Growth

ginning in the early 1840s abortion became, for all intents and purposes, a business, a service openly traded in the free market.... [Pervasive advertising told Americans] not only that many practitioners would provide abortion services, but that some practitioners had made the abortion business their chief livelihood. Indeed, abortions became one of the first specialties in American medical history." [Quoting James Mohr, *Abortion in America: The Origins and Evolution of National Policy* (1978).]

Between 1850 and 1880, the newly formed American Medical Association, through some of its vigorously active members, became the *"single most important factor in altering the legal policies toward abortion in this country."* Nineteenth-century "regular" physicians enlisted state power to limit access to abortion for reasons that are, in retrospect, parochial, and have long since been rejected by organized medicine. The doctors found an audience for their effort to restrict abortion because they appealed to broader concerns: maternal health, consumer protection, a discriminatory idea of the natural subordination of women, nativist fears generated by the fact that elite Protestant women often sought abortions. Some of those seeking these diverse objectives also sought to attribute moral status to the fetus....

The American Medical Association's campaign [in the nineteenth century] to restrict access to abortion succeeded for many reasons. Concerns over the dangers of surgical abortion to women were well founded. Further, physicians persuaded male political leaders that "abortion constituted a threat to social order and to male authority." Since the 1840s, a growing movement for women's suffrage and equality had generated popular fears that women were departing from their purely maternal role. These fears were fueled by the fact that family size declined sharply in the nineteenth century....

Nativism, notably anti-Catholicism, had been part of American politics and culture as early as the Jacksonian period. The Civil War and Reconstruction Era dramatically raised consciousness about national identity and citizenship. Social conservatives in the 1850s articulated an "organicist" ideal in which social unity would predominate over diversity. By the 1870s social thought was turning the insights of Charles Darwin toward racist ends.... The discriminatory immigration policies and nativist fears of the late nineteenth and early twentieth centuries had their roots in a far earlier period, when Americans first became concerned about the creation of an urban population of wage workers....

In the first half of the twentieth century, a two-tiered abortion system emerged in which services depended on the class, race, age and residence of the woman. Poor and rural women obtained illegal abortions, performed by people, physicians and others, who were willing to defy the law out of sympathy for the women or for the fee. More privileged women steadily pressed physicians for legal abortions and many obtained them. . . .

In the 1950s, more restrictive attitudes toward both legal and illegal abortions were part of a conservative response to growing female labor-force participation and independence. The 1960s movement to legalize abortion arose in response to this, rather brief, wave of anti-abortion enforcement. . . .

As a number of states acted to legalize abortion, additional concerns heightened pressure for recognition of constitutional protection for the basic right of abortion choice. Debate over abortion, now revolving around insoluble metaphysical disputes about the moral status of the fetus, preoccupied state legislatures and often prevented them from addressing other vital issues. Class and regional differentiations were accentuated as it became possible for women with resources to travel to states where abortion was legal. In *Roe v. Wade,* this Court responded to all of these forces in holding that constitutional rights of liberty and privacy protect the right of the woman and her physician to choose abortion. . . .

[F]or two core reasons, this Court should reject state efforts to invoke the protection of fetal life to justify restrictions upon women's access to abortion.

First, as this brief has demonstrated, the complex historic grounds for restricting access to abortion are now either socially irrelevant or recognized as constitutionally illegitimate. . . .

Second, and decisively, this Court must affirm *Roe v. Wade,* and reject asserted state interests in protecting prenatal life, because the costs of denying constitutional protection to abortion choice are simply too enormous. Our experience from the 1890s until 1973 amply demonstrates that if women are denied access to legal abortions, many will turn in desperation to self-abortion, folk remedies, or illegal practitioners. Many will die. Others will suffer permanent damage to their reproductive capacity. Still others will bear children for whom they cannot provide adequate care. Apart from these devastating consequences to the lives and health of women, restricting access to abortion will again deny the fundamental legitimacy of women as moral decision-makers.

National Council of Negro Women; National Urban League; American Indian Health Care Association; Asian American Legal Defense Fund; Committee for Hispanic Children and Families; Mexican American Legal Defense and Education Fund; National Black Women's Health Project; National Institute for Women of Color; National Women's Health Network; Organization Nacional De La Salud De Mujer Latina; Organization of Asian Women; Puerto Rican Legal Defense and Education Fund; Women of Color Partnership Program of the Religious Coalition for Abortion Rights; Women of All Red Nations, North Dakota; YWCA of the U.S.A.; and Other Organizations —

> While women of all classes and colors will be endangered by any dismantling of the constitutional framework of *Roe v. Wade,* the burden will fall most heavily and inexorably on poor women, a vastly disproportionate number of whom are women of color—African-American, Latina, Native American and Asian. Women of color were over-represented among the women who died, were left sterile or suffered other serious medical complications as a result of illegal abortions prior to this Court's decision in *Roe v. Wade,* and would be similarly affected by its reversal. . . .
>
> If states are permitted to require hospitalization for abortion throughout pregnancy, the cost of an abortion will increase artificially. The cost of abortions in hospitals is at least five times greater than the cost of clinic abortions. Although a first-trimester abortion in a clinic costs $200–300, the same abortion in a hospital costs $1200–1300. The cost for women who require second-trimester hospital abortions is even greater.

Certain Members of the Congress of the United States (21 Democratic and 4 Republican Senators and 115 Democratic and 5 Republican Representatives) —

> As members of Congress we are concerned that the overruling of *Roe v. Wade* would criminalize conduct that is now constitutionally protected, resulting in a sudden and unprecedented problem of non-compliance with individual state criminal laws. Congress is ill-equipped to design a national response to this problem. Nor can Congress remedy the patchwork of state regulations that will result in burdensome and inequitable treatment of women based on income and, in all likelihood, race. Our respect for the rule of law, along with our recognition of the problems of law enforcement and equality in the administration of justice, lead us to urge this Court to place great weight on *stare decisis* with regard to *Roe v. Wade.* . . .

608 State Legislators from 32 States —

As a practical matter ... overturning *Roe v. Wade* would not endow each state legislature with authority over the regulation of abortion. It could, instead, relegate to New York regulation of abortion for Connecticut, New Jersey, Vermont, and a host of other states. California could in practice regulate abortion for the citizens of its neighboring states. Even if only New York and California retained legalized abortion, over 60 percent of the population of the country would be within 250 miles of a jurisdiction—New York, California, Canada, or Mexico—in which abortion is legal. Thus, those states permitting abortion would have the responsibility of providing for the health not only of their own residents seeking abortion but also of those non-residents coming into the state for that purpose.

Second, in those states prohibiting abortion, many women unable to travel to other states for abortions would instead take the dangerous route of obtaining illegal abortions in their home state. The legislatures of those states would be faced with massive public health problems arising from illegal abortions. Thus, by leaving 50 states to "balance competing interests" regarding abortion, a decision to overrule *Roe v. Wade* would effectively leave legislators in most states unable in practice to further the states' interest in regulating the conduct of a large number of their residents....

National Organization for Women —

Global abortion statistics show that making abortion illegal does not reduce the abortion rate. The abortion rate in the United States now is little different from what it was when abortion was generally unlawful. Abortion rates in countries where abortion is severely restricted, including Brazil, Argentina, and Mexico, are equal to the rate in the United States. In Latin America, where abortions generally are illegal, some 10 to 12 million women nonetheless procure abortions each year. In Ireland, where abortion is illegal, the overall abortion rate (including abortions obtained in foreign countries) is the same as in the Netherlands, where abortions are freely available....

After abortion was legalized in the United States as a result of *Roe v. Wade,* illegal abortions and resultant deaths dropped dramatically. Abortion is now considered an extremely safe procedure, since it is now performed under sanitary conditions by trained medical personnel. The United States Centers for Disease Control reported that in 1985 there were only six deaths from legal abortion in the United States, or one for every 200,000 abortions. For abortions performed during the first trimester of pregnancy the rate is even lower, one in 400,000. Full-term pregnancy and childbirth pose a seven to ten times greater risk of death to a woman than an early abortion. Moreover, medical studies have shown that legal abortion does not lead to any difficulty in subsequent conception or pregnancy.

American Medical Association, American Academy of Child and Adolescent Psychiatry, American Academy of Pediatrics, American College of Obstetricians and Gynecologists, American Fertility Society, American Medical Women's Association, American Psychiatric Association, and American Society of Human Genetics —

Induced abortions are primarily performed on young women, unmarried women, white women, and women who are having their first abortion. Among women age 15–44, more than 21% have had an abortion; if current abortion rates continue, 46% of all American women will have had an abortion by the time they are 45.

Ninety percent of abortions are performed during the first trimester of pregnancy. Only 1% of abortions are performed after 20 weeks of gestation, and approximately 100 abortions a year, or 0.01% of all abortions, occur during the third trimester of pregnancy....

What this discussion of the medical background of abortions, fetal viability and the physical and psychiatric implications of childbirth and abortion reveals is that the Court in *Roe* was correct that "the abortion decision in all its aspects is inherently, and primarily, a medical decision.... "

Catholics for a Free Choice, Chicago Catholic Women, National Coalition of American Nuns, Women in Spirit of Colorado Task Force, et al. —

Amici submit this brief limited to the question of the constitutionality and moral significance of Sec. 1.205 of the Missouri statute, which declares, as a matter of civil law, *inter alia:*

(1) The life of each human being begins at conception;

(2) Unborn children have protectable interests in life, health, and well-being.

Amici are individuals and organizations of persons of the Catholic faith who are committed to principles of religious liberty and constitutional privacy. The religious and moral beliefs and values of *amici* which are deeply rooted in Catholic theology, include the beliefs that the abortion decision is a highly personal one made in the exercise of conscience, informed by an individual's religious and moral teachings and values, and that the individual woman's conscience is the final arbiter of any abortion decision. *Amici* recognize that other religious faiths permit, counsel and even mandate abortion in some circumstances. *Amici* strongly believe that a woman's decision about childbearing must be free of government burden, interference or coercion.

Between 1985 and 1989 those in Congress taking a pro-choice position somewhat moderated their earlier stance, and their numbers grew. When the first pro-choice *amicus* brief on behalf of members of Congress (drafted by Professor Laurence Tribe of Harvard Law School) was filed in 1985, only 10 senators and 69 representatives signed on. Tribe had argued that the right to choose abortion was squarely within the protected liberty of the Fourteenth Amendment and that overturning *Roe* would result in a "bizarre quilt of wildly varying ... laws." In 1989 25 senators and 111 representatives affixed their signatures to a brief drafted by Professor Burke Marshall of Yale Law School, who had headed the Civil Rights Division of the Department of Justice during the Kennedy administration. Marshall emphasized the importance of precedent for the rule of law, the incapacity of Congress to respond fully to *Roe*'s reversal, and the "massive non-compliance" and "disrespect for the rule of law" that would be engendered by the overturning of *Roe*. (See table 6.4, p. 225, for senatorial signatories to pro-choice briefs in 1985 and 1989.)

Impact of *Amici* Briefs and Interest-Group Litigation in *Webster*

What impact did the flood of *amici* briefs have in *Webster*? Certainly, for those outside the Court, they registered the competing political positions and legal strategies of various constituencies and highlighted the attempts of pro-life and pro-choice groups to sway the Court and the country. The bearing such interest-group activities have for the justices is impossible to measure precisely and difficult to isolate from the influence of the briefs filed by the appellants and appellees, the influence of the oral arguments, and the justices' own deliberations. Still, as political scientist Susan Behuniak-Long points out, "The briefs were not only read; they also had impact. Their arguments and information helped shape terms of the Court debate [both during and after hearing oral arguments]. Whether the justices refuted the briefs, modified an argument

TABLE 6.4
SENATORS SIGNING PRO-CHOICE BRIEFS, 1985 AND 1989

Senators	1985 Brief	1989 Brief
B. Adams (D-Washington)		☒
M. Baucus (D-Montana)		☒
J. Bingaman (D-New Mexico)		☒
B. Bradley (D-New Jersey)		☒
Q. Burdick (D-North Dakota)		☒
J. Chafee (R-Rhode Island)	☒	☒
W. Cohen (R-Maine)		☒
A. Cranston (D-California)		☒
C. Dodd (D-Connecticut)	☒	☒
J. Glenn (D-Ohio)		☒
D. Inouye (D-Hawaii)	☒	☒
J. Jeffords (D-Vermont)		☒
N. Kassebaum (R-Kansas)	☒	
E. Kennedy (D-Massachusetts)	☒	☒
J. Kerry (D-Massachusetts)	☒	☒
F. Lautenberg (D-New Jersey)	☒	☒
P. Leahy (D-Vermont)		☒
C. Levin (D-Michigan)		☒
S. Matsunaga (D-Hawaii)	☒	☒
H. Metzenbaum (D-Ohio)	☒	☒
B. Mikulski (D-Maryland)		☒
B. Packwood (R-Oregon)	☒	☒
C. Pell (D-Rhode Island)		☒
D. Riegle (D-Michigan)		☒
P. Simon (D-Illinois)		☒
T. Wirth (D-Colorado)		☒

because of them, or accepted and integrated their points, the *amici* mattered"[15] (see table 6.5, p. 226).

Notably, twelve *amici* briefs—six on each side of the controversy—were cited at least once (for a total of twenty-nine times) in *Webster*. In his opinion for the Court, Chief Justice Rehnquist cited only the *amicus* brief filed by the Reagan and Bush administrations. However, concurring Justice O'Connor (who was in the middle of the controversy within the Court) cited four briefs—all in connection with medical and scientific evidence pertaining to fetal viability. Likewise, dissenting Justice Blackmun made reference to several briefs presenting technical medical information in support of *Roe*'s analysis. In contrast, Justice Stevens focused primarily on the briefs filed by religious organizations and

TABLE 6.5

CITATION OF BRIEFS BY JUSTICES IN *WEBSTER*

| Brief | In Opinion by Justice | | | | | |
	Rehnquist	O'Connor	Scalia	Blackmun	Stevens	Total
Appellant's brief	4				2	6
Appellees' brief	5	3				8
Agudath Israel of America					1	1
American Association of Pro-Life Obstetricians		3				3
American Medical Association		2		2		4
Americans United for Separation of Church and State					2	2
Association of Reproductive Health Professionals		1		1	4	6
Catholics for a Free Choice					2	2
Group of American Law Professors				1		1
Holy Orthodox Church					2	2
Lutheran Church					2	2
Missouri Catholic Conference					1	1
National Association of Public Hospitals		1		1		2
United States Government	1			2		3
Total citations	10	10		7	16	43

SOURCE: Susan Behuniak-Long, "Friendly Fire: Amici Curiae and *Webster v. Reproductive Health Services*," *Judicature* 74 (1991): 261, 269.

groups. As the excerpt of his opinion (reprinted below) indicates, Stevens was the only member to take seriously the freedom of religion assertions made in several *amici* briefs; he was persuaded that Missouri's declaration "life begins at conception" violates the First Amendment (dis)establishment clause.

Those who filed *amici* briefs attacking *Roe* could claim victory by pointing to the chief justice's attack on its "rigid trimester analysis." William Webster's brief had devoted little attention to that aspect of *Roe*, whereas several *amici* briefs denounced it. At the same time, pro-choice groups could take credit for O'Connor's stopping short of completely overturning *Roe*. A number of their briefs had been aimed at O'Connor because she was considered to be pivotal and had previously sharply criticized *Roe*'s trimester approach as "completely unworkable."[16] In particular, citing advances in medical technology, she had stated in 1986 that the point of fetal viability appeared to be moving to an earlier time in a pregnancy; *Roe*'s trimester scheme was on a "collision course with itself."[17] *Amici* briefs filed in *Webster,* though, disabused O'Connor of that understanding of medical and biological developments. Her questioning of counsel during oral arguments and her opinion in *Webster* indicate that she was moved by *amici* briefs to abandon at least that basis for criticizing *Roe.*

The Rehnquist Court Hears Webster

On 26 April 1989, Norma McCorvey and Sarah Weddington returned to the Supreme Court to hear oral arguments in *Webster.* The room was packed. Outside, on the steps of the building, representatives of various organizations and interest groups were giving statements to the press while demonstrators for and against *Roe* marched on the sidewalk. William Webster and Frank Susman, the attorney representing Reproductive Health Services, were each to have a half hour to make their arguments before the bench. In addition, the Rehnquist Court took the unusual step of granting ten minutes to the Bush administration to present its views. The solicitor general had not yet been confirmed by the Senate, and Attorney General Richard Thornburgh had decided not to argue the case. Reagan's former solicitor general, Charles Fried, would once again have his day in Court to press for *Roe*'s reversal.

Webster's strategy was to defend the Missouri law as technically within the limits for state regulation set by *Roe* and to let Fried make the broadside attack on that ruling. Webster bent over backward to downplay the controversial provisions of his state's law. He told the Court, for instance, that the law's preamble, declaring that life begins at conception, that "unborn children have protectable interests in life, health, and well-being," was unenforceable and extended no "substantive right." When Justices Stevens and Kennedy asked about the state's requiring doctors to perform certain tests pertaining to the "gestational age, weight, and lung maturity of" the unborn, Webster declared that such procedures were not mandatory and, in any event, like other provisions of Missouri's law, carried no penalty. As for the state's prohibiting the use of public funds and facilities for abortions, Webster simply pointed to *Maher* and *McRae,* in which similar restrictions had been upheld.

Fried next stood at the lectern. "We are not asking the Court to unravel the fabric ... of privacy rights which this Court has woven in cases like *Meyer* and *Pierce* and *Moore [v. City of East Cleveland,* 431 U.S. 492(1977)] and *Griswold;* rather, we are asking the Court to pull this one thread. And the reason is well stated in *Harris v. McRae:* Abortion is different."

"Your position," asked Justice Kennedy, "then is that *Griswold* is correct and should be retained?" "Exactly," Fried replied, prompting more questions. "Is that," Kennedy probed, "because there is a fundamental right involved in that case?" Fried responded: "In *Griswold* there was a right which was well established in a whole fabric of quite concrete matters, quite concrete. It involved not an abstraction such as the right to control one's body, an abstraction such as the right to be let alone, it involved quite concrete intrusions into the details of marital intimacy. And that was emphasized by the Court and is a very important aspect of the Court's decision."

"Does the case stand for the proposition that there is a right to determine whether to procreate?" Kennedy continued. "*Griswold* surely does not stand for that proposition," replied Fried. But before he could continue Kennedy interrupted, "What is the right involved in *Griswold*?" "The right involved in *Griswold* was the right not to have the state intrude into, in a very violent way, into the details, inquire into the details of marital intimacy. There was a great deal of talk about inquiry into the marital bedroom, and I think that is a very different story from what we have here."

"Do you say there is no fundamental right to decide whether to have a child or not?" O'Connor was moved to interject at that point. "Do you deny that the Constitution protects [the right to procreate]?" Fried hesitated "to formulate the right in such abstract terms," and argued that "the Court prior to *Roe* quite prudently also avoided such sweeping generalities. That was the wisdom of *Griswold*."

O'Connor countered, "Do you think that the state has the right to, if in a future century we had a serious overpopulation problem, has a right to require women to have abortions after so many children?" "I surely do not," Fried shot back, "That would be quite a different matter." "What do you rest that on?" O'Connor wondered aloud. "Unlike abortion, which involves the purposeful termination of future life," claimed Fried, "that would involve not preventing an operation by violently taking hands on, laying hands on a woman and submitting her to an operation and a whole constellation — ."

O'Connor cut Fried off with another question: "You would rest that on substantive due process protection?" "Absolutely," responded Fried.

"How do you define the liberty interests of the woman in that connection?" Kennedy then asked. "The liberty interest against a seizure would be involved," replied Fried. "That is how the Court analyzed the matter in *Griswold*. That is how Justice Harlan analyzed the matter in his dissent in *Poe v. Ullman,* which is, in some sense, the root of this area of law."

Kennedy pressed, "How do you define the interest, the liberty interest, of a woman in an abortion case?" "Well," said Fried, "I would think that there are liberty interests involved in terms perhaps of the contraceptive interest, but there is an interest at all points, however the interest of the woman is defined, at all points it is an interest which is matched by the state's interest in potential life." "I understand it is matched," Kennedy interjected, "but I want to know how you define it." Fried's answer: "I would define it in terms of the concrete impositions on the woman which so offended the Court in *Griswold* and which are not present in the *Roe* situation. Finally, I would like to make quite clear that in our view, if *Roe* were overruled, this Court would have to continue to police the far outer boundaries of abortion regulation under a due process rational basis test and that that test is muscular enough, as Chief Justice Rehnquist said in his dissent in *Roe,* to strike down any regulation which did not make adequate provision — ."

"Mr. Fried, do I correctly read what your brief says," an incredulous Justice Brennan asked, "that *Griswold* is a Fourth Amendment case?" "It is a case which draws on the Fourth Amendment," Fried defensively and deferentially replied. "It is not itself a Fourth Amendment case, it is a Fourteenth Amendment case. But I would like to emphasize that the Court would have ample power under our submission to strike down any regulation which did not make proper provision for cases where the life of the mother was at risk. We are not here today suggesting that the Court would, therefore, allow extreme and extravagant and bloodthirsty regulations and that it would lack the power to strike those down if they were presented to it."

That was not a very fruitful line of argument, and Stevens interrupted to ask whether there was "a difference between the court's power in the case of an abortion that would be life threatening to the woman and an abortion that would merely cause her severe and prolonged disease? Is there a constitutional difference?"

"It is a matter of degree," Fried declared, "and it is perfectly clear that severe health effects shade over into a threat to the life. I cannot promise the Court that our submission would dispense the Federal courts from considering matters like that, but I also very much doubt that the Court would be presented with many such situations. What is necessary is for the Court to return to legislatures an opportunity in some substantial way to express their preference, which the Court says they may express, for normal childbirth over abortion, and *Roe* stands as a significant barrier to that."

When concluding his arguments, Fried implored, "If the Court does not in this case in its prudence decide to reconsider *Roe,* I would ask at least that it say nothing here that would further entrench this decision as a secure premise for reasoning in future cases."

Frank Susman was next at the lectern. His strategy was to argue not only that *Griswold* and *Roe* were inextricably linked but that contraception and abortion were not readily distinguishable. Unlike condoms, modern birth-control pills and IUDs operate as abortifacients. "For better or worse, there no longer exists any bright line between the fundamental right that was established in *Griswold* and the fundamental right of abortion that was established in *Roe.* These two rights, because of advances in medicine and science, now overlap. They coalesce and merge and they are not distinct."

A skeptical Justice Scalia remarked, "Excuse me, you find it hard to draw a line between those two but easy to draw a line between first, second and third trimester." He cut off Susman's response with "I don't see, why a court that can draw that line can't separate abortion from birth control quite readily." Susman was prepared: "If I may suggest the reasons in response to your question, Justice Scalia. The most common forms of what we generically in common parlance call contraconception today, IUD's, low-dose birth-control pills, which are the safest type of birth-control pills available, act as abortifacients. They are correctly labeled as both. Under this statute, which defines fertilization as the point of beginning, those forms of contraception are also abortifacients. Science and medicine refers to them as both. We are not still dealing with the common barrier methods of *Griswold.* We are no longer just talking about condoms and diaphragms. Things have changed. The bright line, if there ever was one, has now been extinguished. That's why I suggest to this Court that we need to deal with one right, the right to procreate. We are no longer talking about two rights."

Kennedy then threw him a curve: "Do you agree that the state can forbid abortions save to preserve the life of the mother after the fetus is, say, eight months old?" "If I understand the question," replied Susman, "I think the health risks of the woman always are supreme at any stage of pregnancy." "Suppose the health rights of the mother are not involved?" Kennedy shot back. "The life or health of the mother is not involved, can the state prohibit an abortion after the fetus is eight months old?" Yes, Susman conceded, "I am willing to recognize the compelling interest granted in *Roe* of the state in potential fetal life after the point of viability." "But that is a line-drawing, isn't it?" Kennedy coldly pressed. "Yes, it is. But that is a line that is more easily drawn." Susman countered by further pointing out that "there are many cogent reasons for picking the point of viability, which is what we have today under *Roe*. First of all, historically, both at common law and in early statutes, this was always the line chosen. Whether it was called quickening or viability, there is little difference time-wise."

"Well," O'Connor now interrupted, "there is a difference, is there not, in those two?" "Technically," replied Susman, "between those two definitions, Justice O'Connor, yes. Quickening had less of a medical significance. It was ... when the woman could first detect movement." "When the fetus was first felt by the mother?" O'Connor knowingly and rhetorically asked. Caught off guard, Susman responded, "A kick, yes, absolutely, approximately two or three weeks before what we would consider viability today." He finally, then, was able to return to his earlier argument:

The second good reason, I think, for remaining with viability as our dividing line in this context, Justice Kennedy, is that it is one that the physician can determine on a case-by-case basis without periodic recourse to the courts.

Thirdly, it is the point that the physician can determine with or without the assistance of the woman. It is a medical judgment, I agree, and not a medical fact. One cannot pinpoint viability to a day or to an hour or to a second. I would suggest again, as I indicated, that the line has now been erased. It is interesting also to note at the same time that the definition of conception or fertilization chosen by this statute does not even comport with the medical definition. The definition of conception promulgated, for example, by the American College of Obstetricians and Gynecologists, starts a week later than the definition that this section has chosen to use.

It is at all stages of procreation, whether before or after conception, that the standards of what constitute fundamental liberty are amply satisfied. Procreational interests are, indeed, implicit in the concept of ordered liberty, and neither liberty nor justice would exist without them.

It is truly a liberty whose exercise is deeply rooted in this nation's history and tradition....

Thirty percent of pregnancies in this country today terminate in abortion. It is a high rate. It is a rate that sometimes astounds people, but it is a rate that has not changed one whit from the time the Constitution was enacted through the 1800's and through the 1900's. That has always been the rate.

It is significantly less than the worldwide rate. Worldwide, 40 percent of all pregnancies terminate in abortion. Abortion today is the most common surgical procedure in the United States with the possible exception of contraception.

It remains today, as it was in the days of Roe, 17 times safer than childbirth, 100 times safer than appendectomy, a safe procedure, minor surgery.

I suggest that there can be no ordered liberty for women without control over their education, their employment, their health, their childbearing and their personal aspirations. There does, in fact, exist a deeply rooted tradition that the government steer clear of decisions affecting the bedroom, childbearing and the doctor-patient relations as it pertains to these concerns.

Susman exhausted his allotted thirty minutes. Later he and Webster stood on the steps of the Court to tell reporters how pleased each was with the arguments in the case. But neither could confidently predict the outcome.

Webster v. Reproductive Health Services, 492 U.S. 490 (1989)

More than two months passed before the Court announced its decision in Webster on 3 July 1989, the last day of the term. O'Connor and Kennedy had already left for England and were conspicuously absent when Rehnquist read aloud portions of his opinion upholding Missouri's regulations and reluctantly declining to jettison Roe.

The bitter divisions among the justices were readily apparent. Only Kennedy and White joined the chief justice's opinion. O'Connor and Scalia concurred in separate opinions. Visibly distressed, Blackmun, the author of Roe, also took the unusual step of reading aloud from his dissenting opinion, which Brennan and Marshall joined. Stevens also read from his separate opinion.

In important and leading cases, chief justices often assign themselves the task of writing the Court's opinion. Chief Justice Rehnquist did this in Webster, but his opinion commanded the support of only two associate justices; he thus spoke for a plurality, not a majority, of the Court. Sixteen years earlier Rehnquist had issued a sharply worded dissenting opinion in Roe, but his opinion in Webster stopped short of overturning that ruling. Although that angered Scalia, it was clear that the fifth vote for overturning *Roe* was lacking. O'Connor held the critical vote and she was not ready to overturn *Roe.*

The chief justice's opinion for the Court consists largely of a systematic discussion of the reasons for upholding Missouri's restrictions on the availability of abortions. However, note that he signals that *Roe* may eventually be overturned when he discusses the value of *stare decisis*—the doctrine that prior decisions should stand—and rejects *Roe's* trimester approach to balancing the interests of women seeking abortions against those of the states in restricting and banning abortions:

🔲 Chief Justice REHNQUIST, with whom Justice WHITE and Justice KENNEDY join, delivers the opinion of the Court.

Decision of this case requires us to address four sections of the Missouri Act: (a) the preamble; (b) the prohibition on the use of public facilities or employees to perform abortions; (c) the prohibition of public funding of abortion counseling; and (d) the requirement that physicians conduct viability tests prior to performing abortions. We address these *seriatim.*

[A] The Act's preamble ... sets forth "findings" by the Missouri legislature that "[t]he life of each human being begins at conception," and that "[u]nborn children have protectable interests in life, health, and well-being." Mo. Rev. Stat. §§ 1.205.1(1), (2) (1986). The Act then mandates that state laws be interpreted to provide unborn children with "all the rights, privileges, and immunities available to other persons, citizens, and residents of this state," subject to the Constitution and this Court's precedents....

In our view, the Court of Appeals misconceived the meaning of the *Akron* [*v. Akron Center for Reproductive Health,* 462 U.S. 416 (1983)] dictum, which was only that a State could not "justify" an abortion regulation otherwise invalid under *Roe v. Wade* on the ground that it embodied the State's view about when life begins. Certainly the preamble does not by its terms regulate abortion or any other aspect of appellees' medical practice. The Court has emphasized that *Roe v. Wade* "implies no limitation on the authority of a State to make a value judgment favoring childbirth over abortion." *Maher v. Roe,* 432 U.S. [464 (1977)]. The preamble can be read simply to express that sort of value judgment....

[B] Section 188.210 provides that "[i]t shall be unlawful for any public employee within the scope of his employment to perform or assist an abortion, not necessary to save the life of the mother," while § 188.215 makes it "unlawful for any public facility to be used for the purpose of performing or assisting an abortion not necessary to save the life of the mother." The Court of Appeals held that these provisions contravened this Court's abortion decisions. We take the contrary view. . . .

Just as Congress' refusal to fund abortions in *McRae* left "an indigent woman with at least the same range of choice in deciding whether to obtain a medically necessary abortion as she would have had if Congress had chosen to subsidize no health care costs at all," Missouri's refusal to allow public employees to perform abortions in public hospitals leaves a pregnant woman with the same choices as if the State had chosen not to operate any public hospitals at all. The challenged provisions only restrict a woman's ability to obtain an abortion to the extent that she chooses to use a physician affiliated with a public hospital. This circumstance is more easily remedied, and thus considerably less burdensome, than indigency, which "may make it difficult—an in some cases, perhaps, impossible—for some women to have abortions" without public funding. *Maher.* Having held that the State's refusal to fund abortions does not violate *Roe v. Wade*, it strains logic to reach a contrary result for the use of public facilities and employees. If the State may "make a value judgment favoring childbirth over abortions and . . . implement that judgment by the allocation of public funds," *Maher,* surely it may do so through the allocation of other public resources, such as hospitals and medical staff. . . .

[D] The viability-testing provision of the Missouri Act is concerned with promoting the State's interest in potential human life rather than in maternal health. Section 188.029 creates what is essentially a presumption of viability at 20 weeks, which the physician must rebut with tests indicating that the fetus is not viable prior to performing an abortion. It also directs the physician's determination as to viability by specifying consideration, if feasible, of gestational age, fetal weight, and lung capacity. The District Court found that "the medical evidence is uncontradicted that a 20-week fetus is *not* viable," and that "23½ to 24 weeks gestation is the earliest point in pregnancy where a reasonable possibility of viability exists." But it also found that there may be a 4-week error in estimating gestational age, which supports testing at 20 weeks. . . .

We think that the doubt cast upon the Missouri statute by these cases is not so much a flaw in the statute as it is a reflection of the fact that the rigid trimester analysis of the course of a pregnancy enunciated in *Roe* has resulted in subsequent cases like *Colautti* and *Akron* making constitutional law in this area a virtual Procrustean bed. Statutes specifying elements of informed consent to be provided abortion patients, for example, were invalidated if they were thought to "structur[e] ... the dialogue between the woman and her physician." *Thornburgh v. American College of Obstetricians and Gynecologists,* 476 U.S. 747 (1986). As the dissenters in *Thornburgh* pointed out, such a statute would have been sustained under any traditional standard of judicial review (WHITE, J., dissenting), or for any other surgical procedure except abortion (BURGER, C.J., dissenting).

Stare decisis is a cornerstone of our legal system, but it has less power in constitutional cases, where, save for constitutional amendments, this Court is the only body able to make needed changes. We have not refrained from reconsideration of a prior construction of the Constitution that has proved "unsound in principle and unworkable in practice." *Garcia v. San Antonio Metropolitan Transit Authority,* 469 U.S. 528 (1985). We think the *Roe* trimester framework falls into that category.

In the first place, the rigid *Roe* framework is hardly consistent with the notion of a Constitution cast in general terms, as ours is, and usually speaking in general principles, as ours does. The key elements of the *Roe* framework—trimesters and viability—are not found in the text of the Constitution or in any place else one would expect to find a constitutional principle. Since the bounds of the inquiry are essentially indeterminate, the result has been a web of legal rules that have become increasingly intricate, resembling a code of regulations rather than a body of constitutional doctrine....

In the second place, we do not see why the State's interest in protecting potential human life should come into existence only at the point of viability, and that there should therefore be a rigid line allowing state regulation after viability but prohibiting it before viability....

The tests that § 188.029 requires the physician to perform are designed to determine viability. The State here has chosen viability as the point at which its interest in potential human life must be safeguarded. See Mo. Rev. Stat. § 188.030 (1986) ("No abortion of a viable unborn child shall be performed unless necessary to preserve the life or health of the woman"). It is true that the tests in question increase the expense of abortion, and regulate the discretion of the physician in determining the viability of the fetus. Since the tests will undoubtedly show in many cases that the fetus is not viable, the tests will have been performed for what were in fact second-trimester abortions. But we are satisfied that the requirement of these tests permissibly furthers the State's interest in protecting potential human life, and we therefore believe § 188.029 to be constitutional....

Both appellants and the United States as *Amicus Curiae* have urged that we overrule our decision in *Roe v. Wade.* The facts of the present case, however, differ from those at issue in *Roe.* Here, Missouri has determined that viability is the point at which its interest in potential human life must be safeguarded. In *Roe,* on the other hand, the Texas statute criminalized the performance of *all* abortions, except when the mother's life was at stake. This case therefore affords us no occasion to revisit the holding of *Roe,* which was that the Texas statute unconstitutionally infringed the right to an abortion derived from the Due Process Clause, and we leave it undisturbed. To the extent indicated in our opinion, we would modify and narrow *Roe* and succeeding cases.... 🖾

O'Connor concurred in *Webster* but disagreed with Rehnquist's analysis of Missouri's requirements for viability testing and, notably, Rehnquist's and Scalia's insistence on reconsidering *Roe.* While maintaining that the underlying analysis in *Roe* remained problematic, O'Connor stepped back from some of the sharp criticism she leveled against *Roe* in her 1983 dissenting opinion in *Akron v. Akron Center for Reproductive Health.* Furthermore, she reaffirmed that she would not uphold restrictive abortion laws that place "undue burden" on women seeking abortions.

🖾 Justice O'CONNOR concurring in part.

Unlike the plurality, I do not understand these viability testing requirements to conflict with any of the Court's past decisions concerning state regulation of abortion. Therefore, there is no necessity to accept the State's invitation to reexamine the constitutionality of *Roe v. Wade,* 410 U.S. 113 (1973).... The Court today has accepted the State's every interpretation of its abortion statute and has upheld, under our existing precedents, every provision of that statute which is properly before us. Precisely for this reason reconsideration of *Roe* falls not into any "good-cause exception" to this "fundamental rule of judicial restraint.... " When the constitutional invalidity of a State's abortion statute actually turns on the constitutional validity of *Roe v. Wade,* there will be time enough to reexamine *Roe.* And to do so carefully....

Finally, and rather half-heartedly, the plurality suggests that the marginal increase in the cost of an abortion created by Missouri's viability testing provision may make § 188.029, even as interpreted, suspect under this Court's decision in *Akron* ... striking down a second-trimester hospitalization requirement.... I dissented from the Court's opinion in *Akron* because it was my view that, even apart from *Roe's* trimester framework which I continue to consider problematic, see *Thornburgh,* the *Akron* majority had distorted and misapplied its own standard for evaluating state regulation of abortion which the Court had applied with fair consistency in the past: that, previability, "a regulation imposed on a lawful abortion is not unconstitutional unless it unduly burdens the right to seek an abortion." ...

It is clear to me that requiring the performance of examinations and tests useful to determining whether a fetus is viable, when viability is possible, and when it would not be medically imprudent to do so, does not impose an undue burden on a woman's abortion decision. On this ground alone I would reject the suggestion that § 188.029 as interpreted is unconstitutional.... 🔲

Although Scalia had not been on the bench when *Roe* came down, he had long been a critic of the ruling and the Court's creation of a constitutional right of privacy. His concurring opinion in *Webster* registers his impatience with the Court's, and in particular O'Connor's, refusal to overturn *Roe.*

🔲 Justice SCALIA concurring in part.

The outcome of today's case will doubtless be heralded as a triumph of judicial statesmanship. It is not that, unless it is statesmanlike needlessly to prolong this Court's self-awarded sovereignty over a field where it has little proper business since the answers to most of the cruel questions posed are political and not juridical—a sovereignty which therefore quite properly, but to the great damage of the Court, makes it the object of the sort of organized public pressure that political institutions in a democracy ought to receive.

Justice O'CONNOR's assertion that a "fundamental rule of judicial restraint" requires us to avoid reconsidering *Roe,* cannot be taken seriously. By finessing *Roe* we do not, as she suggests, adhere to the strict and venerable rule that we should avoid " 'decid[ing] questions of a constitutional nature.' " We have not disposed of this case on some statutory or procedural ground, but have decided, and could not avoid deciding, whether the Missouri statute meets the requirements of the United States

Constitution. The only choice available is whether, in deciding that constitutional question, we should use *Roe v. Wade* as the benchmark, or something else. What is involved, therefore, is not the rule of avoiding constitutional issues where possible, but the quite separate principle that we will not " 'formulate a rule of constitutional law broader than is required by the precise facts to which it is to be applied.' " The latter is a sound general principle, but one often departed from when good reason exists. . . .

The Court has often spoken more broadly than needed in precisely the fashion at issue here, announcing a new rule of constitutional law when it could have reached the identical result by applying the rule thereby displaced. . . .

The real question, then, is whether there are valid reasons to go beyond the most stingy possible holding today. It seems to me there are not only valid but compelling ones. Ordinarily, speaking no more broadly than is absolutely required avoids throwing settled law into confusion; doing so today preserves a chaos that is evident to anyone who can read and count. Alone sufficient to justify a broad holding is the fact that our retaining control, through *Roe,* of what I believe to be, and many of our citizens recognize to be, a political issue, continuously distorts the public perception of the role of this Court. We can now look forward to at least another Term with carts full of mail from the public, and streets full of demonstrators, urging us—their unelected and life-tenured judges who have been awarded those extraordinary, undemocratic characteristics precisely in order that we might follow the law despite the popular will—to follow the popular will. Indeed, I expect we can look forward to even more of that than before, given our indecisive decision today. . . . ▨

For Blackmun, the author of *Roe,* the result and the plurality and concurring opinions in *Webster* were obviously distressing. His separate opinion, in part concurring and dissenting, was impassioned. Note that it offers a strong defense of *Roe's* trimester approach to balancing the interests of women seeking abortions and the interests of the states in prohibiting abortions in emphasizing the Court's responsibility to draw lines between individuals' liberty interests and the coercive powers of government. Blackmun also argued that the line-drawing in *Roe* is basically no different from the lines that the Court draws when it establishes standards for libel and obscenity under the First Amendment's guarantee of freedom of speech and press.

▨ Justice BLACKMUN, with whom Justice BRENNAN and Justice

MARSHALL join, concurring in part and dissenting in part.

Today, *Roe v. Wade,* and the fundamental constitutional right of women to decide whether to terminate a pregnancy, survive but are not secure. Although the court extricates itself from this case without making a single, even incremental, change in the law of abortion, the plurality and Justice SCALIA would overrule *Roe* (the first silently, the other explicitly) and would return to the States virtually unfettered authority to control the quintessentially intimate, personal, and life-directing decision whether to carry a fetus to term. Although today, no less than yesterday, the Constitution and the decisions of the Court prohibit a State from enacting laws that inhibit women from the meaningful exercise of that right, a plurality of this Court implicitly invites every state legislature to enact more and more restrictive abortion regulations in order to provoke more and more test cases, in the hope that sometime down the line the Court will return the law of procreative freedom to the severe limitations that generally prevailed in this country before January 22, 1973. Never in my memory has a plurality announced a judgment of this Court that so foments disregard for the law and for our standing decisions.

With feigned restraint, the plurality announces that its analysis leaves *Roe* "undisturbed," albeit "modif[ied] and narrow[ed]." But this disclaimer is totally meaningless. The plurality opinion is filled with winks, and nods, and knowing glances to those who would do away with *Roe* explicitly, but turns a stone face to anyone in search of what the plurality conceives as the scope of a woman's right under the Due Process Clause to terminate a pregnancy free from the coercive and brooding influence of the State. The simple truth is that *Roe* would not survive the plurality's analysis, and that the plurality provides no substitute for *Roe's* protective umbrella.

I fear for the future. I fear for the liberty and equality of the millions of women who have lived and come of age in the 16 years since *Roe* was decided. I fear for the integrity of, and public esteem for, this Court....

[R]ather than arguing that the text of the Constitution makes no mention of the right to privacy, the plurality complains that the critical elements of the *Roe* framework—trimesters and viability—do not appear in the Constitution and are, therefore, somehow inconsistent with a Constitution cast in general terms.... Were this a true concern, we would have to abandon most of our constitutional jurisprudence. As the plurality well knows, or should know, the "critical elements" of countless constitutional doctrines nowhere appear in the Constitution's text. The Constitution makes no mention, for example, of the First Amendment's "actual malice" standard for proving certain libels, see *New York Times v. Sullivan,* [376 U.S. 254] (1964), or of the standard for determining when speech is obscene. See *Miller v. California,* [413 U.S. 15] (1973). Similarly, the Constitution makes no mention of the rational-basis test, or the specific verbal formulations of intermediate and strict scrutiny by which this Court evaluates claims under the Equal Protection Clause. The reason is simple. Like the *Roe* framework, these tests or standards are not, and do not purport to be, rights protected by the Constitution. Rather, they are judge-made methods for evaluating and measuring the strength and scope of constitutional rights or for balancing the constitutional rights of individuals against the competing interests of government.

With respect to the *Roe* framework, the general constitutional principle, indeed the fundamental constitutional right, for which it was developed is the right to privacy, a species of "liberty" protected by the Due Process Clause, which under our past decisions safeguards the right of women to exercise some control over their own role in procreation. As we recently reaffirmed in *Thornburgh v. American College of Obstetricians and Gynecologists* (1986), few decisions are "more basic to individual dignity and autonomy" or more appropriate to that "certain private sphere of individual liberty" that the Constitution reserves from the intrusive reach of government than the right to make the uniquely personal, intimate, and self-defining decision whether to end a pregnancy. It is this general principle, the " 'moral fact that a person belongs to himself and not others nor to society as a whole,' " that is found in the Constitution. The trimester framework simply defines and limits that right to privacy in the abortion context to accommodate, not destroy, a State's legitimate interest in protecting the health of pregnant women and in preserving potential human life. Fashioning such accommodations between individual rights and the legitimate interests of government, establishing benchmarks and standards with which to evaluate the competing claims of individuals and government, lies at the very heart of constitutional adjudication. To the extent that the trimester framework is useful in this enterprise, it is not only consistent with constitutional interpretation, but necessary to the wise and just exercise of this Court's paramount authority to define the scope of constitutional rights. . . .

Finally, the plurality asserts that the trimester framework cannot stand because the State's interest in potential life is compelling throughout pregnancy, not merely after viability. The opinion contains not one word of rationale for its view of the State's interest. This "it-is-so-because-we-say-so" jurisprudence constitutes nothing other than an attempted exercise of brute force; reason, much less persuasion, has no place. . . .

[T]he plurality pretends that it leaves *Roe* standing, and refuses even to discuss the real issue underlying this case: whether the Constitution includes an unenumerated right to privacy that encompasses a woman's right to decide whether to terminate a pregnancy. To the extent that the plurality does criticize the *Roe* framework, these criticisms are pure *ipse dixit*.

This comes at a cost. The doctrine of *stare decisis* "permits society to presume that bedrock principles are founded in the law rather than in the proclivities of individuals, and thereby contributes to the integrity of our constitutional system of government, both in appearance and in fact." Today's decision involves the most politically divisive domestic legal issue of our time. By refusing to explain or to justify its proposed revolutionary revision in the law of abortion, and by refusing to abide not only by our precedents, but also by our canons for reconsidering those precedents, the plurality invites charges of cowardice and illegitimacy to our door. I cannot say that these would be undeserved.

For today, at least, the law of abortion stands undisturbed. For today, the women of this Nation still retain the liberty to control their destinies. But the signs are evident and very ominous, and a chill wind blows.

I dissent. 🔲

Stevens, after his appointment in 1975 by President Gerald Ford, earned his reputation as a kind of maverick on the bench who often views cases differently than do the appointees of Nixon and Reagan. His separate opinion, in part concurring and dissenting, in *Webster* is notable in this regard. Only Stevens took seriously the arguments that the preamble to Missouri's statute, declaring that "the life of each human being begins at conception" constitutes a governmental endorsement of religion in violation of the First Amendment's guarantee of the separation of church and state.

🔲 Justice STEVENS, concurring in part and dissenting in part.

I am persuaded that the absence of any secular purpose for the legislative declarations that life begins at conception and that conception occurs at fertilization makes the relevant portion of the preamble invalid under the Establishment Clause of the First Amendment to the Federal Constitution. This conclusion does not, and could not, rest on the fact that the statement happens to coincide with the tenets of certain religions, or on the fact that the legislators who voted to enact it may have been motivated by religious considerations. Rather, it rests on the fact that the preamble, an unequivocal endorsement of a religious tenet of some but by no means all Christian faiths, serves no identifiable secular purpose. That fact alone compels a conclusion that the statute violates the Establishment Clause.... ▦

Webster's *Immediate Aftermath*

As if to underscore the Court's new direction in the abortion controversy, on the same day that he handed down *Webster*, Chief Justice Rehnquist also announced that three other abortion cases would be heard the next term. Instead of remanding them to the lower courts to be reconsidered in light of *Webster*, as usually happens when a major ruling bearing on other cases is handed down, a majority on the Court appeared eager to continue to undercut *Roe*. Two of the cases involved challenges to state law requiring parental notification for minors seeking abortions—the same issue that had split the justices 4–4 in 1987, before Kennedy's confirmation.[18]

In *Webster*, the Court invited renewed battles in state legislatures over tougher abortion laws. Even though *Roe* survived, both sides of the controversy predicted that that ruling might well fall in the future. Molly Yard, president of the National Organization for Women, among others, vowed "to take our fight to the people." No less determined and energized were leaders on the other side of the abortion controversy. Operation Rescue's Randall Terry, for one, announced "a two-pronged offensive fight." He and others called on "pro-life Americans to peacefully blockade these killing centers" and to "launch an equal force against state legislatures to chip away at *Roe*."

Although the abortion controversy would continue to dog the Rehnquist Court, *Webster* shifted the attention of pro-choice and antiabortion groups away from the Court and back to marshaling public opinion in support of their respective positions, as well as to carrying on their fight in the halls of state legislatures.

Notes

1. *Hartigan v. Zbaraz,* 484 U.S. 989 (1987).

2. *Thornburgh v. American College of Obstetricians and Gynecologists,* 476 U.S. 747 (1986); discussed in chapter 5.

3. See *Danforth v. Rodgers,* 414 U.S. 1035 (1973).

4. *Planned Parenthood of Central Missouri v. Danforth,* 428 U.S. 52 (1976).

5. *Planned Parenthood Association of Kansas City, Missouri, Inc. v. Ashcroft,* 462 U.S. 476 (1983).

6. See C. Gorney, "Taking Aim at *Roe v. Wade,* " *Washington Post Magazine,* 9 April 1989.

7. See *Reproductive Health Services v. Webster,* 662 F. Supp. 407 (1987).

8. *Maher v. Roe,* 432 U.S. 464 (1977).

9. *Harris v. McRae,* 448 U.S. 297 (1980).

10. *Reproductive Health Services v. Webster,* 851 F.2d 1071, 1080 (1988).

11. Quoted, T. Mauro, "Courtside," *Legal Times,* 20 March 1989.

12. *Regents of the University of California v. Bakke,* 438 U.S. 265 (1978).

13. Quoted, R. Collins, "Abortion Showdown Building," *Atlanta Journal/Constitution,* 9 April 1989, C1. Boxes 6.2 and 6.4 also draw on the Collins article.

14. Quoted, K. Winkler, "Historians Prepare Brief for Supreme Court Arguing U.S. Has Long Supported Abortion," *Chronicle of Higher Education,* 15 March 1989, A5.

15. See Susan Behuniak-Long, "Friendly Fire: Amici Curiae and *Webster v. Reproductive Health Services,*" *Judicature* 74 (1991): 261. See also R. Colker, "Feminist Litigation: An Oxymoron?—A Study of the Briefs Filed in *William L. Webster v. Reproductive Health Services,*" *Harvard Woman's Law Journal* 13 (1990): 137.

16. See *City of Akron v. Akron Center for Reproductive Health,* 462 U.S. 416 (1983) (O'Connor, J., dis. op.), discussed in chapter 5.

17. *Thornburgh v. American College of Obstetricians and Gynecologists.*

18. The Court struck down (5–4) a portion of Minnesota's law that did not provide for a "judicial bypass option" in requiring that a minor notify both parents before obtaining an abortion but upheld the basic requirement that a minor must give parental notification before obtaining an abortion, in *Hodgson v. Minnesota,* 110 S.Ct. 2926 (1990). And in *Ohio v. Akron Center for Reproductive Health,* 110 S.Ct. 2972 (1990), the Court upheld (6–3) Ohio's law that required a minor to notify at least one parent before obtaining an abortion but that also provided a judicial bypass.

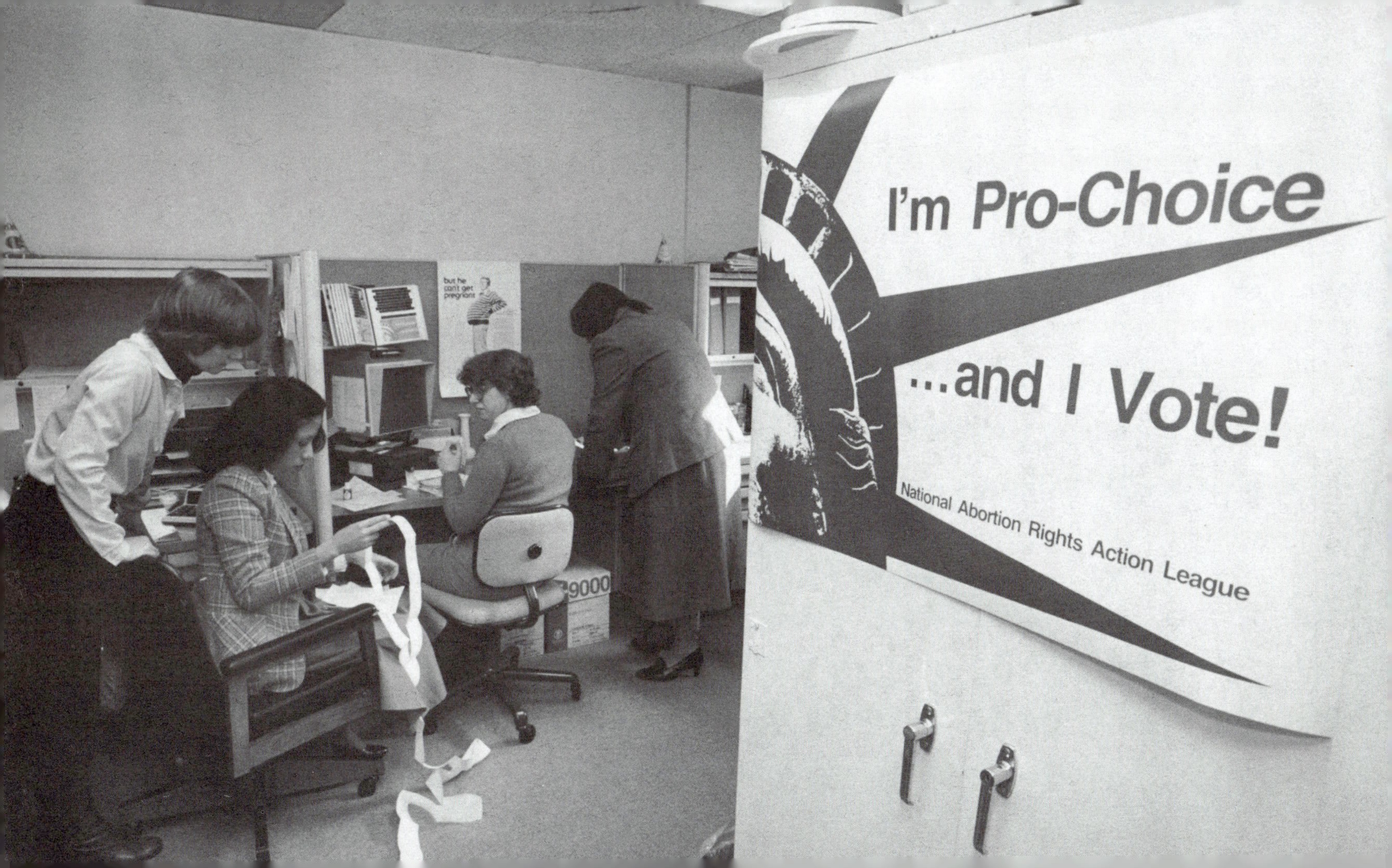
I'm Pro-Choice
...and I Vote!
National Abortion Rights Action League
but he can't get pregnant

CHAPTER 7

Public Opinion and Abortion

Polling organizations moved quickly to measure public reaction to the Supreme Court's 1989 *Webster* decision. A Gallup poll of a representative sample, conducted by telephone within the week, found that 55 percent of those surveyed disapproved of the decision, and only 37 percent approved. Did these results prove majority support for the pro-choice position? Well, yes, no, and maybe.

The poll also found that 29 percent of those disapproving of the *Webster* decision supported overturning *Roe*. Put simply, the 55 percent opposed to the Court's action in *Webster* was made up of people both from the pro-choice side (39 percent), who were unhappy because the Court allowed the states to add new obstacles to a woman's ability to get an abortion, and from the pro-life side (16 percent), who were unhappy because the Court did not overturn *Roe*. Did this prove, then, that a majority (53 percent) favored the pro-life position—the 16 percent disapproving of *Webster* who favored overturning Roe plus the 37 percent who approved of the Court's *Webster* decision? Not if the other questions asked the same interviewees meant anything. When asked specifically if they supported overturning *Roe,* 58 percent said no and only 34 percent said yes. So where does the public stand on the abortion issue? In summing up the results of this poll, Gallup concluded that "Americans remain deeply divided in their attitudes toward the abortion issue. Neither side of the debate can claim to have a majority of the public firmly in its camp."[1]

One reason for the absence of a clear majority position might be that public opinion about abortion is subject to wild fluctuations of the sort that are measured by the so-called mushiness index.[2] The problem,

Opposite: National Abortion Rights League: "I'm Pro-Choice and I Vote" (12 January 1983). *Photo:* Prints and Photographs Division, Library of Congress.

however, is not that the public is "mushy" or subject to dramatic changes in its opinion about abortion. Indeed, public opinion about abortion has remained remarkably stable in the years since *Roe,* but there is little that is straightforward or simple about that opinion. Although the public debate between abortion activists is carried on in absolutist terms, the opinion of the American public is far more complex and ambivalent. As long as the Supreme Court maintained control over abortion policy by holding to *Roe,* public opinion played a minimal role in determining national policy on the issue. Poll results provided potential ammunition for both sides but were not a very powerful weapon for mounting legal attacks or defenses. But the Court's decision in *Webster* allowing state legislatures more flexibility in regulating abortion threw the issue back into the political arena. And elected politicians are far more susceptible to being swayed by opinion polls than judges. Public opinion about abortion, despite all its inconsistencies and confusing contradictions, will play a far more important role in structuring public policy on the issue in the future.

Public Opinion Polls and American Democracy

In a representative democracy the opinion of "the people" matters. To represent, one must know the preferences of those one represents. Before the arrival of modern polling techniques, politicians read the opinion of their constituents, as well as that of the mass public, by hunch, by guess, and by keeping an ear to the ground. Political parties and organized interest groups also played an important role in defining and communicating public opinion to the elected. Public opinion was transmitted but in no regular or precise way. Then, in the 1930s, George H. Gallup and Elmo Roper introduced their "scientific polling methods," which quickly changed electoral politics. Candidates and the media hired pollsters to read the voters' preferences and then used the information to fashion campaign strategies or to predict election results. Polling was quickly expanded to measure public opinion on specific policy issues.

Scientific polling depends on choosing a representative sample, formulating unbiased questions, conducting interviews properly, and tabulating results fairly. Even if considerable care is given to all these aspects, polling is at best inexact, because error can creep in at many points. Questions can be carefully phrased to avoid ambiguity or "loaded words," but the interviewer's approach or demeanor may affect responses. Seemingly neutral questions can elicit different responses depending on the order in which they are asked. Respondents may seem to be cooperating while holding back on their true opinions, or they may refuse to answer some questions, causing the sample on those questions to lose representativeness to some degree. Despite these inherent problems, public opinion polls quickly became, and seem destined to remain, a major factor in the American political process.

Some analysts argue that polls enhance the public's influence by enabling politicians to hear from a broad cross-section of the populace rather than just from powerful pressure groups and elites. Others hold that polls weaken the effect of public opinion in a democracy by undercutting the effectiveness of alternative means of expressing opinions (such as writing letters and demonstrating). Still others worry that political leaders will become slaves to polls or become paralyzed by polls, making them afraid to take unpopular positions or reluctant to take responsibility for educating the public on controversial issues.[3] The public is equally undecided about the value of polls:

> We resent the polls when they become too intrusive.... Yet we are also fascinated by what the polls tell us about ourselves. We are suspicious because we seldom if ever are respondents in a poll, yet we readily cite the surveys conducted by reputable and even disreputable pollsters. We complain about the pervasiveness of polls, yet are apt to raise questions that can be answered only by polls.[4]

As the importance of polls grew, the number of polls proliferated as increasing numbers of polling firms were encouraged to enter the market. Some pollsters succumbed to the temptation to manipulate the polling process to achieve results that would satisfy their clients' wants. This was a risky strategy for the polling industry because ultimately the usefulness of polls depends upon the public's trust and belief in their fairness and validity. If the public grew too skeptical or suspicious, polling could suffer a double defeat. First, willing respondents might become scarce, making it impossible to interview a representative sample. Second, if the public and politicians were to cease believing that poll results matter, the effectiveness of polling would be diminished and paying clients might disappear.

In 1968 the polling profession took the initiative to protect against potential disaster by developing guidelines for policing and monitoring itself. The Code of Disclosure provided that a public report of survey results should include the population surveyed, the size of the sample, how the sample was drawn, the exact wording of the questions, the date of interviewing, and the nature of the interviews (e.g., telephone, face to face, mailed survey instrument, and so on). Later additions required that sponsorship of a poll be made known and that polling organizations encourage the media to include all the disclosure information when reporting poll results. The integrity of the polling profession prompted acceptance and, for the most part, observance of the code. Purposely biased polls are still around, but they are a bit easier to spot and to refute.

The most troubling aspect of polling, perhaps, is sample size. In 95 out of 100 cases a poll with a national sample of about 1500 adults (who have been systematically selected to be representative of the entire adult population of over 180 million) will have an error rate of no more than plus or minus 3 percentage points from the results obtained. In other words, in reference to the Gallup data discussed above, rather than saying that 58 percent of Americans do not support overturning *Roe,* it would be more accurate to say that between 55 and 61 percent of Americans in July 1989 did not support overturning *Roe;* and there is a 5 percent chance that the variance between the high and low ends of that range might be larger if the poll were to be immediately repeated.

It is important also to recognize that as sample size decreases, the potential for error increases. Thus, the meaning of another statement in reference to the same Gallup poll—namely, that 58 percent of whites (subsample, 1075) and 55 percent of nonwhites (subsample, 166) were opposed to overturning *Roe*—is more problematic. For the size of the sample of white respondents, the allowance for error is plus or minus 4 points, which would mean that between 54 and 62 percent of white Americans in July 1989 were opposed to overturning *Roe.* For the smaller sample of nonwhites, however, the allowance for error would be plus or minus 11 points, which would mean that between 44 and 66 percent of nonwhite Americans in July 1989 were opposed to overturning *Roe.*[5] With such a large potential variance, the precision of measurement for the nonwhite opinion category and the significance of the three-point difference between white and nonwhite opinion are open to considerable question.

When using the results of polls, the temptation is always to make much of both small differences between categories of individuals and small movements of opinion change over time. As the abortion issue looms larger in the political arena, public opinion about abortion inevitably will play a critical role. Each change and each difference in the numbers will also become a political weapon for one or the other side in the debate.

Abortion Polls: Results and Meanings

In 1965 and annually thereafter the National Opinion Research Center (NORC), a nonprofit polling organization affiliated with the University of Chicago, asked a series of questions about whether it should be possible for a pregnant woman to obtain an abortion under six different situations. (NORC follows accepted techniques in regard to sample size, sample selection, and question format.) From 1965 to 1973 support grew rather dramatically in all six categories, with amount of support significantly higher for the first three categories (see table 7.1, p. 250, and figure 7.1, p. 251). Not surprisingly, in about a third of the states by the time of *Roe*, legislatures reacted by liberalizing abortion laws. In the first year following *Roe*, support for abortion continued upward slightly and then leveled off until the 1980s, when support dipped slightly (see table 7.2, p. 252, and figure 7.2, p. 253). By 1990 the dip was reversed and some analysts believed the trend was to a slow growth in support for abortion in all cases (see table 7.3, p. 254, and figure 7.3, p. 255).

The "Hard" and "Soft" Reasons

In reviewing poll data, both news media and academic analysts usually divide public opinion about abortion into two categories. The first, often referred to as the "hard-reasons" category—or, as one study concluded, what people view as the "medical-reasons" category—comprises areas covered by the first three conditions named in the NORC's survey question: (1) woman's health seriously endangered, (2) became pregnant as a result of rape, and (3) strong chance of serious defect in the baby.[6] For this set of conditions, the NORC surveys show overwhelming majority opinion support for the availability of legal abortion. Indeed, the results since 1972 show a majority in excess of three-quarters—that is, a majority even larger than the supermajority required to ratify an amendment to the U.S. Constitution.

The second category, usually referred to as the "soft-reasons" or "social-reasons" category, generally includes the situations covered in the last three conditions named in the NORC's survey question: (4) low income and cannot afford more children, (5) not married and does not want to marry the man, and (6) married and does not want any more children. For this set of conditions, support for the availability of legal abortions has hovered just above or just below 50 percent, with the lowest support voiced for question 6; this is the only reason that has not at some point since 1972 hit the 50 percent mark in the NORC surveys.

A seventh condition, concerning whether "pregnancy interfered with work or education," has been named in questions asked recently by some pollsters. It generally receives the lowest level of public support (in a 1989 CBS News/*New York Times* poll only 26 percent of the respondents voiced support for this reason).[7] But public opinion about acceptable reasons for seeking an abortion and public opinion about the reality of why women seek abortions are at considerable odds.

TABLE 7.1

NATIONAL OPINION RESEARCH CENTER
ABORTION OPINION POLL RESULTS,
1965, 1972, 1973

Question(s): "Please tell me whether or not you think it should be possible for a pregnant woman to obtain a legal abortion ...

	1965 (%)	1972 (%)	1973 (%)
[1.] if the woman's health is seriously endangered."			
Yes	73	86	92
No	27	14	7
[2.] if she became pregnant as a result of rape."			
Yes	59	79	84
No	41	21	16
[3.] if there is a strong chance of serious defect in the baby."			
Yes	57	79	85
No	43	21	15
[4.] if the family has low income and cannot afford any more children."			
Yes	22	49	54
No	78	51	46
[5.] if she is not married and does not want to marry the man."			
Yes	18	44	49
No	82	56	51
[6.] if she is married and does not want any more children."			
Yes	16	40	47
No	84	60	53

SOURCE: National Opinion Research Center survey results, as reported in *Public Opinion*, May/June 1989, 37.

NOTE: Percentages are comparisons between those who replied yes or no. Those who replied that they did not know or declined to answer are excluded. The percentage who fall into these two categories varies by question. Question 1 has the lowest average (3.1%) of respondents who did not know or declined; question 5 has the highest (4.6%).

Who Gets Abortions, and Why?

It is estimated that about one-fifth of American women of reproductive age have had an abortion.[8] Approximately 1.5 to 1.6 million abortions are performed in the United States annually, a figure that has remained relatively constant, although the rate of abortions in relation to the number of women of childbearing age dropped about 6 percent between 1980 and 1987. More than half of all abortions are performed on women in their twenties; 70 percent are performed on women between the ages of eighteen and twenty-nine. About half of induced abortions are performed before the ninth week of pregnancy, and less than 1 percent are performed more than twenty weeks after the woman's most recent menstrual period.

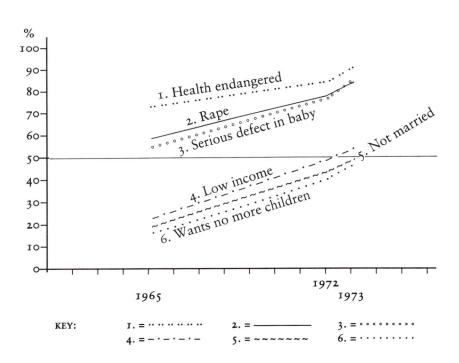

FIGURE 7.1

ABORTION OPINION POLL RESULTS, 1965–73:
TRENDS IN AFFIRMATIVE RESPONSES

SOURCE: National Opinion Research Center survey results as reported in *Public Opinion* May/June 1989, 37.

Questions 1–6: see table 7.1.

TABLE 7.2

NATIONAL OPINION RESEARCH CENTER ABORTION OPINION POLL RESULTS,

AVAILABLE YEARS, 1974–88

Question(s): "Please tell me whether or not you think it should be possible for a pregnant woman to obtain a legal abortion …"

	1974 (%)	1975 (%)	1976 (%)	1977 (%)	1978 (%)	1980 (%)	1982 (%)	1983 (%)	1984 (%)	1985 (%)	1987 (%)	1988 (%)
[1.] if the woman's health is seriously endangered."												
Yes	93	91	91	91	90	90	92	90	90	90	89	89
No	7	9	9	9	10	10	8	10	11	10	11	11
[2.] if she became pregnant as a result of rape."												
Yes	86	83	84	84	84	83	86	83	80	81	81	81
No	14	17	16	16	16	17	14	17	20	19	19	19
[3.] if there is a strong chance of serious defect in the baby."												
Yes	86	83	84	86	82	83	84	79	80	78	79	78
No	14	17	16	14	18	17	16	21	20	22	21	22
[4.] if the family has low income and cannot afford any more children."												
Yes	55	53	53	54	47	52	52	44	46	43	45	42
No	45	47	47	46	53	48	48	56	54	57	55	58
[5.] if she is not married and does not want to marry the man."												
Yes	50	48	50	50	41	48	49	40	44	41	42	40
No	50	52	50	50	59	52	51	61	56	59	58	60
[6.] if she is married and does not want any more children."												
Yes	47	46	46	47	40	47	48	39	43	40	42	40
No	53	54	54	53	60	52	52	61	57	60	58	60

SOURCE: National Opinion Research Center survey results, as reported in *Public Opinion*, May/June 1989, 37. See table 7.1 note.

Few women seek abortions because they have been the victims of rape, or because their lives are threatened, or because of seriously deformed fetuses. In fact, the three reasons combined probably account for less than 5 percent of all abortions.[9] Instead, the explanations most often given are that a baby would change the woman's or the family's life adversely or that a baby cannot be afforded.[10] In 1987 over 80 percent of legal abortions were performed on unmarried women; in that year more than 57 percent of all pregnancies of unmarried women ended in abortion.[11] "Most abortions that take place," one scholar concluded, "do so for precisely the reasons most Americans disapprove: financial or psychological reasons or convenience."[12]

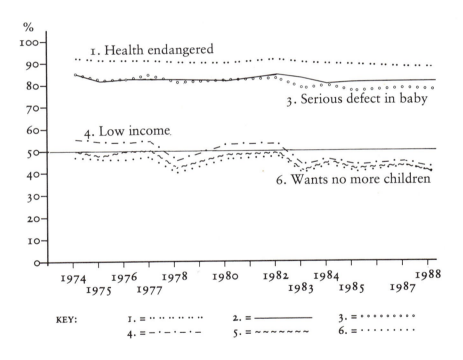

FIGURE 7.2

ABORTION OPINION POLL RESULTS, 1974–88:
TRENDS IN AFFIRMATIVE RESPONSES

SOURCE: National Opinion Research Center survey results as reported in *Public Opinion*, May/June 1989, 37.

Questions 1–6: see table 7.2.

A significant proportion of the women obtaining abortions are members of the religious group that has been the most visible and vociferous opponent of the procedure. Catholic women represent 32.1 percent of the total reproductive-age female population and account for 31.5 percent of the abortions; Protestant women represent 57.9 percent of the total reproductive-age female population and account for 41.9 percent of abortions. As a percentage of their own population, Catholic women are more likely to obtain an abortion than members of any other religious group.[13] Moreover, it is possible that these statistics understate the actual number of Catholic women obtaining abortions. The only catego-

TABLE 7.3

NATIONAL OPINION RESEARCH CENTER

ABORTION OPINION POLL RESULTS,

1989, 1990, 1991

Question(s): "Please tell me whether or not you think it should be possible for a pregnant woman to obtain a legal abortion ...

	1989 (%)	1990 (%)	1991 (%)
[1.] if the woman's health is seriously endangered."			
Yes	94	92	92
No	6	8	8
[2.] if she became pregnant as a result of rape."			
Yes	89	85	86
No	11	15	14
[3.] if there is a strong chance of serious defect in the baby."			
Yes	81	81	83
No	19	19	17
[4.] if the family has low income and cannot afford any more children."			
Yes	46	48	48
No	54	52	52
[5.] if she is not married and does not want to marry the man."			
Yes	44	45	45
No	56	55	55
[6.] if she is married and does not want any more children."			
Yes	40	45	45
No	60	55	55

SOURCE: National Opinion Research Center survey results, as reported in *Public Opinion,* May/June 1989, 37.

See table 7.1 note.

ries in which the proportion of abortions was greater for a group than that group's percentage of the total population of reproductive-aged women were (1) the "other religious denominations" category, which accounted for 3 percent of abortions and 2 percent of the population; and (2) the "no-religious-affiliation" category, which accounted for 22.2 percent of abortions and only 5.5 percent of the total population. The large disparity in the no-religious-affiliation figures (more than four times as many in the abortion population as in the total population) raises the question of whether some women who have abortions are reluctant to reveal their religion. If that is the case, it is a reasonable hypothesis that women from a religious denomination whose leadership is unequivocally opposed to abortion might be inclined to hide their membership from those collecting such statistics. In other words, it is very

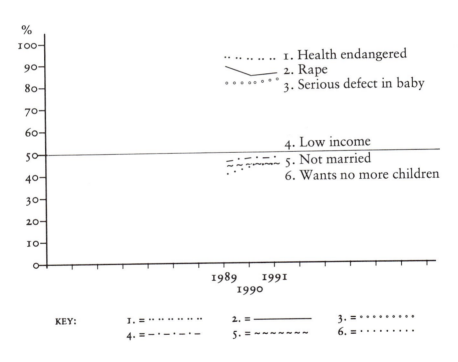

FIGURE 7.3
ABORTION OPINION POLL RESULTS, 1989–91:
TRENDS IN AFFIRMATIVE RESPONSES

SOURCE: National Opinion Research Center survey results as reported in *Public Opinion*, May/June 1989, 37.

Questions 1–6: see table 7.3.

likely that the number of Catholics obtaining abortions is higher than the statistics indicate.

Evangelicals and other fundamentalist religious groups also take a strong public stand in opposition to abortion. Gallup estimates that those claiming a "born-again" religious experience represent about 38 percent of the total population.[14] Based on identification of themselves as "born-again" in a 1987 survey, 15.8 percent of those obtaining abortions were women who claimed this religious experience. Using these measures, born-again women have a lower abortion rate than any other religious category except reproductive-aged Jewish women. Still, nearly a quarter of a million women who claim to have been "born-again" obtained abortions (see table 7.4, p. 257, for details of the demographic characteristics and numbers of legal abortions in the United States in 1987).

Pollsters have consistently reported that blacks are less supportive of abortion than whites, yet the rate of abortions among black women is twice as high as among white women. The spread between white and black opinion about abortion has varied between 6 and 12 percentage points over the past two decades (although more recent figures suggests that this difference is shrinking).[15] Even when social scientists control statistically for socioeconomic status (such as level of education and income) and other variables (such as the greater number of blacks who say that religion is important or very important to them), they find that a significant difference between white and black opinion remains. In his analysis, social scientist Clyde Wilcox concluded that the most important of these factors is the greater religiosity and doctrinal orthodoxy of the black population.[16] But he also found higher support for elective abortion among black women than among white women having similar education, income, and religious affiliation and lower support for abortion among black men than among similarly situated white men. In other words, the difference between the opinions of these groups may be explained by gender plus race, not just race alone.

Demographic Differences in Abortion Opinion

When poll data are broken down into demographic subcategories (tables 7.5, p. 258, and 7.6, p. 260, present results of a 1989 poll and a 1991 poll, respectively, in such a format), some very general descriptions of how abortion opponents and supporters differ can be drawn. It is important, though, to keep in mind several limitations of generalizing from subsets of poll data. One, all statements of opinion are time-bound; that is, they reflect opinion of members of the subgroup at the time the poll was taken. Two, all subcategories represent only a portion of the total sample, hence the error rate of subcategories is always greater than that

TABLE 7.4

DEMOGRAPHIC CHARACTERISTICS OF WOMEN
OBTAINING ABORTIONS, 1987

Characteristics	Number	Percentage of total abortions	Rate per 1000 women of specified group
Total population having abortions	1,559,110	100.0	26.9
Age (years)			
Less than 15	16,090	1.0	9.9
15 to 19	390,700	25.1	43.2
20 to 24	516,340	33.1	52.3
25 to 29	333,420	21.4	30.4
30 to 34	188,920	12.1	17.7
35 to 39	91,660	5.9	9.7
40 and above	21,980	1.4	2.8
Race			
White	1,017,310	65.0	21.1
Other	541,800	34.8	56.0
Marital Status			
Married	275,170	17.6	9.2
Unmarried*a*	1,283,940	82.4	45.6
Religion			
Catholic	491,120	31.5	na
Jewish	21,828	1.4	na
Protestant	653,267	41.9	na
Other	46,773	3.0	na
None	346,122	22.2	na
Claim of			
Born again	246,339	15.8	na
Not born again	1,312,771	84.2	na

SOURCE: Numbers, percentages, and rates per 1000 women for age, race, and marital status come from Stanley K. Henshaw, Lisa M. Koonin, and Jack C. Smith, "Characteristics of U.S. Women Having Abortions, 1987," *Family Planning Perspective*, March/April 1991, 76. Percentages for religion and born-again status come from Stanley K. Henshaw and Jane Silverman, "The Characteristics and Prior Contraceptive Use of U.S. Abortion Patients," *Family Planning Perspective*, July/August 1988, 160. Numbers of abortions for religion and born-again categories were arrived at by multiplying the total number of abortions for 1987 by the reported percentages for these categories.

a. Includes never married, separated, divorced, and widowed.

TABLE 7.5
ABORTION OPINION POLL RESULTS,
BY DEMOGRAPHIC CATEGORY,
1989

Question: "Should abortion be legal as it is now, or legal only in such cases as rape, incest, or to save the life of the mother, or should it not be permitted at all?"[a]

	Legal as it is now (%)	Legal in specified circumstances (%)	Not permitted at all (%)
Total adults	49	39	9
Age (years)			
18-29	56	35	8
30-44	49	40	9
45-64	45	39	12
65 and over	39	45	9
Sex			
Male	51	38	8
Female	47	40	11
Marital Status			
Married men	46	41	8
Married women	42	42	14
Unmarried men	60	31	7
Unmarried women	54	37	7
Education			
Less than high school	37	41	16
High school graduate	47	41	9
Some college	56	35	7
College graduate	58	35	5
Race			
White	49	39	9
Black	45	42	13
Religion[b]			
Protestant	44	44	9
Catholic	48	36	13
Religiosity[c]			
Religion very important—Protestant	34	49	13
Religion very important—Catholic	28	49	22
Not so important–Protestant	61	36	1
Not so important–Catholic	72	22	4

Continued ...

TABLE 7.5 — *Continued*

	Legal as it is now (%)	Legal in specified circumstances (%)	Not permitted at all (%)
Political Philosophy[c]			
Liberal	65	28	5
Moderate	54	38	6
Conservative	38	46	13
Exposure[c]			
Women who say they had an abortion	79	12	9
People who knew someone who had an abortion	58	34	7
People who did not know anyone who had had an abortion	39	44	12

SOURCE: CBS News/*New York Times* Poll, April 1989.

a. Asked between 13 and 16 April 1989 of 1412 adults nationwide, conducted by telephone; those with no opinion not shown.

b. Not enough respondents in Jewish and other subcategories for reliable measurement.

c. Self-selected subcategories.

of the total survey, which means that a difference of four or five percentage points between subcategories is not proof of a real opinion difference. Three, for subcategories in which there are few respondents, survey results are subject to greater potential error; for such subcategories differences as large as ten percentage points may not indicate any real difference of opinion between groups. Four, in some subcategories respondents are asked to place themselves in one of several groups (e.g., Are you a liberal, moderate, or conservative?), and there is virtually no way to measure the accuracy of these self-classifications.

Despite these limitations, it remains possible to make a few generalizations. Recent opinion polls seem to show somewhat greater support for abortion among the young than the old, among unmarried men than married men, among college graduates than those with less than a high school education, and among liberals than conservatives. The difference between overall Catholic and Protestant opinion is negligible to small, depending on the nature of the wording and timing of the poll.

There are really only two characteristics for which there are dramatic differences between abortion rights supporters and abortion op-

TABLE 7.6

ABORTION SUPPORT OPINION POLL RESULTS,
BY DEMOGRAPHIC CATEGORY, 1991

Question(s): "Please tell me whether or not you think it should be possible for a pregnant woman to obtain a legal abortion ...

[1.] if the woman's own health is seriously endangered by the pregnancy."

[2.] if there is a strong chance of serious defect in the baby."

[3.] if she became pregnant as a result of rape."

[4.] if the family has a very low income and cannot afford any more children."

[5.] if she is not married and does not want to marry the man."

[6.] if she is married and does not want any more children."

	Reason for support					
	[1.] Woman's health seriously endangered	[2.] Serious defect in baby likely	[3.] Pregnancy resulted from rape	[4.] Low income, cannot afford more children	[5.] Unmarried; does not want to marry	[6.] Married but does not want more children
	(%)	(%)	(%)	(%)	(%)	(%)
Total adults	92	83	86	48	45	45
Age (years)						
15–29	93	84	92	52	43	46
30–39	94	87	90	56	51	51
40 and over	90	82	84	44	43	41
Sex						
Male	93	87	89	54	51	50
Female	91	81	85	44	40	40
Marital Status						
Married	92	85	85	45	42	40
Unmarried	92	82	88	53	48	49

Continued ...

TABLE 7.6 — *Continued*

	Reason for support					
	[1.] Woman's health seriously endangered	[2.] Serious defect in baby likely	[3.] Pregnancy resulted from rape	[4.] Low income; cannot afford more children	[5.] Unmarried; does not want to marry	[6.] Married but does not want more children
	(%)	(%)	(%)	(%)	(%)	(%)
Education						
Less than high school	85	79	77	36	27	28
High school graduate	94	88	91	45	41	39
Some college	95	82	89	55	52	52
College graduate	91	85	86	59	61	60
Race						
White	92	85	87	50	47	46
Black and others	90	76	83	42	35	40
Religion						
Protestant	92	83	85	44	40	42
Catholic	89	81	87	47	42	39
Jewish	97	93	96	79	78	75
Religiosity						
Strong	85	71	78	34	30	29
Somewhat strong	92	85	90	53	50	50
Not very strong	96	92	91	54	51	51
Political philosophy						
Liberal	96	92	94	66	64	65
Moderate	90	83	86	41	36	36
Conservative	90	80	81	43	40	39

SOURCE: National Opinion Research Center survey, April 1991; data breakdown in James Allan Davis and Tom W. Smith, *General Social Surveys, 1972–1991* (machine-readable data file available from Roper Center for Public Opinion Research, Box U-164, University of Connecticut, Storrs, Conn. 06269).

NOTE: Percentages are based on comparison of those responding "Yes" and "No." The "Don't know" and "No answer" responses (which account for between 3.5 and 4 percent of the total, depending on the question) are not included in percentage computations.

ponents: (1) religiosity (the importance of religion to an individual), and
(2) whether the individual has had an abortion or known someone who
has had one. Among respondents who say that religion is very important, support for abortion is lower than any other subgroup measure,
and that is true for both Catholics and Protestants. Among those who
say religion is not so important, support for abortion is higher than in
any other subgroup, except for women who say they had an abortion
(for this group the figure is 79 percent). Interestingly, the percentage of
support for keeping abortion *legal as it is now* (under *Roe v. Wade*) is
higher for Catholics who say that religion is not so important (72 percent) than for Protestants who make the same declaration (61 percent).
Among those who say that religion is very important, support for keeping abortion *legal as it is now* Catholic support is 28 percent; Protestant
support, 34 percent. The figure for supporting the legality of abortion as
it is now among those who have known a woman who has had an abortion (58 percent) is nineteen percentage points higher than for those who
have not known such a woman (39 percent). If this finding is accurate
and abortion remains legal, "it is likely that support for the right to have
an abortion will grow as more Americans come to know women who
have had an abortion."[17]

The universe of abortion rights opinion seems to be made up of three
groups: those who are absolutely against abortion, except perhaps to
save the woman's life; those who favor a right of abortion on demand;
and those whose position depends on the circumstances. The Gallup poll
asked the following question from 1975 through 1990: "Do you think
abortions should be legal under any circumstances, legal only under certain circumstances, or illegal in all circumstances?" (see figure 7.4). The
percentage supporting each of the alternatives presented in this survey
question, as in the NORC six-question survey discussed above (see figures 7.1–7.3), were remarkably stable from the mid-1970s to the end of
the 1980s; and as with the NORC questions, majority opinion here falls
in the middle, not at either extreme.

Despite all the furor and publicity surrounding the issue and despite
the heralded "Reagan revolution" in the 1980s, the American public
stood firmly upon an ambivalent middle ground with respect to abortion
rights. Indeed, stability and a centrist position are trademarks of American public opinion on most issues. In his firsthand analysis of the American experience in the 1830s, Alexis de Tocqueville noted with surprise
the enduring nature of an opinion once established:

> I hear it said that it is in the nature and the habits of democracies to be
> constantly changing their opinions and feelings. This may be true of

small democratic nations, like those of the ancient world, in which the whole community could be assembled in a public place and then excited at will by an orator. But I saw nothing of the kind among the great democratic people that dwells upon the opposite shores of the Atlantic Ocean. What struck me in the United States was the difficulty of shaking the majority in an opinion once conceived or of drawing it off from a leader once adopted. Neither speaking nor writing can accomplish it; nothing but experience will avail, and even experience must be repeated.[18]

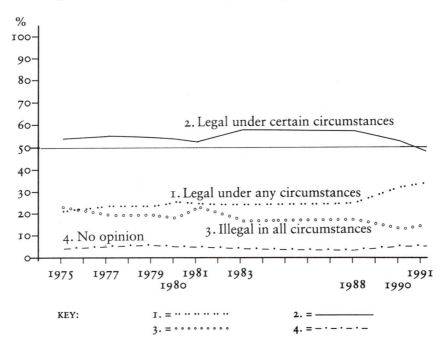

Question: "Do you think abortions should be [1] legal under any circumstances, [2] legal only under certain circumstances, or [3] illegal in all circumstances?" [No opinion = 4.]

FIGURE 7.4

PUBLIC OPINION ON ABORTION, 1975–91:
TRENDS IN AFFIRMATIVE RESPONSES

SOURCE: For 1975–90, *Gallup Poll Monthly,* April 1990, 2; for 1991, *Gallup Poll Monthly,* September 1991.

"Public opinion does change," political scientist Everett Carll Ladd notes, "but the American experience has surely borne out Tocqueville's expectations of a century and a half ago: Stability, not sudden lurchings this way and that, is the norm."[19] Shifts in underlying attitudes occur gradually, usually in response to lasting transformations of social organization. In assessing the new conservatism of the Reagan era in 1984, Daniel Yankelovich, a leading analyst of social trends, did not see a realignment of American politics coming into view. He thought what was happening was a temporary reaction to the sins of 1960s liberalism. He expected that public opinion on abortion, as on other social issues, would go through a sorting-out process that would lead not to a new predominance of conservative opinion but back to a centrist position.[20] Abortion opinion, as measured over time and as it has emerged from the 1980s, seems to support that prediction. Indeed, the nature of American opinion is not one of support for extreme positions on much of anything. "The United States is a profoundly individualistic culture," as one analyst put it. "It is difficult to persuade Americans to ban *anything*—handguns, liquor, pornography, cigarettes, saccharin, or abortions."[21]

Not until the ruling in *Webster* did the composition of the two extreme positions change to any dramatic degree, and even that change left the vast majority, at least in their response to the pollsters, voicing only conditional support for abortion rights. In its analysis of the 1990 poll results in relation to the trend over time, Gallup concluded:

> The percentage of Americans who say abortion should be "legal under any circumstances" has increased from 24 percent two years ago to 31 percent ... representing the sharpest shift recorded by the Gallup poll in its 15 years of measuring opinions about abortions. At the same time, those who choose the other extreme on the scale—abortion should be "illegal under all circumstances"—has declined from 17 percent to 12 percent, the lowest point to date.... This nineteen-point margin of pro-choice over pro-life attitudes is significantly greater than Gallup's measures on this question between 1975 and 1988, when the margin was never more than seven percentage points. However, the majority of Americans continue to say they favor abortion under certain circumstances only.[22]

Problems of Inconsistency in the Polls on Abortion

Consistency in general trends over time in response to specific questions does not translate into consistency on specific findings about abortion opinion at any given moment when responses to differently worded questions are compared. For example, in January 1989 the CBS News /*New York Times* poll asked: "Should abortion be legal as it is now, or legal only in such cases as rape, incest, or to save the life of the mother, or should it not be permitted at all?" The poll found 48 percent choosing abortion should be "legal as it is now"; 43 percent choosing abortion should be limited to "rape, incest, or to save the life of the mother"; and 9 percent choosing abortion should "not be permitted at all."[23] At about the same time a Gallup/*Newsweek* poll asked: "Do you think abortions should be legal under any circumstances, legal under certain circumstances, or illegal in all circumstances?" In that poll 28 percent chose legal under any circumstances; 53 percent, legal under certain circumstances; and 19 percent, illegal in all circumstances[24] (see table 7.7). Thus in 1989 either 9 or 19 percent of the public was totally opposed to abortion, and either 28 percent or 48 percent thought it should be *legal for any reason* or *as it is now* (which is almost, but not quite, the equivalent of "any reason").

Because both 1989 polls were taken at about the same time and both were based on normal representative sample sizes, why the difference? The answer is quite simple: Respondents were not given the same alternatives. In the CBS News/ *New York Times* poll, the "certain circumstances" are explicitly stated and they all fit the "hard-reasons" or "medical-reasons" category described above. In fact, two "hard reasons"—*health of the woman* and *fetal deformity*—are not among the CBS News/*New York Times* alternatives. If a respondent supported

TABLE 7.7

TWO ABORTION OPINION POLLS' RESULTS, 1989

Poll	Respondents' choices		
CBS News/*New York Times*			
	Legal as now	Legal for rape, incest, and to protect woman's life	Not permitted at all
	48%	43%	9%
Gallup/*Newsweek*			
	Legal under any circumstances	Legal in certain circumstances	Illegal in all circumstances
	28%	53%	19%

SOURCE: CBS News/*New York Times* poll, 12–15 January 1989, and Gallup/*Newsweek* poll, both as reported in *Public Opinion*, May/June 1989, 36.

abortion for just these two reasons in addition to what the question offered and wanted so to indicate, she or he would be left with only one
response: legal as it is now. If the percentages of the population that support the full list of "hard reasons" as shown in the eighteen years of sur-
veying done by NORC have any meaning, there should be a goodly
number of folks who might opt to place themselves in the less restrictive
category, which would explain the twenty-point difference in the two
polls on the support-of-abortion side.

Explaining the ten-point difference between *illegal in all circumstances* and *not permitted at all* is more difficult. Perhaps the mushy,
open-ended nature of the choice *legal in certain circumstances* caused it
to look as if it might be stretched to cover more circumstances than
some respondents might want to support, making them unwilling to endorse it. If that was the case, they were left with only the *illegal in all
circumstances* or *no response* choices. Inasmuch as opposition to abortion for any but the "hard reasons" is usually a more strongly felt position than support for abortion (see table 7.8, p. 271) and the discussion
below on this point), it is possible that the temptation to voice some
clear opposition to the alternative of permissive abortion would cause
such respondents to settle on illegality.

There are many other problems with the inconsistency of abortion
poll results. For example, compare the results to the following questions
in two separate 1989 polls:

> *Question 1:* If a woman wants to have an abortion and her doctor
> agrees to it, should she be allowed to have an abortion or not?
> YES: 63%[25]

> *Question 2:* Please tell me whether or not it should be possible for a
> pregnant woman to obtain a legal abortion if she wants it for any rea-
> son?
> YES: 36%[26]

On the surface each question appears to ask if a woman can obtain an
abortion if she wants one; the only difference is the involvement of "her
doctor" in Question 1. Apparently, the implied stamp of approval provided by the doctor's agreement led nearly twice as many people to say
yes. This seems a pointless distinction. Because doctors perform abortions, then logically a "doctor" agrees in virtually every case. Perhaps
the public views the involvement of a doctor more specifically in light of
the word *her*. Did respondents envision a family practitioner well ac-
quainted with the patient and her situation who would carefully weigh
the moral and medical reasons in deciding for abortion? In this era of

group practice, clinics, and health maintenance organizations, the notion that women rely on a good old family-friend doctor for advice rests more on myth than reality.

The phrasing of and answers to two questions asked in 1982 polls add even more confusion to the meaning of abortion opinion poll results.[27]

> *Question 1:* Do you agree or disagree with the following statement: Every woman who wants to have an abortion should be able to have one?
> AGREE: 61%
>
> *Question 2:* Please tell me whether or not it should be possible for a pregnant woman to obtain a legal abortion if she wants it for any reason?
> YES: 41%

What, really, is the substantive difference between *"every women who wants to have"* and *"if she wants it for any reason"*? Both leave the reason to the woman and neither limits the reason in any way. Yet 20 percent of the population apparently was swayed to support or oppose the equivalent of abortion on demand depending wholly on a seemingly minor difference in wording. Why? Perhaps the words *"any reason"* convey the impression that the abortion decision could be made for selfish reasons or that it would be made without an appreciation of its moral complexity. *"Any reason"* could include trivial reasons. For what might be termed the "reluctant abortion supporters," the perceived tone might be sufficiently off-putting to cause them to withhold support.

"People are extremely uncomfortable with the idea of abortion," comments one social scientist. "They think it is wrong, but they seem reluctant to make moral decisions about it for others."[28] For many people, abortion is a personal ethical question that is dependent on context. In a perfect world, women would get pregnant only when they wanted to and their circumstances allowed them to bear a child. But the world is not perfect, and there is "a profound commitment to tolerance on the part of a sizable percentage of the American public" that leads them to support the legality of abortion despite personal doubts about its morality.[29] Moreover, there is a tacit understanding that, for any number of reasons, any woman, the wife or partner of any man, might sometime find herself unwantedly pregnant. Implicit in support for any public policy making abortion illegal is the potential denial to oneself of the individual liberty to make an abortion decision. Doubts about morality may dissipate when the reality of an unwanted pregnancy strikes home and the abortion question is weighed within one's own network of relations and personal circumstances. Abortion in the abstract may not be the best solution in the minds of the majority that gives it conditional support; but such people may also recognize that for individuals facing grim alternatives—which they might themselves someday face —it might be the rational answer.

Any question that seems in its phrasing or tone to ignore the need to weigh such decisions with care, or that appears to approach abortion in a frivolous way, is likely to lose many of the reluctant supporters. The reason that is singled out by the fewest respondents in the NORC surveys—"*married and does not want any more children*"—may suffer from a problem of tone. There is no apparent extenuating circumstance compelling the decision (not penury or fear of divorce or the needs of existing children, for example). It probably takes presentation of a real situation and the human predicaments therein to gain the understanding and support of the reluctants. And this is difficult to convey in a general question asked outside the context of an actual situation. As the director of the annual General Social Survey for NORC points out: "You have to be very careful to write a clean, clear question, because, on something like abortion, if there are any secondary issues raised by the question it can skew your results."[30] For a significant percentage—perhaps a majority—of Americans, there is always a secondary issue in connection with abortion; personal imperatives and conventional moral values are continually in conflict. Abortion poll data are replete with examples of the ambivalence occasioned by this moral tug-of-war.

In 1980 the CBS News/*New York Times* asked whether there should be a constitutional amendment prohibiting abortion. Only 29 percent said yes. The same respondents were then asked if there should be a constitutional amendment protecting the life of the unborn child. And 50 percent said yes![31] Compare the conflicting results that seem to come from the following questions:

Do you agree or disagree with this statement: "Abortion is murder"?
[March 1989]

Abortion is murder:	62%
Abortion is not murder:	38%

If a woman wants to have an abortion and her doctor agrees to it, should she be allowed to have an abortion or not? [January 1989]

Should not:	26%
Should be allowed:	63%
It depends:	11%

Do you believe abortion is morally right or morally wrong? [March 1989]

Morally wrong:	61%
Morally right:	22%
Not sure/refused:	13%
Indifferent:	4%

Do you favor or oppose a constitutional amendment to *ban* legalized abortions? [January 1989]

Favor a constitutional amendment:	30%
Oppose a constitutional amendment:	70%

If the Supreme Court reversed its 1973 ruling and let each state make its own abortion laws, abortion could become legal in some states and illegal in others. Would you want abortion to be legal or illegal in your state? [March 1989]

Would not want abortion legal:	39%
Would want abortion legal:	61% [32]

Other important factors that can influence poll results are the order and the context of questions. Studies have shown that it matters whether a general question is posed before or after a specific question. If a specific question comes first, it may undercut support for the general question that follows. In their attempt to explain the effect of question order, Howard Schuman, Stanley Presser, and Jacob Ludwig experimented by asking two of the NORC questions in different order. If the question referring to "married and does not want any more children" was asked before the question about "chance of serious defect in the baby" it got a much higher support. When the order was reversed (as it is in the NORC surveys), support for the "married and does not want any more children" alternative declined. The researchers speculated that the reason for the difference was that reluctant abortion supporters were relieved of the need to show their response for the more general "does not want any more" reasoning if they had just endorsed a specific reason like fetal defect that was more acceptable to them.[33]

What do these seemingly contradictory findings mean? The overall picture that emerges is that a majority supports leaving abortion legal and available to women unfortunate enough to need it, though many in that majority remain concerned about the moral implications. Part of the majority support for abortion may be reluctant, but it is nonetheless present. Perhaps the clearest measure of this public sentiment lies in the responses to this survey question: "Do you agree or disagree with this statement? I personally feel that abortion is morally wrong, but I also feel that whether or not to have an abortion is a decision that has to be made by every woman for herself." It elicited agreement from 78 percent of the respondents and disagreement from only 22 percent.[34] If the figures accurately reflect public opinion, more than three-quarters of Americans basically support leaving abortion legal and up to the woman involved. One wonders, then, why the issue is so resistant to political resolution. Measurements of the intensity, centrality, and behavioral components of opinion in the abortion struggle may hold part of the answer.

Measuring the Strength: Numbers versus Commitment

Strength of feeling about abortion has two aspects: (1) centrality, or how important for the individual the issue is in relation to other issues; and (2) intensity, or how deeply the individual feels about his or her own position. When asked what issues they consider most important, only a small minority of the public (less than 0.5 percent) include abortion. When given a list of twenty-five issues to rank in order of importance, respondents put abortion last.[35] When asked in October 1989 just how important a candidate's stand on abortion is to them when voting, only 14 percent of respondents replied that it was "one of the most important" considerations. (Abortion opponents had the edge here: 27 percent said it was one of their most important considerations; only 8 percent of abortion supporters said the same.)[36] Compared with other issues and even standing alone, though, the political importance that the abortion issue commands is not reflected in poll responses. It seems clear that very vocal minorities on both sides have been able to keep the issue politically on stage.

Polls have been used to assess public opinion about some of the most visible groups that publicly act on behalf of the abortion issue. On this measure, the supporters of abortion enjoy a commanding lead. More than two-thirds of every demographic subgroup in a 1989 poll rated Planned Parenthood Federation of America in the top two categories—"very favorable" and "mostly favorable"—and 79 percent overall rated it in those categories (11 percent rated it as unfavorable). The National Right to Life Committee received an overall 54 percent rating in the top two categories with fewer than half of the college-graduate and higher-income respondents rating it as very or mostly favorable (32 percent rated it as unfavorable).[37]

The Gallup poll measures intensity by asking whether a respondent's feelings are extremely strong, very strong, fairly strong, or not strong at all about his or her position. Table 7.8 presents the intensity information regarding the overturning of *Roe*.

TABLE 7.8

FEELINGS ABOUT OVERTURNING *ROE,*

POLL RESULTS, 1989

Question(s): "Compared to how you feel on other public issues, are your feelings about abortion ...

	Intensity of feelings			
	Extremely strong	*Very strong*	*Fairly strong*	*Not strong at all*
Of the 32 percent who favor overturning *Roe*	41%	33%	29%	6%
Of the 62 percent who oppose overturning *Roe*	17	26	41	16

SOURCE: Adapted from *Gallup Poll Monthly,* October 1989, 18.

What does the rather dramatic difference in the intensity in how opponents and supporters of abortion feel about their position mean? Does the opponents' 74 percent in the top two categories of intensity give them the political edge? Or do the supporters' greater numbers (62 percent of all respondents) give them the edge? The political inequality might look like this: Is

(41% extremely strong + 33% very strong) × 32% of the total

less than or equal to or greater than

(17% extremely strong + 26% very strong) × 62% of the total?

The answer, however, remains elusive. Perhaps it will be found in how the politics of the abortion issue plays out in the future.

Another measure of political commitment is behavior: How willing are supporters and opponents to act on their convictions? But the overwhelming majority on both sides of the abortion issue are not willing to do much of anything about abortion (see table 7.9).

When responses in a 1989 survey were broken down by demographic category, only two activities showed any significant difference between groups. College graduates were 22 percent more likely to have written or given money than those with less than a high school education. And those in households with an annual income in excess of $50,000 were 14 percent more likely to have done so than those in households with

TABLE 7.9

ABORTION ACTIVISM, POLL RESULTS,

OCTOBER 1989

Question: "Have you ever written a letter to a public official expressing your views on abortion, or given money to an organization concerned with this issue?"

	Wrote a letter	Gave money	Wrote a letter and gave money	Neither
Favor overturning *Roe* (abortion opponents)	8%	11%	8%	73%
Oppose overturning *Roe* (abortion supporters)	4	7	4	85

SOURCE: *Gallup Poll Monthly,* October 1989, 20.

less than $20,000 income. One analysis of the results of this poll held that it proved that the pro-choicers had "dramatically stepped up their activism on the issue."[38] Compared with ten years ago (1979), abortion rights supporters were twice as likely in 1989 to have written letters to public officials or to have donated money to organizations supporting their position (15 percent in 1989 versus 7 percent in 1979—more than a 100 percent increase). On the other side, pro-life activism in these two categories increased from 20 to 27 percent —about a 33 percent increase. Does the more dramatic growth to a lower level of activism on the side that is statistically twice as large (in the same poll 61 percent of the respondents opposed overturning *Roe*; 33 percent favored overturning it) equal more or less political clout? Another political equation sets out the problem; but since the effectiveness of such activism is unknown, the solution to the equation provides no answer to the question of which side has more political clout. Is

15% × 61% of the total population

less than or equal to or greater than

27% × 33% of the total population?

After the failures of preelection polls during the 1989 Virginia gubernatorial and New York City mayoral races, Everett Carll Ladd commented:

The fact is we don't *know* just why it is that polls are having a harder time estimating the vote. And, if election polling is having trouble, it's likely other forms of opinion research are as well, though in less evident ways. We need to know what has happened. I don't think the polls should go away. High among their merits, they require the political community—press included—to reach outside its own closed circle and confront *vox populi*. . . . [But] opinion research must demonstrate that it is in fact able to amplify—not distort—the public's voice.[39]

The inconsistency and confusion in abortion poll results raises the question of whether abortion is an issue for which public opinion polls can serve a useful purpose. There is no doubt that they amplify the volume of the debate, although just what it is that is being amplified remains problematic. There is the very real possibility that the inability of polls to measure nuances in opinion—the very essence of abortion opinion—results in distortion rather than clarification of the majority sentiment. Ladd concludes that the majority's opinion about abortion is quite clear: "Abortion should not be categorically banned, but it should not be established as an absolute right."[40] This greatly oversimplifies the matter. It is undoubtedly correct that the majority is not prepared to accept abortion as a "right" with the positive glow that surrounds that concept. Still, if the polls are looked at in toto, it does seem fair to conclude that the majority does recognize abortion as *a troublesome, problematic, morally wrenching, wish it would go away, occasional necessity that I hope it never does but may someday face me, and in case it does I want the option (though I doubt I would want to exercise it) to decide what to do myself.* And though most people are uncomfortable about discussing the issue in terms of rights, there does seem to be a rather strong majority that wants to keep it legal and available for those who need it whatever the Court does with its *Roe* decision. This position might be best described as a *right in effect,* if not *in effect a right.*

Ladd and others use the responses to the six NORC questions to suggest that majority support is not present for so-called birth-control reasons, or simply to end an unwanted and unplanned-for pregnancy. When, however, the NORC questions are placed in the context of others (like the one discussed above, in which 78 percent agreed that they personally feel that abortion is wrong but also feel that the abortion decision has to be made by each woman for herself), the proof that the majority does not want abortion available for unwanted pregnancy (in other words, for birth-control reasons) is not so certain at all.

What is even more troublesome than the confused message of the polls is the potential for manipulation and misuse of poll results in the political process. The results of individual questions can be, and are, misused by the media and all the players in the abortion debate to further their own ends, and neither side has to resort to survey shenanigans to accomplish its purpose. Even the most reputable polling organizations—Gallup, Roper, and NORC—continue to ask questions that, depending on their wording, result in the majority's sentiments appearing now on one side, now on the other. Careful assessment of combinations of these questions can provide a somewhat clearer picture of the complex public stance on abortion, and tracking of individual questions over time can provide some clue to how mass opinion has changed (or not changed); but this is not the norm. Abortion poll results are most often used as weapons to escalate an already inflamed public debate. This practice is likely to continue as the issue moves into state legislative arenas.

What the Polls Say about Possible Abortion Restrictions

A number of polls have asked questions about specific restrictions that were being considered by some states following the Court's lifting in *Webster* of the prohibition on state regulation of abortion. Table 7.10 presents the results of one such poll, which found majority support for requiring minors under the age of eighteen to get parental consent for an abortion (67 percent), for performing abortions in public hospitals only to save the woman's life (54 percent), and for permitting abortions in the fifth month only after a test for fetal viability (52 percent). The majority was opposed to prohibiting abortions for sex selection (55 percent) or to making it difficult for clinics to provide abortions (59 percent). An earlier Gallup poll (September 1988) found 66 percent opposed to the Reagan administration's decision to withhold federal financing from family-planning clinics that provide counseling about abortion. Other polls have found a much higher percentage (85 percent in the *Los Angeles Times* March 1989 poll) voicing support for requiring a minor to have parental permission before getting an abortion. Interestingly, 67 percent at the same time thought that making abortion illegal would not reduce the number of abortions in the United States, and 93 percent thought that if abortion were illegal in their state that it would not stop most women from having abortions because they would go to a state where abortion was legal.[41] Support for abortion restrictions does not seem to have anything to do with the expectation that the number of abortions will be affected. Perhaps it is like many other unpleasant policy problems: People recognize that abortion exists and will continue to exist but would just as soon not have it exist in their own back yards.

If abortion becomes a state policy issue, some states will move to ban abortion, some will move to try to restrict abortion, and some will con-

TABLE 7.10
POSSIBLE ABORTION RESTRICTIONS,
POLL RESULTS, JULY 1989

Question(s): "As I read some restrictions on abortion that are being considered in some states, tell me if you would favor or oppose such a restriction in your state.

	Favor (%)	Oppose (%)	No opinion (%)
[1.] Not allowing abortions to be performed in public hospitals unless the abortion is to save a woman's life?"	54	43	3
[2.] In cases where the mother is five months pregnant, requiring a test to see if the fetus might survive outside the womb before allowing the abortion?"	52	41	7
[3.] Requiring that women under 18 years of age get parental consent before they are allowed to have an abortion?"	67	29	4
[4.] Prohibiting abortions that are performed because the parents want a child of the other sex?"	41	55	4
[5.] Passing laws and regulations that would make it very difficult for women's clinics that perform abortions to continue to operate?"	35	59	5

SOURCE: *Gallup Poll Monthly,* July 1989, 10.

tinue to make it legal as it is now. The state legislative battles will be contentious, witness the Idaho and Connecticut battles (discussed in chapter 8). If the Supreme Court overturns or moves further back from *Roe,* the battles will be exacerbated. Although Capitol Hill has played a minimal role in the national abortion struggle since *Webster* (discussed in chapter 9), if *Roe* is overturned, a reluctant Congress may find it impossible not to become reentangled in abortion politics. Endless opinion polls will undoubtedly become tactical weapons of activists on both sides. It seems unlikely that the politicians making the policy decisions will take the time to digest the complex messages carried in those polls.

Arguments about the meaning and use of abortion poll data will go on and on. Claims and counterclaims will continue to fill the air. In abortion polling there is plenty of ammunition to arm both sides. Ironically, the public opinion survey has become so commonplace in our society that questions about its utility and validity in the democratic process are all but ignored. It is difficult to imagine a subject that raises such questions more pointedly than abortion, yet the polls grind on and the controversies over what those polls mean continue.

Notes

1. *Gallup Poll Monthly Report,* July 1989, 5; for a full report on the July poll, see pages 6–12.

2. This index was developed by Yankelovich, Skelly, and White and designed to measure the volatility in the public's views on issues. The index has four components: how much the issue affects the respondent individually; how well informed the respondent is on the issue; how much and how often the person has discussed the issue with family and friends; and the respondent's own assessment of how likely his or her views will change on the issue.

3. For a discussion of various points of view about democracy and polling, see Herbert Asher, *Polling and the Public* (Washington, D.C.: CQ Press, 1988), 150–55.

4. Ibid., 155.

5. Sampling error figures are taken from the Gallup poll's recommended allowance for sampling error tables. See *Gallup Poll Monthly,* January 1991, 60–61.

6. See Hyman Rodman, Betty Sarvis, and Joy Walker Bonar, *The Abortion Question* (New York: Columbia University Press, 1987), 136.

7. CBS News/*New York Times* poll of 1412 adults conducted by telephone 13–16 April 1989, as reported in the *New York Times,* 26 April 1989, A1.

8. Figures from the Alan Guttmacher Institute, as reported in the *Washington Post,* 21 March 1989, A1, and 26 April 1991, I12.

9. See Senate Committee on the Judiciary, Subcommittee on the Constitution, *Hearings,* 97th Cong., 1st sess., 1981, 412, for one estimate of these categories.

10. *Washington Post,* 21 March 1989, A1.

11. Stanley K. Henshaw, Lisa M. Koonin, and Jack C. Smith, "Characteristics of U.S. Women Having Abortions, 1987," *Family Planning Perspectives,* March/April 1991, 76.

12. Victoria A. Sackett, "Between Pro-Life and Pro-Choice," *Public Opinion,* April/May 1985, 55.

13. Figures for overall percentage of U.S. female population by religious group are from a national survey on family growth cycles, as reported in *Public Opinion,* April/May 1988, 52.

14. See "Opinion Roundup," *Public Opinion,* April/May 1981, 22. Using three additional measures to differentiate between born-agains and Evangelicals, Gallup estimates that Evangelicals make up about 19 percent of the total population. Gallup figures for born-agains and Evangelicals are not broken down into the subcategory of "women of childbearing age." As a percentage of women of childbearing age, born-agains might be somewhat smaller or larger.

15. For example, see Michael W. Combs and Susan Welch, "Blacks, Whites, and Attitudes Toward Abortion," *Public Opinion Quarterly* 46 (1982):510–20;

and Elaine J. Hall and Myra Marx Ferree, "Race Differences in Abortion Attitudes," *Public Opinion Quarterly* 50 (1986): 193–207; Clyde Wilcox, "Race Differences in Abortion Attitudes: Some Additional Evidence," *Public Opinion Quarterly* 54 (1990): 248–55.

16. Wilcox, "Race Differences in Abortion Attitudes," 254.

17. *New York Times,* 26 April 1989, A25.

18. *Democracy in America,* 2 vols. (New York: Vintage Books, 1960), 2:272

19. Everett Carll Ladd, "Public Opinion: Questions at the Quinquennial," *Public Opinion,* April/May 1983, 31.

20. "A Conversation with Daniel Yankelovich—American Values: Change and Stability," *Public Opinion,* January 1984, 3–8.

21. William Schneider, "Trouble for the GOP," *Public Opinion,* May/June 1989, 60.

22. George Gallup, Jr., and Dr. Frank Newport, "Americans Shift Toward Pro-choice Position," *Gallup Poll Monthly,* March 1990, 2.

23. CBS News/*New York Times* survey, 12–15 January 1989, as reported in *Public Opinion,* May/June 1989, 36.

24. Gallup/*Newsweek* 1989 poll, as reported, ibid.

25. *New York Times,* 26 April 1989, A25.

26. *Public Opinion,* May/June 1989, 36.

27. Question 1 asked 18–19 January 1982, by NBC News/AP poll; Question 2 asked February–April 1982, NORC-GSS; both as reported in *Public Opinion,* April/May 1983, 31.

28. Sackett, "Between Pro-Life and Pro-Choice," 53.

29. Rodman, Sarvis, and Bonar, *The Abortion Question,* 145.

30. *New York Times,* 22 January 1989, 21.

31. Ibid.

32. *Public Opinion,* May/June 1989, 35, 38.

33. Howard Schuman, Stanley Presser, and Jacob Ludwig, "Context Effects on Survey Responses to Questions about Abortion," *Public Opinion Quarterly* 45 (1981): 216–23.

34. *Los Angeles Times* survey, 3–10 March 1989, as reported in *Public Opinion,* May/June 1989, 35.

35. John E. Jackson and Maris A. Vinovskis, "The 'Single-Issue' Issue," in *The Abortion Dispute and the American System,* ed. Gilbert Y. Steiner (Washington, D.C.: Brookings Institution, 1983), 68.

36. *Gallup Poll Monthly,* October 1989, 19.

37. *Gallup Poll Monthly,* April 1989, 26–27.

38. Diane Colasanto and Linda DeStefano, "'Pro-Choice' Position Stirs Increased Activism in Abortion Battle," *Gallup Poll Monthly,* October 1989, 16.

39. "The Polls: 1948 Looks Better and Better," *Christian Science Monitor,* 17 November 1989, 18.

40. "The Partisan Consequences," *Public Opinion,* May/June 1989, 4.

41. *Public Opinion,* May/June 1989, 38, reporting on results from the *Los Angeles Times,* poll conducted 3–10 March 1989 and an AP Media General poll conducted 6–15 March 1989.

CHAPTER 8

Abortion and State Politics
after *Webster*

Advocates on both sides of the abortion issue predicted a bitter fifty-state battle following *Webster,* and state-level politicians were all too aware that their votes were the prize sought by both sides. "It's terrible to have this issue back again," lamented Mel Miller, former Speaker of the New York State Assembly.[1] But back it was. "I have been contacted by at least 150 organizations and hundreds of women from my district who have never contacted me before," commented one state lawmaker just a month after *Webster.*[2] "The disaster facing America's state legislators," one editorial noted, "is that they may have to address an issue of public policy on which their constituents have strong and irreconcilable opinions. This they hate to do and are skilled at avoiding, even though it is what they are paid for."[3]

The timing of *Webster* limited immediate action because the 1989 legislative sessions had ended in many states. While politicians in most states "ducked and hedged or pondered,"[4] Florida Governor Bob Martinez, a strong opponent of abortion, promptly announced that he planned to convene a special session solely to address new abortion restrictions. When the legislators gathered in Tallahassee in the fall of 1989, though, his proposed restrictions were resoundingly defeated. Very few wanted to follow the governor out on his precarious pro-life limb. State opinion polls by then were reporting that six in ten Floridians were opposed to the special session; six in ten believed that the decision on abortion should be between a woman and her doctor; and seven in ten favored either no change or liberalization of the Florida abortion law. Pro-choice supporters quickly claimed Florida as a victory for their

Opposite: Hollywood stars and feminist leaders at the head of a pro-choice march on the Capitol, 9 April 1989. *Photo:* UPI/Bettmann Newsphotos.

side. Dozens of abortion restrictions were introduced in state houses around the nation, but only Pennsylvania actually passed a new abortion law in 1989; and although its restrictions were all procedural, pro-life supporters claimed a major success there.

The first post-*Webster* year seemed to end in a draw. Still, most predictions regarding the political lay of the land in the states were not encouraging to the pro-choice camp. Nine states and the District of Columbia were tagged as likely to keep abortion legal; nineteen were assumed likely to add restrictions or move to apply existing restrictions that had been unenforceable prior to *Webster*. The remaining twenty-two states were deemed toss-ups: action would depend on political forces such as the strength of the lobbying, public opinion, and struggles between legislatures and governors (see table 8.1).

Some predictions concerning states' abortion actions proved accurate, others not. By the end of 1991 nine states and Guam, a U.S. territory, had passed new restrictions. Michigan, Nebraska, and South Carolina, all of which had statutory requirements for parental notification for minors seeking abortions prior to *Webster*, revised their requirements to include the judicial bypass called for as constitutionally necessary by the Supreme Court in *Webster*. In 1990, Guam passed one of the most restrictive laws, permitting abortion only to save the life of the woman and prohibiting the giving of information concerning where an abortion may be obtained. Mississippi, North Dakota, and Ohio passed laws in 1991 requiring both a waiting period and a "lecture" about alternatives and the dangers of the procedure before an abortion could be performed. Louisiana and Utah passed extremely restrictive laws in 1991 limiting abortions to situations involving rape or incest, in which the life of the woman is at stake, and in which an infant with grave defects might be born.

Of the nine states that enacted new abortion laws between *Webster* and the end of 1991, six were among those considered most likely to do so (Louisiana, Mississippi, Nebraska, Pennsylvania, South Carolina, and Utah). Nebraska and South Carolina merely clarified existing law requiring parental notification for minors, though they had been thought to be among the states most likely to pass tough new abortion laws. From the toss-up category, only Michigan, North Dakota, and Ohio passed new procedural restrictions on abortion.

On the pro-choice side, four states, three designated as toss-up states (Connecticut, Maryland, and Nevada) and one state from the most-likely-to-keep-abortion-legal category (Washington) passed laws liberalizing abortion after *Webster*. The Connecticut General Assembly acted in 1990 to legalize all abortions prior to viability (in effect writing *Roe*

TABLE 8.1

PROBABLE ABORTION ACTION IN THE STATES

AFTER *WEBSTER*

States most likely to keep abortion legal

Alaska	○ Hawaii	New York
○ California	Iowa	○ Vermont
District of	Maine	○ Washington[a]
Columbia	New Mexico	

States most likely to restrict abortion further

① Alabama	① Louisiana[b]	① Pennsylvania[c]
Arkansas	Minnesota	① South Carolina[d]
Florida	① Mississippi[d]	Texas
Georgia	① Missouri[d]	① Utah[c]
Idaho	① Nebraska[d]	① West Virginia
Indiana	Oklahoma	Wyoming
Kentucky		

Battlegrounds: contest too close to predict winner

Arizona	① Michigan[d]	① Ohio[d]
Colorado	Montana	○ Oregon
○ Connecticut[e]	Nevada[f]	Rhode Island
Delaware	New Hampshire	① South Dakota
Illinois	New Jersey	Tennessee
Kansas	○ North Carolina	Virginia
Maryland[e]	North Dakota[d]	① Wisconsin
Massachusetts		

SOURCE: Categories based on information from *Newsweek*, 17 July 1989, 24.

① = states later deemed by the National Abortions Rights Action League (NARAL) most likely to pass restrictive laws if *Roe* is overturned (*Who Decides? A State-by-State Review of Abortion Rights*, 3d ed. [Washington, D.C.: NARAL Foundation, 1992]).

○ = states, according to NARAL, that pose the lowest risks for the loss of abortion rights if *Roe* is overturned (ibid.).

a. Passed liberalized law by referendum, 1990.

b. Passed restrictions and limits, 1991.

c. Passed restrictions, 1989.

d. Passed restrictions, 1991.

e. Liberalized, 1990.

f. Liberalized by referendum, 1991.

into state law), but required counseling for minors under sixteen. Maryland passed a similar law in 1991, which included a requirement for parental notification for minors. A successful ballot initiative drive required voters to approve the referendum in the November 1992 election. By a 2 to 1 margin, Maryland's voters approved the measure, which basically codifies *Roe*'s guarantees except that the law also requires minors seeking abortions to have parental permission. Nevada voters passed a similar codification of *Roe* by a ballot initiative in 1990, which included a provision that the law cannot be amended, repealed, or otherwise changed except by the vote of the people. And in November 1991, by a vote of 756,812 to 752,588 (a margin of less than three-tenths of one percent of the total vote), Washington state voters passed the Reproductive Privacy Act, which provides that a woman has a fundamental right to choose or refuse birth control or an abortion and that a woman eligible for maternity care benefits from any state program cannot be denied benefits for a voluntary abortion. The voters of Oregon turned down two ballot questions in 1990: one that would have limited abortions to cases in which the woman's life was at risk or in cases of rape or incest, and one that would have eliminated state public funding of abortions.

Ascertaining the winning side in the battles over state abortion laws is more complicated than the simple statistics: nine for the pro-life side, five for the pro-choice side. If a pro-life win is measured by the elimination of all abortions except those performed to save the life of the woman (the position of the most committed pro-life activists) and a pro-choice win is measured by no regulation over abortion (the position of the most committed pro-choice activists), then only in Washington was there a clear "win," and it is on the pro-choice side. Tiny Guam (population 130,000) could be called an absolute win for the pro-life side. The rest of the new laws only lean in one direction or the other. Utah and Louisiana enacted very strong antiabortion statutes, even though they allow exceptions for rape or incest, severe fetal deformity, and severe damage to the health of the woman. Just as clearly the Connecticut, Maryland, and Nevada laws are strongly pro-abortion, even though they require counseling or parental notification for minors. The other new laws all add significant new procedural obstacles, but none limits the reasons for abortion—even though most of these states were likely candidates for doing so.

The question of who is winning is further complicated by state legislative actions that have not yet resulted in final laws. For example, in March 1990 the Idaho legislature sent to the governor what was up to that point the nation's strictest antiabortion bill. It limited abortions to three situations: in a case of rape if reported within seven days or of incest for women under eighteen if reported before the abortion; in the case of profound fetal deformity; and in the case that a woman's life or physical health would be threatened. Political pressure on Idaho's Democratic Governor Cecil D. Andrus, a long-time opponent of abortion, was intense. Pro-life callers threatened to withdraw their support for a fourth term, a significant concern for a Democratic candidate in an overwhelmingly Republican state. Pro-choice callers threatened a nationwide boycott of Idaho potatoes (which account for about a third of the nation's supply) and other products, and, especially troublesome, a boycott of tourism, the fastest growing segment of the state's economy ($1.5 billion annually). Andrus vetoed the bill, in his message lashing out at antiabortion groups outside Idaho that had written the bill and pressed it on the Idaho legislature for the "sole purpose of getting this issue back before the Supreme Court. The bill is drawn so narrowly that it would punitively and without compassion further harm an Idaho woman who may find herself in the horrible, unthinkable position of confronting a pregnancy that resulted from rape or incest."[5] The veto message suggested that had the legislation not included a reporting limit on abortions in the case of pregnancy from rape or incest, Andrus would have signed it. This hardly makes his stance pro-choice, yet the western director of the National Right to Life Movement said the governor no longer could call himself pro-life.[6] On the other hand, a subsequent report by the National Abortion Rights Action League rated Andrus as strongly antiabortion.[7] It seems there was little payoff from either camp—he has a foot in neither. His actions did not hurt his popularity with Idaho voters; he handily won 67 percent of the ballots cast in the November 1990 election (compared to a squeaker in 1986, when he received just over 50 percent). Either Idaho voters approved of his veto or the abortion issue is not as important to most of them as activists on both sides assert; or other, more salient issues, such as the weakening economy, caused abortion to recede as a factor.

State abortion politics has at least as many variations as there are states. No two battles are quite the same. The composition of both houses of the legislature, the position of the governor, the relative strength of the pro-choice and pro-life lobbies, the demographics of the population, and the nature of competing issues—which as the 1990s got under way focused on the recession, rising unemployment, and budget deficits—are all critical factors in determining structure and outcome. Comparing the political struggle in two states that passed permissive abortion laws and the struggle in two states that passed restrictive abortion laws illustrates the point.

Connecticut and Maryland —
Two Pro-Choice "Wins"

As the third-most-Catholic state (1,375,000 Roman Catholics in a population of 3.3 million), Connecticut seems an unlikely state for passing a liberal abortion statute, yet it was the first to do so following *Webster*. Connecticut's antiabortion laws, passed just after the Civil War, were among the harshest, providing sentences of up to five years in prison for anyone performing an abortion and two years in prison for any woman receiving an abortion for any reason. Though *Roe* effectively made them unenforceable, Connecticut never removed these laws from the books; if *Roe* were overturned, the criminal penalties could be thus enforced.

By the time *Webster* was announced, the Connecticut General Assembly had adjourned for the year, enabling the legislators to avoid the issue in 1989. State Representative Richard D. Tulisano, cochair of the Judiciary Committee, though, predicted that "all political hell will break loose come the next session."[8] With 1990 being an election year, groups on both sides of the issue would be out in force. It would be impossible to avoid coming to grips with abortion.

Connecticut has long had an active and politically effective prochoice lobby, the Connecticut Coalition for Choice, which is made up of several large organizations including state chapters of the National Abortion Rights Action League, the National Organization for Women, Planned Parenthood, and the Connecticut Civil Liberties Union. No antiabortion legislation had even come close to passage since *Roe*. Despite its large Catholic sector, Connecticut is usually considered to be a strong abortion rights state. Though the governor at the time (Democrat William A. O'Neill) was a Roman Catholic and personally opposed to abortion, his public position was to support *Roe*. Public opinion polls in the state showed that a large majority favored leaving abortion legal, even among those who declared membership in the Catholic church. The political climate, the balance of power between the abortion lobbies, the membership of the legislature, and the acceptance (if not the support) of the governor favored an abortion rights position. In the immediate aftermath of *Webster*, the calculus of power tipped even more toward the pro-choice position.

Webster galvanized dozens of groups that had been on the sidelines of the state pro-choice movement. The Coalition for Choice quickly expanded to include more than fifty groups, including the League of Women Voters and the United Church of Christ. With a sense of burgeoning power, the coalition initially set an ambitious goal: elimination of all governmental power over abortion. This effective expansion of *Roe* (which allows for state regulation in the third-trimester) was to be accomplished by the following proposed statutory language: "The State of Connecticut, and all political subdivisions and agencies thereof, shall not interfere with a woman's personal decision to prevent, commence, terminate or continue a pregnancy."

On the other side, the Pro-Life Council of Connecticut, led by a former state senator who also served as a paid consultant to Connecticut's Catholic bishops, had a more modest legislative agenda. The council sought to require parental notification by minors, limits on abortion after viability, and tests for viability before abortions would be allowed. Five bills were offered advancing these goals in various combinations. Many abortion opponents were not satisfied with the limited objectives, but the lack of success in previous efforts in Connecticut to achieve limitations on abortions made more stringent restrictions a dim political prospect.

That Connecticut ultimately passed a strong pro-choice law is largely due to the efforts of two legislators: Representative Tulisano and State Senator Anthony Avallone, both Democrats, Catholics, and cochairs of the powerful Judiciary Committee. Tulisano is pro-life; Avallone is pro-choice. Both, however, are political realists, and both understood that the only way to manage the abortion issue was to get control of it before it got control of them. "Richard and I believed there was a consensus on abortion," said Avallone. "Nobody else but he and I believed that."[9] The consensus they saw leaned far more toward the pro-choice than the pro-life camp, but they knew that for any bill to pass it would have to have something for the pro-life side. The problem was to fashion an acceptable compromise. To that end they sought to contain the contentiousness of the issue.

Tulisano and Avallone began by holding a series of "informational hearings" during the summer with carefully chosen participants from both sides who, they believed, would be reasonable and willing to carry on a dialogue without the emotional rhetoric of some abortion debates. Though more militant groups objected to this strategy and sought to be included, the two legislators refused. One common ground was identified from these meetings: Both sides agreed that the state's criminal statutes ought to be repealed. Beyond that, however, consensus and compromise seemed at best a remote possibility. The cochairmen then switched to a behind-the-scenes negotiation in an effort to identify what the pro-choice side would accept as limitations on choice to keep the pro-life side aboard, and what concessions to choice the pro-life side would accept, if grudgingly, to keep its partisans from fighting a bill that liberalized access to abortion.

As is often the case for politicians, protection of one's public image was an important consideration in the process of achieving compromise. One gesture Tulisano insisted upon was that the Judiciary Committee vote to schedule all five of the pro-life bills for public hearings along with the pro-choice bill. Pro-choice groups pressed committee members to vote against including the pro-life bills. The groups knew from experience that the best way to keep an antiabortion bill from passing was to stop it at the start. Without a hearing, legislative procedure would prevent floor action on the bills and no floor action was the safest bet.

"Avallone went through the roof."[10] He was angry, and he let the pro-choice lobbyists know it in a confrontational meeting. Shouting, he came down hard on the fairness issue: "How do you negotiate if everybody's not at the table and you don't want the other side at the table?"[11] Chagrined by this attack from one of their own, the coalition, after some heated internal debate, abandoned its absolutist position. This did not mean the pro-choice people were prepared to give away any rights they already had, but they were forced to recognize that there was no possibility of expanding those rights. They sought instead to protect the position of *Roe*. The line they drew in the sand was *no regulation before viability* and *no parental notification*.

On the pro-life side, limits on abortion after viability and parental notification were the prime goals. Neither of these requirements would have much effect on the number of abortions performed in the state (see table 8.2), but pro-lifers saw them as important first steps in limiting abortions.

In March 1990 the Judiciary Committee held public hearings on all the abortion bills. This was the chance for everyone to be heard. The hearing room was packed with spectators, but only fifteen of the thirty committee members were present. Members were not eager to get into the fray.

Tulisano opened the hearing, sounding like a schoolmaster admonishing an unruly class: "No shouting. No booing. No cheering. No standing in the aisles. Nothing. Or else, I'll tell you now, we'll adjourn the hearing and no one will be heard."[12] Nearly 190 people then took turns at the witness table; 110 identified themselves as pro-life. Some read poetry. Some quoted from the Bible. Some presented scientific research. Some made impassioned pleas or told abortion horror stories. No one expected that any minds on the committee or in the audience would be changed. "It's a place for people to vent their feelings," Tulisano said.[13] He hoped that the emotional catharsis of testifying in public would produce a lull in the activists' fervor long enough to get some compromises accepted and legislation passed.

After the hearing, committee members continued to haggle for weeks

TABLE 8.2

CONNECTICUT ABORTION STATISTICS, 1987

Number of abortions performed		19,994
Number of abortions after twenty weeks[a]		7
Number of abortions on females under		
age sixteen		471
Number aged 15	282	
Number aged 14	92	
Number aged 13	21	
Number aged 12 or under	76	
Number of abortions paid for with state funds[b]		2,485
Total cost of state-funded abortions		$773,100

SOURCE: "Official State Health Statistics for 1987," *Hartford Courant,* 2 February 1990, A11.

a. Viability is usually pegged at between twenty-four and twenty-eight weeks, but the U.S. Supreme Court has upheld a standard of twenty weeks to provide a four-week margin of error in estimating gestational age.

b. Under a state court order issued in 1981 and made permanent in 1986, the state must pay for abortions for indigent women when a doctor certifies the procedure is "medically necessary."

over the precise wording for a final bill that was to be reported to the floor. Everything was a source of contention, even the title. "An Act Concerning Abortion" and "An Act Concerning Counseling" were rejected as potential red flags. The committee finally settled on the innocuous and obfuscating "An Act Concerning the Repeal of Certain Statutes."

The principal substantive sticking points in the committee negotiations were how to define viability; what sort of threat to a woman's health after viability would justify an abortion; and whether to include a parental notification requirement. Members debated using "serious" or "significant" to qualify the health risk to the woman but, as one representative commented, this "gets you on the slippery slope of weighing the fetus's life against the mother's health. And once you get on that slope we don't know where to get off."[14] Tulisano wanted viability set at twenty-two weeks; abortion rights supporters wanted twenty-eight weeks. The notification issue degenerated into a battle royal, with the pro-choice people unwilling to budge. "In abortion politics," one pro-choice legislator noted when underscoring the importance of perception in this political struggle, "passage of a parental-notification measure would be considered a major abortion-rights defeat."[15] In the end, the pro-life side gave in (some later said the reality was that they were rolled by the pressure and power of the committee chairmen). The Judiciary Committee reported out a bill that merely repealed the old criminal statues and provided counseling for pregnant girls under sixteen.

The pro-choice side was ebullient. If the bill became state law and *Roe* were overturned, Connecticut would be left with no law on abortion other than the counseling portion. Effectively, this would mean that the pro-choicers' original goal of no state regulation would be realized. It did not take long for the pro-life legislators to figure this out. Tulisano was definitely not happy with such a potential result. "We wanted something everybody could vote on, and maybe not be happy with, but at least support," he said. The bill lacked "anything anti-abortion legislators could 'bring home' to their constituencies."[16] The counseling provision was not enough to compensate for unfettered abortion as Connecticut policy. What he wanted was a provision that limited abortions after viability. What he knew he could not get politically was testing to determine viability. A compromise was finally struck that in effect adopted the regulatory scheme set out in *Roe*.

The Connecticut bill stated: "The decision to terminate a pregnancy prior to the viability of the fetus shall be solely that of the pregnant woman in consultation with her physician. No abortion may be performed upon a pregnant woman after viability of the fetus except when necessary to protect the life and health of the pregnant woman." Viability was not defined in the law nor was the nature of the health risk to the mother specified. Tulisano called it a viability provision because abortion after viability was limited. Pro-choice members called it a codification of *Roe* because it prevented regulation of abortion before viability. Both sides could publicly claim some victory. Tulisano signed on.

With both Judiciary Committee chairs behind the bill, antiabortion leaders felt they had been presented with a fait accompli. Reluctantly, the Pro-Life Council agreed to accept the compromise. Because the chief spokeswoman for the council was also a hired lobbyist for the Catholic bishops, members of the state legislature assumed the Catholic church was not going to oppose the bill either. In fact, the church did not actively oppose the bill, but whether that represented support, resignation, or the fact that the rest of the legislative process moved so fast that they did not get organized in time remained open to conjecture. After the bill passed, one antiabortion legislator asserted that the church had not signed on at all and that his side had gotten "snookered."

In introducing the committee bill on the floor of the House, abortion-opponent Tulisano stressed its consensus nature. "This bill begins to work on developing those issues which people agree upon."[17] As abortion rights supporters had feared, an amendment was immediately offered to require parental notification. Its sponsors presented it as nothing more than "common sense." "There is virtually no other medical procedure that I can think of," remarked one member, "where our society has somehow adopted the rule that parents aren't notified.... This is not a consent statute. It says simply that they've been notified. It does not require that they agree to the procedure."[18]

Other supporters pushed the amendment as a "family-values" issue. One conservative member harangued his colleagues for their lack of compassion and understanding:

> I think everyone in this room here has family values. I think we love our kids and we love our grandchildren and I think if they're in trouble, we welcome them to come home and talk to us ... for anybody to suggest that's the wrong way to go, is an idiot in my book and doesn't know what the facts of life are.... I suggest anybody who thinks it's a bad amendment, like one speaker prior to myself, have a family, raise some kids and you'll know what the hell life is all about before you get up on this floor and make ridiculous statements.[19]

It was not a particularly persuasive approach, but perhaps the speaker recognized that the amendment stood no chance and was just voicing his frustration.

Opponents did not see the amendment as a plus for family values. One legislator stated:

> It's a wolf in sheep's clothing. It does nothing of what it purports to do, yet it imposes an extraordinary burden on a group in our society pathetically unable to defend themselves in the political process and unprepared to deal with the requirements set forth in this amendment.... [T]he young women of this state will not benefit from this bill.... The only parties that I can see that benefit are the anti-choice lobbies and the groups who would like to bring home a victory today and say that we did something for family relations.[20]

Another railed against Congress:

> We wouldn't be in this mess if Congress had taken its responsibility. Everyone says this decision has been given to the states. It needn't have been. Congress could make laws regarding abortion and they would be

standard throughout the country. We wouldn't have to talk about going from Hartford, Providence, Boston to Albany. They could have standardized it. But Congress has no more desire than we politically to act on this measure. They have wimped out.[21]

Yet another member cautioned that as legislators "we can not stand on this floor and say what's good for parents or children." He read from a father's letter about the grief another state law had wrought:

> My daughter Becky made a mistake and became pregnant.... Parent consent laws, very similar to those you are considering today, dictated that in order to terminate her pregnancy she must obtain approval of her parents, petition the courts or travel to another state that would allow her safe, clinical abortions or seek back alley assistance. She died of an illegal abortion. In confiding with her friends, she said, "I don't want to disappoint Mom and Dad. I love them so much." ... My daughter was a quality child. She was raised in a functional family environment.... How can we legislate or dictate that families communicate.... If I understand correctly, the legislation before you offers no accommodation for a real life situation like that of Becky Bell, nor does it consider that the young lady [may be] from a dysfunctional home who may fear [for] her physical well-being. These laws speak to theories. They do not address real life.... Rebecca Sue Bell was not a theory. She was a beautiful human being. She was my daughter taken away because others thought that they had all the answers. The bill before you does not have all the answers.[22]

Supporters countered by pointing out that the amendment was not a consent bill and that it provided a bypass arrangement allowing a pregnant young woman to notify others besides her parents (grandparents, an aunt, or a probate court judge), but their explanations were unsuccessful. The amendment lost: 48 voting for it, 101 against. Two other amendments were similarly defeated, and in the end the committee bill passed 136–12. The lopsided vote made the results look close to consensus. Many of those in the "aye" column, however, were less than happy. To the assertion that "everyone's aboard," one member who ultimately voted for the committee bill countered, "Believe me, I'm not on board. I have got a foot on board and a foot on the ground, and I think many other people here do too."[23]

Tulisano, nonetheless, was content with the results. Though he firmly reasserted his preference for a more restrictive law, he also stated that he believed that "it is futile and wrong to try to stop abortion until society can offer women better alternatives."[24] Until then, he was prepared to "accept" abortion though he did not pretend to like it. Most of all he was proud that the legislature had faced the abortion issue and acquitted itself well:

> I think our example here in Connecticut ... will be an example to the nation that a very difficult issue, an issue which has rended our country asunder, can be dealt with by a democratically elected body, that we can, rather than trying to have a victory for one side or the other, begin to develop a consensus among individuals, to begin to put into legislative language those items which we agree upon. I see this as a beginning, not the end. I do not believe that many of the issues that are still out there have gone away and that we will never see them again in the future. I think we will. But at long last ... leaders from both groups are beginning to talk to each other ... and to build into law a respect for each other and a solid foundation for the future.[25]

Ten days later, the State Senate voted overwhelmingly in favor of the bill and the governor quickly signed it into law.

One factor that undoubtedly affected the outcome in Connecticut was timing. In early 1990 the political winds seemed to be blowing hard toward the pro-choice position. By the end of the year the direction of public opinion and the perception of the balance between pro-choice and pro-life political power were not quite so clear, however. Nationally, pro-life forces were back in action, and whether their Connecticut allies would have been so accepting of the "codification-of-*Roe*" compromise is debatable.

The National Abortions Rights Action League called Connecticut a "very important victory,"[26] but there is no assurance that the victory is final. A statutory protection of a "right" is a far less powerful shield against its future denial than a constitutional protection. By 1992, when the Supreme Court seemed poised to overturn *Roe,* one pro-choice legislator warned: "Connecticut's [abortion] law is not sacrosanct.... It's about as safe as the Lemon Law [the law aimed at protecting new-car buyers]. It's subject to election once every two years."[27] Both sides in the abortion struggle were well aware of that reality; both continued to expend considerable energy and funds trying to change or protect the balance of power in the legislature by supporting candidates who favor their positions and mounting attacks against candidates who oppose those positions.

If the abortion issue reappears in Connecticut, it will matter who is governor and who controls the legislature. The power of incumbency is considerably less in statehouses than on Capitol Hill, so significant change in membership as time passes is a given. Will the working relationship and potential for consensus among Connecticut abortion activists that Tulisano and Avallone forged endure? Will the two lawmakers still be there, or will there be new leaders? Just a year after the General Assembly passed the compromise abortion law, it was embroiled in a battle over a state income tax in which demagogy, stalemate, and acrimony ruled. Working relationships even within the same party were ravaged. There are no guarantees that consensus and compromise will rule the next time the state deals with the abortion issue.

Only one other state followed Connecticut's legislative example. In Maryland, an act similar to the Connecticut abortion statute was signed into law in February 1991. The road to passage was much bumpier and the legislative process far more acrimonious. During 1990 efforts in the Maryland legislature to deal with the abortion issue had ended in gridlock when sixteen state senators held the pro-abortion bill hostage to an eight-day filibuster. When the Senate attempted to resolve the impasse by passing both a pro-abortion bill and an antiabortion bill, leaving it to the voters to decide by referendum which they wanted, the House rebelled and killed both.

Part of the problem in getting action through the legislature was the reluctance of Governor William D. Schaefer to take a stand on the issue of abortion. Not until just before the fall 1990 elections did he make his position public: He personally opposed abortion but as governor would veto legislation that did not give women wide discretion in choosing early-term abortion. When the state legislature convened in early 1991, both houses quickly passed legislation protecting a woman's right to abortion (84–52 in the House, 29–18 in the Senate). The governor signed the bill immediately.

Elected politicians' overwhelming support of the Maryland law did not translate into its acceptance by the pro-life activist camp, even though the law included a parental-notification requirement. Fast action had moved the issue out of the legislature (to the relief of most members) but had not given pro-life supporters a sense of participation—a feeling that their concerns had been considered and their efforts had won something, as had been the case in Connecticut. Though the law was scheduled to go into effect on 1 July 1991, pro-life groups moved energetically to collect enough signatures before then to force a referendum. Because they were successful in this effort, the liberalized abortion law was placed on the ballot for Maryland's November 1992 elections. Voters approved it by a 2 to 1 margin.

Fast Action in Louisiana and Utah —
Two Pro-Life "Wins"

Within days of the *Webster* decision, the Louisiana legislature acted to restrict abortions. By 81–13 in the House and a unanimous vote in the Senate, the legislators passed a resolution asking the state's district attorneys to enforce its 134-year-old state law banning abortions under any circumstances and imposing criminal penalties of up to ten years in prison at hard labor for those performing the procedure. The resolution was not binding, but it was the best the legislature could immediately accomplish; it was then in a special session to balance the budget and could not take up other substantive matters. One legislator explained: "In the late 70s we passed an act that said if *Roe v. Wade* was overturned, all of our previous laws would have continued vitality. What we are doing in a friendly way is instructing the D.A.s to enforce the criminal statutes."[28]

The old criminal antiabortion law—along with several other laws that banned abortion clinic advertising, the sale or distribution of drugs and devices designed to induce abortion, and advertising concerning birth control—was subject to a thirteen-year-old court injunction that prohibited enforcement. Within a few months of the resolution's passage, lawyers for the New Orleans district attorney and the state attorney general were in federal court asking that the injunction be lifted. "The tide is turning in favor of more restrictive abortion laws," declared the state's counsel before the court. There could be no doubt that change in the law had occurred, he argued, and that "this change is significant." In consequence, he argued, the injunction should be dissolved, thereby avoiding "the loss of the most intrinsic and basic right there is, the right to life itself."[29] The ACLU attorney arguing for the other side, Rachael Pine, countered that there were no new standards for abortion that would support lifting of the injunction on the most restrictive criminal abortion law in the country. "Nothing short of overruling *Roe* would allow Louisiana law to be enforced," she said.[30] Pine's initial assumption was that the lawsuit would be quickly dismissed as frivolous, but following oral arguments the three Reagan-appointed judges hearing the case requested additional briefing. It was clear that they were considering the state's request seriously.

A poll taken in July 1989 showed that a majority of Louisiana voters (56 percent) believed that a woman should have the right to make her own decision about abortion. The same poll found that 29 percent of the voters were "definitely" in favor of making abortion a crime except in cases of rape or incest, and 30 percent were "definitely" against making it a crime.[31] This information about voter opinion, however, did not dissuade many legislators. While the legal strategy to enforce the old laws progressed slowly through the courts, the legislature moved on its own. In 1990 two new stringent abortion bills were vetoed by Governor Buddy Roemer. Override efforts ran into procedural snarls, and the legislature adjourned for the year.

In April 1991 antiabortion legislators tried again. Democratic State Representative Sam Theriot introduced a bill providing that "life begins at conception" and outlawing all abortions unless necessary to preserve the woman's life or unless the pregnancy was the result of rape or incest. The bill further required that a rape victim had to (1) have reported the rape to law enforcement officials within seven days of the rape; (2) have obtained a physical examination within five days of the rape to determine that she was not pregnant prior to the rape; and (3) have the abortion within thirteen weeks of conception. Similar restrictions applied in situations involving incest. There were to be no loopholes that might allow a false assertion of rape in order to obtain an abortion. The penalty for performing an illegal abortion was a prison term of one to ten years and a fine of $10,000 to $100,000.

The governor proposed a number of amendments, including one that would have allowed abortion in the case of a tubal pregnancy and in the case of a fetus with a life-threatening deformity. They were soundly defeated. By overwhelming majorities (72–31 in the House, 29–9 in the Senate) Theriot's bill sailed through.

Governor Roemer again exercised his veto. "The open window for abortions must be closed in order to protect the life of the unborn," he said in his veto message, "but meaningful exceptions must be drawn in order to protect the life and rights of the woman involved."[32] This was not a pro-choice governor versus a pro-life legislature; rather, it was a struggle over marginal differences at the extreme end of regulation. As had Governor Andrus in the Idaho case discussed above, Roemer wanted only a few more exceptions in the law. But where Andrus's veto stood, Roemer's second veto was quickly overridden. Whether the difference is attributable to the personal popularity of Andrus compared to Roemer's stormy relationship with his legislature (exacerbated by his switch from Democrat to Republican after his 1987 election), or whether the legislators were simply more pro-life in Louisiana than in Idaho is unclear. What was clear is that in both states opinion polls showed that a majority of the people did not want abortion to be made illegal.[33]

One special source of outrage for many women in the state was to see the abortion issue debated and decided by a body almost exclusively male. Louisiana has the lowest percentage of women serving in its state legislature (2.1 percent) of any state in the Union (the average is 18.1 percent). Only 3 women serve in its 105-member House, none in the Senate.

The day after the bill became law, the American Civil Liberties Union was in federal district court in New Orleans challenging its constitutionality and seeking an injunction to keep it from going into effect while the court case proceeded. The ACLU's action was neither a surprise nor an unwelcome action to the bill's supporters. "I am anxious that this case reach the U.S. Supreme Court as soon as possible," commented the state's attorney general. "We believe that this law will be found constitutional and *Roe vs. Wade* will be overturned."[34] Louisiana abortion opponents were hopeful that their law would be the vehicle the Court would use to scuttle *Roe.* When the district court judge found the law unconstitutional and issued an injunction against its enforcement in August 1991, the state immediately appealed. The race was on to be the first case to reach the Supreme Court. But, following the Court's ruling in *Planned Parenthood of Southeastern Pennsylvania v. Casey* (see chapter 10), the justices declined to review Louisiana's appeal, leaving the lower court's invalidation of the state's restrictive abortion law intact.

Meanwhile, Utah took all of three days to bring a strict new antiabortion law into existence. In this state where 70 percent of the population and 90 percent of the legislators are members of the Mormon church, which considers abortion a sin except in the most extreme medical circumstances, such expeditiousness was a matter of course.

On the eighteenth anniversary of *Roe,* 23 January 1991, the Utah Senate passed two bills: one would make anyone who performed an illegal abortion guilty of a second-class felony, carrying a penalty of up to $10,000 and up to fifteen years in jail; the other would make performance of an abortion a third-class felony, carrying a $5,000 fine and up to five years in jail. The next day the House passed the less restrictive alternative. The following day the Senate accepted the House action, and within hours the governor signed the act into law.

Commenting on the result, the executive director of Planned Parenthood in Utah charged that the governor and legislature were ignoring the will of the majority; she cited two polls reporting that the majority of Utah citizens did not want more restrictive laws. "This really has come down to the Legislature and the Governor versus the people," she said.[35] Utah retains its ranking as the second-highest risk for abortion rights in the nation according to the National Abortion Rights Action League, outranked only by Louisiana.

Elections and the Abortion Issue:
The Power Equation Changes

For state politicians after *Webster,* the issue of abortion became not only a policy issue but a critical election campaign issue as well. So long as the Supreme Court stood behind *Roe,* the pro-life forces were predominant in pressing state legislatures to change the status quo. Candidates who advocated the pro-life position were rewarded with votes. Those who did not chanced a negative campaign waged by pro-life groups. It usually did not cost candidates much in terms of organized opposition from the pro-choice camp to climb on the pro-life bandwagon (although it undoubtedly cost them some votes). Because the states had little power over the abortion issue, pro-choice supporters felt freer to mark their ballots on the basis of candidates' other policy stands or on party preference. There was no real threat; pro-choice advocates could count on the federal courts to strike down antiabortion laws passed by state legislatures.

Webster changed that. Although a loss for the pro-choice side, it produced what the National Abortion Rights Action League's political director termed "the smoking gun we needed to mobilize our people."[36] The league's executive director, Kate Michelman, declared, "We're all energized with the idea that we can turn this around. We have made a commitment to work in a Bork-like fashion to make this happen."[37] "We intend to go on the offensive," warned Eleanor Smeal of the Fund for the Feminist Majority.

Public opinion seemed to be shifting. For the first time in a decade, polls began to show that sentiment for keeping abortion legal was growing. News coverage of reaction to *Webster* added to the perception that a sleeping bear of pro-choice support was awakening across the country. A number of initial successes in state legislative races, in stopping Florida Governor Martinez's antiabortion proposals, and in congressional votes (see chapter 9) added up to a "terrific psychological advantage."[38]

In the year after *Webster,* membership in the National Abortion Rights Action League jumped from 150,000 to 400,000; in the National Organization for Women, from 170,000 to 250,000.[39] In response to intensive fund-raising efforts money flowed into the pro-choice groups' coffers. The National Abortion Rights Action League nearly tripled its income (from $4.3 million in 1988 to $11.9 million in 1989); the National Organization for Women nearly doubled its income (from $5.5 million in 1988 to $10.6 million in 1989), as did Planned Parenthood Federation of America (from $7 million in 1988 to $13 million in 1989).[40]

Webster was a victory of sorts for the pro-life forces. Its immediate effect, though, was that some steam went out of the pro-life drive. Anti-abortion leaders conceded that they had lost energy but insisted it was little more than "the natural ebb and flow of ardor that occurs in any long-standing national debate."[41] Paige Cunningham of Americans United for Life explained: "The pro-life movement has been organized and active for twenty years, and some of us are tired. The pro-choice movement is fresh so they're operating with a much greater energy reserve. They've really rallied in light of *Webster*."[42]

The 1989 Elections: Pro-Choice Shows Its Muscle
Full coffers enabled the pro-choice groups to mount impressive public relations efforts aimed at generating support and targeting critical election campaigns. There was a sense of urgency following *Webster* to demonstrate newfound muscle, but in 1989 there were not many campaign arenas in which to do so. Only two governorships were up—Virginia and New Jersey. The mayoralty in New York City and a handful of state legislative seats were the only other races of any significance. All told, they were few in number, but they could not have been more propitious for pro-choice supporters.

Virginia's Democratic candidate for governor, L. Douglas Wilder, made his pro-choice position the centerpiece of his campaign against Republican Marshall Coleman, who had promised to veto any legislation that allowed abortions. One of Wilder's televised campaign commercials, picturing a backdrop of a fluttering American flag and a statue of Thomas Jefferson, warned:

> In Virginia we have a strong tradition of freedom and individual liberty—rights that are now in danger in the race for governor. On the issue of abortion, Marshall Coleman wants to take away your right to choose and give it to the politicians. He wants to go back to outlawing abortion, even in cases of rape and incest. Doug Wilder believes the government shouldn't interfere in your right to choose. He wants to keep the politicians out of your personal life. Don't let Marshall Coleman take us back. To keep Virginia moving forward Doug Wilder is the clear choice.[43]

It was a contest offering a clear choice on the abortion issue. Wilder became the first African-American to be elected to a governorship. As University of Virginia political scientist Larry Sabato commented just before the election, though, "The real story of this election is more one of abortion than race. It's certainly been the central issue in Virginia."[44]

It could cause 2 to 3 percent of the electorate to switch sides, Sabato claimed, which could be enough to decide the election. Based on exit polls, 32 percent of 1147 voters interviewed said that abortion was one of the two issues that mattered most to them in making their decisions. Of those who mentioned abortion, 55 percent supported Wilder. According to postelection news analyses, Wilder's ability to attract the suburban, young professionals away from the Republican column was key to his winning, and his stand on the abortion issue was credited for that feat.

In New Jersey the abortion issue also played an important role in the defeat of Republican Jim Courter by Democrat James J. Florio for the governorship. Opinion polls conducted by the Eagleton Institute at Rutgers University a few months before the election found 68 percent of those surveyed opposed to new state laws restricting abortions and 80 percent agreeing with the statement "The decision to have an abortion is a private matter that should be left to the woman to decide without government intervention."[45]

In light of those figures, Courter tried to play down his antiabortion stand during the election, but the National Abortion Rights Action League used television, radio, newspapers, direct mail, and phone banks to keep the abortion issue in the public eye. It was a hard-fought campaign and a critical test of pro-choice political strength. "If we can't win with Jim Florio versus Jim Courter, we are through nationally," a New Jersey state senator warned National Abortion Rights Action League volunteers. "If we don't do it this year, women's rights nationally are in trouble."[46] Florio garnered 62 percent of the vote. Courter's best showing came among the 18-to-29-year-old voters, who gave Florio the edge by only 52 to 47 percent. But when the returns from this cohort were broken down by sex, women voted for Florio by 60 to 39 percent. This was the population most heavily targeted by the pro-choice effort, and the effort seemed to have paid off.

Perhaps the most visible power of the abortion issue in state legislative races in 1989 was in a state senate race in California. When Roman Catholic Bishop Leo T. Maher refused to permit Democratic candidate Lucy Killea to receive communion because of her abortion rights position, he set off a nationwide uproar. This was the first time a political candidate had been singled out for such a proscription. Newspaper polls showed that an overwhelming majority of Catholics and non-Catholics objected to the action as an intrusion of religion into secular politics. The result for Killea was national media attention leading to a narrow upset victory over her Republican pro-life opponent in a conservative and heavily Republican district.

Within months another bishop made national news for his warning to New York Governor Mario M. Cuomo that he was "in serious risk of going to hell" for supporting abortion rights, but he stopped short of excommunicating or otherwise punishing Governor Cuomo.[47] In South Texas another bishop excommunicated the director of the local Reproduction Services Clinic and an obstetrician who performed abortions there.[48] Faced with the growing pro-choice power, some officials of the Roman Catholic church were taking matters into their own hands. Their national political organ, the National Conference of Catholic Bishops, seemed equally concerned. In April 1990 it hired a public relations firm, Hill and Knowlton, to help design an estimated $5 million counteroffensive that the bishops hoped would shift the debate and alter the political climate on the issue. It was the first time the bishops had sought such help in a public-policy debate, and again the issue of separation of church and state came to the fore.[49]

Commenting on the results of the November 1989 elections, U.S. Senator Bob Packwood (R-Oregon) said that "Republicans got the bejabbers beat out of them because of abortion."[50] Congressman Jim Leach (R-Iowa) worried that the GOP's failure to pay attention to the views of its rank-and-file members on matters of reproductive freedom of choice and family planning threatened the ability of the party ever to attain a governing majority. He blamed the election defeats on the fact that the "Republican Party and its candidates were perceived as holding rigid narrow views on one of the most difficult and divisive issues of our time."[51]

A Supreme Court decision had once again politically energized the losing side. But the political fallout from *Webster* was quite different from that following *Roe*. Pro-life forces were initially put off stride, but not for long. As one abortion rights consultant warned, "Those of us in the pro-choice movement ought not to be dazzled to the point of losing sight that we're in a very long-term battle that's going to be played in forum after forum in the country."[52] Soon there were two powerful, determined, and politically active forces—one on each side of the abortion issue—and caught in the middle were the state politicians.

The 1990 Election Campaigns: Muddied Waters

"Immediately after *Webster*," commented one pollster, "you could get an impact from abortion on a race for dogcatcher."[53] Pro-choice supporters hoped that abortion would stay in the limelight and that its continued saliency would work to their benefit as it had in 1989. In 1990 every U.S. House seat, thirty-four U.S. Senate seats, thirty-six governorships, and thousands of statehouse seats were on the line. By then, though, the prominence and clarity of the abortion issue in election campaigns was considerably diminished. Issue avoidance, recession, impending war, and political waffling intervened.

Politicians are fast learners when it comes to sidestepping threatening or controversial issues. As evidence mounted about the danger of taking a straightforward antiabortion position, dozens of pro-life politicians began to soft-pedal their rigid antiabortion stance. One technique was to return to reasserting personal opposition to abortion while denying the appropriateness of imposing one's personal views on others. This way a politician could vote pro-choice while mouthing pro-life. Another was to accept abortion reluctantly in the most widely supported circumstances (health danger to the woman, rape or incest, fetal deformity) while favoring parental permission or at least notification for minors and the elimination of abortion for "birth-control" reasons. This tactic included the counteroffensive of pressing pro-choice opponents to take unequivocal positions on these more popular (at least as measured by the specific poll questions) abortion restrictions.

Even the chairman of the Republican National Committee, Lee Atwater, entered the waffling game, characterizing his party as really just a "big tent" with room for all viewpoints, despite the party's longstanding antiabortion platform plank. As one Democratic National Committee staffer pointed out, "The great abortion debate of 1990 is rapidly disappearing on us because, lo and behold, politicians out there are trying to avoid talking about it."[54] Races between strong, unambiguous pro-life and pro-choice candidates were harder to find. And hence a clear referendum was equally hard to find among the results. Commenting on another problem with abortion as a campaign issue, one GOP pollster noted, "There's a yearning among the public that they don't want to discuss it. There's a feeling that they want it to go away." A Democratic pollster agreed that the public "hates that [abortion's] been politicized. They don't want it to dominate campaigns, and they hate politicians who try to make it the dominant issue."[55]

As the national mood swing toward the abortion rights position that immediately followed the *Webster* decision slowed, the scramble to get on the pro-choice bandwagon abated as well. In February of 1989, just before the *Webster* decision, the American Bar Association (ABA) voted to support a constitutional right to abortion. In August of 1990 the ABA Assembly, urged on by U.S. Attorney General Richard Thornburgh, voted 885–837 to rescind that stand.[56] That same month the governing body of the AFL-CIO decided by voice vote to remain neutral on the abortion issue.[57] Both the NAACP and the League of United Latin American Citizens were also reluctant to join the pro-choice coalition because of the split of opinion among their members.[58]

Still, abortion played a role in some races in the 1990 state elections. "The three most coveted prizes in yesterday's election, governors' seats in Florida, Texas, and California, shifted from anti- to pro-choice hands, and each of these prizes was wrapped in pro-choice votes," declared Kate Michelman of the National Abortion Rights Action League. "Choice was a bigger issue in more races in 1990 than at any time in history."[59] In California, gubernatorial candidates Democrat Dianne Feinstein and Republican Pete Wilson both favored abortion rights, so pro-choice had a sure win there. In Florida, Democrat Lawton Chiles (the winner) ran on an abortion rights position (though he had taken several antiabortion positions when he was in the U.S. Senate) against Republican Governor Martinez, whose call for the 1989 special session to pass abortion restrictions had outraged pro-choice supporters. Indicative of the level of anger Martinez engendered was the bumper sticker *"Abort Martinez before a second term!"*[60] The race in Texas also offered a clear choice between abortion rights supporter Democrat Ann Richards and abortion opponent Republican Clayton Williams. Williams tried repeatedly but unsuccessfully to reframe the debate by pressing Richards to join him in backing parental notification. Political analysts credit Richards's abortion rights views for attracting support among Republican women.

Overall, 1990 was a good year for pro-choice candidates. The elections increased the number of governors who favor keeping abortion legal from sixteen to twenty-seven, and the number of state legislative bodies that favor keeping abortion legal from twenty-three to forty-five.[61] Much of the growth in measurable pro-choice support, however, came from efforts to force incumbents to take a stand rather than from defeats of pro-life incumbents. (For example, in 1989 eleven governors had no position on abortion; by the close of the 1990 elections, the position of every governor was known.)

On the other side, Sandra Faucher, the National Right to Life Committee's political action director, claimed victories in the gubernatorial races in Alaska, Kansas, and Ohio, and in several key congressional elections. "One year ago, pro-abortion groups and commentators were predicting that any candidate who suggested that unborn children be protected would be defeated," Faucher pointed out. "This year you can't say that with a straight face."[62] In Ohio the Democratic candidate, Anthony Celebrezze, Jr., switched from his career-long antiabortion position to support abortion rights in response to pressure from many women in his party. The strategy did not help him beat Republican George V. Voinovich; other issues, especially ethical lapses in the incumbent Democratic administration, however, seemed to weigh more heavily in voters' minds than abortion. Several pro-life incumbent governors considered potentially vulnerable on the issue (Republican Governors Terry E. Branstad of Iowa, Tommy G. Thompson of Wisconsin, and Judd Gregg of New Hampshire, and Democratic Governor Robert P. Casey of Pennsylvania) all won handily, apparently not harmed by their abortion position. There was a net loss of one governor in the total who favored outlawing abortion (from twenty-three before the election to twenty-two after).

The 1991 Elections and Beyond: The Battle Goes On

Meanwhile the firebombing of clinics continued. Operation Rescue demonstrations returned in force. And annual national and state-level marches by both sides became the norm. But the public was largely focused on other issues. When President Bush announced the start of bombing against Iraq in January of 1991, the nation's attention was riveted for the next several months on CNN and its war-in-the-Gulf coverage. The stunning success of the ground operations in only one week of battle inaugurated a season of flag-waving patriotism that left abortion and many other public issues in the shade.

Then as 1991 progressed and the "short" corrective recession dragged on, the economy again took over as the momentous issue. The war's afterglow that the president and national government had enjoyed dimmed. Doubts about the win and what it meant began to creep into public dialogue. Resentment grew over a perceived greater concern in Washington, and especially on the part of the president, for foreign policy than for the problems at home.

There were not many political races of national import in 1991, but the special senatorial election in Pennsylvania to fill the seat of deceased Republican Senator John Heinz was one. The favored candidate in that race was former governer and U.S. attorney general, as well as close Bush ally, Richard Thornburgh. He was trounced by a little-known Democratic challenger, Harris Wofford, by more than 340,000 votes, a ten-percentage-point margin. The deciding factor, however, was not abortion. Wofford campaigned on extended unemployment benefits, middle-class tax relief, and a national health insurance program. The economy and taxes were blamed also for the unseating of a number of Democrats—most notably by Ray Mabus in Mississippi. It looked as if abortion had receded to an electoral nonissue.

Following the November 1991 elections, the Supreme Court announced it was accepting a challenge to Pennsylvania's post-*Webster* restrictive abortion law, in the case of *Planned Parenthood of Southeastern Pennsylvania v. Casey.* Abortion was again propelled back onto the national political stage. With the presidency, congressional seats, and many state offices at stake in the 1992 elections, the big question became, again, how and to what extent the abortion issue would play in electoral politics. Only one thing was certain: The abortion battle would go on. Or, to be more precise, far-flung battles would go on, and the skirmishes would be hard fought, won, lost, and refought by both sides.

A news article related the exasperation of one young woman from Wichita, Kansas (where Operation Rescue staged daily incidents at abortion clinics throughout the summer of 1991), on a visit in Washington state, where Initiative 120, legalizing abortion, was on the fall 1991 ballot. When faced with demonstrators passing out pro- and anti-Initiative 120 pamphlets: "I am sick of the abortion debate," she said, crumpling the pamphlets and tossing them into a nearby garbage can. "And no, I don't want to give you my name. All I want is for people to stop —stop arguing about abortion. Is there nowhere people are not fighting about abortion?"[63] The article's answer? "Probably not."

Notes

1. Quoted, *Time,* 17 July 1989, 96.
2. Missouri State Representative Charles Troupe, quoted, *USA Today,* 10 August 1989, 7A.
3. Michael Kinsley, essay, "The New Politics of Abortion," *Time,* 17 July 1989, 96.
4. *Washington Post,* 1 August 1989, A3.
5. Quoted, *New York Times,* 30 March 1990, 1.
6. Ibid., 8.
7. *Who Decides? A State-by-State Review of Abortion Rights,* 3d ed. (Washington, D.C.: NARAL Foundation, 1992).
8. Quoted, *Hartford Courant,* 11 March 1990, B2.
9. Information on the Connecticut General Assembly's 1990 abortion battle comes from "The Green Light: Behind the Legislative Scenes with Richard Tulisano—and the 'Impossible Consensus' on the Most Divisive Issue of Our Time," by Joel Lang, *Northeast Magazine* section, *Hartford Courant,* 12 August 1990, 12–17, 20; quotation, 14.
10. Ibid., 16.
11. Ibid.
12. Quoted, *Hartford Courant,* 3 March 1990, A1.
13. Ibid., A4.
14. Lang, "The Green Light," 16.
15. Ibid., 17.
16. Ibid.
17. Connecticut General Assembly debate of House Bill 5447, 17 April 1990, 84.
18. Ibid., 104.

19. Ibid., 109, 113.

20. Ibid., 91, 102.

21. Ibid., 205.

22. Ibid., 116–18.

23. Ibid., 289.

24. Lang, "The Green Light," 20.

25. Connecticut General Assembly debate of House Bill 5447, 17 April 1990, 220.

26. *New York Times*, 28 April, 1990, 1.

27. *Hartford Courant*, 23 January 1992, C11.

28. Quoted, *New York Times*, 8 July 1989, 7.

29. Quoted, ibid., 7 October 1989, 9.

30. Ibid.

31. Poll of 800 Louisiana voters conducted by Jim Carville and Joe Walker, political consultants in New Orleans, *New York Times*, 7 October 1989, 9. (Sampling error is plus or minus three percentage points.)

32. *New York Times*, 15 June 1991, 9.

33. Roemer was defeated in his 1991 reelection bid, but there was little evidence that it was because of his abortion stand. Louisiana was facing a deteriorating economy by then and an incumbent governor is a lightning rod for voter ire in that circumstance.

34. Ibid.

35. Quoted, *New York Times*, 26 January 1991, I10.

36. *Legal Times*, 3 July 1989, 11.

37. Both quotations from *Washington Post*, 8 July 1989, A2.

38. *Legal Times*, 3 July 1989, 11.

39. Figures from interviews with NARAL and NOW staff as reported in Michael J. Huppe, "Beyond Adjudication: The Impact of the United States Supreme Court upon Public Opinion" (Honors thesis, University of Virginia, April 1990), 67. As pointed out in chapter 2, membership counts for organizations are often slippery figures. These counts are self-reported by the organizations.

40. *Wall Street Journal*, 26 December 1989, A10.

41. *New York Times*, 15 October 1989, sect. 4, 1.

42. Ibid.

43. *New York Times*, 29 October 1989, 30.

44. Ibid.

45. *Washington Post*, 17 July 1989, A6.

46. Ibid.

47. *New York Times*, 1 February 1990, A1.

48. *New York Times*, 2 July 1990, A11.

49. *Washington Post*, 6 April 1990, A10.

50. *Washington Post*, 10 November 1989, A26.

51. Ibid.

52. *New York Times*, 29 October 1989, 30.

53. *Washington Post*, 11 September 1989, 1.

54. Ibid.

55. *Washington Post*, 11 September 1989, A6.

56. *Wall Street Journal*, 7 August 1990, B2.

57. *New York Times,* 1 August 1990, A10.
58. *Legal Times,* 31 July 1989, 1, 10.
59. *New York Times,* 8 November 1990, B10.
60. *Congressional Quarterly Weekly Report,* 10 November 1990, 3841.
61. *Who Decides?* i.
62. *New York Times,* 8 November 1990, B10.
63. *Hartford Courant,* 9 September 1991, A5.

CHAPTER 9

Abortion and National Politics

"We say to the political leadership of this country and to the Supreme Court and particularly to President Bush, we will not go back," shouted a determined Molly Yard, president of the National Organization for Women to the cheering, banner-waving crowd.[1] On the second Sunday in November 1989, more than 150,000 abortion rights supporters descended on the nation's capital. It was a replay of the April march that had brought 300,000 abortion rights supporters to Washington, D.C., to send a message to the Supreme Court.

The ruling in *Webster* had proved that earlier effort unavailing. Nevertheless, the pro-choice groups returned to march again. There are few visible means for drawing public attention to an interest group's determination, but none captures media attention more successfully than a huge demonstration. But after *Webster* pro-choice groups needed to aim their efforts where they would be most needed. The major arenas would be not only the nation's capital but cities in virtually every state. The strategy for the November 1989 "Mobilize for Women's Lives" demonstrations represented this new political reality. It would not do for everyone to travel to Washington; their numbers would have to be dispersed nationwide. Rallies were held that day across the country—supporters claimed over a thousand in all—in more than 150 cities and towns.

Early that morning more than 2500 defenders of legalized abortion gathered at the First Parish Unitarian Church in Kennebunkport, Maine, just a few miles from President Bush's summer home, to hold a candlelight vigil. "A thousand points of light for a women's right to choice," they called it. "We hold our candles high to banish the darkness," declared Faye Wattleton, president of Planned Parenthood Federation of

---

Opposite: Patricia Ireland, president of the National Organization for Women, addressing a rally outside the Supreme Court, 12 March 1993. *Photo:* Reuters/ Bettmann Newsphotos.

America. "Where better to begin than on our president's back porch?"[2] In Missouri, birthplace of the *Webster* case, a rally took place on the steps of the state capitol. "They didn't think you were here. They didn't think you were in Missouri," Harriett Woods, a former lieutenant governor, told the thousands gathered at the statehouse. State treasurer Wendell Bailey, a Republican, joined in the *Webster*-bashing: "The decision is infamous, and we're going to de-Websterize Missouri."[3] An old-time gospel revival in New Orleans was attended by 15,000. In Los Angeles more than 50,000 marchers caused a gigantic traffic jam.

Congress Responds: Efforts to Loosen Abortion Restrictions

Abortion rights activists were not giving up on Washington, but to win the battle there required overcoming a powerful and seemingly immovable obstacle: the president. Within weeks of *Webster*, the House of Representatives had voted (219–206), to allow the District of Columbia once again to use its own tax revenues to pay for abortions for the poor. It was the first time in over a decade that the House voted against a restrictive abortion-funding rider. (Just the year before, when Congress first had imposed the restriction over the district's use of its own funds, the House had voted 222–186 in favor of the restriction.) "All across the country, a newly energized pro-choice movement is going to say," warned Congressman Les AuCoin (D-Oregon), " 'If you are anti-choice, when we the voters go to the ballot box, we won't choose you.' "[4] Many of his colleagues apparently took note. But President Bush sounded his own warning in a letter to the chairman of the House appropriations subcommittee in charge of the bill: He would veto any bill that "permits the use of appropriated funds to pay for abortions other than those where the life of the mother would be endangered if the fetus were carried to term."[5] When the Senate approved a spending bill that also eliminated the ban on the district's use of its own funds for abortions, the president made good his word when the conference measure reached his desk. Congress repassed the law with the abortion funding restriction still absent, and the president vetoed it again. Congress then gave in and sent a bill to the White House that met the president's demands.

A similar scenario followed in the congressional effort to allow federal funding of abortions for poor women whose pregnanacy was caused by rape or incest. On 11 October 1989, the House passed by a vote of 216–206 the Labor–Health and Human Services appropriations bill that included the rape and incest exception language. Twenty Democrats and six Republicans had switched from their 1988 positions on a parallel bill. The about-face of one member, John G. Rowland (R-Connecticut), who was soon to announce his candidacy for the governor's chair in Hartford, was editorially attacked: "Charitable people will say that the congressman is a pragmatist. The uncharitable will call him unprincipled. Mr. Rowland does not come off as a mature statesman either way. Whatever his motives, this is the kind of behavior that makes people cynical about politics."⁶

Rowland was hardly alone, whatever the motive. Following *Webster*, dozens of members of Congress attempted to reposition themselves on the abortion issue. Perhaps the explanation given by Senator Sam Nunn (D-Georgia) for his shift from a long-held antiabortion position expressed the most pragmatic line:

> I do not believe that large segments of the American people and the medical profession will accept or obey a law making early-term abortions a criminal act after all those years. The law can only accomplish so much, and with respect to abortion I believe the only enforceable line the law can draw is to protect the unborn child when it is clear an independent life is involved.⁷

At the time Nunn "relaxed" his position, as the news media termed it, he was frequently mentioned as a potential Democratic candidate for the presidency in 1992. Election politics was again the suspected motive.

It briefly appeared that the president himself might also be ready to relent in his opposition, at least regarding an exception to allow abortions in the case of pregnancies caused by rape or incest. During a news conference on 13 October 1989, Bush had seemed to soften: "We're going to be meeting with some of the various, most interested congressional parties on this and see what can be resolved; I'm not looking for any conflict over this. I'm not going to change my position any. But let's see how these negotiations come out."⁸ There thus appeared at least a chance that the growing pro-choice power might persuade the president to follow the lead of the vote changers in Congress. That inference was wrong.

Just two weeks after its passage, Bush vetoed the Labor–HHS appropriations bill, reiterating his intent to veto any measure that "permitted the use of appropriated funds to pay for abortions other than those in which the life of the mother would be endangered."⁹ The Senate margin of victory had been great enough to overturn a veto, but the House fell short of the two-thirds necessary. (The margin in favor of allowing federal funding increased substantially, however, from 216 in favor on the

first vote to 231 on the override vote—191 against or 51 votes shy of an
override.) Angered by the ability of the minority to triumph, pro-choice
members lashed out at the president, calling his actions "a cruel, cow-
ardly, punitive veto that makes female victims incubate the child of the
rapist."[10]

One of the first actions in Congress following the *Webster* decision
was the introduction of Reproductive Rights bills in the House (HR
3700) and Senate (S1912). An attempt to write the trimester framework
of *Roe* into law, the legislation simply said: "A state may not restrict the
right of a woman to choose to terminate a pregnancy before fetal viability or at any time, if such termination is necessary to protect the life or
health of the woman." But even one of the key cosponsors, Congressman AuCoin, said, "It would be a very serious mistake to try to move
the measure now."[11] For the most part the effort was a demonstration of
support for the pro-choice groups, especially as the 1990 elections approached. No one supposed that a presidential veto would not be sustained.

As the pro-choice groups began to gain ground after *Webster*, abortion opponents were on the defensive. What they saw as their small
gains in outlawing federal expenditures for abortions were increasingly
threatened by efforts to loosen existing restrictions. They soon devised a
counterstrategy. As the polls show, one of the most broadly supported
restrictions on abortion is a requirement that parents be notified prior to
performing an abortion on a minor child. A survey commissioned in late
1989 by EMILY's List, a group that sponsors female candidates who advocate abortion rights, found that nearly 70 percent of voters support requiring parental consent (a far more restrictive measure than just notification) for teenagers seeking abortions.[12] After Minnesota passed a law
requiring that both parents be notified before a minor could obtain an
abortion, a study showing a decline in the number of teen pregnancies
and abortions was published in the March 1991 *American Journal of
Public Health*. Needless to say, abortion opponents found the survey
and the study to be of considerable use.

Few members of Congress are eager to go on record in opposition to
parental notification. Yet abortion rights advocates are reluctant to accept parental notification because of give-them-an-inch-and-they'll-take-
a-mile thinking or because they believe that it is not possible to mandate
good family relations and fear the results of trying to do so. Abortion
opponents believe that the best way to stop abortion rights legislation is
to offer parental-notification amendments. This "poison-pill" strategy
leaves the abortion rights supporters with a difficult choice: to go forward with what they see as negatively piggybacked efforts, or to give up

on their legislative strategy. Work to reauthorize the earlier family-planning program was brought to a standstill in 1991 by a parental-notification amendment, and several other attempts to modify abortion restrictions were likewise thwarted. When their parental-notification approach failed, though, abortion opponents had the ultimate fallback: the president and his veto.

As the 1992 elections neared, the Reproductive Rights Bill under a new name—the Freedom of Choice Bill—again received considerable congressional attention. With 131 cosponsors in the House and 31 cosponsors in the Senate, the bill was gaining momentum. Though there were still clearly not enough votes to overcome a presidential veto, election politics might serve as a forcing mechanism. Interest-group politics and party politics might combine to provide an impetus for action. But there was little realistic prospect of that happening until after the Rehnquist Court handed down its decision in a case challenging Pennsylvania's antiabortion law, *Planned Parenthood of Southeastern Pennsylvania v. Casey* (which is discussed in the next chapter). If the Court had overturned *Roe* in deciding *Casey,* as some in the pro-choice movement suspected it might, the inevitable uproar from pro-choice supporters might have been sufficient to force Congress's hand. Though a presidential veto was virtually certain, the Democratic leadership saw an advantage therein: The backlash might aid the Democrats' 1992 reelection campaigns. In the end, though, Democrats in Congress could not agree on a bill that would force Bush's hand on the issue before the election.

Each piece of legislation loosening abortion funding restrictions after *Webster* has met with a presidential veto.[13] In most cases, the Senate had the votes to override, but in every case the House did not. Even after the 1990 elections, which sent a few more pro-choice legislators to Capitol Hill, there were not enough votes. As long as the president stood pat and there is a minority of one-third plus one in either house prepared to hold the pro-life line, Congress will remain stymied.

Proof of the veto-override deadlock in Congress was made stark in November 1991. Following the Rehnquist Court's 1991 decision in *Rust v. Sullivan* (see chapter 10, pp. 331–32) upholding a 1988 Reagan administration Health and Human Services regulation banning abortion counseling in any federally funded family-planning clinic, there was an uproar in the national press. One editorial writer voiced the concerns of many citizens:

Perhaps the outrage stirred by *Rust v. Sullivan* will reinvigorate the moribund "debate" over social issues. It should. The decision's implications are stunning. It could allow the government to dictate what may or may not be said, taught or advocated by anyone receiving federal funds. Potentially, it could even allow bureaucrats to dictate what must be said, taught or advocated.[14]

The Court's 5–4 decision meant that the nearly 4000 family-planning clinics around the country faced a choice: no longer providing abortion counseling or giving up federal subsidies. Title X of the federal family-planning program in 1991 provided $141 million—$30 million to Planned Parenthood alone—to clinics that serve some 4 million women a year. As the *Christian Science Monitor* put it, "In one stroke, the United States Supreme Court has thrown the women's movement into a frenzy, federally funded family-planning clinics into crisis, and pro-choice advocates in Congress into high gear."[15] The only way to overturn the regulation was for Congress to pass legislation. With the free-speech issue raised by the gag rule, abortion rights supporters were hopeful that they could muster the two-thirds in both houses that would be necessary to overcome a Bush veto—a veto that the president made clear would result if there were any attempt to overturn the regulation.

Legislation to strike the abortion-counseling prohibition had been stalled by parental-notification amendments in 1990, but after *Rust* it sailed through the Senate with little debate because, as Senate Majority Leader George Mitchell declared, the counseling ban supported by the president was "so unfair, so harsh, and so unfeeling that there has been very little public debate supporting his position."[16] The vote in the Senate, 72–25, was more than enough to override a presidential veto; but in the House the vote of 272–156 was fourteen short of the number necessary to override a veto.

Republican political consultant John Deardourff described an attempt at negotiating a compromise that he alleged was sabotaged by White House Chief of Staff John Sununu. At the president's direction, chief domestic policy adviser Roger Porter began talks with Republican Senator John Chaffee of Rhode Island and Republican Congressman John Porter of Illinois, both sponsors of legislation to prevent implementation of the gag rule. At one point it appeared that an agreement had been reached that would allow a clinic to provide information about medically reliable abortion services in its area if a patient specifically requested it. Deardourff explains what apparently happened next.

While Porter, at the president's request, was negotiating privately with Chaffee, reports from various House Republicans indicate that [John] Sununu [then White House Chief of Staff] was calling and meeting with antiabortion Republicans in the House, rallying them for an all-out public battle to sustain a gag rule veto. Chaffee's office was notified that Sununu "had problems" with the agreement worked out over months of private discussion. Then Chaffee was sent new language from the White House, which took the negotiations almost all the way back to ground zero. Apparently to assure antiabortion leaders that Sununu was busy defending their cause, word "leaked" from the White House itself that Sununu had torpedoed the Chaffee-Porter negotiations.[17]

Deardourff wondered about Sununu's role. Was he playing a "lone hand" or was he "simply playing the heavy in a complex, devious political game in which the president and all his men are engaged, hoping somehow to placate gag rule opponents without offending their 'core vote' on the religious right?"[18] Whatever the "truth," the result was a presidential veto. Because the Senate had the votes to override, the battlefield was in the House. Speaker Thomas Foley was so convinced that the votes were there that he publicly predicted an eventual victory. He was wrong; the House came up twelve short of the necessary two-thirds. Just before the House tally, the White House released a memo from the president to Secretary of Health and Human Services Louis W. Sullivan stating that the Department of Health and Human Services ought to revise its rule to permit doctors to inform women about their right to full information about family-planning alternatives. Precisely what the memo meant was unclear, and whether it caused some hesitant members to vote to sustain the veto was equally unclear. When HHS issued its new guidelines in March 1992 on the basis of the presidential memo, the skimpiness of the relaxation of the ban became apparent. Doctors, but not other clinic workers, could mention abortion, but even doctors could not refer patients to abortion providers. Because most counseling at family-planning clinics is done by nurses and counselors, the exception was relatively meaningless. Ironically, then, on the day of the 1992 presidential election the Court of Appeals for the District of Columbia Circuit struck down HHS's revised regulations on procedural grounds (as further discussed in the next chapter).

Abortion and Party Politics

Republican strategists in Congress and out increasingly worried about the effect of the president's abortion position on the party's electoral future. Three separate groups of elected Republican officials and other party members organized to combat the party's antiabortion image: the National Republican Coalition for Choice, Pro-Choice America, and Republicans for Choice. Some Republican governors urged the party to ease its antiabortion stance, and the Young Republican National Federation voted to ask the party to remove the antiabortion plank that had been central to the GOP platform since 1980.

The president had his own electoral concern: holding onto his conservative constituency. After being attacked by many conservatives for abandoning his read-my-lips-no-new-taxes pledge, he seemed determined to stand firm on some issue dear to conservatives. Apparently, abortion was to be *the issue,* and Bush seemed prepared to use all his weapons—his veto, the appointment and direction of members of his administration, and his appointive power in connection with the federal bench—to accomplish his purpose.

All was not tranquil in the Democratic party either. In April 1989 fifty House Democrats sent a letter to the chairman of the National Democratic Committee seeking a change in the platform. "We ... believe the principle and practice of abortion on demand is wrong," they stated. "We ... think it is politically wrongheaded for our party to be on the record as favoring the use of taxpayer dollars to fund an alleged 'fundamental right' which is so strongly opposed in conscience by millions of Americans and by ourselves."[19] The signatories belied the conventional wisdom that all antiabortion Democrats are from either the South or heavily Catholic districts. Although half the signers were Roman Catholic and thirteen more were southerners, sixteen others did not fit the stereotype. Many were from northern liberal states and five were powerful committee chairmen, part of the party's own congressional leadership. On 12 November 1989, another twenty-four House Democrats wrote to the Speaker objecting to language in the military appropriations bill that would require overseas bases to provide abortions to military personnel and dependents (a provision that did not ultimately pass).

In the past, the Democratic leadership had not put any pressure on antiabortion Democrats, leaving them to "vote their conscience." As the future of *Roe* became increasingly perilous and pressure grew on Congress to act, the leadership proved not so considerate. As a campaign issue, many liberal Democrats would like to promote their party as the party of abortion rights, but that claim is shaky in light of the split among House Democrats. Even in the effort to overturn the gag rule, House Democrats provided the margin of victory for sustaining the presidential veto: 43 Democrats joined with 113 Republicans. Among the Democrat defectors were five committee chairmen: Agriculture Chairman E. "Kika" de la Garza, Texas; Select Hunger Chairman Tony P. Hall, Ohio; Small Business Chairman John J. LaFalce, New York; Veterans' Affairs Chairman G.V. "Sonny" Montgomery, Mississippi; and Public Works and Transportation Chairman Robert A. Roe, New Jersey. One House Democrat blamed the loss on a "lack of discipline in the caucus where we allow the privileges of office to go to five full committee chairmen, who on a crucial vote with the party in battle against the president, leave us."[20]

Abortion and the Presidency

Following *Webster*, Solicitor General Kenneth W. Starr moved at the first opportunity to seek the overturn of *Roe*. On 13 October 1989, the very day that Bush appeared to be opening the door to some compromise on the rape and incest exception, the Justice Department filed a brief in *Hodgson v. Minnesota* urging the Supreme Court to uphold a Minnesota law; "the administration continues to believe that *Roe* was wrongly decided and should be overruled."[21] An ebullient National Right to Life Committee spokesman gloated, "This [brief] should quiet those pundits who have been suggesting that the president is backing off from his pro-life commitment."[22]

The Bush administration further demonstrated its stand by filing *amici* briefs in the abortion-counseling case of *Rust v. Sullivan* (see pp. 331–32) and in support of Pennsylvania's antiabortion law in *Planned Parenthood of Southeastern Pennsylvania v. Casey* as well as in *Bray v. Alexandria Women's Health Clinic. Bray* had been scheduled for oral arguments and decision during the Court's 1991–92 term but was carried over to the Court's following term (see p. 355). *Bray* posed the question of whether federal courts may enjoin antiabortion protesters from blockading abortion clinics. In the 1980s, some antiabortion protesters, led by the head of Operation Rescue, started staging sit-ins and blockades of abortion clinics around the country (see chapter 2). In some cases, the protesters were arrested for violating state trespass laws and ordinances against disturbing the peace. In addition, several federal courts also enjoined Operation Rescue and other antiabortion groups from blockading abortion clinics under an 1871 law that prohibits conspiracies to deprive people of their civil rights. The law, known as the Ku Klux Klan Act, was passed in response to attacks on blacks after the Civil War.

Prior to the Court's ruling in *Bray*, the Justice Department filed an identical brief in support of Operation Rescue in the federal district court in Wichita, Kansas. During the summer of 1991, Operation Rescue orchestrated a huge and at times violent blockade and "rescue" at abortion clinics in Wichita. The events drew thousands of protesters from as far away as San Francisco and New York. After repeated warnings and hearings, Judge Patrick Kelly ordered U.S. marshals to maintain peace and to arrest those who violated his orders. Over 2500 arrests were made; among those arrested were a number of very young children. The Bush administration's brief in the Wichita case drew heavy fire for encouraging the protesters to disobey the district court's orders and the law. Indeed, in response to the brief, Judge Kelly took the highly unusual step of defending his ruling on ABC's "Nightline" and criticized the administration for putting its "imprimatur upon this ... illegal action." When antiabortion protesters continued blocking entrances to abortion clinics and were arrested, Bush told reporters that "breaking the law is excessive. Some of the people have been convicted, so I disapprove of that.... When you hurt somebody else's rights, that's what I disagree about."[23]

No less important have been President Bush's appointments to the Supreme Court. Less than a month after the Rehnquist Court handed down its decision in *Webster*, one of *Roe*'s strongest defenders on the bench, Justice William J. Brennan, Jr., retired. Bush had his first opportunity to strengthen the conservative bloc on the Rehnquist Court.

Within three days of Brennan's announced retirement, Bush nominated Judge David Hackett Souter, whom less than a year earlier he had appointed to the Court of Appeals for the First Circuit. In the year and a half since Bush's inauguration, the White House counsel had pared a list of fifty potential nominees, which had been inherited from the Reagan administration, to eighteen, and by Brennan's retirement, to eight. Bush's choice came down to Souter or forty-one-year-old federal court Judge Edith Jones, a southerner whose judicial record was deemed at the time to be potentially too controversial.

At age fifty, Souter, a bachelor, was the same age as Brennan had been when he was named to the high bench. Souter had been a Rhodes scholar at Oxford University and had received his law degree from Harvard Law School. In the late 1970s he served as New Hampshire's attorney general, and was appointed in 1983 to that state's supreme court by then-governor (and subsequently Bush's White House chief of staff) John Sununu. On the state supreme court, Souter wrote more than two hundred opinions, none with great flair and none that sparked controversy. On the appellate bench, he had no published opinions by the time of his nomination to the Supreme Court.

Souter testified for three days before the Senate Judiciary Committee, which also heard two days of testimony from witnesses for and against him. The hearings revealed less about Souter than about the senators. As expected, Souter maintained a studied presence and portrayed himself as a learned man with a "heart." Anticipating vigorous questioning, Souter had been well prepared by a month spent in reading, mock committee sessions with White House staff, and reviewing videotapes of the Senate's hearings on Judge Robert Bork.

Unlike Bork, Souter was reluctant to explain his views on controversial issues of the day. It would be "inappropriate" to comment, as he appropriately and wryly put it, on "the lone case which has been on everyone's lips since the moment of my nomination—*Roe v. Wade.*" Not only his reticence distinguished Souter from Bork. Without promising how he would decide particular cases, Souter characterized himself as a "centrist" in the mold of moderately conservative Justice John M. Harlan. For instance, he did not dismiss out of hand a constitutional "right of privacy," even though he asserted that not all aspects of the right of privacy were "fundamental." The Ninth Amendment, he allowed, recognized protection for such unenumerated rights, but he declined to reveal whether he deemed it to embrace a woman's decision on abortion. At the same time, he distanced himself from the hard-line states'-rights position of conservative senators like South Carolina's Republican Strom Thurmond.

Throughout his testimony, Souter endeavored to reassure senators that he had no agenda or commitment to a rigid philosophy of "original intent." The "majestic clauses" of the Constitution were broad, he declared, and required attention to history and precedent as well as text. He also disclaimed adherence to some sharply conservative positions that he had taken as New Hampshire's attorney general: "That was then, this is now." Some Republicans and "movement conservatives" were wary of the nominee; some liberals remained unpersuaded. His evasive answers inspired some media commentators to dub him "the stealth candidate."

Despite concerns that Souter would vote for *Roe*'s reversal, and the opposition of the National Organization for Women, Planned Parenthood Federation of America, and the National Abortion Rights Action League, the Senate Judiciary Committee recommended confirmation by a vote of 13–1 (Massachusetts Democratic Senator Edward Kennedy dissenting). On 2 October 1990 the full Senate confirmed his appointment 90–9, with only a handful of liberal Democratic senators voting against him.

Sworn into office as the 105th justice on 8 October, Souter has proved cautious and conservative on the high bench. In his first term, he frequently voted with Chief Justice William Rehnquist and Justice Sandra Day O'Connor. Notably, he cast the deciding vote (and in the opposite direction than would have Justice Brennan) in a number of important 5–4 rulings,[24] including on the restriction on abortion counseling and the First Amendment in *Rust v. Sullivan*. Abortion rights supporters viewed his vote in *Rust* as justification for their anxieties about his view of *Roe*. But his opinion, in conjunction with O'Connor and Justice Anthony Kennedy, in *Casey* established that this was less clear and that he is a more traditional judicial conservative who believes in precedent and does not share the hardline views of others on the bench like Chief Justice Rehnquist and Justice Antonin Scalia.

Less than a year after naming Souter, Bush had a second opportunity to fill a vacancy on the Court. On the last day of the 1990-91 term, Justice Thurgood Marshall retired after twenty-four years' service. Bush promptly selected Judge Clarence Thomas, a young black conservative, relatively unseasoned jurist. Fresh from attacking Congress for its inclusion of what he said were "quotas" in its civil rights bills, Bush reacted combatively to charges that his choice of Thomas was just such a "quota." Yet, in choosing Thomas, Bush banked on the political symbolism of naming an African-American to replace Marshall to overshadow the nominee's inexperience and controversial views.

With only fourteen months on the Court of Appeals for the District of Columbia Circuit, Thomas had written fewer than two dozen opinions. In 1990 Bush had appointed him to the seat once held by Judge Bork, and prior to that Thomas had served for eight years as head of the Equal Employment Opportunities Commission. Unlike Bush's first nominee, Thomas had a substantial record of outspoken and controversial conservative views. On several occasions he had sharply attacked affirmative action, for example, and the reasoning (though not the result) in the 1954 landmark school desegregation decision in *Brown v. Board of Education of Topeka, Kansas,* along with the civil rights movement's efforts to achieve integration.[25] Thomas advocated a "Booker T. Washington philosophy of self-help" for blacks. In his words, "I firmly insist that the Constitution be interpreted in a colorblind fashion. It is futile to talk of a colorblind society unless this constitutional principle is first established. Hence, I emphasize black self-help, as opposed to racial quotas and other race-conscious legal devices that only further and deepen the original problem."[26]

Contrary to Bork and Justice Scalia, however, Thomas also rejected the theory that the Court should interpret the Constitution on the basis of the "original intentions" of its Framers. Instead, he associated himself with the even more controversial theory that constitutional interpretation should rest on principles of "natural law" as embodied in the Declaration of Independence.[27]

With regard to the vexing abortion controversy, in a press conference the president flatly stated, "I don't know, [and] I didn't ask about" Judge Thomas's view of *Roe* and abortion.[28] Yet Bush's advisers knew that Thomas had sided with those opposing *Roe* in a speech delivered to the conservative Heritage Foundation. There, he praised an article by Lewis Lehrman that had appeared in the *American Spectator.* Lehrman attacked the Court's "conjured right to abortion" and called for constitutional protection for "the inalienable right to life of the child-about-to-be-born." Thomas called the article a "splendid example of applying natural law."[29]

Not surprisingly, within a couple of days of Thomas's nomination, the National Organization for Women (NOW) announced its opposition, as it had with the nominations of Bork, Kennedy, and Souter. "We're going to Bork him," announced Flo Kennedy, a feminist lawyer.[30] NOW was followed by the liberal Alliance for Justice, the Women's Legal Defense Fund, the National Education Association, the Women's Political Caucus, and the National Abortion Rights Action League, among other groups. At the same time, the Eagle Forum, the Family Research Council, Concerned Women for America, the U.S. Chamber of Commerce, and other conservative groups defended him.

An outspoken conservative, who grew up in the extreme poverty of the small town of Pinpoint, Georgia, raised by his grandfather, Thomas went on to graduate from Yale Law School and to work in the Reagan administration. His racial identity and his roots clashed with his conservative politics and caused a bitter split in the civil rights community. The National Association for the Advancement of Colored People (NAACP), other black and Hispanic organizations, and the AFL-CIO united in opposing his confirmation. Still, in July, when he was nominated, public opinion polls of blacks found that 54 percent approved of his nomination and 52 percent said that he reflected the views of most blacks.[31]

When the Senate Judiciary Committee began its hearings on the Thomas nomination in September 1991, the House and Senate were voting on legislation to suspend the administration ban on abortion counseling and referrals that the Supreme Court had upheld in *Rust v. Sullivan* in May. Abortion was a central issue in Congress and hence —even though the Court already seemed to have an antiabortion majority—inevitably a central issue in the confirmation hearings. Pro-choice senators were not about to lose the opportunity to draw public attention and support to their cause. At one point Senator Orrin Hatch of Utah charged that Democratic committee members were asking an excessive number of questions about Thomas's views on abortion. By Hatch's count, Thomas had been asked at least seventy times to address the abortion debate, while Souter had been asked only thirty-seven times.[32] Hatch seemed to think the difference reflected racial discrimination; more likely it reflected the realization that failure to pin Souter down had cost abortion rights supporters the deciding vote in *Rust!*

There was also considerable doubt about Thomas's claim that he had never "personally" engaged in discussions about abortion. Columnist Ellen Goodman voiced this skepticism:

> After two decades of heated debate, it seems everyone has an opinion about abortion. Just this week, the latest in a never-ending series of polls asked Americans whether they generally favor or generally oppose a woman's right to decide. Only 1 percent of them answered "Don't know."
>
> So it may be that the only thinking, breathing, newspaper-reading, television-watching person in America between 12 and 94 years of age who appears to have no opinion whatsoever on this subject is the current nominee for the Supreme Court.... In six days of questioning, we discovered that this man, who was in law school when *Roe vs. Wade* was decided, never discussed the case with his fellow students. "Senator," he said, "I cannot remember personally engaging in those discussions." He was married, he explained, and went right home from class.
>
> We discover that in the past 18 years of knock-down-drag-out fighting over this case, Thomas had discussed *Roe vs. Wade,* "only in the most general sense." He said, "If you're asking me whether or not I've ever debated the contents of it, the answer to that is no, senator."[33]

Other analysts were even more incredulous. One charged that Thomas was a nominee with "less than a year and a half of judicial experience; [who] lacked any coherent judicial philosophy; and was in all probability willing to lie to get the job, since it is unlikely in the extreme that a lawyer of his generation never discussed *Roe v. Wade.*"[34]

Later, when law Professor Anita Hill's charges of sexual harassment against her former boss Thomas—made under a guarantee of anonymity to the Senate Judiciary Committee—were somehow leaked to the media, public pressure mounted to address them. Thomas's earlier extreme claims about his obliviousness to *Roe* fueled doubts about his declarations of innocence in connection with the harassment charge. The televised Senate hearings on Hill's accusations and Thomas's denials in October turned into an absurd public spectacle. Members of the Senate judiciary—all white males, mostly older—variously assumed the roles of pop psychologist, indignant moralist, and blustering prosecutor. The abortion issue lost out to sex, human pathos, and the self-degradation of the national legislature. When the drama ended, the Senate confirmed

Thomas by a vote of 52 to 48, making his confirmation one of the closest in history.

Abortion and National Election Politics

The role of the abortion issue in election politics is uncertain. After the limited experience gained in the few 1989 races, it seemed destined to become one, if not the most, critical issue in national campaigns. Then as the war in the Persian Gulf heated up throughout the fall of 1990, abortion receded in importance.

In the 1990 congressional elections, the pro-life forces estimated a net loss of eight antiabortion votes in the House; the pro-choice forces estimated that they had picked up between seven and ten votes. In the Senate, abortion opponents lost two votes: one with the defeat of Minnesota incumbent Rudy Boschwitz to abortion rights supporter Paul Wellstone; and an open seat in Colorado, previously held by antiabortion Senator William L. Armstrong that was won by a Republican who generally supports abortion rights. In races where abortion was a central issue, results were mixed. Senator Jesse Helms in North Carolina held his seat against an abortion rights supporter; in Virginia an abortion rights Democrat defeated an antiabortion incumbent Republican in a nasty fight.

In early 1991, nothing could compete with the war. The nation was almost wholly focused on the events in the Gulf. Some months after U.S. and UN troops claimed victory in March, the war mania was replaced by recession worries. The Rehnquist Court momentarily thrust abortion back onto the national political center stage when it announced its decision in *Rust v. Sullivan*. Yet, after Bush vetoed legislation to overturn those regulations and Congress was unable to override his veto, abortion again receded as a national issue.

By contrast, in 1992 the abortion controversy again loomed larger. That was due to the Rehnquist Court's granting review to a challenge to Pennsylvania's antiabortion law in *Planned Parenthood of Southeastern Pennsylvania v. Casey,* amid heightened speculation that *Roe* would be overturned. Following that decision, which is examined in the next chapter, pro-life and pro-choice forces then focused on the 1992 presidential and congressional elections. The Democratic party once again reaffirmed its support for a woman's right to choose. Besides keeping a plank in its platform supporting the pro-choice side of the controversy, Democratic leadership denied Pennsylvania's governor Robert Casey the opportunity to represent antiabortion forces on the podium at its convention. For its part, the Republican party retained in its platform a strong antiabortion plank calling as in 1980, 1984, and 1988 for a constitutional amendment and the appointment of federal judges who oppose abortion. Within its ranks, however, pro-choice forces grew more visible when unsuccessfully fighting against the inclusion of that plank, and Massachusetts Governor William Weld was allowed to address the convention in support of women's right to choose abortion. Barbara Bush, moreover, in a television interview for the first time expressed her disapproval of her party's strong antiabortion position; abortion, she said, was a private matter that had no place in the platform. Still, President Bush counted on conservative pro-life supporters to help him win reelection. But the economy and Bush's lack of leadership proved overwhelming in the 1992 election. With the victory of Democratic presidential candidate Bill Clinton (discussed in chapter 10), the shape and direction of the abortion controversy was certain to change again.

Notes

1. *Washington Post,* 13 November 1989, A15.
2. Ibid.
3. Ibid.
4. *Washington Post,* 3 August 1989, A13.
5. *Congressional Quarterly Almanac,* 101st Cong., 1st sess., 1989, 759.
6. *Hartford Courant,* 15 October 1989, C2.
7. *New York Times,* 5 September 1990, A20.
8. *Congressional Quarterly Almanac,* 101st Cong., 1st sess., 1989, 303.
9. Ibid.
10. *Washington Post,* 26 October 1989, A12.
11. *Congressional Quarterly Weekly Report,* 31 March 1990, 1004.
12. *Congressional Quarterly Weekly Report,* 19 May 1990, 1573.
13. Since *Webster,* Congress has tried to loosen abortion restrictions with amendments to the federal family-planning program authorizations, Labor–HHS appropriations, National Institutes of Health appropriations (concerning fetal research), defense authorization covering military hospitals, D.C. appropriations, foreign operations appropriations, and foreign aid authorizations. All have failed either by presidential veto, Senate filibuster, or conference committee negotiations.
14. *Washington Post National Weekly Edition,* 10–16 June 1991, 25.
15. *Christian Science Monitor,* 28 May 1991, 6.
16. *New York Times,* 13 September 1991, A1.
17. *Washington Post,* 6 November 1991, A25.
18. Ibid.
19. *Congressional Quarterly Weekly Report,* 14 December 1991, 3541.
20. *Congressional Quarterly Weekly Report,* 23 November 1991, 3457.
21. *Hartford Courant,* 15 October 1989, A6.
22. Ibid.

23. *Washington Post,* 10 August 1991, A13.

24. For a further discussion of Justice Souter's record, see David M. O'Brien, *Supreme Court Watch — 1991* (New York: Norton, 1991).

25. See, e.g., Clarence Thomas, "Civil Rights as a Principle versus Civil Rights as an Interest," in *Assessing the Reagan Years,* ed. David Boaz (Washington, D.C.: Cato Institute, 1983), 391; "Affirmative Action Goals and Timetables: Too Tough? Not Tough Enough!" *Yale Law and Policy Review,* 1987, 402; and "Affirmative Action: Cure or Contradiction?" *Center Magazine,* November/December 1987, 20.

26. Clarence Thomas, "Letter to the Editor," *Wall Street Journal,* 20 February 1987, 21.

27. Clarence Thomas, "Toward a 'Plain Reading' of the Constitution—The Declaration of Independence in Constitutional Interpretation," *Howard Law Journal* 30 (1987): 983; "The Higher Law Background of the Privilege or Immunities Clause of the Fourteenth Amendment," *Harvard Journal of Law and Public Policy* 12 (1989): 63.

28. *New York Times,* 2 July 1991, A14.

29. *Washington Post,* 3 July 1991, A15.

30. *Washington Post,* 6 July 1991.

31. *USA Today,* 5 July 1991, A1.

32. *Hartford Courant,* 13 September 1991, A12.

33. *Hartford Courant,* 20 September 1991, D15.

34. Deborah A. Stone, "Race, Gender, and the Supreme Court," *American Prospect,* Winter 1992, 65.

Planned Parenthood of Southeastern Pennsylvania v. Casey, the Rehnquist Court, and American Politics

"George Bush's Court has left *Roe v. Wade* an empty shell that is one Justice Thomas away from being destroyed," proclaimed Kate Michelman, president of the National Abortion Rights Action League (NARAL).[1] The National Organization for Women's president, Patricia Ireland, declared, "*Roe* is dead."[2] But the other side of the controversy was no less disheartened by the decision in *Planned Parenthood of Southeastern Pennsylvania v. Casey.*[3] Operation Rescue's founder, Randall Terry, angrily denounced Justices Sandra Day O'Connor, Anthony Kennedy, and David Souter for voting with Justices Harry Blackmun and John Paul Stevens to uphold *Roe:* "Three Reagan/Bush appointees stabbed the pro-life movement in the back."[4] Former Reagan administration official and president of the conservative National Research Council, Gary Bauer, echoed Terry's dismay at "the emergence on the Court of a Wimp Block who are quickly becoming an embarrassment to the presidents who appointed them."[5]

So it went in the hours immediately following the announcement of *Casey* on 29 June 1992. On the steps of the Supreme Court's building pro-choice and antiabortion advocates alike scurried before television cameras and talked with reporters. Nor were politicians any less eager to give their reactions. The White House issued a statement expressing President George Bush's agreement with the decision and reaffirming his opposition to "abortion in all cases except rape or incest or where the life of the mother is at stake."[6] Pennsylvania's Democratic Governor

Opposite: The Rehnquist Court in 1992. *Seated, left to right:* Justices John Paul Stevens, Byron White, Chief Justice William Rehnquist, Justices Harry A. Blackmun, Sandra Day O'Connor. *Standing, left to right:* Justices David Souter, Antonin Scalia, Anthony Kennedy, Clarence Thomas. *Photo:* National Geographic Society/Supreme Court Historical Society.

Robert Casey, who defended his state's restrictions and had asked the Court to overrule *Roe,* also tried to cast the ruling in a positive light: "The decision, while not overturning *Roe,* clearly returns to the people the power to regulate abortion in reasonable ways, so as to protect maternal health and reduce the number of abortions in our country."[7] By contrast, Senate Majority Leader George Mitchell (D-Maine) joined other pro-choice supporters in warning that "the Court is one vote away from reversal of *Roe v. Wade.*"[8]

Across the country activists on both sides rushed to hold press conferences. For the moment, the struggle was a war of words waged through the media. "Make no mistake," charged Norma McCorvey, the woman who had become known to millions as Jane Roe, "*Roe* is still the law of the land for women of wealth." But, she added, the Court has "issued teenagers, indigent women and rural women their own death warrant"; they "have become Jane Roe."[9] Sarah Weddington, who twenty years earlier had argued McCorvey's case before the Court, sought as well to put *Casey* into perspective. "In theory, *Roe v. Wade* is still on the books, but in terms of how it impacts women's lives, it is a shadow of its former self. Up to now, the Court has said, 'It's a woman's decision, and you people in the legislature, leave her alone.' Now they're saying, 'It's still her decision, but you people in the legislature can erect hurdles and roadblocks so that only women who are the most determined, who have the most money, who are the most sophisticated make it through.'" "Patronizing" to women was how Weddington characterized the ruling and Pennsylvania's law requiring women to undergo counseling, give their informed consent, and then wait twenty-four hours before obtaining an abortion. "The only surgery that you have to, by law, wait 24 hours for," Weddington underscored, "is abortion—as if women don't think about it before they get to the clinic."[10]

In the days following the decision each side put its own spin on *Casey.* Although major newspapers published excerpts from the decision, Democratic strategist Tony Podesta pointed out, "Very few Americans will read the actual decision, so we are now in a definitional battle of how people will view [*Casey*]."[11] And that would affect how much force each side might marshal in future face-offs.

In seeking to define for the public the meaning of *Casey,* neither side gave ground. "[The pro-choice people] got exactly what they wanted," charged Tom Jipping, an attorney associated with the conservative Free Congress Foundation. "It is in their interest to claim defeat so that they can say that they need a legislative response."[12] Andrea Sheldon of the Traditional Values Coalition complained, "These women will never be happy until they have everything. They won. They know they won."[13]

Pro-choice advocates like Ruth Jones, counsel to the NOW Legal Defense and Education Fund in New York, countered "that most people wouldn't understand how deeply *Roe v. Wade* was dismantled." *Roe,* according to Jones, "stood for more than the proposition that states cannot make abortion illegal."[14] Both sides, in the words of pro-choice attorney Estelle Rogers, had "a genuine difference of opinion about what *Roe* meant."[15]

Both sides banked on the fact that few Americans—and even few lawyers—would indeed read the five opinions handed down by the justices, in a total of 184 pages. The opinions were complex and revealed competing judicial philosophies and approaches to constitutional interpretation, precedent, and the Court's role in politics. *Casey* had fragmented the Court in surprising ways. A bare majority firmly drew a line in reaffirming (while at the same time redefining) *Roe*'s "central holding." That bare yet apparently solid majority would not uphold laws that "unduly burden" access to abortion or ban abortion early in pregnancy. Still, four justices—Chief Justice William Rehnquist and Justices Scalia, Clarence Thomas, and Byron White—voted expressly to overturn *Roe.* Only Justice Blackmun would have stricken all of Pennsylvania's restrictions; Justice Stevens voted to uphold the informed consent and reporting requirements but to invalidate the provisions for abortion counseling, a twenty-four-hour waiting period, and spousal notification. The balance was momentarily held by a newly forged plurality: Justices O'Connor, Kennedy, and Souter. Those three justices issued an extraordinary joint opinion announcing the decision to uphold Pennsylvania's regulations except for its requirements for spousal notification, and reporting and public disclosure of spousal notification.

The result reached in *Casey* virtually mirrored opinion polls. Following the decision in *Webster,* support for legalized abortion had grown —how much depended on the question asked.[16] But ambivalence still reigned in the court of public opinion. The vast majority of Americans support legalized abortion while also favoring restrictions. The day after *Casey* came down, a *USA Today*/CNN/Gallup poll reported that 82 percent of the public supported legalized abortion with some or no restrictions. In keeping with other polls, 34 percent supported unrestricted access to abortion, 48 percent favored some restrictions, while 13 percent thought abortion should be illegal, and 5 percent had no opinion.[17] In addition, more than 70 percent supported each of the restrictions at stake in *Casey.* That led Republican pollster Linda DiVall to proclaim, "The Supreme Court reached a decision that reflects mainstream American opinion;"[18] "abortion should not be made illegal, yet certain restrictions ought to apply."[19]

The surprising result and fragmentation of the high bench raised questions about whether the controlling plurality of Reagan and Bush appointees—O'Connor, Kennedy, and Souter—had tailored their opinion to the polls in a calculated move to deflate the controversy prior to the 1992 presidential election or, alternatively, whether it was merely coincidental that they came down about where the polls did. Scalia accused them of playing politics and following "not a principle of law ... but the principle of Realpolitik." Regardless, White House advisers were relieved that *Roe* was not reversed. They had feared a possible backlash from women and young Republicans that might cost the election. One reporter summed up their view: "Bush has it both ways in political terms—he retains right-to-life support for appointing judges in hopes they would reverse *Roe,* without paying the political cost of reversing *Roe.*"[20] *Casey* represented the kind of political compromise within the Court that was destined neither to please activists on either side nor to lay the controversy to rest. This chapter examines the issues, strategies, and arguments, along with the judicial politics behind the justices' opinions and the Court's ruling, as well as how *Casey* may affect the continuing fight over abortion in American politics.

The Issues in Casey

In 1988 and 1989, following the Court's ruling in *Webster,* Pennsylvania amended its abortion law to include more restrictions on access to abortion. It was not alone in doing so. Its new restrictions were not as severe as those passed by Utah and Louisiana and by the Territory of Guam. Utah outlawed abortion, except when a woman's health is gravely endangered by the pregnancy and in cases of rape or incest that have been reported to police. Louisiana's legislature overrode the governor's veto to enact sweeping new antiabortion legislation. Its law, which a lower federal court invalidated, would have permitted abortion only when necessary to save a woman's life and in certain cases when a pregnancy was due to rape or incest. Louisiana was also the first state to criminalize abortions once again. Doctors who performed abortions would have been subject to prison terms of up to ten years and fines as high as $100,000.

Pennsylvania's restrictions aimed at forcing the Court to uphold more restrictive conditions than those in *Webster* and into possibly reversing *Roe.* Indeed, several of the restrictions were almost identical to those struck down in an earlier Pennsylvania case, *Thornburgh v. Ameri-*

can College of Obstetricians and Gynecologists (1986). *Thornburgh* had split the Court 5–4, but the Court's composition had significantly changed since then. Reagan had elevated Rehnquist to chief justice and named Scalia and Kennedy. They were followed by Bush's appointments of Souter and, by the time oral arguments were heard in *Casey,* Thomas. The only member remaining on the bench who had voted with the majority in *Roe* was its author. Pennsylvania's legislators and governor, moreover, were reassured by the signal in *Webster* that at least a plurality of the Court was willing to reverse *Roe.*

Five principal restrictions enacted by Pennsylvania were at stake and immediately challenged in the courts. They provided for the following:

1. *Abortion counseling and a woman's informed consent* — requiring doctors to counsel women on the specifics and risks of abortion; to describe and provide materials detailing each stage of fetal development; to furnish information on, as well as a list of, providers offering "alternatives to abortion"; and to obtain a woman's written consent to an abortion.
2. *A waiting period* — requiring a woman, after giving her informed consent, to wait twenty-four hours before obtaining an abortion.
3. *Parental consent* — requiring an unmarried woman under the age of eighteen to obtain the written consent of at least one parent, or alternatively a judge, before having an abortion; also requiring a parent to accompany the teenager for abortion counseling.
4. *Spousal notification* — requiring a married woman to sign a statement certifying that she had notified her husband, except when the husband is not the father or cannot be located "after diligent effort"; if the pregnancy is the result of a "spousal sexual assault" that has been reported to police; or if she has reason to believe that she faces "bodily injury" as a result of the notification.
5. *Reporting and public disclosure requirements* — requiring a doctor to report to state authorities on each abortion performed, including supplying copies of the woman's informed consent and, if applicable, the parental consent or spousal notification. The reports were to be open to the public.

Several other abortion clinics in the state joined Planned Parenthood of Southeastern Pennsylvania and a doctor in challenging the constitutionality of the requirements under the due process clause of the Fourteenth Amendment. Subsequently, federal district court Judge Daniel

Huyett—a Republican and an appointee of President Richard Nixon—
struck down the informed consent, parental consent, spousal notification, and reporting requirements, along with the provision for public
disclosure of the doctors' reports.[21] He upheld the other regulations.
Both Planned Parenthood and the state appealed to the Court of Appeals
for the Third Circuit.

Much of Huyett's ruling was later reversed by a three-judge panel of
the Third Circuit.[22] Judge Collins Seitz (a Democrat and appointee of
President Lyndon Johnson) joined Judge Walter K. Stapleton (a Republican and Nixon appointee) in upholding four of the restrictions: those requiring that the woman (1) be informed by the doctor about fetal development and abortion procedures; (2) give consent or, if a minor, obtain
parental consent; and (3) wait at least twenty-four hours after giving
consent before obtaining an abortion; and (4) the provisions imposing reporting requirements on doctors and clinics performing abortions.

Despite the fact that virtually identical provisions had been invalidated in *Thornburgh,* Stapleton emphasized that *Webster* had substantially undercut support for a woman's "fundamental right" to obtain an
abortion. Based on his reading of *Webster,* at best four justices adhered
to *Roe*'s recognition of a woman's "fundamental right" and to the
"strict scrutiny" test. Four others appeared inclined to uphold restrictions so long as they had a "rational basis." O'Connor had appeared to
command the pivotal position. On her "undue-burden" analysis in *Akron I* and *Webster,* "strict scrutiny" appeared to apply only when a law
unduly burdened the woman; otherwise, restrictions merely needed to
meet the "rational-basis" test. "In sum," observed Stapleton, "O'Connor's undue burden standard is the law of the land." He concluded that
none of the above four restrictions constituted an undue burden or failed
the rational-basis test.

Along with Seitz, Stapleton found the spousal notification provision
to unduly burden the woman in exposing her to potential spousal abuse,
violence, and economic duress at the hands of a husband; it could not
survive the strict-scrutiny test. The third judge on the panel—Samuel A.
Alito, whom Bush had named to the court in 1990—strongly disagreed;
spousal notification was neither an undue burden nor unreasonable. He
observed, "We have no authority to overrule that legislative judgment
even if we deem it 'unwise' or worse."[23]

Planned Parenthood again prepared to appeal—this time to the Supreme Court. Its leadership was far from confident. Besides *Webster,* the
Rehnquist Court had upheld the Reagan and Bush administrations' "gag
order" on abortion counseling by family-planning clinics that receive
federal funding under Title X of the Public Health Service Act.

Rust v. Sullivan *and the Federal Ban*
on Abortion Counseling

When Congress enacted Title X of the Public Health Service Act of 1970, it authorized the secretary of the Department of Health and Human Services (HHS) to make grants to public and private organizations offering family-planning services. A section of the act provided that "[n]one of the funds appropriated under this subchapter shall be used in programs where abortion is a method of family planning." Still, for eighteen years organizations providing abortion-related services received funding under the program, although they could not directly spend any federal funds on those services.

In 1988 Louis W. Sullivan, the Reagan administration's secretary of HHS, set down new regulations attaching three principal conditions to a grant of federal funds under Title X. First, a "Title X project may not provide counseling concerning the use of abortion as a method of family planning or provide referral for abortion as a method of family planning." Second, grant recipients may not carry out activities that "encourage, promote or advocate abortion as a method of family planning." Third, organizations engaged in family planning and receiving federal funding must be so organized that they are "physically and financially separate" from prohibited abortion activities.

HHS's new regulations were immediately challenged on the grounds that they were not authorized by Title X and that they violated the First and Fifth Amendment rights of doctors and of women seeking abortions. In one of several cases filed in federal courts challenging HHS's new regulations, Irving Rust, a doctor who worked at a clinic which received funding under Title X, sued HHS's secretary, Louis Sullivan. A federal district court, however, upheld HHS's regulations and the Court of Appeals for the Second Circuit affirmed its ruling. But, in other cases challenging the regulations in the first and tenth circuits, appellate courts struck down the regulations. When Rust subsequently appealed the Second Circuit's ruling to the Supreme Court, his petition for *certiorari* was granted review because it presented a substantial question of federal law on which appellate courts were split. In resolving that intercircuit conflict over the constitutionality of HHS's antiabortion counseling regulations in *Rust v. Sullivan*, the justices split 5–4 on upholding the regulations.[24]

Joined by Kennedy, Scalia, Souter, and White, Chief Justice Rehnquist held that Title X was ambiguous in regard to Congress's intent to permit or prohibit such funding and, in cases of ambiguous statutory language, the federal courts should defer to the executive branch's interpretation of the law. In rejecting the argument that the "gag order" ran afoul of the First Amendment's guarantee for free speech, Rehnquist said, "Congress has ... not denied [organizations receiving federal funding] the right to engage in abortion-related activities. Congress has merely refused to fund such activities ... and the Secretary has simply required a certain degree of separation from the Title X project...." As for the Fifth-Amendment-based assertion that the restrictions violated a woman's fundamental rights, Rehnquist observed: "The difficulty that a woman encounters when a Title X project does not provide abortion counseling or referral leaves her in no different position than she would have been if the government had not enacted Title X."

Blackmun, Marshall, Stevens, and O'Connor dissented. Stevens contended that Congress in fact had indicated its approval of such funding in both its continuing appropriations and its choice of the language in Title X. O'Connor thought the issue ought to be left for Congress to decide. Blackmun criticized the majority's treatment of the free speech and privacy claims, explaining,

> Whatever may be the Government's power to condition the receipt of its largess upon the relinquishment of constitutional rights, it surely does not extend to a condition that suppresses the recipient's cherished freedom of speech based solely upon the content or viewpoint of that speech.... By suppressing medically pertinent information and injecting a restrictive ideological message unrelated to considerations of maternal health, the Government places formidable obstacles in the path of Title X clients' freedom of choice and thereby violates their Fifth Amendment rights.

The Strategies and Arguments in Casey

In *Rust v. Sullivan* (1991) Chief Justice Rehnquist had commanded a bare majority that included Justices Kennedy, Scalia, Souter, and White. Justices Blackmun, Thurgood Marshall, O'Connor, and Stevens had dissented. In Planned Parenthood's estimation, the balance on the Court further shifted against it with the appointment of Thomas. In addition, Planned Parenthood had failed in 1991 to persuade the Court to grant review of *Planned Parenthood v. Agency for International Development* (1991),[25] which concerned another of the Reagan administration's regulatory reforms designed to cut back on the availability of abortion. In 1984 the administration had abruptly barred federal funding for foreign health-care organizations, which also rely on money from other sources, if any part of an organization receiving funding from the Agency for International Development (AID) provides abortion counseling.

Planned Parenthood and other abortion rights groups were determined to raise the stakes politically. To intensify the abortion debate before the 1992 presidential election, the leadership decided not only to appeal but also to ask the justices either to abandon *Roe* or to reaffirm that women have a "fundamental right" under the Fourteenth Amendment.

The leaders' strategy was revealed at a press conference on 7 November 1991 by Faye Wattleton, then president of Planned Parenthood Federation of America; Kate Michelman of NARAL; Nadine Strossen, president of the American Civil Liberties Union; and Kathryn Kolbert, an attorney who had successfully challenged Pennsylvania's law in *Thornburgh* and who would spearhead the attack in *Casey*. "Even if [the Court's ruling] does not come before the election," Wattleton explained, "it will still be a major issue in this election. This is not whether it's better for us politically, but what is better for women. We will not permit the courts to have the last word on this ever again, and we will show our strength in the polls because we simply will not go back."[26]

Subsequently, Pennsylvania's attorney general, Ernest Preate, Jr., appealed. He too asked the Court to "end the current uncertainty in the law of abortion." In April the Bush administration joined *Casey* with an *amicus* brief urging the Court to overrule *Roe*. "As we explained in our briefs in *Akron I, Thornburgh, Webster, Hodgson,* and *Rust v. Sullivan,*" Solicitor General Kenneth Starr wrote, "*Roe v. Wade* was wrongly decided and should be overruled. We strongly adhere to that position in this case."[27] In their briefs, Preate and Starr agreed that the Court should explicitly reject the view that women have a "fundamental right" to abortion and that courts must apply the "strict-scrutiny" test when reviewing restrictions on abortion. They asked the Court to endorse squarely the less rigorous "rational-basis" test that a plurality of the Court had embraced in *Webster;* on that basis all of Pennsylvania's restrictions were constitutional.

Both sides were supported by hundreds of organizations and individuals who joined in *amici* briefs, but only thirty-two *amici* briefs were filed in *Casey,* far short of the record number in *Webster.* Besides the federal government, Pennsylvania was supported in briefs from University Faculty for Life, Feminists for Life of America, Catholics United for Life, the United States Catholic Conference, the National Legal Foundation, the Knights of Columbus, the Rutherford Institute, the National Right to Life, Inc., the State of Utah, and the American Association of Pro Life Obstetricians, among others.

Filing *amici* briefs on the other side, Planned Parenthood's allies from previous court battles included, among others, 250 American Historians, the American Psychological Association, the Alan Guttmacher Institute, the NAACP Legal Defense and Education Fund, the City of New York, fourteen states, and the District of Columbia, as well as 178 organizations, including the Abortion Rights Mobilization.

Members of Congress once again signed on to *amici* briefs for both sides, though fewer than did so in *Webster*. A longtime champion of the antiabortion cause, Representative Henry Hyde (R-Illinois) was joined this time around by only three Republican senators and thirty-seven representatives (twenty-eight Republicans and nine Democrats). Their brief was written by Rutgers University School of Law Professor Albert Blaustein and Kevin Todd of Americans United for Life. Besides contending that *Roe* had lost much of its precedential value, they argued that the doctrine of *stare decisis* did not preclude reversal. *Roe* was wrongly decided and ought to be jettisoned.

Planned Parenthood received support in an *amicus* brief from 157 members of Congress: 29 senators (5 Republicans and 24 Democrats) and 128 representatives (7 Republicans and 121 Democrats). Duke Law School Professor Walter Dellinger and Washington, D.C., attorney and insider Lloyd Cutler submitted their brief. They called for a reaffirmation of *Roe*'s recognition of a woman's "fundamental liberty" to have an abortion based on arguments for respecting *Roe*'s precedential value.

Although the briefs contained many of the same medical, historical, socioeconomic, and constitutional arguments and counterarguments made in *Webster*, most also touched on the issue of precedent and the doctrine of *stare decisis*. The doctrine of *stare decisis* was also central to Kolbert's strategy. Although six years earlier she had successfully argued *Thornburgh,* she appreciated that the changes in the Court's composition had left O'Connor, Kennedy, and Souter in pivotal positions. Kolbert would have to convince them of the importance of *stare decisis* and settled societal expectations about the law.[28]

On 23 April 1992 the Court heard oral arguments in *Casey* in a courtroom crowded beyond capacity. For seven uninterrupted minutes Kolbert argued that if Pennsylvania's law were upheld upon the rational-basis test, *Roe* would be essentially overturned, regardless of what the Court said. Then O'Connor inquired whether Kolbert was going to address the specific provisions of Pennsylvania's law. Kolbert did turn to the provisions but continued to stress the importance and consequences of the Court's standard of review, and of women's expectations about their constitutional right to choose.

Kennedy appeared to search for a compromise that would allow the Court to uphold Pennsylvania's law without catapulting the abortion issue into the 1992 presidential election by expressly overruling *Roe*. But

Kolbert was unyielding when responding to his suggestion that "our sustaining these statutory provisions does not necessarily undercut all of the holding of *Roe v. Wade.*" "It is our position, Your Honor, that if this court were to change the standard of strict scrutiny, which has been the central core of that holding, that in fact, that will undercut the holdings of this court and effectively overrule *Roe v. Wade.*"

When Preate took to the lectern, he initially defended Pennsylvania's law not on the basis of *Roe*'s strict-scrutiny test or *Webster*'s rational-basis test but O'Connor's "undue-burden" test. But O'Connor appeared unpersuaded by how far Preate wanted to push that analysis when defending the spousal-notification requirement. The justice wondered why, if the state's interest was in fact in protecting the unborn, it did not require notification of fathers who were not husbands or that unmarried women notify their sexual partners? Preate said that the state's interest was the same in such situations but enforcement would be "problematic." O'Connor agreed, yet continued probing until Scalia interrupted to ask whether the undue-burden test applied across the board or on a case-by-case basis. In an about-face Preate declared that "there is no undue burden in our statute, anywhere in our statute, and if the undue burden test is, as applied or understood by this Court causes our statute to fall, then we ask this Court to adopt rational basis as the appropriate analysis." That led to further questions from O'Connor.

Solicitor General Kenneth Starr received the toughest questioning from the bench. He began well enough until Stevens wanted to know the administration's position on "whether a fetus is a person within the meaning of the Fourteenth Amendment." "We do not have a position on that question," Starr responded. Stevens persisted, pointing out that *Roe* had addressed that issue. "That is correct," Starr conceded, while insisting that the Court need not now address that extraordinarily difficult issue. "Does the United States have a position on that question?" Stevens reiterated, launching Starr into the following exchange:

> *Mr. Starr:* We do not, because we think it would be an extraordinarily difficult and sensitive issue by virtue of a number of questions that would flow from that, including equal protections and so forth.
>
> *Justice O'Connor:* Well, the Court decided that in *Roe*, did it not?
>
> *Mr. Starr:* The Court did, in fact, decide that there is a very keen interest on the part of the state in what the *Roe* Court called potential life, and that's my —
>
> *Justice O'Connor:* Yes, but said the fetus is not a person under the Fourteenth Amendment.
>
> *Mr. Starr:* Well, I think that that is the necessary consequence of *Roe*

v. Wade. But I think that the key point is that a number of the Justices of this Court have said that regardless of that legal question, that constitutional question, that the state does have a compelling interest in the potential life, in fetal life, and that that interest runs throughout pregnancy.

Justice Scalia: We did not say in *Roe* that a state could not have a position on whether a fetus is a person, did we?

Mr. Starr: Certainly the Court —

Justice Scalia: We said that the Constitution takes no position on whether a fetus is a person, and/or that it does takes a position that a fetus is not protected by the Constitution.

Mr. Starr: The Court seemed to admit of the possibility of state regulation to protect the unborn at all stages.

Justice Scalia: Including state regulation on the basis of the people's determination within that state that a fetus is a person. There's nothing in *Roe* that says a state may not make that judgment, if it wishes.

Starr agreed. But after fielding further questions from Souter, Starr faced renewed questioning from Stevens. "What is the textual basis for your position that there's a compelling interest in something that is not a person within the meaning of the Fourteenth Amendment?" Starr appeared caught off guard. Chiding him for being nonresponsive, Stevens repeated the question. Appealing to the powers reserved to the states under the Tenth Amendment, Starr asserted that "the state can order its relationships in ways that reflect the morality of the people, with limits."

Scalia came to Starr's rescue with a leading question: "Why does there have to be something in the Constitution? There's nothing in the Constitution that requires the state to protect the environment, is there?" "Of course not," Starr replied. "And yet that can be a compelling state interest," Scalia resounded. "Yes," Starr agreed, adding that "the Constitution does not seek to order and to ordain. These are interests in which the state can have, and our nature of government — " Scalia cut him off to make his own point, which radically reinterpreted *Roe:* "All that *Roe* says is that the Constitution does not protect the fetus under the Fourteenth Amendment. It does not say that a state may not choose to do so."

Starr's concluding colloquy with the justices centered on whether the rational-basis test would allow states to prohibit abortions absolutely. Starr repeatedly hedged that it was important not to answer in the abstract. However, Stevens remained on his track, rather sarcastically summarizing his argument for him: "Rational basis under your analysis: there's an interest in preserving fetal life at all times during pregnancy.

It's rational, under your view. Ergo it follows that a total prohibition, protected by criminal penalties, would be rational, it would meet your standard."

Judicial Politics, Casey, *and the Fragmentation of the Rehnquist Court*

Almost four months after hearing oral arguments, on the last day of the Court's term, the Court announced its decision. O'Connor, Kennedy, and Souter each read portions of their joint opinion for the Court. They were followed by the other justices, who filed opinions in part concurring in and dissenting from the ruling.

The Plurality's Fine Lines

From the first page of their sixty-page opinion, O'Connor read the plurality's bottom line:

> After considering the fundamental constitutional questions resolved by *Roe,* principles of institutional integrity, and the rule of *stare decisis,* we are led to conclude this: the essential holding of *Roe v. Wade* should be retained and once again reaffirmed.
>
> It must be stated at the outset and with clarity that *Roe's* essential holding, the holding we reaffirm, has three parts. First is a recognition of the right of the woman to choose to have an abortion before viability and to obtain it without undue interference from the State. Before viability, the State's interests are not strong enough to support a prohibition of abortion or the imposition of a substantial obstacle to the woman's effective right to elect the procedure. Second is a confirmation of the State's power to restrict abortions after fetal viability, if the law contains exceptions for pregnancies which endanger a woman's life or health. And third is the principle that the State has legitimate interests from the outset of the pregnancy in protecting the health of the woman and the life of the fetus that may become a child. These principles do not contradict one another; and we adhere to each.

It became clear later that the plurality had rejected or significantly redefined much of what *Roe* stood for. Besides rejecting *Roe's* trimester analysis for balancing the interests of the woman and the state, the plurality overturned portions of rulings in *City of Akron v. Akron Center for Reproductive Health, Inc.* (1983) and *Thornburgh v. American Col-*

lege of Obstetricians and Gynecologists (1986), which had struck down informed consent, parental consent, and requirements for abortion counseling, among other provisions. Even more significant, the plurality (and an overwhelming majority of the justices) no longer recognized *Roe* as guaranteeing women a "fundamental right." Instead, O'Connor, Kennedy, and Souter redefined the "central principle" of *Roe* as guaranteeing the woman a liberty interest under the Fourteenth Amendment "to choose to terminate or continue her pregnancy before viability."

In replacing *Roe*'s analysis with an "undue-burden" standard, the plurality said in regard to overly restrictive regulations:

> ⚖ We conclude the line should be drawn at viability, so that before that time the woman has a right to choose to terminate her pregnancy. We adhere to this principle for two reasons. First, ... is the doctrine of *stare decisis*. ... *Roe* was a reasoned statement, elaborated with great care. We have twice reaffirmed it in the face of great opposition. Although we must overrule those parts of *Thornburgh* and *Akron I* which, in our view, are inconsistent with *Roe*'s statement that the State has a legitimate interest in promoting the life or potential life of the unborn, the central premise of those cases represents an unbroken commitment by this Court to the essential holding of *Roe*. ...
>
> The second reason is that the concept of viability, as we noted in *Roe*, is the time at which there is a realistic possibility of maintaining and nourishing a life outside the womb, so that the independent existence of the second life can in reason and all fairness be the object of state protection that now overrides the rights of the woman. Consistent with other constitutional norms, legislatures may draw lines which appear arbitrary without the necessity of offering a justification. But courts may not. We must justify the lines we draw. And there is no line other than viability which is more workable....
>
> The woman's right to terminate her pregnancy before viability is the most central principle of *Roe v. Wade*. It is a rule of law and a component of liberty we cannot renounce....
>
> What is at stake is the woman's right to make the ultimate decision, not a right to be insulated from all others in doing so. Regulations which do no more than create a structural mechanism by which the State, or the parent or guardian of a minor, may express profound respect for the life of the unborn are permitted, if they are not a substantial obstacle to the woman's exercise of the right to choose. Unless it has that effect on her right of choice, a state measure designed to persuade her to choose

childbirth over abortion will be upheld if reasonably related to that goal. Regulations designed to foster the health of a woman seeking an abortion are valid if they do not constitute an undue burden. 🖼

O'Connor, Kennedy, and Souter offered the following summary of the principles that had guided their decision.

🖼 (a) To protect the central right recognized by *Roe v. Wade* while at the same time accommodating the State's profound interest in potential life, we will employ the undue burden analysis as explained in this opinion. An undue burden exists, and therefore a provision of law is invalid, if its purpose or effect is to place a substantial obstacle in the path of a woman seeking an abortion before the fetus attains viability.

(b) We reject the rigid trimester framework of *Roe v. Wade.* To promote the State's profound interest in potential life, throughout pregnancy the State may take measures to ensure that the woman's choice is informed, and measures designed to advance this interest will not be invalidated as long as their purpose is to persuade the woman to choose childbirth over abortion. These measures must not be an undue burden on the right.

(c) As with any medical procedure, the State may enact regulations to further the health or safety of a woman seeking an abortion. Unnecessary health regulations that have the purpose or effect of presenting a substantial obstacle to a woman seeking an abortion impose an undue burden on the right.

(d) Our adoption of the undue burden analysis does not disturb the central holding of *Roe v. Wade,* and we reaffirm that holding. Regardless of whether exceptions are made for particular circumstances, a State may not prohibit any woman from making the ultimate decision to terminate her pregnancy before viability.

(e) We also reaffirm *Roe's* holding that "subsequent to viability, the State in promoting its interest in the potentiality of human life may, if it chooses, regulate, and even proscribe, abortion except where it is necessary, in appropriate medical judgment, for the preservation of the life or health of the mother." 🖼

The central and longest section of the plurality's opinion was sixteen pages written by Souter. It dealt with the doctrine of *stare decisis* and offered the plurality's reasoning for not overruling *Roe.* It was also the section that drew the most fire from Rehnquist and Scalia.

As Souter read aloud portions of the opinion, it was evident that *stare decisis* had been given a new twist in order to rationalize the plurality's reaffirmation of *Roe*. There were only two comparable controversial constitutional doctrines in the past century, Souter said, that might be deemed analogous to *Roe* and its progeny. Both had been eventually abandoned by the Court but, according to the plurality, *Roe* was analogous to neither.

First was the line of cases associated with *Lochner v. New York* (1905)[29] and *Adkins v. Children's Hospital of the District of Columbia* (1923).[30] In those and other cases the Court struck down progressive economic legislation—such as minimum wage and maximum hours laws—on the basis of a "liberty of contract" that the Court invented and read into the Fourteenth Amendment. That contributed to the constitutional crisis of 1937 and to FDR's "Court-packing" plan, which would have increased the number of justices from nine to fifteen. The crisis was averted when the Court backed down in its proverbial switch-in-time-that-saved-nine (see chapter 1).[31] The Court's abandonment of its doctrine and its overturning of *Adkins* in *West Coast Hotel v. Parrish* (1937)[32] was prudent because, in the plurality's words, "the Depression had come and, with it, the lesson that seemed unmistakable to most people by 1937, that the interpretation of contractual freedom protected in *Adkins* [and *Lochner*] rested on fundamentally false factual assumptions about the capacity of a relatively unregulated market to satisfy minimal levels of human welfare."

The second comparison was the Court's overruling of the doctrine of "separate but equal." That doctrine had initially been given constitutional force in *Plessy v. Ferguson* (1896)[33] and had effectively been overruled by the school desegregation ruling in *Brown v. Board of Education* (1954).[34]

Plessy had rested on the proposition that if racial segregation "stamps the colored race with a badge of inferiority," that effect was "solely because the colored race chooses to put that construction upon it." By the time of *Brown,* it was clear that legally sanctioned segregation did indeed stamp blacks with a "badge of inferiority." And, the plurality asserted, "Society's understanding of the facts upon which a constitutional ruling was sought in 1954 was thus fundamentally different from the basis claimed for the decision in 1896."

In other words, the plurality sought to establish that "*West Coast Hotel* and *Brown* each rested on facts, or an understanding of facts, changed from those which furnished the claimed justifications for the earlier constitutional revolutions," and that circumstance justified the Court's abandoning the "liberty of contract" and "separate but equal" doctrines. The Court had correctly recognized that the constitutional *cum* factual suppositions on which *Lochner, Adkins,* and *Plessy* rested no longer held true and, the plurality contended, that changes in the country justified the Court's overruling of those decisions. Moreover, O'Connor, Kennedy, and Souter declared that the Court and the country would have paid a "terrible price" if *West Coast Hotel* and *Brown* had not overturned those earlier decisions. The same could not be said for *Roe. Roe* was not analogous to either *Lochner* or *Plessy* because "neither the factual underpinnings of *Roe*'s central holding nor our understanding of it has changed."

In addition to that novel argument for upholding *Roe*'s precedential value, the plurality maintained that reversing *Roe* would badly damage the Court.

> [The Court's] legitimacy is ... expressed in the Court's opinions, and our contemporary understanding is such that a decision without principled justification would be no judicial act at all. But even when justification is furnished by apposite legal principle, something more is required.... [T]he justification claimed must be beyond dispute. The Court must take care to speak and act in ways that allow people to accept its decisions on the terms the Court claims for them, as grounded truly in principle, not as compromises with social and political pressures....
>
> ... A decision to overrule *Roe*'s essential holding under the existing circumstances would address error, if error there was, at the cost of both profound and unnecessary damage to the Court's legitimacy, and to the Nation's commitment to the rule of law. It is therefore imperative to adhere to the essence of *Roe*'s original decision, and we do so today.

Finally, the plurality turned to the specific provisions of Pennsylvania's law. All were permissible, except for the requirement of spousal notification and the related reporting and public-disclosure requirements. Spousal notification went too far because, as the plurality put it, "there are millions of women in this country who are the victims of regular physical and psychological abuse at the hands of their husbands. Should these women become pregnant, they may have very good reasons for not wishing to inform their husbands of their decision to obtain an abortion.... The unfortunate yet persisting conditions ... will mean that in a large fraction of the cases in which [spousal notification] is relevant, it will operate as a substantial obstacle to a woman's choice to undergo an abortion. It is an undue burden, and therefore invalid."

The plurality's opinion was extraordinary and surprising in many ways. In contrast to the detailed and heavily footnoted review of medical literature and history of abortion going back to the ancient Greeks in *Roe*, it focused on the doctrine of *stare decisis* and the Court's role in relation to societal expectations about the rule of law. O'Connor made it unmistakably clear that she was not bound to reverse *Roe* completely. Even more remarkable was Kennedy's and Souter's desertion from Rehnquist's side. Until that term Kennedy had generally aligned himself with the chief justice, as he did when signing on to Rehnquist's opinions in *Webster* and *Rust v. Sullivan*. But, here and in a few other cases,[35] he turned out to be a more traditional conservative than the justices on the far right. So too did Souter break with the chief justice after having joined his opinion in *Rust*. A plurality controlled on this issue and emerged as moderate conservatives who believed in restraint with respect to interpreting the Constitution and reversing precedent and societal expectations.

"Make no mistake," observed Blackmun in his opinion in *Casey*, "the joint opinion of Justices O'Connor, Kennedy, and Souter is an act of personal courage and constitutional principle." The four dissenters in *Casey* and their fellow critics charged precisely the opposite: the plurality lacked courage, bending to pressure from the supporters of *Roe* and failing to respect crucial constitutional principles. Ill-fated Supreme Court nominee Robert H. Bork, for one, labeled O'Connor, Kennedy, and Souter, constitutional "radicals," "given more to liberal activism than to adherence to the principles of the Constitution as originally understood."[36] Bork left no doubt—and seemingly none of the members of the Court doubted—that had his nomination been confirmed in 1987, and he were now sitting in the seat occupied by Kennedy, *Roe* would have been completely overturned in *Casey*.

Roe's Last Two Staunch Defenders

In separate opinions, each concurring and dissenting in part, Stevens and Blackmun expressed agreement with some of the plurality's opinion and disagreement with some of it and with the plurality's reasoning. Stevens disagreed with the plurality's analysis of *Roe*'s trimester approach and would have struck down Pennsylvania's requirements for abortion counseling, a twenty-four-hour waiting period, and spousal notification.

Blackmun's opinion was impassioned. He underscored that "five Members of this Court today recognize that 'the Constitution protects a woman's right to terminate her pregnancy in its early stages,'" and emphasized the precariousness of what remained of *Roe*. He alone was wedded to *Roe* and would have invalidated all of Pennsylvania's restrictions. But, as he put it, "If there is reason to applaud the advances made by the joint opinion today, there is more to fear from the Chief Justice's opinion."

Much of Blackmun's opinion countered Rehnquist's and the other dissenter's insistence on *Roe*'s reversal. Neither Blackmun nor Rehnquist had budged from his position in *Roe,* but Rehnquist was now chief justice, the balance on the bench had shifted, and the justices' arguments had grown more personal and rhetorical. Rehnquist's criticism of *Roe,* insisted Blackmun, stemmed from his "stunted conception of individual liberty" and extreme deference to the electoral system and majoritarian democracy on such matters. At bottom, Rehnquist and Blackmun represented sharply opposing conceptions of the constitutional system and the Court's role in American politics. According to Rehnquist, elections should determine controversies like that over abortion, and courts should defer to the operation of majoritarian democracy on such matters. Blackmun insisted that the Constitution did not create a majoritarian democracy per se but, rather, a republic or representative democracy with built-in constitutional checks and balances—including judicial review—to protect the liberties and rights of individuals and minorities.[37] In his words, "While there is much to be praised about our democracy, our country since its founding has recognized that there are certain fundamental liberties that are not to be left to the whims of an election. A woman's right to reproductive choice is one of those fundamental liberties. Accordingly, that liberty need not seek refuge at the ballot box."

Blackmun concluded on a highly personal note, pointing up the importance of the electoral process: "In one sense, the Court's approach is worlds apart from that of the Chief Justice and Justice Scalia. And yet, in another sense, the distance between the two approaches is short—the distance is but a single vote. I am 83 years old. I cannot remain on this Court forever, and when I do step down, the confirmation process for my successor may well focus on the issue before us today. That, I regret, may be exactly where the choice between the two worlds will be made."

Waiting for One More Vote: The Dissenters

The balance in *Casey* clearly shifted to allowing states to impose more conditions on the availability of abortions, particularly after the first trimester. But it had not tipped far enough for Rehnquist, Scalia, Thomas, and White. In separate opinions Rehnquist and Scalia joined those parts of the plurality's opinion upholding sections of Pennsylvania's law but otherwise vehemently dissented. They attacked the plurality's "undue-burden" test as "standardless" and ridiculed its treatment of *stare decisis.* Their bitterness at the refusal to overturn *Roe* was unmistakable. Scalia's spirited dissent, in particular, invited speculation that he may have overplayed his hand here and in *Webster,* contributing to a moderate-conservative position on *Roe* by the more judicially tempered O'Connor, Kennedy, and Souter.

Rehnquist offered a detailed critique of the plurality's reasoning for upholding *Roe;* its theory of *stare decisis* was incoherent and disingenuous, and precious little of *Roe* remained. "*Roe* decided that a woman had a fundamental right to an abortion. The joint opinion rejects that view. *Roe* decided that abortion regulations were to be subjected to 'strict scrutiny' and could be justified only in the light of 'compelling state interests.' The joint opinion rejects that view. *Roe* analyzed abortion regulation under a rigid trimester framework, a framework which has guided this Court's decisionmaking for 19 years. The joint opinion rejects that framework.... *Roe* continues to exist, but ... [as] a mere facade to give the illusion of reality."

Rehnquist bore down on the rationale for adhering to *Roe.* If the Court overturned *Roe* when it was "under fire," the plurality asserted, it would be widely perceived as "surrendering to political pressure." But "there are two sides to every controversy," Rehnquist shot back, blasting the plurality for succumbing to the pressures of *Roe*'s supporters. Neither the Court's legitimacy nor *stare decisis,* he contended, were served by adhering to a ruling wrongly and improperly arrived at. Nor did the chief justice find the plurality's reasoning any more persuasive with respect to distinguishing *Roe* from *Lochner* and *Plessy:*

> The joint opinion discusses several *stare decisis* factors which, it asserts, point toward retaining a portion of *Roe.* Two of these factors are that the main "factual underpinning" of *Roe* has remained the same, and that its doctrinal foundation is no weaker now than it was in 1973. Of course, what might be called the basic facts which gave rise to *Roe* have remained the same—women become pregnant, there is a point somewhere, depending on medical technology, where a fetus becomes viable, and women give birth to children. But this is only to say that the same facts which gave rise to *Roe* will continue to give rise to similar cases. It is not a reason, in and of itself, why those cases must be decided in the same incorrect manner as was the first case to deal with the question. And surely there is no requirement, in considering whether to depart from *stare decisis* in a constitutional case, that a decision be more wrong now than it was at the time it was rendered. If that were true, the most outlandish constitutional decision could survive forever, based simply on the fact that it was no more outlandish later than it was when originally rendered....

In the end, ... the joint opinion's argument is based solely on generalized assertions about the national psyche, on a belief that the people of this country have grown accustomed to the *Roe* decision over the last 19 years and have "ordered their thinking and living around" it. As an initial matter, one might inquire how the joint opinion can view the "central holding" of *Roe* as so deeply rooted in our constitutional culture, when it so casually uproots and disposes of that same decision's trimester framework. Furthermore, at various points in the past, the same could have been said about this Court's erroneous decisions that the Constitution allowed "separate but equal" treatment of minorities, or that "liberty" under the Due Process Clause protected "freedom of contract." The "separate but equal" doctrine lasted 58 years after *Plessy,* and *Lochner*'s protection of contractual freedom lasted 32 years. However, the simple fact that a generation or more had grown used to these major decisions did not prevent the Court from correcting its errors in those cases, nor should it prevent us from correctly interpreting the Constitution here....

The joint opinion agrees that the Court's stature would have been seriously damaged if in *Brown* and *West Coast Hotel* it had dug in its heels and refused to apply normal principles of *stare decisis* to the earlier decisions. But the opinion contends that the Court was entitled to overrule *Plessy* and *Lochner* in those cases, despite the existence of opposition to the original decisions, only because both the Nation and the Court had learned new lessons in the interim. This is at best a feebly supported, post hoc rationalization for those decisions....

The sum of the joint opinion's labors in the name of *stare decisis* and "legitimacy" is this: *Roe v. Wade* stands as a sort of judicial Potemkin Village, which may be pointed out to passers by as a monument to the importance of adhering to precedent. But behind the facade, an entirely new method of analysis, without any roots in constitutional law, is imported to decide the constitutionality of state laws regulating abortion. Neither *stare decisis* nor "legitimacy" are truly served by such an effort. 🔳

Scalia's opinion reiterated his call in *Webster* for *Roe*'s reversal, and again laid bare his approach to constitutional interpretation and the Court's role in politics: The Court "should get out of this area, where we have no right to be, and where we do neither ourselves nor the country any good in remaining." The reason:

🔲 The permissibility of abortion, and the limitations upon it, are to be resolved like most important questions in our democracy: by citizens trying to persuade one another and then voting.... A State's choice between two positions on which reasonable people can disagree is constitutional even when (as is often the case) it intrudes upon a "liberty" in the absolute sense.

... The issue is whether [a woman's claim to a constitutional right to have an abortion] is a liberty protected by the Constitution of the United States. I am sure it is not ... I reach [that] conclusion ... because of two simple facts: (1) the Constitution says absolutely nothing about it, and (2) the longstanding traditions of American society have permitted it to be legally proscribed.... 🔲

Scalia also dismissed the plurality's theory of *stare decisis* as "contrived" at best. Characterizing the theory as a "new, keep-what-you-want-and-throw-away-the-rest version," he offered the following list:

🔲 • Under *Roe,* requiring that a woman seeking an abortion be provided truthful information about abortion before giving informed written consent is unconstitutional, if the information is designed to influence her choice, *Thornburgh, Akron I.* Under the joint opinion's "undue burden" regime (as applied today, at least) such a requirement is constitutional.

• Under *Roe,* requiring that information be provided by a doctor, rather than by nonphysician counselors, is unconstitutional, *Akron I.* Under the "undue burden" regime (as applied today, at least) it is not. Under *Roe,* requiring a 24-hour waiting period between the time the woman gives her informed consent and the time of the abortion is unconstitutional, *Akron I.* Under the "undue burden" regime (as applied today, at least) it is not.

• Under *Roe,* requiring detailed reports that include demographic data about each woman who seeks an abortion and various information about each abortion is unconstitutional, *Thornburgh.* Under the "undue burden" regime (as applied today, at least) it generally is not. 🔲

Concluding, Scalia lamented—like Blackmun, though for different reasons—that *Roe*'s fate may rest with the next nominee to the Court, virtually guaranteeing a bitter confirmation battle. "*Roe* fanned into life an issue that has inflamed our national politics in general, and has obscured with its smoke the selection of Justices to this Court in particular, ever since. And by keeping us in the abortion-umpiring business, it is the perpetuation of that disruption, rather than of any pax Roeana, that the Court's new majority decrees."

Into the Future

"Really, what this all means is full employment for reproductive law-yers."[38] That is how Kathryn Kolbert summed up the inevitable ques-tions that arose in *Casey*'s aftermath and that would confront legislators and courts. Burke Balch, the state legislative director for the National Right to Life Committee agreed: "We're back to where we were in the 1970s and 1980s testing the limits of what the Court will allow."[39] Ac-cording to one estimate, in 1992 thirty-eight states had abortion-related bills pending in legislatures.[40]

For the moment, the Rehnquist Court had achieved a kind of com-promise—a compromise contingent on how and how soon the composi-tion of the bench changed. A bare majority was unwilling to uphold un-duly restrictive regulations, such as spousal-notification provisions and bans on abortion prior to viability. At the same time *Casey* invited more state regulation, particularly with respect to counseling, informed and parental consent, and a waiting period for the woman seeking an abor-tion.

Depending on political climate, the strength of contending forces, and legislation and legal challenges proposed or under way, *Casey* would affect each state differently. It was not the last word in the struggle over abortion, any more than *Roe* had been. Instead, it signaled another squaring off between the parties in myriad public arenas. In drawing new lines on abortion regulation, *Casey* raised more questions than it laid to rest. Ten states, for example, have regulations similar to Pennsylvania's twenty-four-hour waiting requirement, but requiring any-where from two- to forty-eight-hour waits. Those mandating more than a twenty-four-hour delay invite further challenges as a way of forcing the Court to fine-tune its ruling in *Casey*. In Nebraska, for instance, the principal abortion facilities are in Omaha, more than five hundred miles from the western end of the state. Some women would face the burden of either traveling out of state for abortions or taking, if possible, one or two days off from work to meet the waiting requirements. Waiting peri-ods and parental or informed consent also increase the cost of abortions. They may, as well, contribute to an increase in second-trimester abor-tions, especially for minors; after Minnesota's parental consent law went into effect in 1990, there was a 26.5 percent rise.[41] And second-trimester abortions are more expensive. A first-trimester abortion typically costs $250, whereas at fifteen weeks the cost increases to about $400, and at twenty weeks to $1000.[42] In addition, *Casey* indicated that states may impose significant restraints on second- and third-trimester abortions, perhaps even banning all except those necessary to save women's lives. State restrictions that individually do not present an undue burden therefore may be challenged for constituting an undue burden in combination and in relation to the availability of abortion in different regions. In short, what may not amount to an undue burden in one state may amount to just that in another state, as the head of the Center for Reproductive Law and Policy, Janet Benshoof, points out, "because of geography, lack of facilities, and travel distance."[43]

A Renewed Struggle in the States

Each side in *Casey* had twenty-five days to ask the Court to rehear the case. If neither did so, the case would be remanded to the Third Circuit and on to Judge Huyett so he could lift the injunction against the law's enforcement. In the meantime Planned Parenthood began gathering data on the effects of the waiting period and other requirements with a view to challenging again the law's enforcement as posing an undue burden "in practice, if not in theory." One of the authors of the law, Republican State Representative Stephen Freind, said that after studying *Casey* he would push for more restrictions "if we believe it allows us to go further";[44] and Pennsylvania pro-choice activists set up a telephone hotline and an "overground railroad" to help minors travel to New Jersey, which does not have a parental-consent law, to obtain abortions. As the head of a New Jersey clinic put it, "It's going to be easier just to come over the bridge into New Jersey than to deal with the courts."[45]

Reactions varied across the country. The Utah state attorney general and lawyer Mary Ann Wood, who had been hired to defend that state's post-*Webster* law, announced that its major restrictions were unconstitutional; Utah would no longer defend in federal court its outlawing of most abortions.[46] Officials in other states announced that *Casey* would have no effect. In Florida, for example, voters in 1980 had approved a state constitutional amendment, "Every natural person has the right to be let alone and free from government intrusion into his private life except as otherwise provided herein." Subsequently, in 1989 the Florida supreme court ruled that the amendment guarantees a woman the right to have an abortion and observed that its ruling "is beyond the reach" of the Supreme Court because the latter is "a bystander when it comes to interpreting state constitutions."[47]

As in Florida, state supreme courts in California,[48] Connecticut,[49]

Michigan,[50] Massachusetts,[51] and New Jersey[52] have construed their state constitutions to be protective of the right to abortion.[53] And some state legislatures, like that in Connecticut (see chapter 8) and those in Maryland, Nevada, and Washington, passed post-*Webster* legislation permitting abortion in the event the Court overruled *Roe*.

In at least eleven states—Alabama, Louisiana, Michigan, Mississippi, Missouri, Nebraska, Ohio, Pennsylvania, Utah, West Virginia, and Wisconsin—more restrictive legislation was expected. The legislatures and governors were on record as supporting the criminalization of abortion, as Utah and Louisiana had tried to do; hence antiabortion forces would press their cause in these and some other states. *Casey* invited that much, but antiabortion activists also faced the fact that until the Court's composition changed, they could not prevail. "Tragically," lamented the National Right to Life Committee's Burke Balch, "there is no way the Louisiana law would be upheld by this Court."[54] Moreover, antiabortion activists could take little comfort in the fact that the justices voting to overrule *Roe* had done so on federalist grounds, not because they believed that the Constitution protects the unborn; they would simply return the issue to each state and leave it to turn on political geography.

How the battles in the states shape up, and whether and what kinds of new restrictions on abortion emerge depend on the politics of each state. In 1992 twenty-nine governors supported keeping abortion legal, up from twenty-seven in 1991 and sixteen in 1989. According to the National Abortion Rights Action League Foundation, both houses of legislatures in nineteen states favored keeping abortion legal; those in fifteen states favored criminalizing abortion. In the Illinois, South Carolina, and Texas legislatures both houses were closely divided. In six others—Delaware, Idaho, Iowa, New York, Virginia, and West Virginia—one house supported keeping abortion legal and the other is divided. In the remaining seven states—Arkansas, Indiana, Nevada, Oklahoma, Rhode Island, South Dakota, and Tennessee—one house was bitterly divided and the other is supportive of restrictions.[55] Table 10.1 (pp. 351–53) presents for each state the positions of the governor and legislature, the number of abortions performed, the number of abortion providers, and a summary of the restrictions on the books in 1991–92.

Increased Pressure on Congress and Focus on the Presidency

Following the ruling in *Webster,* pro-choice groups slowly mounted pressure on Congress to pass legislation barring states from enacting the kinds of restrictions upheld in *Webster* and guaranteeing abortion rights. Scuffling over the so-called Freedom of Choice Act escalated during 1991–92 in anticipation of the decision in *Casey*. As with any controversial legislation, it took time to move Congress and to forge compromises. Even Democrats supportive of pro-choice had to be prodded. Senate Majority Leader George Mitchell (D-Maine), for one, initially opposed the act on the dubious ground that Congress should not by majority vote determine "fundamental constitutional rights." In February 1992 he called the act "a very dangerous precedent" because a majority of Congress could always undo it by passing new legislation. At the time Mitchell favored instead a constitutional amendment, which would require a two-thirds vote in both houses of Congress and ratification by three-fourths of the states.[56] The matter was not as simple as Mitchell presented it and he knew it, but his reasoning gave him a way temporarily to duck the issue.

As the possibility that *Roe* might be reversed in *Casey* loomed larger, pro-choice Democrats and activists pressed Mitchell and others in Congress harder. A constitutional amendment seemed out of reach. The very same obstacles that had led antiabortion advocates in the early 1980s to abandon their effort for an amendment favoring their cause still seemed insurmountable. Backers of the Freedom of Choice Act also doubted that they could muster the votes to override a presidential veto. Bush had vetoed seven bills with tacked-on provisions supportive of abortion, though none had been squarely pro-abortion. The Freedom of Choice Act would be a way to force his hand and to turn his veto into a major issue in the 1992 campaign. By June 1992 Mitchell had come around and had introduced a bill in the Senate that would codify *Roe*. While it would forbid states from outlawing abortion, it would nevertheless allow them to refuse funding and to require parental notification.

The day after the announcement of the ruling in *Casey*, the House Judiciary Committee approved the Freedom of Choice Act by a 20 to 13 vote. The vote split along party lines with certain exceptions: Democrats Romano Mazzoli (Kentucky), George Sangmeister (Illinois), and Harley Staggers (West Virginia) voted with Republicans against the bill; Tom Campbell (R-California) and Jim Ramstad (R-Minnesota) voted with the Democrats. By 23–10 the committee rejected an amendment that would have allowed the states to require abortion counseling on fetal development and to impose a twenty-four-hour waiting period. A bare majority (17–16) also approved a "conscience-clause" amendment permitting "health-care workers to refuse to perform abortions if they were unwilling to do so for moral or religious reasons."

On 1 July 1992 the Senate Labor and Human Resources Committee approved a similar measure. Committee chairman Edward Kennedy (D-Massachusetts) led the fight, declaring, "We must safeguard a woman's right to make this deeply personal choice." An unsuccessful battle

TABLE 10.1
ABORTION AND THE STATES, 1991–92

State	Governor	Senate	House	Number of abortions	Number of providers	Type of regulations in place
Alabama	N	N	N	18,220	20	A, B(2), F(1), M+, V
Alaska	N	Y	Y	2,390	12	A, F(2)
Arizona	Y	Y	N	23,070	29	A, B(2)-, F(1), M-, P
Arkansas	Y	C	N	6,250	10	B(2)-, F(1), M+
California	Y	Y	Y	311,720	608	B(2)-, F(2), M-
Colorado	Y	Y	Y	18,740	61	B(2)-, F(1), S-, M
Connecticut	Y	Y	Y	23,630	43	B-, F(2), L(2), M-
Delaware	Y	C	Y	5,710	17	A-, B(2)-, F(1), M-, W-
Florida	Y	Y	Y	82,850	143	A-, B-, F(1), I, S-
Georgia	Y	Y	Y	36,720	55	B-, F(1), M+
Hawaii	Y	Y	Y	11,170	53	F(2)
Idaho	N	Y	N	1,920	9	A, B-, I,M,
Illinois	Y	C	C	72,570	52	B, F(1), L(1), M-, S-
Indiana	Y	C	N	15,760	24	A, B-, F(1), M+, W
Iowa	N	C	Y	9,420	16	B
Kansas	N	Y	Y	11,440	19	B(2)-, F(1)
Kentucky	Y	N	N	11,520	9	A-, B-, F-, L(1), M-, P-, S-, W-
Louisiana	N	N	N	17,340	13	A, B(1)-, F(1), L(1), M+, P, V
Maine	Y	Y	Y	4,620	21	A, B, F(1), M+, W-
Maryland	Y	Y	Y	32,670	53	A-, B(2)-, F(2), M-, W-
Massachusetts	Y	Y	Y	43,720	64	A-, B(2)-, F(1), M+, W-
Michigan	N	N	N	63,410	78	B(2)-, M+
Minnesota	Y	N	N	18,580	13	A, B, F(1), M+

Continued ...

TABLE 10.1 — Continued.

State	Governor	Senate	House	Number of abortions	Number of providers	Type of regulations in place
Mississippi	N	N	N	5,120	5	A-, B(2)-, F(1), M-, W-
Missouri	N	N	N	19,490	20	A, B, F(1), M+, P, S-, V, W-
Montana	N	Y	Y	3,050	13	A, B, F(1), M, I, S-
Nebraska[a]	N	N	N	6,490	9	A, B, M+, W
Nevada	N	C	N	10,190	20	A, B-, F(1), L(2), M-
New Hampshire	N	Y	Y	4,710	15	B(2)-, F(1)
New Jersey	Y	Y	N	63,900	89	F(2)
New Mexico	Y	Y	Y	6,810	24	A-, B(2)-, F(1), M, S-, W-
New York	Y	Y	Y	183,980	305	B(2), F(2)
North Carolina	Y	Y	Y	39,720	97	B(2), F(2)
North Dakota	Y	N	N	2,230	3	A, B(1)-, F(1), P, M+, S-
Ohio	N	N	N	53,400	53	A-, F(1), M+, W-
Oklahoma	Y	C	N	12,120	13	B(2)-, F(1)
Oregon	Y	Y	Y	15,960	45	F(2)
Pennsylvania	N	N	N	51,830	90	A, B(2)-, M, P, S-, W
Rhode Island	Y	N	C	7,190	6	A-, B(1)-, F(1), M+, S-
South Carolina	N	C	C	14,160	15	B(1)-, F(1), M+, S-
South Dakota	N	C	N	900	1	A-, B(1)-, F(1), L(1), M-, W-
Tennessee	Y	C	N	22,090	41	A, B, F(1), M-, W-
Texas	Y	C	C	100,690	91	B(2)-, F(1)
Utah	N	N	N	5,030	8	A, B(1), F(1), M+, S-
Vermont	Y	Y	Y	3,580	16	B(2)-, F(2)
Virginia	Y	C	Y	35,420	73	A, B-
Washington	Y	Y	Y	31,220	68	F(2), L(2)
West Virginia	N	N	N	3,270	6	B(2)-, F(2), M+
Wisconsin	N	N	N	18,040	17	A, B(2)-, M, W-

Wyoming	N	C	Y		B-, M+
Total abortions			600	7	
Total providers			1,555,630		2552
Total Y	29	20	24		
Total N	21	17	21		
Total C		4	4		

SOURCES: Compiled from The National Abortion Rights Action League Foundation, *Who Decides? A State-by-State Review of Abortion Rights*, 3d ed. (Washington, D.C.: NARAL, 1992). Data on the number of abortions performed comes from M. Hall, "In the States: Abortion Laws State by State," *USA Today*, 30 June 1992, 8A.

N = Opposes abortion or wants restrictions   Y = Supports abortion rights   C = Too close to call

a. Nebraska's one-house legislature opposes abortion.

A = Abortion counseling requirement
B(1) = Abortion banned after viability or similar restriction, but may allow for certain exceptions as in cases of rape; passed after *Roe*
B(2) = Abortion banned after viability or similar restrictions, but may allow for certain exceptions as in cases of rape; passed before *Roe* and though unenforced still on the books
F(1) = Prohibits Medicaid funding for abortions
F(2) = Provides funding for most abortions
I = Informed consent required
L(1) = Legislative declaration that if *Roe* is overturned, abortion will be prohibited
L(2) = Legislative declaration that if *Roe* is overturned, right to obtain an abortion will be guaranteed under state law
M = Parental notification and/or consent requirements
M+ = Parental notification and/or consent requirements enforced
P = Prohibits use of public facilities for abortions
S = Spousal notification and/or consent requirement
W = Waiting period required
V = Requires doctors to perform fetal viability tests before performing an abortion
- = Provisions ruled unconstitutional by state or federal courts

against the bill was waged by Orrin Hatch (R-Utah). He attacked it as an intrusion upon the powers of the states and a misuse of Congress's powers under the commerce clause and the Fourteenth Amendment. Hatch and others reiterated the position, staked out two decades earlier by Rehnquist in his dissent in *Roe,* that "the resolution of the conflicting interests in the very difficult and troubling matter of abortion is best worked out under our constitutional system by the people in each state through their elected representatives." Nonetheless, Republicans Nancy Kassebaum (Kansas) and James Jeffords (Vermont) joined ten Democrats on the committee in voting for the bill. Republicans Hatch, Dan Coats (Indiana), Strom Thurmond (South Carolina), Dave Durenberger (Minnesota), and Thad Cochran (Mississippi) voted against it.

Senate Majority Leader Mitchell and House Speaker Thomas Foley (D-Washington) vowed to push for a vote on the bill in each of their houses before the presidential election. Bush promised a veto, and his supporters charged that Congress was wasting its time. "We'll go through the exercise on the House floor, pass it and the President will veto it and that will be the end of it," predicted Congressman Hamilton Fish, Jr. (R-New York).[57] Supporters of the Freedom of Choice Act countered that it would be a "rallying point" for the forthcoming presidential and congressional elections. But that proved incorrect; about all that the two sides agreed on was that legislative battles would go on after the 1992 elections.

Abortion struggles were certain to take new directions following the election of Democratic presidential candidate Bill Clinton. Coincidentally, on election day, 3 November 1992, a three-judge panel (composed of Democratic appointees) on the Court of Appeals for the District of Columbia Circuit struck down the Bush administration's revised ban on abortion counseling by organizations that receive federal funding. Following the ruling in *Rust v. Sullivan,* the Bush administration faced pressure to revise, if not abandon, its ban on abortion counseling. After months of negotiations Bush's Department of Health and Human Services issued a new regulation allowing doctors, but not nurses or clinic counselors, to advise women about abortion. But, then, in *National Family Planning and Reproductive Health Association, Inc.* v. *Sullivan,* the Court of Appeals for the District of Columbia ruled that HHS in promulgating its revised regulation had failed to comply with the Administrative Procedure Act's requirement that agencies provide an opportunity for public notice and comment on proposed regulatory changes before making them. Subsequently, two days after his inauguration, President Clinton fulfilled a campaign promise by issuing an executive order repealing the Reagan-Bush administration's ban on abortion counseling. Clinton also rescinded a ban on fetal tissue research, among other policy changes. At the same time, pro-life forces pledged to renew their efforts in the states to enact more restrictive abortion laws. And some Republicans and conservative interest groups, such as the Free Congress Foundation, began gearing up for battles over Clinton's nominees to the federal bench. Defeated Supreme Court nominee Robert Bork joined with others in forming an organization to monitor and to fight Senate confirmation of Clinton's judicial nominees. In the Senate, Utah's Republican Senator Orrin Hatch announced that he would take over the position of ranking minority member on the Senate Judiciary Committee in order to spearhead Republicans' opposition to Clinton's judicial appointees and attempt to shift the direction of the federal courts after twelve years of Republican appointees.

The Court and the Continuing Battle over Abortion
Along with *Planned Parenthood of Southeastern Pennsylvania v. Casey,* the Rehnquist Court agreed to decide another controversial abortion case. *Bray v. Alexandria Women's Health Clinic* raised the question of whether federal courts may enjoin Operation Rescue and other antiabortion protesters from blockading abortion clinics (see chapters 2 and 9 for further discussion). Several federal courts had done so under an 1871 law that prohibits conspiracies to deprive people of their civil rights. The law is known as the Ku Klux Klan Act because it was enacted in response to attacks on blacks after the Civil War. According to the National Abortion Federation, between January 1987 and December 1990 over 26,000 antiabortion protesters were arrested at 419 blockades of clinics.

Bray began in 1989 when Operation Rescue announced plans to block access to several northern Virginia abortion clinics. The clinics and others promptly sued Operation Rescue; its founder, Randall Terry; and other antiabortion activists, including convicted abortion-clinic bomber Michael Bray. A federal district judge's injunction against blockading the clinics was affirmed by a federal appellate court and Bray appealed to the Supreme Court. In *Bray,* however, the justices initially failed to reach a decision after hearing oral arguments. And the case was scheduled to be reargued during the Court's 1992–93 term. Finally, in mid-January 1993 the Rehnquist Court handed down its ruling in *Bray,* denying federal jurisdiction over antiabortion protesters under the 1871 law. Writing for the majority, Justice Scalia dismissed out-of-hand arguments for extending federal court jurisdiction. Justices Stevens and O'Connor, joined by Justice Blackmun, took strong exception to the majority's reasoning and result in bitter dissenting opinions.

As if to underscore the majority's unwillingness for the time to revisit the abortion controversy and to refine further the lines drawn in *Casey,* the Rehnquist Court by a vote of six to three denied review of *Ada v. Guam Society of Obstetricians and Gynecologists.*[58] In that case the governor of the Territory of Guam appealed a ruling by the Court of Appeals for the Ninth Circuit that invalidated as overly broad Guam's 1990 post-*Webster* law barring virtually all abortions, except for those required by a medical emergency. In a dissenting opinion joined by Chief Justice Rehnquist and Justice White, however, Justice Scalia argued that the appeal of that ruling should have been granted because under the Court's overbreadth doctrine not all applications of a statute may be unconstitutional. In Scalia's view, there was "no reason why the Guam law would not be constitutional at least in its application to abortions conducted after the point at which the child may live outside the womb." The dissenters were nonetheless unable to persuade a fourth member of the Court, as required by the justices' informal rule of four, to vote to grant review. Notably, Justice Thomas, who voted with the three other dissenters in *Casey,* offered no explanation for his failure to vote to revisit the abortion controversy in *Ada* and to consider Scalia's suggested application of the overbreadth doctrine to restrictive abortion laws.

In addition and without explanation the Rehnquist Court also denied an appeal of a decision by the Court of Appeals for the Fifth Circuit that upheld Mississippi's 1991 abortion law. That law requires women seeking an abortion to wait twenty-four hours after giving their consent and having their doctors explain the medical risks of abortion, describe fetal development, as well as discuss pregnancy prevention and alternatives to abortion, along with notifying them "that the father is liable to assist in the support of [the] child." In light of *Casey,* the appellate court held that these requirements did not unduly burden women and were thus constitutional.[59] The Rehnquist Court also denied review to another appellate court ruling, which struck down Louisiana's 1991 law banning all abortions except those necessary to save a woman's life and in cases of rape or incest. In denying review of those lower court decisions, the Rehnquist Court signaled that it would uphold states' restrictive abortion laws that are similar to that approved in *Casey.* The Court signaled as well that, at least until its composition changed further, it was unlikely to chart a major new course in the controversy over abortion.

Conclusion

Two days after *Casey* came down a twenty-nine-year-old pregnant woman, Leona Benten, was arrested at John F. Kennedy International

Airport for bringing RU486 abortion pills into the United States. Benten had been recruited by officers of the San Francisco Medical Society, who had also notified the U.S. Customs Service that she was bringing the French abortion pills into the country. Steve Heilig, the society's director, later explained that Benten had been selected to "fit the clinical profile for the drug. She had to be very early in pregnancy, have no hypertension and not be a smoker. She also had to be brave." "In recruiting, we had to be very clear that [the woman selected for the test case] could become another Jane Roe."[60]

The plan for a legal challenge originated with Lawrence Lader, president of Abortion Rights Mobilization in New York. Lader had been in the forefront of the pro-choice struggle since the 1960s, when he successfully challenged state restrictions on the use of contraceptives. Lader and other doctors had grown frustrated in their efforts to test RU486 and to win approval for its use from the Food and Drug Administration (FDA). The manufacturer, Roussel Uclaf, declined to test and market RU486 in the United States because of the threat of boycotts by antiabortion groups.[61] RU486 is not a contraceptive, like Norplant (a recently developed implant that lasts up to five years), but an abortifacient that causes a miscarriage. It is taken as soon as a pregnancy is confirmed and is followed forty-eight hours later by another pill containing the hormone prostaglandin, which enhances the pill's effect and reduces the risk of hemorrhaging. RU486 is available by prescription in England, France, and Sweden.

Antiabortion leaders strongly oppose RU486. People on the prochoice side argue that it could become "even more important when the Court continues to allow states to restrict and harass women," in the words of Eleanor Smeal, president of the Fund for a Feminist Majority.[62] Some look for developments like RU486 to provide a solution to the abortion controversy, but that appears unlikely, in the near future at least. Robert McFadden of the Ad Hoc Committee in Defense of Life, among others in the antiabortion camp, dismissively terms RU486 "an abortion." And Lisa Kaeser of the Alan Guttmacher Institute points out that there still would be a great demand for abortion because use of RU486 is limited to the first nine weeks of a pregnancy, requires monitoring by doctors, and is not recommended for women over thirty-five or women who smoke. "A lot of people think you can keep a bottle of [RU486] in your cabinet at home," Kaeser emphasizes, "and that is not the case."[63]

Roussel Uclaf was deterred from introducing RU486 into the United States by the FDA as well. The FDA has authority to approve the use of new drugs, foods, and cosmetics, after reviewing tests for reliability and safety. Under its mandate from Congress it may also prevent the importation of unapproved drugs. The controversy over RU486 erupted in 1989, when the Bush administration's FDA modified its policy on the importation of unapproved drugs. The new guidelines allowed certain unapproved drugs, such as those for the treatment of AIDS and cancer, to be brought into the country for "personal use." After protests from antiabortion groups, the FDA announced that RU486 was not among the eligible drugs. Lader and the San Francisco Medical Society went about creating a test case to challenge the policy on procedural grounds. In their view, the policy against RU486 was unwise and illegal because the FDA had failed to comply with federal requirements that agencies publish notice of and allow public comment on all proposed rules and regulations.

"This is a lawsuit waiting to happen," declared U.S. District Court Judge Charles P. Sifton, when holding that the FDA had illegally seized Benten's pills and had failed to follow proper administrative procedures in proscribing the importation of RU486. "The record before this court, reveals a history of political and bureaucratic timidity mixed with well-intentioned blundering in dealing with two of the most charged and significant issues of our time: AIDS and abortion." A Jimmy Carter appointee, Sifton sharply commented, "In the face of political outcry, a retreat was ordered by the FDA, again without the investigation, notice, or [public] comment required by law." Sifton ordered the pills returned to Benten but stopped short of invalidating FDA policy on RU486.

Sifton's order was immediately appealed by the Bush administration, and later that same day a three-judge panel for the Court of Appeals for the Second Circuit stayed the order. The panel included three Reagan appointees: Frank X. Altimari, Daniel J. Mahoney, and John M. Walker; Walker, a cousin of Bush's, had been named to a district court by Reagan and later elevated by Bush. Benten, Lader, and their supporters applied for a stay from the Supreme Court. But, with Justices Blackmun and Stevens dissenting, the Rehnquist Court denied a stay and declined to review *Benten v. Kessler.*[64]

Benten's arrest within days of the Rehnquist Court's ruling in *Casey* was coincidental. That coincidence was a sign of the times and how the struggle over abortion could take new twists and turns in the 1990s. Moreover, the controversy over abortion is certain to move in new directions due to the 1992 election of Democratic presidential candidate Bill Clinton. Not only did the Clinton administration reverse course by rescinding the Reagan and Bush administrations' antiabortion policies that restricted abortion counseling by organizations receiving federal funding or barred fetal-tissue research. President Clinton also has the op-

opportunity to appoint hundreds of federal judges and fill one or more seats on the Supreme Court, thereby influencing the direction of judicial policymaking in this and other areas. Less than two months after Clinton was sworn into office, the only remaining Democratic appointee on the high bench, Justice Byron White, announced that he would retire at the end of the 1992–93 term. Appointed by President John F. Kennedy in 1962, Justice White generally voted with conservatives and staunchly opposed the ruling in *Roe v. Wade*, dissenting from that and subsequent rulings down to *Casey*, which affirmed a woman's constitutional right to choose an abortion. In naming Justice White's successor, Clinton thus had the opportunity to shift the balance on the Court. Both sides of the abortion controversy would nevertheless continue to seek the advantage in the constitutional politics of the federal system, in the competition between Congress and the president in determining public policy, and in influencing the changing composition of the Supreme Court as well as its deliberations and direction. The tenacious problems of securing liberty against government and of reconciling tensions between rights and responsibilities, private versus public morality, and self-determination against majoritarianism and communitarianism give no sign of letup. The abortion controversy will remain a driving force in and a reflection of American politics.

Notes

1. Quoted, S. McCarthy, "Abortion's Empty Rhetoric," *Newsday*, 1 July 1992, 8.
2. Ibid.
3. *Planned Parenthood of Southeastern Pennsylvania v. Casey*, 112 S.Ct. 2791 (1992).
4. Quoted, "The Conflict Continues: Differing Views of a Controversial Decision," *San Francisco Chronicle*, 30 June 1992, A5.
5. Ibid.
6. Quoted, transcript of broadcast, ABC News "Nightline," "Abortion: From Legal Battles to Political Wars," 30 June 1992.
7. Quoted from *Harrisburg Patriot-News*, 30 June 1992, in "Abortion Report—Supreme Court II: Selected Reactions," *Lexis*, 30 June 1992.
8. Quoted, M. Hall, "Disappointment on Both Sides," *USA Today*, 30 June 1992, A3.
9. Quoted, J. Solomon, "Original 'Jane Roe' Sees 'Death Warrant,'" *Boston Globe*, 1 July 1992, 10; note 4 supra.
10. Quoted, K. Freifeld, "Rights Eroding, *Roe* Lawyer Says; Law 'Shadow of Former Self,'" *Newsday*, 30 June 1992, 86.
11. Quoted, R. Ciolli, "Next: Fight Shifts to Legislatures," *Newsday*, 30 June 1992, 4.

12. Quoted, N. Roman, "Pro-Choice Groups See Defeat; Abortion Battle Moves to Congress," *Washington Times,* 1 July 1992, A1.

13. Quoted, ibid.

14. Quoted, ibid.

15. Quoted, ibid.

16. See chapter 7; "Abortion: Presidential Politics," *Public Perspective* 3 (May/June 1992): 98–99.

17. See M. Hall, "Activists Aside, Justices' Ruling Pleases Many," *USA Today,* 1 July 1992, 3A.

18. Quoted, ibid.

19. Quoted, E. Dionne, "Justices' Abortion Ruling Mirrors Public Opinion," *Washington Post,* 1 July 1992, A4.

20. Quoted from *New York Post* in "Abortion Report—Supreme Court I: Effect Muddled on Presidential Election," *Lexis,* 30 June 1992.

21. *Planned Parenthood of Southeastern Pennsylvania v. Casey,* 744 F.Supp. 1323 (1990).

22. *Planned Parenthood of Southeastern Pennsylvania v. Casey,* 947 F.2d 682 (1991).

23. Ibid., 726 (J. Alito, con. and dis. op.).

24. *Rust v. Sullivan,* 111 S.Ct. 1759 (1991).

25. *Planned Parenthood v. Agency for International Development,* 111 S.Ct. 335 (1991).

26. Quoted, R. Berke, "Groups That Back Right to Abortion Ask Court to Act," *New York Times,* 8 November 1991, A1.

27. *Brief for the United States as Amicus Curiae Supporting Respondents* in *Planned Parenthood of Southeastern Pennsylvania v. Casey* (October term 1991), 8.

28. For a discussion of precedent and an empirical study of the Court's reversal rates, see C. Banks, "The Supreme Court and Precedent: An Analysis of Natural Courts and Reversal Trends," *Judicature* 75 (1992): 262.

29. *Lochner v. New York* 198 U.S. 45 (1905).

30. *Adkins v. Children's Hospital of the District of Columbia,* 261 U.S. 525 (1923).

31. For further discussion, see chapter 1; D. O'Brien, *Storm Center: The Supreme Court in American Politics,* 2d ed. (New York: Norton, 1990), chap. 2.

32. *West Coast Hotel Co. v. Parrish,* 300 U.S. 379 (1937).

33. *Plessy v. Ferguson,* 163 U.S. 537 (1896).

34. *Brown v. Board of Education,* 347 U.S. 483 (1954).

35. For a discussion and other cases, such as *Lee v. Weisman,* 112 S.Ct. 2649 (1992), in which Kennedy broke with Rehnquist, see D. O'Brien, *Supreme Court Watch—1992* (New York: Norton, 1992).

36. R. Bork, "Again, a Struggle for the Soul of the Court," *New York Times,* 8 July 1992, A19.

37. See D. O'Brien, "The Framers' Muse on Republicanism, the Supreme Court, and Pragmatic Constitutional Interpretivism," *Review of Politics* 53 (1991): 251.

38. Quoted, R. Marcus, "Court's Ruling Assures More Abortion Litigation," *Washington Post,* 1 July 1992, A1.

39. Quoted, ibid., A7.

40. See D. Howlett, "Abortion Issue Now Key to State, Governors' Races," *USA Today,* 30 June 1992, 8A.

41. See C. Simmons, "Planned Parenthood Explains How It Will Comply with Parental Consent Law," United Press International, Regional News (Wisconsin), 1 July 1992.

42. S. Henshaw, "The Accessibility of Abortion Services in the United States," *Family Planning Perspectives* 23 (November/December 1991): 246.

43. Quoted, "The High and Middle Ground," *Economist,* 4 July 1992, 25.

44. Quoted from *Philadelphia Daily News,* 30 June 1992, in "Abortion Report—Supreme Court III: What Now in Pa.?" *Lexis,* 30 June 1992.

45. Quoted from *Philadelphia Inquirer,* 30 June 1992, in "Abortion Report—State Report," *Lexis,* 30 June 1992; see also F. Kummer, "Clinics Expect Increase in Abortion Requests, Protests" (Gannett News Service), *Bridgewater Courier-News,* 1 July 1992.

46. Reported in "Abortion Report—Utah: State's Ban on Abortion Now Unconstitutional," *Lexis,* 1 July 1992.

47. *In re T.W.,* 551 So.2d 1186 (Fla. 1989).

48. See *Comm. to Defend Reproductive Rights v. Myers,* 29 Cal. 3d 252, 625 P.2d 779 (Cal. 1981) (requiring state funding for abortion); see also *Conservatorship of Valerie,* 40 Cal. 3d 143, 707 P.2d 760 (Cal. 1985).

49. See *Doe v. Maher,* 515 A.2d 134 (Conn. Super. 1986).

50. See *Doe v. Director of Michigan Dep't of Social Services,* 468 N.W. 2d 862 (Mich. App. 1991).

51. See *Moe v. Sec. of Administration,* 417 N.E. 2d 387 (Mass. 1981).

52. See *Right to Choose v. Byrne,* 450 A.2d 925 (N.J. 1982).

53. See also J. Devlin, "State Constitutional Autonomy Rights in an Age of Federal Retrenchment," *Emerging Issues in State Constitutional Law* 3 (1990): 195, arguing that the history of the adoption of amendments to the state constitutions of Alaska, Hawaii, Illinois, and Louisiana provides evidence for judicial recognition of rights of personal and family autonomy in these states as a matter of state constitutional law.

54. Quoted, J. Pope, *New Orleans Times Picayune,* 30 June 1992, in "Abortion Report—State Report," note 45 supra.

55. See National Abortion Rights Action League Foundation, *Who Decides? A State-by-State Review of Abortion Rights,* 3d ed. (Washington, D.C.: 1992).

56. G. Mitchell, quoted in "Talking Points," *Washington Post,* 4 February 1992, A13.

57. Quoted, E. Ferguson, "Fish: Freedom of Choice Bill Is Waste of Time," Gannett News Service, 30 June 1992.

58. *Ada v. Guam Society of Obstetricians and Gynecologists,* 113 S.Ct. 663 (1992).

59. *Barnes v. Moore,* 970 F.2d 12 (1992).

60. Quoted, S. Russell, "Bay Group Planned Try on Abortion Pill," *San Francisco Chronicle,* 3 July 1992, A1.

61. A. Riding, "Maker of Abortion Pill Said to Fear U.S. Reprisals," *International Herald Tribune,* 30 July 1992, 3. See also Note, "I Want a New Drug: RU-486 and the Right to Choose," *Southern California Law Review* 63 (1990): 1061.

62. Quoted, M. Clements, "Interest Renewed in Abortion Pill" (Gannett News Service), *Detroit News*, 30 June 1992.

63. Quoted, ibid.

64. *Benten v. Kessler*, 112 S.Ct. 2929 (1992).

Selected Bibliography

Aberbach, Joel D. *Keeping a Watchful Eye: The Politics of Congressional Oversight.* Washington, D.C.: Brookings, 1990.

Abraham, Henry J. *The Judicial Process.* 6th ed. New York: Oxford University Press, 1991.

———. *Justices and Presidents.* 3d ed. New York: Oxford University Press, 1991.

Abramson, Paul R. *Political Attitudes in America.* San Francisco: Freeman, 1983.

Adamany, David. "The Supreme Court's Role in Critical Elections." In *Realignment in American Politics,* edited by Bruce Campbell and Richard Trilling. Austin: University of Texas Press, 1980.

Alan Guttmacher Institute. *Abortion, 1974–1975: Need and Services in the United States, Each State and Metropolitan Area.* New York: Planned Parenthood Federation of America, 1976.

———. *Abortions and the Poor: Private Morality, Public Responsibility.* New York: Alan Guttmacher Institute, 1979.

Alumbaugh, Steve, and C.K. Rowland. "The Links between Platform-Based Appointment Criteria and Trial Judges' Abortion Judgments." *Judicature* 74 (1990): 153–62.

Aron, Nan. *Liberty and Justice for All: Public Interest Law in the 1980s and Beyond.* Boulder, Colo.: Westview Press, 1989.

Asher, Herbert. *Polling and the Public: What Every Citizen Should Know.* Washington, D.C.: CQ Press, 1988.

Baehr, Ninia. *Abortion without Apology: A Radical History for the 1990s.* Boston: South End Press, 1990.

Baum, Lawrence. *The Supreme Court.* Washington, D.C.: CQ Press, 1989.

Becker, Theodore L., and Malcolm M. Feeley, eds. *The Impact of Supreme Court Decisions.* 2d ed. New York: Oxford University Press, 1973.

Behuniak-Long, Susan. "Friendly Fire: Amici Curiae and *Webster v. Reproductive Health Services.*" *Judicature* 74 (1991): 261–70.

Berry, Jeffrey M. *The Interest Group Society.* Glenview, Ill.: Scott, Foresman, 1989.

Blasi, Vincent, ed. *The Burger Court: The Counter-Revolution That Wasn't.* New Haven: Yale University Press, 1983.

Bogart, Leo. *Polls and the Awareness of Public Opinion.* 2d ed. New Brunswick, N.J.: Transaction, 1985.

Bond, Jon R., and Charles A. Johnson. "Implementing a Permissive Policy:

Hospital Abortion Services after *Roe v. Wade.*" *American Journal of Political Science* 26 (1982): 1–24.

Bronner, Ethan. *Battle for Justice: How the Bork Nomination Shook America.* New York: Norton, 1989.

Butler, J. Douglas, and David F. Walbert, eds. *Abortion, Medicine, and the Law.* New York: Facts on File, 1986.

Callahan, Daniel. *Abortion: Law, Choice, and Morality.* New York: Macmillan, 1970.

Campbell, Colin, and Bert A. Rockman, eds. *The Bush Presidency: First Appraisals.* Chatham, N.J.: Chatham House, 1991.

Cannon, Mark, and David M. O'Brien, eds. *Views from the Bench: The Judiciary and Constitutional Politics.* Chatham, N.J.: Chatham House, 1985.

Caplin, Lincoln. *The Tenth Justice: The Solicitor General and the Rule of Law.* New York: Knopf, 1987.

Choper, Jesse. *Judicial Review and the National Political Process.* Chicago: University of Chicago Press, 1980.

Cigler, Allan J., and Burdett A. Loomis, eds. *Interest Group Politics.* 2d ed. Washington, D.C.: CQ Press, 1986.

Condit, Celeste Michelle. *Decoding Abortion Rhetoric: Communicating Social Change.* Urbana: University of Illinois Press, 1990.

Conover, Pamela Johnston, and Virginia Gray. *Feminism and the New Right: Conflict over the American Family.* New York: Praeger, 1983.

Crawford, Alan. *Thunder on the Right.* New York: Pantheon, 1980.

Dahl, Robert. "Decision-Making in a Democracy: The Supreme Court as a National Policy Maker." *Journal of Public Law* 6 (1957): 279–95.

———. *Dilemmas of Pluralist Democracy.* New Haven: Yale University Press, 1982.

Davidson, Roger H., ed. *The Postreform Congress.* New York: St. Martin's Press, 1992.

Davidson, Roger H., and Walter J. Oleszek. *Congress and Its Members.* 3d ed. Washington, D.C.: CQ Press, 1990.

Davis, James. *The American Presidency.* New York: Harper & Row, 1987.

Devlin, John. "Privacy and Abortion Rights under the Louisiana State Constitution: Could *Roe v. Wade* Be Alive and Well in the Bayou State?" *Louisiana Law Review* 51 (1991): 685–732.

Dodd, Lawrence C., and Bruce I. Oppenheimer, eds. *Congress Reconsidered.* 4th ed. Washington, D.C.: CQ Press, 1989.

Ely, John Hart. *Democracy and Distrust.* Cambridge: Harvard University Press, 1980.

Epstein, Lee. *Conservatives in Court.* Knoxville: University of Tennessee Press, 1985.

Epstein, Lee, and C.K. Rowland. "Interest Groups in the Courts: Do Groups Fare Better?" In *Interest Group Politics,* 2d ed., edited by A.J. Cigler and B.A. Loomis. Washington, D.C.: CQ Press, 1986.

Falik, Marilyn. *Ideology and Abortion Policy Politics.* New York: Praeger, 1983.

Faux, Marian. *Roe v. Wade.* New York: Macmillan, 1988.

Fenno, Richard F., Jr. *Congressmen in Committees.* Boston: Little, Brown, 1973.

———. *Home Style.* Boston: Little, Brown, 1978.

Ferejohn, John A., and James H. Kuklinski, eds. *Information and Democratic Processes.* Urbana: University of Illinois Press, 1990.

Fiorina, Morris P. *Congress: Keystone of the Washington Establishment.* 2d ed. New Haven: Yale University Press, 1989.

Fried, Charles. *Order and Law: Arguing the Reagan Revolution—A Firsthand Account.* New York: Simon and Schuster, 1991.

Friendly, Fred, and Martha J.H. Elliott. *The Constitution: That Delicate Balance.* New York: Random House, 1984.

Gates, John B., and Charles A. Johnson, eds. *The American Courts: A Critical Assessment.* Washington, D.C.: CQ Press, 1991.

Glendon, Mary Ann. *Abortion and Divorce in Western Law.* Cambridge: Harvard University Press, 1987.

Goldman, Sheldon. "Judicial Appointments and the Presidential Agenda." In *The Presidency in American Politics,* edited by Paul Brace, Christine B. Harrington, and Gary King. New York: New York University Press, 1989.

———. "Reagan's Judicial Legacy: Completing the Puzzle and Summing Up." *Judicature* 72 (1989): 318–30.

Goldman, Sheldon, and Thomas P. Jahnige. *The Federal Courts as a Political System.* 3d ed. New York: Harper & Row, 1985.

Granberg, Donald. "The Abortion Activist." *Family Planning Perspectives* 13 (1981): 157–63.

Halpern, Stephen, and Charles Lamb, eds. *Supreme Court Activism and Restraint.* Lexington, Mass.: Lexington Books, 1982.

Hansen, Susan B. "State Implementation of Supreme Court Decisions: Abortion Rates since *Roe v. Wade.*" *Journal of Politics* 42 (1980): 372–95.

Hertz, Sue. *Caught in the Crossfire: A Year on Abortion's Front Line.* New York: Prentice-Hall, 1991.

Hinckley, Barbara. *Stability and Change in Congress.* 4th ed. New York: HarperCollins, 1988.

Hrebner, Ronald J., and Ruth K. Scott. *Interest Group Politics in America.* Englewood Cliffs, N.J.: Prentice-Hall, 1982.

Jaffe, Frederick S., Barbara L. Lindheim, and Phillip R. Lee. *Abortion Politics: Private Morality and Public Policy.* New York: McGraw-Hill, 1981.

Johnson, Charles A., and Jon R. Bond. "Coercive and Noncoercive Abortion Deterrence Policies: A Comparative State Analysis." *Law and Policy Quarterly* 2 (1980): 106–28.

Johnson, Charles A., and Bradley C. Canon. *Judicial Policies: Implementation and Impact.* Washington, D.C.: CQ Press, 1984.

Jung, Patricia Beattie, and Thomas A. Shannon, eds. *Abortion and Catholicism: The American Debate.* New York: Crossroad, 1988.

Keefe, William J. *Congress and the American People.* 3d ed. Englewood Cliffs, N.J.: Prentice-Hall, 1988.

Key, V.O., Jr. *Public Opinion in American Democracy.* New York: Knopf, 1961.

Keynes, Edward, with Randall K. Miller. *The Court vs. Congress: Prayer, Busing and Abortion.* Durham: Duke University Press, 1989.

Kingdon, John W. *Agendas, Alternatives and Public Policies.* Boston: Little, Brown, 1984.

Lamb, Charles M., and Stephen C. Halpern, eds. *The Burger Court: Political and Judicial Profiles.* Urbana: University of Illinois Press, 1991.

Laswell, Harold D. *Democracy through Public Opinion*. Menasha, Wis.: George Banta, 1941.

Laufer, Romain. *Marketing Democracy: Public Opinion and Media Formation in Democratic Societies*. New Brunswick, N.J.: Transaction, 1990.

Levy, Leonard W. *Original Intent and the Framers' Constitution*. New York: Macmillan, 1988.

Liebman, Robert C., and Robert Wuthnow. *The New Christian Right*. New York: Aldine, 1983.

Light, Paul C. *Forging Legislation*. New York: Norton, 1992.

Lindblom, Charles Edward. *The Intelligence of Democracy: Decision Making through Mutual Adjustment*. New York: Free Press, 1965.

Lovenduski, Joni, and Joyce Outshoorn, eds. *The New Politics of Abortion*. London: Sage, 1986.

Lowi, Theodore J. *The End of Liberalism*. New York: Norton, 1969.

Luker, Kristin. *Abortion and the Politics of Motherhood*. Berkeley: University of California Press, 1984.

McCormick, Patricia E. *Attitudes toward Abortion: Experiences of Selected Black and White Women*. Lexington, Mass.: Lexington Books, 1975.

McGuigan, Patrick B., and Dawn M. Weyrich. *Ninth Justice: The Fight for Bork*. Washington, D.C.: Free Congress Research and Educational Foundation, 1990.

Maloy, Kate, and Maggie Patterson. *Birth or Abortion? Private Struggles in a Political World*. New York: Plenum, 1992.

Margolis, Michael, and Kevin Neary. "Pressure Politics Revisited: The Anti-Abortion Campaign." *Policy Studies Journal* 8 (1980): 698–716.

Moe, Terry M. *The Organization of Interests*. Chicago: University of Chicago Press, 1980.

Mohr, James C. *Abortion in America: The Origins and Evolution of National Policy, 1800 to 1900*. New York: Oxford University Press, 1978.

Morowitz, Harold, and James Trefil. *The Facts of Life*. New York: Oxford University Press, 1992.

Murphy, Walter. "Lower Court Checks on Supreme Court Power." *American Political Science Review* 53 (1959): 1017–31.

Murphy, Walter, and C. Herman Pritchett. *Courts, Judges, and Politics*. New York: Random House, 1985.

Neuman, W. Russell. *The Paradox of Mass Politics: Knowledge and Opinion in the American Electorate*. Cambridge: Harvard University Press, 1986.

Neustadt, Richard E. *Presidential Power and the Modern Presidents*. New York: Free Press, 1990.

Nice, David C. *Federalism*. New York: St. Martin's Press, 1987.

Noonan, John T. *The Morality of Abortion*. Cambridge: Harvard University Press, 1970.

Note, "I Want a New Drug: RU-486 and the Right to Choose." *Southern California Law Review* 63 (1990): 1061–1149.

Note, "'Of Winks and Nods'—*Webster*'s Uncertain Effect on Current and Future Abortion Legislation." *Missouri Law Review* 50 (1990): 163–217.

Note, "Webster, Privacy, and RU486." *Journal of Contemporary Health Law and Policy* 6 (1990): 277–96.

O'Brien, David M. *Privacy, Law, and Public Policy*. New York: Praeger, 1979.

———. *Judicial Roulette: The Report of the Twentieth Century Fund Task*

Force on the Appointment of Federal Judges. New York: Twentieth Century Fund/Priority Press, 1988.

——. "The Reagan Judges: His Most Enduring Legacy?" In *The Reagan Legacy,* edited by Charles O. Jones. Chatham, N.J.: Chatham House, 1988.

——. "Federalism as a Metaphor in the Constitutional Politics of Public Administration." *Public Administration Review* 49 (1989): 411–19.

——. *Storm Center: The Supreme Court in American Politics.* 2d ed. New York: Norton, 1990.

——. *Constitutional Law and Politics.* Vol. 2, *Civil Rights and Civil Liberties.* New York: Norton, 1991.

——. "The Framers' Muse on Republicanism, the Supreme Court, and Pragmatic Constitutional Interpretivism." *Review of Politics* 53 (1991): 251–88.

O'Connor, Karen. *Women's Organizations' Use of the Courts.* Lexington, Mass.: Heath, 1980.

O'Connor, Karen, and Lee Epstein. "A Research Note: Amicus Curiae Participation in U.S. Supreme Court Litigation." *Law and Society Review* 16 (1982): 311–20.

Oleszek, Walter J. *Congressional Procedures and the Policy Process.* 3d ed. Washington, D.C.: CQ Press, 1989.

Olsen, Frances. "Unraveling Compromise." *Harvard Law Review* 103 (1989): 105–55.

Ornstein, Norman J., Thomas E. Mann, and Michael Malbin. *Vital Statistics on Congress, 1989–90.* Washington, D.C.: CQ Press, 1990.

Orren, Karen. "Standing to Sue: Interest Group Conflict in the Federal Courts." *American Political Science Review* 70 (1976): 723–41.

Pertschuk, Michael, and Wendy Schaetzel. *The People Rising: The Campaign against the Bork Nomination.* New York: Thunder's Mouth, 1989.

Petchesky, Rosalind. *Abortion and Woman's Choice: The State, Sexuality, and Reproductive Freedom.* Boston: Northeastern University Press, 1985.

Pious, Richard M. *The American Presidency.* New York: Basic Books, 1979.

Porter, Mary Cornelia, and G. Alan Tarr, eds. *State Supreme Courts: Policymakers in the Federal System.* Westport, Conn.: Greenwood Press, 1982.

Pyle, Christopher, and Richard M. Pious, eds. *The President, Congress, and the Constitution.* New York: Free Press, 1984.

Riker, William. *Federalism: Origins, Operation, Significance.* Boston: Little, Brown, 1974.

Ripley, Randall T., and Grace A. Franklin. *Congress, the Bureaucracy and Public Policy.* 5th ed. Chicago: Dorsey Press, 1990.

Rodman, Hyman, Betty Sarvis, and Joy Walker Bonar. *The Abortion Question.* New York: Columbia University Press, 1987.

Roll, Charles W. *Polls: Their Use and Misuse in Politics.* New York: Basic Books, 1972.

Rosenberg, Gerald N. *The Hollow Hope: Can Courts Bring About Social Change?* Chicago: University of Chicago Press, 1991.

Rossiter, Clinton. *1787: The Grand Convention.* New York: Macmillan, 1966.

Rubin, Eva R. *Abortion, Politics, and the Courts: Roe v. Wade and Its Aftermath.* 2d ed. Westport, Conn.: Greenwood Press, 1987.

Rubin, Irene S. *The Politics of Public Budgeting: Getting and Spending, Borrowing and Balancing*. Chatham, N.J.: Chatham House, 1990.

Sarvis, Betty, and Hyman Rodman. *The Abortion Controversy*. New York: Columbia University Press, 1973.

Schattschneider, E.E. *The Semisovereign People*. Hinsdale, Ill.: Dryden Press, 1960.

Schlozman, Kay Lehman, and John T. Tierney. *Organized Interests and American Democracy*. New York: Harper & Row, 1986.

Schwartz, Bernard. *Packing the Courts: the Conservative Campaign to Rewrite the Constitution*. New York: Scribner's, 1988.

———. *The New Right and the Constitution*. Boston: Northeastern University Press, 1990.

———, ed. *The Unpublished Opinions of the Burger Court*. New York: Oxford University Press, 1988.

———, ed. *The Ascent of Pragmatism: The Burger Court in Action*. Reading, Mass.: Addison-Wesley, 1990.

Segers, Mary C. "Governing Abortion Policy." In *Governing Through Courts*, edited by Richard A.L. Gambitta, Marilyn L. May, and James C. Foster. Beverly Hills: Sage Publications, 1981.

Seidman, Harold. *Politics, Position, and Power: The Dynamics of Federal Organization*. 3d ed. New York: Oxford University Press, 1980.

Simon, James F. *In His Own Image: The Supreme Court in Richard Nixon's America*. New York: McKay, 1974.

Smith, Hedrick. *The Power Game: How Washington Works*. New York: Random House, 1988.

Smith, Steven S., and Christopher J. Deering. *Committees in Congress*. Washington, D.C.: CQ Press, 1990.

Staggenborg, Suzanne. *The Pro-Choice Movement: Organization and Activism in the Abortion Conflict*. New York: Oxford University Press, 1992.

Steiner, Gilbert Y., et al., eds. *The Abortion Dispute and the American System*. Washington, D.C.: Brookings, 1983.

Steinhoff, Patricia G. *Abortion Politics: The Hawaii Experience*. Honolulu: University Press of Hawaii, 1977.

Stetson, Dorothy McBride. *Women's Rights in the USA: Policy Debates and Gender Roles*. Pacific Grove, Calif.: Brooks/Cole, 1991.

Sundquist, James L. *The Decline and Resurgence of Congress*. Washington, D.C.: Brookings, 1981.

Sussman, Barry. *What Americans Really Think: And Why Our Politicians Pay No Attention*. New York: Pantheon, 1988.

Tatalovich, Raymond, and Byron W. Daynes. *The Politics of Abortion: A Study of Community Conflict in Public Policymaking*. New York: Praeger, 1981.

Tribe, Laurence. *God Save This Honorable Court: How the Choice of Supreme Court Justices Shapes Our History*. New York: Random House, 1985.

———. *Abortion: The Clash of Absolutes*. New York: Norton, 1990.

Truman, David B. *The Governmental Process*. New York: Knopf, 1951.

Van Horn, Carl, ed. *The State of the States*. Washington, D.C.: CQ Press, 1989.

Viguerie, Richard A. *The New Right: We're Ready to Lead*. Falls Church, Va.: Viguerie, 1981.

Wasby, Stephen. *The Impact of the United States Supreme Court.* Homewood, Ill.: Dorsey Press, 1970.

––––––. "Civil Rights Litigation by Organizations: Constraints and Choices." *Judicature* 68 (1985): 337–52.

Wayne, Stephen J. *The Legislative Presidency.* New York: Harper & Row, 1978.

––––––. *The Road to the White House.* New York: St. Martin's Press, 1991.

Weddington, Sarah. *A Question of Choice.* New York: Grosset/Putnam, 1992.

Wildavsky, Aaron. *The New Politics of the Budgetary Process.* Glenview, Ill.: Scott, Foresman, 1988.

Yankelovich, Daniel. *Coming to Public Judgment: Making Democracy Work in a Complex World.* Syracuse: Syracuse University Press, 1991.

Young, Michael L. *The Classics of Polling.* Metuchen, N.J.: Scarecrow Press, 1990.

Index of Cases

Boldface numerals indicate excerpts from judicial opinions.

Ada v. Guam Society of Obstetricians and Gynecologists, 356, 361n58

Adkins v. Children's Hospital of the District of Columbia, 340, 341, 360n30

Akron I ("one"): see *City of Akron v. Akron Center for Reproductive Health*

Baker v. Carr, 33n4

Barnes v. Moore, 361n59

Beal v. Doe, 92, 98, 152n29

Bellotti v. Baird, 90, 97

Benten v. Kessler, 358, 362n64

Bigelow v. Virginia, 81, **82,** 97

Bowen v. Kendrick, 188

Bowers v. Hardwick, 209

Boyd v. United States, 26

Bray v. Alexandria Women's Health Clinic, 315, 355

Brown v. Allen, 68n1

Brown v. Board of Education of Topeka, Kansas, 318, 340, 341, 345, 360n34

Buck v. Bell, 8

Buckley v. Valeo, 150n7

Carey v. Population Services International, 82, 98

City of Akron v. Akron Center for Reproductive Health, 80, 87, 90–91, 98–99, 186, 194n39, 233, 234, 236, 237, 243n16, 330, 333, 337, 346

Colautti v. Franklin, 84, **98,** 234

Committee to Defend Reproductive Rights v. Myers, 361n48

Connally v. General Construction Co., 13

Danforth v. Rodgers, 101n22, 243n3

Doe v. Bolton, 97, 103

Doe v. Director of Michigan Department of Social Services, 361n50

Doe v. Maher, 361n49

Dombrowski v. Pfister, 33n13

Eisenstadt v. Baird, 8, 9, 26, 28

Garcia v. San Antonio Metropolitan Transit Authority, 235

Griswold v. Connecticut, 6–7, 8, 9, 10, 15, 18, 26, 28, 30, 33n6, 182, 227–30 passim

Grove City College v. Bell, 155 nn75–76

H.L. v. Matheson, 90, 98

Harris v. McRae, 153n49, 164, 201, 227, 228, 243n9

Hartigan v. Zbaraz, 194 n41, 243 n1

Hodgson v. Minnesota, 91, 100, 243n18, 315, 333

Katz v. United States, 26

Lee v. Weisman, 360n35

Leigh v. Olson, 101n21

Lochner v. New York, 340, 341, 344, 360n29

Loving v. Virginia, 9, 26

McRae v. Califano, 152n25

Maher v. Roe, **92–94,** 98, 152n29, 163, 201, 227, 233, 234, 243n8

Mapp v. Ohio, 33n5

Meyer v. Nebraska, 26, 28, 227

Miller v. California, 240

Miranda v. Arizona, 33n5

Moe v. Secretary of Administration, 361n51

Moore v. City of East Cleveland, 227

National Family Planning and Reproductive Health Association, Inc. v. Sullivan, 354

New State Ice Co. v. Liebmann, 101n2

New York Times v. Sullivan, 240

Ohio v. Akron Center for Reproductive Health, 91, 100, 243n18

Olmstead v. United States, 26

Palko v. Connecticut, 26
People v. Norton, 101n20
People v. Orser, 101n21
Pierce v. Society of Sisters, 8, 26, 28,
    227
Planned Parenthood Association of Kan-
    sas City, Missouri, Inc. v. Ashcroft,
    80, 99, 101n22, 199, 201, 243n5
Planned Parenthood Federation of Amer-
    ica v. Agency for International De-
    velopment, 195n51
Planned Parenthood of Central Missouri
    v. Danforth, 84–85, 87, 88, 97,
    101n18, 101n22, 192n7, 199,
    243n4
Planned Parenthood of Southeastern
    Pennsylvania v. Casey, 32, 295, 302,
    311, 315, 321, 325, 326–27,
    328–30, 333, 334, 337–41,
    342–44, 344–46, 347, 348, 349,
    355, 356, 359, 360n21, 360n22,
    360n27
Planned Parenthood v. Agency for Inter-
    national Development, 332, 360n25
Plessy v. Ferguson, 340, 341, 344,
    360n33
Poe v. Ullman, 6, 7, 229
Poelker v. Doe, 92, 98, 101n12, 152n29
Prince v. Massachusetts, 26

Regents of the University of California v.
    Bakke, 204, 243n12
Reproductive Health Services v. Web-
    ster, 243n7, 243n10
Right to Choose v. Byrne, 361n52
Roe v. Wade, 1, 4–5, 12–13, 14–32, 24,
    25–30, 31–32, 32, 33n1, 33n13,
    42–43, 54–56 passim, 59, 62, 64,
    65, 73, 74, 77, 78, 79, 103, 162,

169, 182, 186, 187, 192, 198, 201,
    206, 208–13 passim, 220–25 passim,
    226–27, 229, 233, 234, 236–39 pas-
    sim, 241, 242, 243n6, 245, 248, 262,
    272, 275, 284, 286, 288, 293, 295,
    299, 310, 311, 317, 320, 325–29
    passim, 333–36 passim, 339, 341,
    344, 345, 346, 350, 354, 359
Rust v. Sullivan, 191, 311, 315, 318,
    319–20, 321, 331–32, 333, 342,
    354, 360n24

Simopoulos v. Virginia, 80, 99
Skinner v. Oklahoma, 8, 26, 28
Stanley v. Georgia, 26, 28
State v. New York Times, 101n21

Terry v. Ohio, 26
Thornburgh v. American College of Ob-
    stetricians and Gynecologists, 62,
    63, 99, 187, 194n40, 198, 206, 235,
    237, 240, 243n2, 243n17, 329, 330,
    333, 334, 337–38, 346
Tileston v. Ullman, 6

Union Pacific R. Co. v. Botsford, 26
United States v. Vuitch, 15, 16, 20, 23,
    33n14

Webster v. Reproductive Health Services,
    32, 63, 65, 67, 83, 99, 101n22, 187,
    191, 198, 201, 204, 206, 224,
    232–42, 243n15, 245, 264, 275,
    279, 280, 284, 296, 299, 300, 307,
    308, 315, 327–30 passim, 333, 334,
    342, 343, 345, 348, 349
West Coast Hotel v. Parrish, 340, 341,
    345, 360n32
Williamson v. Lee Optical Co., 31
Wolfe v. Schroering, 101n17

Index of Names and Subjects

ABC's "Nightline," 316

Abortion(s): advertising and promotion of, 81–84, 97; and American federalism, 73–78; and common law, 26; Congress and, 103–55; counseling, 90, 188–90; 329, 331–32; criminalizing, 97; demographic characteristics of (1987), 257; facilities for, 91–94, 191; and fetal-protection statutes, 98; frequency of, 159; and HEW appropriations, 110–32; history of, 25–26, 213, 219–20; hospitals permitting, 78; as legislative weapon, 147–50; as litmus test in politics, 48; medicalized, 40; out-of-state, 76, 78; and party platforms, 166–68; proposals, 110; and public funding, 91–94, 98; regulation of, by review groups, 40–41; and religious affiliation, 262; who gets and why, 251–56

Abortion Control Act (PA), 84

Abortion in America: The Origins and Evolution of National Policy (Mohr), 211

Abortion laws: extent of, 42; liberalization of, 9–10; state and local, 41, 74–75, 78–79, 99. *See also* individual states

Abortion marches, turnouts for, 51

"Abortion on demand," 30, 85, 89

Abortion opinion polls: and abortion restrictions, 274–76; by demographic categories, 258–61; inconsistency in, 264–70; of National Opinion Research Center, 250–55

Abortion opinions: characteristic differences of, 254–62; demographic differences in, 256–64; measuring strengths of, 270–74

Abortion politics, terminology used in, *xv*

Abzug, Bella, 103, 114

Ad Hoc Committee in Defense of Life, 367

Adolescent Family Life Act (1981), 172, 188

Affirmative action, 318

AFL-CIO, 300, 319

Age Discrimination Act (1975), 148

Agency for International Development (AID), 332

Akron, Ohio, informed-consent ordinance of, 85, 87

Akron Center for Reproductive Health, 85

Alan Guttmacher Institute, 45, 276n8

Alaska, abortion law of, 74

Alito, Samuel A., 330

Allen, James B., 103

Alliance for Justice, 319

Altimari, Frank X., 358

Alumbaugh, Steve, 178, 194n34

American Academy of Child and Adolescent Psychiatry, 223

American Academy of Pediatrics, 223

American Association of Pro Life Obstetricians and Gynecologists, 204, 206, 208

American Association of Pro-Life Pediatricians, 208

American Baptist Friends for Life, 211

American Bar Association, 4, 300

American Civil Liberties Union (ACLU), 59, 65, 149, 181–82, 204, 284, 295

American College of Obstetricians and Gynecologists, 85, 223

American Conservative Union, 64

American Fertility Society, 223

American Indian Health Care Association, 221

American Journal of Public Health, 310

American Law Institute (ALI), 74

American Life Lobby, 145

American Medical Association, 40, 74, 85, 219, 223

American Medical Women's Association, 223

American Psychiatric Association, 223

American Society of Human Genetics, 223

American Spectator, 319

Americans United for Life, 55, 67, 334

Amici curiae briefs: in *Casey,* 333–34; defined, 185–86; impact of, 224–27; for

Reproductive Health Services, 214–18; in *Roe*, 204–11; in *Webster*, 204, 205–11, 224–27
Andrews, Joan, 56–57
Andrus, Cecil D., 283
Antiabortion amendments, proposals for, 55
Antiabortionists, march on Court (1989), 66–67
Apple, R.W., Jr., 71n58
Appropriations, legislative, 108, 110, 132–37
Armstrong, William L., 321
Arnold, Richard, 201
Asher, Herbert, 276n3
Asian American Legal Defense Fund, 221
Association for Public Justice, 204
Atlanta Constitution poll, 184
Atwater, Lee, 300
AuCoin, Les, 308, 310
Avallone, Anthony, 285–86, 292

Babbitt, Bruce, 179
Bailey, Wendell, 308
Baird, William, 89
Baker, Howard, 121, 130, 143, 144, 146, 182
Balch, Burke, 347, 349
Banks, C., 360n28
Baptists for Life, 211
Bartlett, Dewey F., 116–17
Bartlett Amendment, 117–18
Baucus, Max, 141, 143, 144
Bauer, Gary, 325
Bayh, Birch, 123
Behuniak–Long, Susan, 224, 243n15
Bell, Griffin, 175
Benshoof, Janet, 348
Benten, Leona, 356–57
Berke, R., 360n26
Berkson, Larry, 193n26
Bernardin, Joseph, 160
Berry, Jeffrey M., 38, 68n8, 69n17
Bibby, John F., 151n12
Biden, Joseph, 141, 177, 183
Bigelow, Jeffrey C., 81–82
Bill of Rights, penumbras of (Douglas), 7, 10
Black, Hugo, 4
Blackmun, Harry, 4, 15, 91, 92, 163, 187, 225, 232, 327, 355; on *Bigelow*, 82; on *Casey*, 342–43; on Fourteenth Amendment, 25; on *Maher*, 93–94; memo on reargument of *Roe*, 21; on parental consent, 90; on *Roe*, 18,

23–24, 25–30; on *Rust*, 332; on spousal consent, 88; on *Webster*, 238–41
Blacks, and abortion, 256
Blake, Judith, 101n6
Blaustein, Albert, 334
Boggs, Lindy, 117
Bonar, Joy Walker, 276n6, 277n29
Bork, Robert H., 63–64, 159, 174, 177, 178, 194, 317, 342, 355, 360n36; confirmation hearings of, 181–85
Boschwitz, Rudy, 321
Bowen, Otis R., 188
Boxer, Barbara, 67
Brandeis, Louis D., 73–74, 182
Branstad, Terry E., 302
Bray, Michael, 355
Breen, James, 85
Brennan, William J., Jr., 2, 6, 15, 91, 92, 163, 229, 232, 316
Bronner, Ethan, 194n37
Brooke, Edward, 117, 124–26, 131, 135
Brownell, Herbert, 154n59
Brozan, Nadine, 101n5
Buchanan, John, 52
Buckley, James, 45, 109
Budget Impoundment and Control Act (1974), 104, 108
Budget reform, and deficit politics, 108–9
Burger, Warren E., 3, 15, 18, 30, 62, 63, 179, 183, 187
Bush, Barbara, 322
Bush, George, 64, 165, 170, 302, 314, 315, 322, 325; appointments of, to Court, 316–21; and Freedom of Choice Act, 354; presidency of, 191–92; road to defeat of, 28–31
Buxton, Dr., 6
Byrd, Harry F., 3
Byrd, Robert C., 129–31, 141, 184

Califano, Joseph, 125, 126, 164
California, abortion law in, 42
Campbell, Tom, 350
Cannon, Mark, 194n38
Carbon, Susan, 193n26
Carswell, G. Harrold, 4
Carter, Jimmy, 3, 134, 160, 183; and abortion, 164–69; selecting of judges by, 174
Carter, Tim Lee, 115
Carville, Jim, 304n31
Case review, justices needed for, 197
Casey, Robert P., 302, 321, 326
Casey: issues in, 328–30; strategies and arguments in, 332–37
Casper, Gerhart, 33n16

Catholic League for Religious and Civil Rights, 204
Catholics, 147; population of, 43. *See also* U.S. Catholic Bishops Conference
Catholics for a Free Choice, 46, 263
Catholics for Life, 204
Catholics United for Life, 211
Cavanaugh-O'Keefe, John, 70n39
CBS News/*New York Times* poll (1980), 268; (1989), 250, 264–68
Celebrezze, Anthony, Jr., 301
"Cemetery of the Innocents," 67
Center for Judicial Studies, 207, 210–11
Center for Reproductive Law, 348
Chaffee, John, 312
Checks and balances, in U.S. government, *xiv*
Chicago Catholic Women, 223
Chiles, Lawton, 121, 301
Christian Action Council, 211
Christianity, early, and abortion, 40
Christian Science Monitor, 312
Christian Voice, 52
Church, Frank, 121
Ciolli, R., 359n11
Civiletti, Benjamin, 154n59
Civil Rights Act (1964), 2, 148
Clark, Ramsey, 154n59
Clark, Tom C., 6
Clinton, Bill, 3, 322, 354–55, 358–59
Cloture rule (Senate), 130
Coats, Dan, 354
Cochran, Thad, 354
Code of Disclosure, 247
Coffee, Linda, 4–5, 8, 9–10, 14, 15–18 passim
Colasanto, Diane, 277n38
Coleman, Marshall, 297
Colker, R., 243
Collins, R., 243n13
Combs, Michael W., 276n15
"Compelling point," 29
Concerned Women for America, 64, 319
Congress: birth of modern, 104–9; campaign costs of, 106; and committee recruitment, 153–54; and loosening of abortion restrictions, 308–13; hearings in, 138–39; law-making procedures of, 118; and lobbyists, 106; politics and abortion issue, 109–17; pressure on re abortion, 349–55; proposals to undo *Roe,* 103–4
Congressional Black Caucus, 149
Conn, Erin A., 88–89
Connecticut: and abortion funding,

92–94; abortion statistics (1987), 287; as pro-choice "win," 284–92
Connecticut Coalition for Choice, 284
Consent statutes, 84–91; informed, 98–99; parental, 90, 98–99; spousal, 90
Conservative Caucus, 36
Constitutional amendment(s), on abortion, 137–47, 172; procedures for, 137–46
Conte, Silvio O., 118–19
Contraception, information on and prescribing of, 6–7, 8, 10
Cooke, Terence Cardinal, 32
Costanza, Midge, 164
Courter, Jim, 298
Cox, William, 127
Craig, Barbara Hinkson, 151nn9, 17
Cunningham, Paige, 67, 297
Cuomo, Mario M., 299
Cutler, Lloyd, 334

Dahl, Robert, 152n37
Danforth, John C., 83, 209
Darwin, Charles, 219
Davidson, Roger, 150n8, 151n11
Deardourff, John, 312
Debt-ceiling bills, 132–44
DeConcini, Dennis, 141, 184
deFeo, Louis, 200
de la Garza, E. "Kika," 314
Delay, as protection of liberties, *xiv*
Dellinger, Walter, 334
Demonstrations, counting heads at, 49–50
Denton, Jeremiah, 139, 141, 175
Derwinski, Edward J., 128
DeStefano, Linda, 277n38
Devlin, J., 361n53
Dionne, E.J., 360n19
District court, three-judge panels of, 12
District of Columbia, 15–16, 74, 135
DiVall, Linda, 327
Doerflinger, Richard, 54
Dole, Robert, 141, 184
Dooling, John, 118, 120
Dornan, Robert K., 49, 134
Douglas, William O., 6–10, 30, 150
Dowdy, John, 150n4
Durenberger, Dave, 354

Eagle Forum, 319
Eagleton, Thomas F., 146, 155n66
Eagleton Institute (Rutgers University), 298
East, John P., 139, 141, 175
Education Act Amendments (1972), 148
Edwards, Don, 154n58

Eighteenth Amendment, 31
Eisenhower, Dwight D., 2
Election reform, consequences of, 104–7
Elections: national, and abortion,
   321–22; 1980, 54; 1989, 297–99;
   1990, 299–302; 1991, 302–3; 1992,
   311; state, and abortion issue, 296–303
Ely, John Hart, 33n27
EMILY's list, 310
Equal Rights Amendment, 148, 153n41,
   164
Eugenics movement, 8

Fair Deal, 1
Falwell, Jerry, 50, 52
Family-planning clinics, 77–78
"Family rating," of members of Congress,
   52
Family Research Council, 319
Faucher, Sandra, 301
Federal Election Campaign Act (1974),
   104, 105, 150n7
Federalism, American, and abortion,
   73–78
Fein, Bruce, 173
Feinstein, Dianne, 301
Fenwick, Millicent, 117
Ferguson, E., 361n57
Ferree, Myra Marx, 277n15
"Fetal-protection statutes," 83–84
Fetus, as "person," 20–22
Fielding, Fred, 175
Filibuster (Senate), 130, 143, 155n69
Finkbine, Sherri, 41
Fish, Hamilton, Jr., 354
Florio, James J., 298
Flowers, Robert C., 22
Floyd, Jay, 17–18
Foley, Thomas, 313, 354
Food and Drug Administration (FDA),
   357–58
Ford, Betty, 160
Ford, Gerald R., 158, 159–60, 164, 183;
   on abortions, 160–61
Forrest, J., 101n13
Fortas, Abe, 3
Fourteenth Amendment, 18, 20, 22, 25,
   27, 29, 31, 140
Franklin, Grace A., 68n7
Free Congress Foundation, 326, 355
Freedom of Choice Act, 311, 349–50
Freifield, K., 359n10
Freind, Stephen, 348
Frey, Andrew, 175
Fried, Charles, 169, 186, 194n42, 204,

227–30
Fund for the Feminist Majority, 66, 357
Funding-ban rider for HEW bills: 1974,
   110–13; 1976, 118–19; 1977, 119–27;
   1978, 127–32
Funston, Richard, 33n10

Gallagher, Mark, 44–45, 47
Gallup, George H., 246, 277n22
Gallup/Newsweek poll (1989), 265–68
Gallup polls, 245, 262, 264, 271. See also
   Abortion opinion polls
Garn, Jake, 122
Giaimo, Robert, 115
Gingrich, Newt, 207
Ginsburg, Douglas H., 178, 181, 184
Goldberg, Arthur, 6
Goldman, Sheldon, 193n26
Goldwater, Barry, 133–34, 159
Goodman, Ellen, 320
Gorney, C., 243n6
Granberg, Donald, 69n23
Grassley, Charles, 139, 141, 179, 185
Great Society program, 2
Gregg, Judd, 302
Griswold, Esther, 6
Guttmacher, Alan, 32

Habitual Criminal Sterilization Act (OK),
   8–9
Hall, Elaine J., 276n15
Hall, M. 359n8, 360
Hall, Tony P., 314
Hallford, James H., 10, 13
Harlan, John M., 4, 15, 317
Hatch, Orrin, 32, 117, 123, 131, 140–42,
   144–45, 175, 180, 185, 206, 319–20,
   354, 355
Hatfield, Mark, 135, 146–47
Hawaii, abortion law of, 74
Hayakawa, S.I. ("Sam"), 126
Haynsworth, Clement, 4
Health regulations, of states, 79–81
Heckler, Margaret, 117
Heflin, Howell, 184
Heilig, Steve, 357
Heinz, John, 302
Helms, Jesse, 54, 117, 122, 136, 142–46,
   177, 321
Helms's bill, regarding status of fetuses,
   139–40, 143–44
Henn, John H., 70n46
Henshaw, Stanley K., 101n10, 276n11,
   361n42
Heritage Foundation, 319

Hill, Anita, 320
History of Abortion in America (Mohr), 143
Hogan, Lawrence J., 114
Hollywood Women's Political Committee, 67
Holt, Marjorie, 117
Holtzman, Elizabeth, 66, 117
"Holy Week Rescue" (1989), 58
House, Toni, 65
House of Representatives, floor procedure in, 142
Howlett, D., 361n40
Hughes, Charles Evans, 66
Hughes, Sarah T., 12
Humphrey, Gordon, 49, 185
Humphrey, Hubert H., 121
Hunt, E. Howard, Jr., 158
Huppe, Michael J., 304n39
Huyett, Daniel, 329–30, 348
Hyde, Henry, 44, 121, 124, 128, 154n58, 334
Hyde Amendment, 48, 110–17, 162. *See also* Funding-ban rider for HEW bills

Interest groups, 36–39, 39–43, 204
Ireland, Patricia, 326

Jackson, John E., 69n24, 277n35
Jackson, Robert, 35
Jeffords, James, 354
Jepsen, Roger, 179
Jipping, Tom, 326
John Paul II (pope), 57
Johnson, Douglas, 189
Johnson, Lyndon B., 1, 2–3, 158
Johnston, J. Bennett, 187
Jones, Charles O., 193n20
Jones, Edith, 316
Jones, Ruth, 327
Judges, confirmation of, 176
"Judicial bypass" option," 90–91, 100
Justices, citation of briefs by in *Webster*, 226

Kaeser, Lisa, 357
Kassebaum, Nancy, 354
Katzenbach, Nicholas, 154n59
Kennedy, Anthony M., 64, 91, 178, 184, 185, 227–29 passim, 232, 327, 331, 334, 338, 342
Kennedy, Edward, 121, 139, 141, 176, 180, 181, 189, 317, 350, 354
Kennedy, Flo, 319
Kennedy, John F., 2

Killea, Lucy, 298
King, Coretta Scott, 64
Kinsley, Michael, 303n3
Knights of Columbus, 204, 209
Kolbert, Kathryn, 204, 333–35, 347
Koonin, Lisa M., 276n11
Koop, C. Everett, 188
Krol, John Cardinal, 32
Ku Klux Klan Act, 315, 355
Kummer, F., 361n45
Kurland, Philip, 33n16

Ladd, Everett Carll, 151n10, 264, 272–73, 277n19
Lader, Lawrence, 74, 101n4, 257, 358
LaFalce, John J., 314
Lang, Joel, 303nn9, 14; 304n24
Laxalt, Paul, 141
Lay, Donald, 201
Leach, Jim, 299
League of United Latin American Citizens, 300
League of Women Voters, 284
Leahy, Patrick, 121, 141, 177, 182
Lee, Rex, 85, 186
Lee, Samuel, 198, 200
Lehrman, Lewis, 319
Levi, Edward H., 180
Levy, Leonard, 33n10
Life Amendment Political Action Committee, 141
Lindblom, Charles, 108, 151n14
Lloyd, Marilyn, 117
Lobbies, 106
Loesch, Juli, 57
Louisiana, abortion law of, 74, 293–95
Ludwig, Jacob, 269, 277n33
Luker, Kristin, 46–47, 69n10
Lutherans for Life, 211

Mabus, Ray, 302
McCarthy, S., 359n1
McCloskey, Henry, Jr., 5
McCord, James W., Jr., 158
McCormick, Ellen, 48
McCorvey, Norma, 5–6, 9–10, 12, 77, 227, 326
McCree, Wade, 164
McFadden, Robert, 357
McGovern, George, 159
McMillan, Theodore, 201
Magnuson, Warren, 125, 126, 130
Maher, Leo T., 298
Mahone, George, 128
Mahoney, Daniel J., 358

Malbin, Michael J., 151n12
Mann, Thomas E., 151n12
March for Life, 48, 141, 170
March for Women's Equality/Women's
    Lives, 201
March for Women's Lives, 62
Marcus, R., 360n38
Markman, Stephen, 174–75
Marshall, Burke, 224
Marshall, Thurgood, 15, 56–57, 91, 92,
    93–94, 232, 318, 332; on public fund-
    ing for abortions, 163
Martinez, Bob, 279, 296, 301
Maryland, abortion laws of, 284–92
Massachusetts, abortion laws of, 89
Mathias, Charles, 141
Mauro, T., 243n11
Mazzoli, Romano, 350
Medicaid, 92, 109. See also Public fund-
    ing
Meese, Edwin III, 173, 174
Metzenbaum, Howard, 109–10, 141, 149
Mexican American Legal Defense and Ed-
    ucation Fund, 221
Michel, Robert H., 154n58
Michelman, Kate, 296, 301, 325, 332
Miller, George, 128
Miller, Mel, 279
Miscegenation law, 9
Mississippi, abortion law of, 74
Missouri, abortion laws of, 63, 83,
    198–204
Missouri Catholic Conference, 200
Mitchell, George, 312, 326, 350, 361n56
Mobilize for Women's Lives, 49, 307
Model Penal Code (ALI), 74
Mohr, James C., 143, 211–12
Mollohan, Alan B., 209
Montgomery, G.V. ("Sonny"), 315
Moral Majority, 38, 50, 52, 179. See also
    New Right
Moran, Alfred F., 77
Moravians for Life, 211
Morrison, Alan, 71n52
"Motherhood Bill," 131–32
Murphy, George, 150n4
Muskie, Edmund, 121

National Abortion Federation, 355
National Abortion Rights Action League
    (NARAL), 59, 62, 68, 283, 284, 291,
    295, 296, 298, 301, 319, 325, 349
National Abortion Rights League, 50,
    145
National Affairs Briefing, 52

National Association for the Advancement
    of Colored People (NAACP), 5, 38, 56,
    64, 300, 319; strategies of, 68n7
National Association for the Repeal of
    Abortion Laws, 74
National Black Women's Health Project,
    221
National Christian Action Coalition, 52
National Coalition of American Nuns, 223
National Committee for a Human Life
    Amendment, 44–45, 55, 127
National Conference of Catholic Bishops,
    141, 160, 299. See also National Coun-
    cil of Catholic Bishops
National Conservative Political Action
    Committee (NCPAC), 182
National Council of Catholic Bishops, 47.
    See also National Conference of Catho-
    lic Bishops
National Council of Negro Women, 221
National Education Association, 64, 319
National Institute for Women of Color,
    221
National Legal Foundation, 204
National Opinion Research Center
    (NORC) surveys, 266–68. See also
    Abortion opinion polls
National Organization for Women, 45–46,
    59, 64, 65, 145, 185, 201, 222–23, 284,
    296, 319
National Organization of Episcopalians
    for Life, 211
National politics, and abortion, 307–23
National Pro-Life Political Action Com-
    mittee, 141
National Religious Broadcasters, 170–72
National Republican Coalition for Choice,
    313
National Right to Life Committee, 50, 65,
    141, 145, 179, 206, 209, 270
National Right to Life Movement, 283
National Right to Life party, 57
National Urban League, 221
National Women's Health Network, 221
Nativism, 219
New Deal, 2
New Frontier, 2
New Hampshire, abortion law of, 74
Newport, Frank, 277n22
New Right, 50–59, 185. See also Moral
    Majority
New York State, abortion law in, 42, 74
New York Times, 1, 15, 36
Nixon, Richard M., 3–4, 17, 18, 104–5,
    108, 157–58

Noonan, John T., Jr., 56
Norplant, 357
Notification laws, 84–91; parental, 90, 282, 287, 289, 310–11; spousal, 329, 341
Nunn, Sam, 121, 309
Nurses Association of the Obstetrical College, 85

Oakar, Mary Rose, 117
Oberstar, James, 128
Obey, David R., 114, 115, 131; on protracted debate, 128–29
O'Brien, David M., 33n6, 101n1, 192n8, 193nn23, 25; 194nn28, 31, 32, 38; 323, 325n24, 360n37
O'Connor, Sandra Day, 62, 91, 178–79, 186, 187, 225, 228–31 passim, 232, 327, 330, 332, 355; on *Akron*, 87–88; and plurality view on *Casey*, 337–39, 341, 342; on *Webster*, 236–37
Oleszek, Walter J., 138–39, 150n8, 151nn11, 18; 153n56
Omnibus bill, appropriations (1982), 142
Omnibus resolutions, and abortion, 132–37
O'Neill, William A., 284
On-site participants, rules for, 60–61
Operation Rescue, *xv*, 57–59, 170, 302, 303, 315, 355; and rules for on-site participants, 60–61
Organization Nacional De La Salud De Mujer Latina, 221
Organization of Asian Women, 221
Ornstein, Norman J., 64–65, 151n12

Packwood, Robert, 117, 121, 122, 136, 143–44, 150n3, 299
PACs. *See* Political action committee
Paltrow, Lynn, 195n54
Parental consent. *See* Consent statutes
Parental notification. *See* Notification
Parents Aid Society, 89
Party politics, and abortion, 313–15
"Pastoral Plan for Pro-Life Activities," 47
Pastore, John O., 116
Pennsylvania, abortion law of, 74. *See also Casey*
People for the American Way, 64, 182
Person, and constitutional definition (Blackmun), 27–28
Phillips, Howard, 36
"Pill, the," popular use of, 41
Pine, Rachael, 293
Planned Parenthood Federation, 54, 59,

65, 77, 83–84, 145, 149, 189, 190, 200, 201, 204, 270, 284, 295, 296
Podesta, Tony, 326
Political action committee (PAC), 37, 150–51; defined, 105; financing by, 105
Poll data: analysis of, 246–47; limitations of subsets of, 256–59; misuse of, 274
Pope, J., 361n54
Porter, John, 312
Porter, Roger, 312
Postviability, 83–84
Powell, Lewis F., Jr., 4, 63, 178, 181; on *Maher*, 92–93
Preate, Ernest, Jr., 333, 335
Presbyterians for Life, 211
Presidency: abortion and, 315–21; increased pressure on re abortion, 349–55. *See also* individual presidents
Presser, Stanley, 269, 277n33
"Prisoners of Christ," 58
Pritchett, C. Herman, 33n3
Privacy, developing constitutional law of, 6–9
Pro-choice: demographic profile of, 46–47; reawakening of, 59–68. *See also* individual pro-choice organizations
Pro-Choice America, 313
Prohibition, 36
Pro-life, demographic profile of, 46–47. *See also* individual pro-life organizations
Pro-Life Action League, 64
Pro-Life Council of Connecticut, 285
Pro-life Nonviolent Action Project (PNAP), 57
Proposition 13 (California), 131
Protestantism, "born again" evangelical, 45
Public facilities, use of for abortions, 91–94
Public funding, of abortions, 55, 56, 91–94, 95, 98, 110, 116, 136, 159, 161, 190–91
Public Health Service Act (1970), 172, 188–90. *See also* Title X
Public opinion, on abortion (1975–91), 263
Public opinion polls: and American democracy, 246–48; and hard and soft reasons, 249–50. *See also* Abortion opinion polls
Puerto Rican Legal Defense and Education Fund, 221
Puzder, Andrew, 198, 199–200

"Quickening," 9, 26

Quorum rule (Senate), 130

Ramstad, Jim, 350
Reagan, Ronald, 53, 135, 137, 145, 149,
    157, 159, 169, 171–72; and abortion
    legislation, 172; appointments of, to
    Supreme Court, 173–85; conservative
    agenda of, 55; crusade of before Burger
    and Rehnquist courts, 185–87; record
    of with congressional legislation, 172.
    See also Reagan Revolution
Reagan Revolution, abortion and,
    169–91
Rees, Grover III, 194n36
Regulatory reform, changing law
    through, 187–91
Rehabilitation Act (1973), 148
Rehnquist, William H., 4, 62, 63, 65–66,
    82, 87, 91, 179, 180, 186, 187, 225,
    327, 331–32, 343, 356; on Casey,
    344–45; composition of Court of, 196;
    and Court opinion re Webster, 233–36;
    in dissenting Roe, 30–31
Religious Roundtable, 52
Reproductive Freedom Project of ACLU,
    189
Reproductive Health Services, 200
Reproductive Privacy Act (WA), 282
Reproductive Rights bills (House and
    Senate), 310, 311. See also Freedom
    of Choice Act
Reproductive Services Clinic, 299
Republicans for Choice, 313–14
Reynolds, William Bradford, 187, 197
Richards, Ann, 301
Richardson, Elliot, 154n59
Riding, A., 361n61
Right-to-life movement: early years of,
    43–50; first, 40; New Right joins,
    50–59; second, 43–59
Right to Life party, 48
Ripley, Randall B., 68n7
Robinson, James, 70n29, 71n29
Rodino, Peter, 139, 153n57
Rodman, Hyman, 276n6, 277n29
Roe, Robert A., 315
Roemer, Buddy, 294
Roe v. Wade: and constitutional politics
    between Court and states, 94–100; dis-
    senters, 30–32; filing of suit, 9–12; im-
    mediate aftermath of, 32; last two
    staunch defenders in Casey, 342–43;
    and mootness, 24; opinion of the Court
    (Blackmun), 25–30; and reargument,
    19–23; and review of Supreme Court,

14–24; as test case for changing times,
    5–9
Rogers, Estelle, 327
Rogers, Paul, 134
Roman, N., 360n12
Roncallo, Angelo D., amendment to HEW
    appropriation bill, 110–14
Roper, Elmo, 246
Roosevelt, Franklin D., 1–2
Rosenberg, Gerald, 78, 101, 190, 195n53
Rousselot, John, 128
Roussel Uclaf, 357
Rowland, C.K., 178, 194n34, 309
Roy, William R., on Roncallo amendment,
    114–15
Rubin, Eva, 101n7
Russell, S., 361nn57, 60
Rust, Irving, 331

Sabato, Larry, 297–98
Sackett, Victoria, 276n12, 277n28
San Francisco Medical Society, 357, 358
Sangmeister, George, 350
Sarasin, Ronald, 153n43
Sarvis, Betty, 276n6, 277n29
Saxbe, William, 154n59
Scalia, Antonin, 63, 91, 179, 180–81, 230,
    232, 327, 331, 343, 355, 356; on Casey,
    345–47; on Webster, 237–38
Schaefer, William D., 292
Schattschneider, E.E., 53–54, 70n32
Scheidler, Joseph, 57
Schlozman, Kay Lehman, 68n9
Schneider, John, 200
Schneider, William, 277n21
Schroeder, Patricia, 129
Schuman, Howard, 277n33
Schweiker, Richard, 126
Segal, Jeffrey, 33n7
Seitz, Collins, 330
Senate, and abortion funding proposals,
    131
Senators: signing antiabortion briefs (1985
    and 1989), 207; signing pro-choice
    briefs in Webster (1985 and 1989), 225
Sevareid, Eric, 129
Shearer, Lloyd, 33n12
Sifton, Charles P., 358
Simmons, C., 361n41
Simpson, Alan, 141
Skinner, Jack, 8–9
Slotnick, Elliot, 193n26
Smeal, Eleanor, 66, 179, 296, 357
Smith, Christopher, 49, 209
Smith, Jack C., 276n11

Smith, Virginia, 117
Smith, William French, 174
Solomon, J., 359n9
Songer, Donald, 194n33
Souter, David Hackett, 316–18, 327, 331, 338, 339, 342; on *Casey,* 340–41
Southern Baptists for Life, 211
Spaeth, Harold, 33n7
Specter, Arlen, 141, 183, 184, 194n44
Spousal consent. *See* Consent statutes
Spousal notification. *See* Notification
Staggers, Harley, 350
Standing, and the constitutional law of privacy, 6–8
Stapleton, Walter K., 330
Stare decisis, 342
Starr, Kenneth, 333, 335–37
State politics, and abortion after *Webster,* 279–305
States: and abortion laws after *Casey,* 348–49; and abortion policy, 274–75, 351–53; advertising and promotion regulations on abortion, 81–84; and constitutional politics between, and Supreme Court, 94–100; and health regulations, 79–91; informed consent requirements, 88; and probable abortion action after *Webster,* 281; sovereignty of, 74
Steinem, Gloria, 165
Steiner, Gilbert, 69n24, 70n24
Stennis, John, 125
Stevens, John Paul, 91, 159, 163, 183, 225–26, 227–29 passim, 232, 327, 332, 335, 336–37, 342, 355; on *Webster,* 241–42
Stewart, Potter, 6, 15, 30, 31, 179; on public funding for abortions, 162–63
Stone, Deborah A., 323n34
Stone, Harlan, 2, 183
Stopgap funding, 154n64
Strossen, Nadine, 333
"Subcommittee bill of rights," 104
Sullivan, E., 101n13
Sullivan, Louis W., 192, 313, 331
Sundquist, James L., 151n10
Sununu, John, 312, 316
Supreme Court: and constitutional politics between, and the states, 94–100; and continuing battle over abortion, 355–56; decision-making process of, 4; as guardian of civil rights and liberties, 2; internal dynamics of, 18–20; and "judicial activism," 3; and "reapportionment revolution," 2. *See also* Index

of Cases; individual justices
Susman, Frank, 227, 230, 232
SWAG system, 49

Task Force of United Methodists on Abortion and Sexuality, 211
Teeter, Robert, 164
Terry, Randall A., 57, 58, 325, 355
Texas abortion laws, 11–16, 23
Thalidomide, 41
Theriot, Sam, 294
Thomas, Clarence, 318–21, 327, 356
Thompson, Tommy G., 302
Thornburgh, Richard, 186, 227, 300, 302
Thurmond, Strom, 139, 141, 155n65, 176–77, 354
Tierney, John T., 69n9
Tietze, C., 101n13
Title X, 188–89, 312, 330, 331
Todd, Kevin, 334
Tocqueville, Alexis de, 262–63
Totenberg, Nina, 175
Traditional Values Coalition, 326
Tribe, Laurence, 224
Trimester, first, and mortality (Blackmun), 29–30
Troupe, Charles, 303n2
Truman, David B., 37, 68n6
Tulisano, Richard D., 284, 285–86, 288, 290, 292
Twenty-First Amendment, 36
Tydings, Joseph D., 150n4

"Unduly burdensome" standard, 87
United Center for Disease Control, 222
United Church of Christ, 284
United Church of Christ Friends for Life, 211
U.S. Catholic Conference, 43–44, 149
U.S. Chamber of Commerce, 319
Urban League. *See* National Urban League
USA Today, 36
USA Today/CNN/Gallup poll (1992), 327
Utah, abortion laws, 90, 293–95

Viability, 83–84, 288
Vinovskis, Maris A., 69n24, 277n35
Voinovich, George W., 301
Voting Rights Act of 1965, 2

Wade, Henry, 10, 12
Walker, Joe, 304n3
Walker, John M., 358
War on Poverty, 158
Warren, Earl, 2–3, 6

Washington (state): abortion laws of, 74; Reproduction Privacy Act, 282
Washington Post, 35, 135
Washington Post/ABC News poll, 184
Watergate, 157–58
Wattleton, Faye, 65, 141–42, 307–8, 333
Webster, William, 187, 197, 201, 226, 227
Webster: amici curiae briefs in, 205–24; decision and opinions, 232–42; hearing, 227–32; impact of *amici* briefs in, 224–27; Missouri law, 198–204
Weddington, Sarah, 5–6, 8, 9–10, 14, 15–18 passim, 74–75, 227, 316; and reargument, 20–23
Weicker, Lowell, 106, 117, 136, 144, 148
Weinstock, Edward, 192n6
Weiss, Ted, 153n44
Welch, Susan, 276n15
Weld, William, 322
Wellstone, Paul, 321
White, Byron, 4, 6, 15, 62, 82, 87, 91, 163, 183, 186, 187, 232, 327, 331, 356, 359
White House Judicial Selection Committee, 175
Whittaker, Charles E., 6
Whittaker, Judith, 175
Wilcox, Clyde, 277n15
Wilder, L. Douglas, 297
Wilke, J.C., 141

Williams, Clayton, 301
Wills, Gary, 70n41
Wilson, James Q., 68n7
Wilson, Pete, 301
Winkler, K., 243n14
Wofford, Harris, 302
Women, in abortion fight, 46–47
Women in Spirit of Colorado Task Force, 223
Women of All Red Nations, North Dakota, 221
Women of Color Partnership Program of the Religious Coalition for Abortion Rights, 221
Women's Law Project, 204
Women's Legal Defense Fund, 319
Women's Liberation Zap Action Brigade, 140
Women's movement, in mid-1960s, 41
Women's Political Caucus, 319
Wood, Mary Ann, 348
Woods, Harriett, 308
Wright, Jim, 127
Wright, Scott O., 200
Writ of *certiorari,* defined, 14

Yankelovich, Daniel, 264
Yard, Molly, 66, 307
Young Republican National Federation, 314
YWCA of the U.S.A., 221